The Political Economy of Communication

The Political Economy of Communication

Second Edition

Vincent Mosco

Los Angeles | London | New Delhi
Singapore | Washington DC

First published 1996
This edition 2009
Reprinted 2010

SAGE Publications Ltd
1 Oliver's Yard
55 City Road
London EC1Y 1SP

SAGE Publications Inc.
2455 Teller Road
Thousand Oaks, California 91320

SAGE Publications India Pvt Ltd
B1/I 1 Mohan Cooperative Industrial Area
Mathura Road, New Delhi 110 044
India

SAGE Publications Asia-Pacific Pte Ltd
33 Pekin Street #02-01
Far East Square
Singapore 048763

Library of Congress Control Number: 2008934404

British Library Cataloguing in Publication data

A catalogue record for this book is available
from the British Library

ISBN 978-1-4129-4700-8
ISBN 978-1-4129-4701-5

Typeset by C&M Digitals (P) Ltd, Chennai, India
Printed in Great Britain by the MPG Books Group
Printed on paper from sustainable resources

Mixed Sources
Product group from well-managed
forests and other controlled sources
www.fsc.org Cert no. TT-COC-2082
© 1996 Forest Stewardship Council
FSC

CONTENTS

PREFACE

The second edition of *The Political Economy of Communication* substantially revises and updates the 1996 first edition. I decided to write this book because the field has grown substantially over the last decade and the new edition provides an opportunity to address this work and to incorporate comments about the first edition. In addition to addressing new work, my goals were to deepen understanding of the enduring themes that have animated the field for many years, to address the new issues that are revitalizing it, and to do so in an accessible style that nevertheless respects the need for precise language. Here are some of the more important specific changes.

Some have suggested that it would be useful to provide a short overview of the political economy approach which also identifies some of the key books and articles in the field. Hence, the book begins with a one-chapter overview. I also thought it would make the book more accessible to break up some of the larger chapters into smaller ones. So I have taken a lengthy chapter on the general field of political economy and divided it into two chapters. Chapter 2 defines the political economy approach and takes up its major characteristics. Chapter 3 addresses major schools of thought. I have done something similar with a long chapter that mapped the history and current state of the political economy of communication. Chapter 4 begins with a section on the meaning of communication that provides a more detailed treatment of the concept than did the original edition. The chapter proceeds to describe the social and intellectual influences on the field and Chapter 5 examines the history of research in the political economy of communication.

Chapter 6 contains a completely new chapter that addresses five current trends in the political economy of communication. These include globalization of the field, the growing attention to new forms of history, an increasing emphasis on standpoints of resistance, especially feminism and labor, a focus on new media, especially the Internet, and on media reform and democracy. These themes animate the entire book but I also thought that it would be useful to gather them together in one chapter on new developments in the political economy of communication.

Chapters 7 to 10 follow the general pattern of the first edition but with key changes. For example, Chapter 7 begins with a new section on the philosophical foundation upon which to build a theory of the political economy of communication. The chapter then proceeds to examine the process of commodification and resistance to it. Chapter 8 on spatialization gives more weight to the concept of globalization and its relationship to nationalism, terrorism, and fundamentalism. Chapter 9 pays greater attention to labor and to differences within the study of social class, gender, and race.

Finally, in addition to highlighting the closer connections between political economy and cultural studies, Chapter 10 concludes by identifying two major new challenges for political economy: engaging with science and technology studies, including actor network theory, and making a contribution to debates about the relationship of the sciences to the humanities.

It is impossible to thank everyone who has helped me to produce this book. I have lived its ideas for sixty years and have engaged with them intellectually for forty years. My thanks goes again to all of those mentioned in the first edition's Acknowledgements section. Among these, I would like to single out Dallas Smythe, Herbert Schiller, James Halloran, Thomas Guback, Janet Wasko, Peter Golding, Graham Murdock, and Nicholas Garnham, who gave me formal interviews for the first edition. Sadly, the first three are no longer with us, but their work lives on, as does the memory of their commitment to critical research.

2009 marks the thirtieth anniversary of the largest nuclear accident in US history at Three Mile Island, Pennsylvania. As I flew over that state on the weekend of the event, I wondered whether my life was about to change substantially. I soon learned that it would, but not because of the near meltdown at a nuclear plant. My flight took me from Washington, DC, where I taught sociology at Georgetown University, to the University of Illinois, which was holding a "Working Conference" officially sponsored by the Political Economy Section of the International Association of Mass Communication Research. It was there that I met for the first time Dallas Smythe, Thomas Guback, Janet Wasko, Oscar Gandy, Eileen Meehan, and Manjunath Pendakur. As these pages describe, each of them has made a significant contribution to the political economy of communication. Over that weekend, I also met Fred Fejes, Jennifer Slack, Sari Thomas, Carolyn Marvin, Timothy Haight, and others whose research enriched critical communication studies over the years. Because it provided me with an intellectual home in the political economy of communication, that weekend did change my life. So I salute all of those who shared a memorable weekend of intellectual excitement and environmental trepidation thirty years ago. And here's to the many of you who have enriched my life ever since.

Since the first edition appeared, I have enjoyed the opportunity to speak about the political economy of communication in many places. I would like to single out for special thanks the people I have met in China and Taiwan who have been among the most eager to learn about the political economy of communication. The first edition appeared in two Chinese versions, one from Taiwan and the other from the mainland. I have visited both places several times over the years to speak on the subject. Thanks to these institutions whose students and faculty welcomed me with generosity and often intense discussion: Beijing University, Fudan University, Hong Kong Baptist University, National Cheng Chi University (Taiwan), National Chung Cheng University (Taiwan), Shanghai University, Zhejiang University, and Zhejiang Media University. I am also grateful for the opportunity to speak on the political economy of communication and specifically on the need for media democracy at the 2007 Beijing Forum. I will always cherish the memory of giving this address in the Great Hall of the People. Indeed, whenever my motivation to complete this new edition diminished, my thoughts would inevitably return to intense discussions in lecture halls, at meals, in cars, and on the streets, and I would invariably replenish my spirit and get back to work.

I am also grateful for the support of the Social Sciences and Humanities Research Council of Canada, the Canada Research Chairs Program, and Queen's University.

I would like to conclude by thanking a few people who were especially helpful in the preparation of this second edition. First, I owe a special note of appreciation to Dan Schiller, whom I met soon after that "Three Mile Island" event and with whom I have carried on a nearly thirty-year conversation in Philadelphia, San Diego, Ottawa, Kingston, Vancouver, New York, Washington, DC, Urbana, Illinois, Boulder, Colorado, Ankara, Beijing, Paris, and elsewhere. Whatever the city, our meetings typically turn from reviews of the latest books into debates about political economy, including the merits of history versus theory, of instrumentalist versus structuralist understandings of power, of the resilience versus the stress points of capitalism, of reform versus revolution, and so on. These encounters often result in each of us taking the other's position and more often than not the only resolution is our agreement that we have the most wonderful children in the world. Whatever our positions on the issues of the day, I can say with certainty that I owe a great debt to Dan for enriching my understanding of the political economy of communication.

I also want to thank two students who provided invaluable help on this project. When I approached my then research assistant and now doctoral candidate at York University David Lavin with the request that he find everything written since 1996 on every theme in the first edition, David did not flinch. Instead, he brought back annotated bibliographies and boxes of materials on every chapter of the book. Thank you David for your assistance at the start of what I know will be your own lifetime contribution to political economy and to sociology. I would also like to thank Andrew Stevens, my current doctoral student at Queen's, who took the original 1996 manuscript and put it into a form that I could work with for this new edition. Andrew also made very useful suggestions for this edition and helped me through a thicket of referencing issues. Thank you Andrew. I know that you too will make great contributions in the future.

Finally, I want to thank Catherine McKercher, my partner in life for over thirty years and in research for most of the last six. Since you overcame the greatest challenge of your life, you and I have completed three book projects together on labor in the communication industries, have walked to exhaustion through the streets of Europe, China, the United States, and Canada, and carried on intense discussions about the political economy of communication. Thank you for everything.

1

OVERVIEW OF THE POLITICAL
ECONOMY OF COMMUNICATION

Political economy is a major perspective in communication research. Since the 1940s, the approach has guided the work of scholars around the world and its global expansion continues today (Cao and Zhao, 2007; McChesney, 2007). This first chapter identifies the major ideas that subsequent chapters develop in depth and calls attention to key references that are drawn from throughout the book.

The book begins its map of the political economy approach by defining it, identifying its fundamental characteristics, and providing a guide to its major schools of thought. From here, it proceeds to examine how communication scholars have drawn on the theoretical framework to carry out research on communication media and information technologies. The section highlights recent trends, including the globalization of political economic research, the growth of historical research and of studies that concentrate on resistance to dominant media. It also emphasizes the transition from old to new media and the spread of communication activism.

The book then turns to the philosophical foundation of a political economic approach in order to better understand the enduring and new issues that need to be addressed in communication studies. Specifically, it calls for an approach to understanding that accepts as real both the concepts or ideas that guide our thinking as well as our observations or what we perceive with our senses. It thereby rejects the view, prominent in some theories, that only our ideas or only our observations, but not both, are real. It also rejects the view that reality is little more than a chimera or a figment of our imagination and that neither ideas nor observations are in any sense real. Moreover, this perspective means that reality is established or constituted by many sources and cannot be reduced to the essentialism of either economics (e.g. money alone drives the media) or culture (e.g. people's values drive the media). The approach also brings to the forefront the concepts of social change, social processes, and social relations, even if that means re-evaluating the emphasis that political economy has traditionally placed on social institutions, like media businesses, or on seeing social class as a category rather than, as this approach suggests, as a social relationship.

Putting these ideas into practice, the book moves on to identify three processes that make up the main starting points for a political economy of communication.

Commodification is the process of transforming things valued for their use into marketable products that are valued for what they can bring in exchange. This can be seen, for example, in the process of turning a story that friends enjoy into a film or a novel to be sold in the marketplace. How does the human act of communication become a product produced for a profit? *Spatialization* is the process of overcoming the constraints of geographical space with, among other things, mass media and communication technologies. For example, television overcomes distance by bringing images of world events to every part of the globe and companies increasingly use computer communication to organize business on a worldwide basis, thereby allowing them greater access to markets and the flexibility to move rapidly when conditions make it less favorable for them to stay in one place. What happens when communication goes global and when businesses use communication to create and manufacture their products worldwide? Finally *structuration* is the process of creating social relations, mainly those organized around social class, gender, and race. For example, with respect to social class, political economy describes how access to the mass media and new communication technologies is influenced by inequalities in income and wealth which enable some to afford access and others to be left out. The book wraps up by describing how the political economy of communication responds to challenges from disciplines on its borders, specifically from cultural studies and public choice theory by building bridges across theoretical divides. The book concludes with a brief coda on new bridges to build.

What is Political Economy?

Let's put more detail into this overview by taking a closer look at the makeup of this book. Chapter 2 covers the meaning of political economy, first by defining it and then by considering the main characteristics of the approach.

Two definitions of political economy capture the wide range of approaches to the discipline. In the narrow sense, *political economy is the study of the social relations, particularly the power relations, that mutually constitute the production, distribution, and consumption of resources, including communication resources.* This formulation has a certain practical value because it calls attention to how the communication business operates. It leads us to examine, for example, how communications products move through a chain of producers, such as a Hollywood film studio, to distributors, and, finally, to consumers in theaters or in their living rooms. It also directs us to the ways consumer choices, such as the websites we visit and the television shows we watch, are fed back into decisions that companies make about new media products. Furthermore, it asks us to focus on how information about these choices and even our attention to media become products for sale in the marketplace. The definition directs the political economist to understand the operation of power, a concept that addresses how people get what they want even when others do not want them to get it. It also leads us to think about what it means to be a producer, distributor, or consumer, and to appreciate the growing ambiguity about what constitutes these categories.

A more general and ambitious definition of political economy is *the study of control and survival in social life*. Control refers specifically to how a society organizes itself, manages its affairs and adapts, or fails to adapt, to the inevitable changes that all societies face. Survival means how people produce what they need to reproduce themselves and to keep their society going. According to this interpretation, control is a *political* process because it shapes the relationships within a community, and survival is mainly *economic* because it involves the process of production and reproduction. The strength of this definition is that it gives political economy the breadth to encompass at least all human activity and, arguably, all living processes. This definition was initially suggested to me by Dallas Smythe, one of the founding figures of the political economy of communication, in an interview for the first edition of this book. But since that time, it has been advanced by other political economists who are concerned about how humans relate to our increasingly threatened environment (Foster, 2002). Similar views have been advanced as well by leading figures in the rapidly developing field of science and technology studies (Haraway, 2003; Latour, 2005). The principal drawback of this broad definition is that it can lead one to overlook what distinguishes human political economy, principally our consciousness or awareness, from general processes of control and survival in nature.

Another way to describe political economy is to broaden its meaning beyond what is typically considered in definitions by focusing on a set of central qualities that characterize the approach. This section of Chapter 2 focuses on four ideas: history, the social totality, moral philosophy, and praxis. These are qualities that all schools of political economic thought tend to share, whatever their other differences.

Political economy has consistently placed in the foreground the goal of understanding social change and *historical* transformation. For the founding figures of political economy, people such as Adam Smith, David Ricardo, and John Stuart Mill, who were leading figures in European intellectual life in the eighteenth and nineteenth centuries, this meant explaining the great capitalist revolution, the vast social upheaval that transformed societies based primarily on agricultural labor into commercial, manufacturing, and, eventually, industrial societies. Responding to this first wave of political economy thinking, Karl Marx shifted the debate by critically examining the dynamic forces within capitalism and the relationship between capitalism and other forms of political economic organization. He did this specifically in order to understand the processes of social change that would, he contended, ultimately lead from capitalism to socialism. The issue of explaining social change remains central for the political economist today but the debate has shifted to include the question of whether we are now entering an information society. Specifically, is ours a new kind of society, as was capitalism, or is it just a form of capitalism, perhaps to be called informational capitalism? Are the forces of new communication and information technology so revolutionary that they are bringing about a radical restructuring that will lead to the transformation or even the dissolution of capitalism? Whatever the differences among political economists on this issue, there is no lack of attention and debate over it.

Political economy is also characterized by an interest in examining the social whole or the *totality of social relations* that make up the economic, political, social, and cultural areas of life. Political economy has always believed that there is a big picture of society and that we should try to understand it. Adam Smith was not constrained to look at only those things that a narrow discipline told him to see. He cared about the relationships among all facets of social life, including the political, economic, moral, and cultural. The same applied to Karl Marx, as it also does to today's political economists, whether they belong to the institutional, conservative, neo-Marxian, autonomist, feminist, or environmental schools of political economic thought. They differ on many points but all aim to build on the unity of the political and the economic by accounting for their mutual influence and for their relationship to wider social and symbolic spheres of activity. The political economist asks: How are power and wealth related and how are these in turn connected to cultural and social life? The political economist of communication wants to know how all of these influence and are influenced by our systems of mass media, information, and entertainment.

Political economy is also noted for its commitment to *moral philosophy*, which means that it cares about the values that help to create social behavior and about those moral principles that *ought* to guide efforts to change it. For Adam Smith, as evidenced in his *Theory of Moral Sentiments* (1976), a book he favored more than the much more popular *Wealth of Nations* (1937), this meant understanding values like self-interest, materialism, and individual freedom, that were contributing to the rise of commercial capitalism. Whereas for Karl Marx (1973, 1976a), moral philosophy meant the ongoing conflict between viewing human labor as a source of individual fulfilment and social benefit, as he hoped would be the case, or simply as a marketable commodity, as he concluded was the case in capitalism. Contemporary political economy supports a range of moral positions but, on balance, tends to favor the value of extending democracy to all aspects of social life. This includes the political realm, where democracy means the right to participate in government, but it also extends to the economic, social, and cultural domains where supporters of democracy call for income equality, access to education, full public participation in cultural production, and a guaranteed right to communicate freely.

The fourth characteristic of political economy is *social praxis*, or the fundamental unity of thinking and doing. Specifically, against traditional academic positions which separate research from social intervention and the researcher from the activist, political economists have consistently viewed intellectual life as a means of bringing about social change and social intervention as a means of advancing knowledge. This is in keeping with a tradition tracing its roots to ancient practices of providing advice and counsel to leaders. Political economists certainly differed on what should characterize intervention. Thomas Malthus so feared that population growth would outstrip the food supply that he supported open sewers because the spread of disease is one way to control population. On the other hand, there was Karl Marx, who called on workers to seize power. Notwithstanding these differences, political economists are united in the view that the division between research and action is artificial and must be overturned.

Chapter 3 documents how the political economy approach is also distinguished by the many schools of thought that guarantee a significant variety of viewpoints and vigorous internal debate. Arguably, the most important divide emerged in responses to the classical or founding political economy of Adam Smith and his followers. One set of reactions, which eventually established contemporary economics, focused on the individual as the primary unit of analysis and the market as the principal structure, both coming together through the individual's decision to register wants or demands in the marketplace. Over time, this approach progressively eliminated classical political economy's concerns for history, the social totality, moral philosophy, and praxis. In doing so, it transformed political economy into the science of economics founded on empirical investigation of marketplace behavior presented in the language of mathematics. Broadly understood as *neoclassical economics,* or simply, in recognition of its dominant position as today's orthodoxy, *economics,* it is a perspective which reduces labor to just one among the factors of production. According to this view, labor, along with land and capital, is valued solely for its productivity, or the ability to enhance the market value of a final product (Jevons, 1965; Marshall, 1961). Whether human or non-human, organic or inorganic, matter is assessed to the extent that it can be used productively to create wealth. Whereas political economy was founded on the idea that power is central to society, economics largely ignored it (Foley, 2006).

A second set of responses to the classic political economy of Adam Smith opposed the tendencies of neoclassical economics by retaining the concern for history, the social whole, moral philosophy, and praxis, even if that meant giving up the goal of creating the science of economics. This set constitutes the wide variety of approaches to *political economy*. A first wave was led by a number of groups, including *conservatives,* who sought to replace marketplace individualism with the collective authority of tradition (Carlyle, 1984). It also included *Utopian Socialists,* who accepted the classical faith in social intervention but urged putting community ahead of the market (Owen, 1851). Finally, the first wave also included *Marxian* thinkers, who returned labor and the struggle between social classes to the center of political economy. Subsequent formulations built on these perspectives, leaving us with a wide range of contemporary formulations.

On the right-wing side of the academic political spectrum, a *neo-conservative political economy* builds on the work of people like George J. Stigler (1971, 2003), James M. Buchanan (1999), and Ronald Coase (Coase, 1991; Coase and Barrett, 1968), all recipients of the Nobel prize in economics. These thinkers applied the categories of neoclassical economics to all social behavior with the aim of expanding individual freedom. A recent extension of this approach is called the *new institutional economics,* a school of thought that is gaining adherents and is exemplified in the work of Oliver Williamson (2000). Central to this view is the continuing use of neoclassical economic tools to examine the market as the universal and most natural of institutions (Ankarloo and Palermo, 2004). All other ways of organizing social life are seen as institutional alternatives that serve only to shore up the market on those occasions when it is deficient in meeting social goals (Boettke and Storr, 2002).

On the center left of the academic spectrum an older form of *institutional political economy* focuses critically on how institutional and technological constraints shape markets to the advantage of those corporations and governments large enough and powerful enough to control them (Galbraith, 1985, 2004; Lawson, 2005; Veblen, 1932, 1934). Institutionalists created the framework for communication research that documents how large media companies can control the production and distribution of media products and, by doing so, restrict the diversity of content, specifically by keeping out work that challenges pro-business views. *Neo-Marxian* approaches, including theories of post-Fordism (Jessop, 2002; Lipietz, 1988), world systems theory (Wallerstein, 2004), and others engaged in the debate over globalization (Harvey, 2006; Sassen, 2007), continue to place social class at the center of analysis, and are principally responsible for debates on the relationship between monopoly capitalism, the automation and deskilling of work, and the growth of an international division of labor. Recent research has sought out common ground between institutional and neo-Marxian theories (O'Hara, 2000, 2002). Finally, social movements have spawned their own schools of political economy. These include primarily *feminist political economy*, which addresses the persistence of patriarchy and the lack of attention to household and other reproductive labor (Huws, 2003; McLaughlin, 2004; Peterson, 2005), *environmental* or *ecological political economy*, which concentrates on the links between social behavior and the wider organic environment (Foster, 2002; Rosewarne, 2002; Wall, 2006), and a political economy that melds the analysis of social movements with the Italian *autonomous* theoretical tradition (Hardt and Negri, 2000, 2004). Dyer-Witheford (1999) and Terranova (2004) have made the most productive use of this tradition in communication studies.

The Political Economy of Communication

Chapters 4, 5, and 6 take up the development of a political economy tradition in communication research and describe its development throughout the world. Chapter 4 begins with the definition of communication. It is interesting to observe the vast range of fields that have found it necessary to address the meaning of communication from their specific vantage points. Areas of study and practice, including engineering, computer science, sociology, information studies, philosophy, linguistics, architecture, and several others, including, of course, communication and media studies, have examined the nature of communication. In keeping with a basic theme of this book, there is no single definition that works across all fields. But for the purpose of exploring the political economy of communication, it is useful to see it as *a social exchange of meaning whose outcome is the measure or mark of a social relationship*. From this perspective, communication is more than the transmission of data or information; it is *the social production of meaning that constitutes a relationship*. Chapter 4 proceeds to examine the specific characteristics of the political economy of communication by taking up the social and intellectual forces that propelled its development.

Chapter 5 examines the foundational work in the political economy of communication. North American research has been extensively influenced by the contributions of two founding figures, Dallas Smythe and Herbert Schiller. Smythe taught the first course in the political economy of communication at the University of Illinois and is the first of four generations of scholars linked together in this research tradition. Schiller, who followed Smythe at the University of Illinois, similarly influenced several generations of political economists. Their approach to communication studies drew on both the *institutional* and *Marxian* traditions. A concern about the growing size and power of transnational communication businesses places them squarely in the institutional school, but their interest in social class and in media imperialism gives their work a definite Marxian focus. However, they were less interested than, for example, European scholars, in providing an explicit theoretical account of communication. Rather, their work and, through their influence, a great deal of the research in North America has been driven more explicitly by a sense of injustice that the communication industry has become an integral part of a wider corporate order which is both exploitative and undemocratic. Although Smythe and Schiller were concerned with the impact in North America, they both developed a research program that charts the growth in power and influence of transnational media companies throughout the world (Maxwell, 2003; Schiller, 1989, 1992, 1996, 2000; Smythe, 1981).

Partly owing to their influence, North American research has produced a large literature on transnational corporate and government power, coupled with active involvement in social movements to change the dominant media and to create alternatives to its commercial emphasis (McChesney, 2007; Mosco and McKercher, 2008; Schiller, 2007a; Wasko, 2003). One objective of this work is to advance public interest concerns before government regulatory and policy organs. This includes support for those movements that have taken an active role before international organizations, in defense of a new international economic, information, and communication order (Mosco and Schiller, 2001). North American communication scholarship has called for a renewed critique of global capitalism, including its use of information and communication technologies, and its media practices. Authors working in this tradition highlight the continuing significance and unique vantage point of Marxism for media and communication studies. While those who employ a Marxian framework do disagree on some of the specifics, they all insist on the necessity of including power and social class relations in media and communication studies as well as committing to praxis by combing research and action to advance a more democratic society (Artz, Macek, and Cloud, 2006; Schiller, 2007a).

European research has been less clearly linked to specific founding figures and, although it is also connected to movements for social change, particularly in defense of public service media systems, the leading work in this region was, from the start, more concerned to integrate communication research within various neo-Marxian and institutional theoretical traditions. Of the two principal directions this research has taken, one, most prominent in the work of Garnham (2000, 2003) and in that of Golding and Murdock (Murdock, 2004; Murdock and Golding, 2000), has emphasized *class power* and the fundamental inequalities that continue to divide rich from poor. Building on the Frankfurt School tradition, as well as on the work of Raymond Williams (1975), it documents the vast expansion and integration of the communication industry, its connection to government power, and its integration into the wider system of capitalism. Media reinforce social class divisions and help to build solidarity within a dominant class.

A second stream of research foregrounds *class struggle* and is most prominent in the work of Armand Mattelart (2000; Mattelart and Mattelart, 1992; Mattelart and Siegelaub, 1979, 1983). Mattelart has drawn from a range of traditions, including dependency theory, Western Marxism, and the worldwide experience of national liberation movements to understand communication as one among the principal sources of *resistance* to power. His work has demonstrated how people in the less developed world, particularly in Latin America, where Mattelart was an advisor to the government of Chile before it was overthrown in a 1973 military coup, used the mass media to oppose Western control and create indigenous news and entertainment media.

Two scholars who provide good examples of how to put these perspectives into practice, particularly in their analysis of labor in the media industries, are Bernard Miège and Peter Waterman. From a class power perspective, Miège (1989, 2003) offers an assessment of different labor processes that tend to cohere with different forms of media production within the overall logic of capitalist social relations. He suggests that there is a connection between the type of media product, the structure of corporate control, and the nature of the labor process. Research on labor and class struggle has also been prominent in the work of Waterman (2001), who has documented labor and trade union use of the mass media and new communication technologies to promote democracy and the common interests of workers worldwide.

Communication research from and about the less developed world has covered a wide area of interests, although a major stream of political economy research arose in response to the modernization or developmentalist theory that originated in Western, particularly US, attempts to emphasize the role of the media in its particular vision of economic and social development. The modernization thesis held that the media were resources which, along with urbanization, education, and other social forces, would mutually stimulate economic, social, and cultural development. As a result, media growth was viewed as a sign of development. According to this view, societies became modern when they demonstrated a specific level of media development, including newspapers, broadcasting stations, and movie theaters. Drawing on several streams of international neo-Marxian political economy, including world systems and dependency theory, political economists challenged the fundamental premises of the developmentalist model, particularly its technological determinism and the omission of practically any interest in the power relations that shape the terms of relationships between rich and poor nations and the multilayered class relations between and within them (Melkote and Steeves, 2001; Mody, 2003; Pendakur, 2003; Wheeler, 2003; Zhao, 2008).

When massive media investment failed to promote development, modernization theorists went in search of revised models that include telecommunication and new computer technologies (Jussawalla, 1993; Jussawalla and Taylor, 2003). While Asia, especially China and India, have made extensive use of network technologies to speed economic growth, political economy emphasizes that the former has done so with precious little progress toward democracy (Lee, 2001; Zhao, 2008) and the latter remains overwhelmingly impoverished with a few big companies and over half the population without electricity (Kapur, 2007; Kumar, 2003; Mosco and McKercher, 2008).

Africa is the poorest, most marginalized continent and has been subject to numerous development schemes. With the growth of the Internet and the rise of a global information economy, the proliferation of new information and communication technologies, like media growth, is now seen as a key index of development. It is assumed by some in influential academic and policy-making circles that their wide dissemination will cause progressive social, cultural, political, and economic change in a simple, direct, and linear manner. In addition to their neoliberal orthodoxy, which insists that developing countries take a market-based approach with as little government intervention as possible, these dominant views are clearly situated within the developmentalist paradigm and take technological determinist positions. Such visions and policy formulations have been subjected to considerable critique as they have so far fallen short of their promises and predictions in relation to actual accomplishments in most of Africa (Alzouma, 2005; Mercer, 2004; Tetty, 2001; Thompson, 2004; Van Audenhove, et. al., 1999; Wheeler, 2003; Ya'u, 2004).

Political economists have also responded by addressing the power of these new technologies to integrate a global division of labor. A first wave of research saw the division largely in territorial terms: unskilled labor concentrated in the poorest nations, semi-skilled and more complex assembly labor in semi-peripheral societies, and research, development, and strategic planning limited to first-world corporate headquarters to where the bulk of profit would flow. Current research acknowledges that class divisions cut across territorial lines and maintains that what is central to the evolving international division of labor is the growth in flexibility, or flexible accumulation as it is called, so that firms can overcome any constraints on their ability to control markets and make money (McKercher and Mosco, 2007; Pellow and Park, 2002; Schiller, 2007a; Sussman and Lent, 1998).

Chapter 6 concludes this section by identifying five major current trends in the political economy of communication, starting with the globalization of research. The field is no longer characterized by specific regional tendencies, nor does North American and European research dominate its agenda to the extent that it once did. Political economy research is now international in that it is carried out by scholars from all over the world who are increasingly interested in addressing global issues.

The field has also expanded its commitment to communication history, especially the history of opposition to dominant powers in industry and government. In doing so, it has uncovered the unexamined stories of attempts to build alternatives to the dominant commercial system that fed into wider resistance movements in society. Political economy has also broadened its traditional focus on examining dominant powers and processes of exploitation to address standpoints of resistance. These especially include feminist and labor perspectives on media and communication.

Political economy has begun to make the transition from its established strength in examining how power operates in older media to a variety of approaches to new media, especially to the Internet. As it has in the past, the field continues to account for continuities between old and new media, including describing how dominant powers use both to make money. But it also now examines discontinuities by considering the challenges that new media pose for traditional patterns of capitalist development. Moreover, political economists have documented the connections between the promises made about old and new media and, more importantly, they have linked efforts to create a technological utopia, present from the telegraph to the Internet, to systems of power in society. Political economists are also taking on social issues that new media make especially prominent. These include control over intellectual property, electronic surveillance, and the significance of a network economy.

The fifth and final current trend in political economy research is the expansion of political activism. This includes the continued growth of established organizations such as the Union for Democratic Communications and the International Association for Media and Communication Research. The trend is embodied most substantially by the media reform movement in the United States. But it is also exemplified in the success of new national (Free Press) and international (the World Summit on the Information Society) movements.

Philosophical Foundation

Having mapped the field and examined current trends, Chapters 7 through 9 provide a specific theoretical grounding for the political economy of communication. Chapter 7 begins with the philosophical foundation by advancing basic *epistemological* and *ontological* principles. An epistemology is an approach to understanding how we know things. The political economy of communication is grounded in a realist, inclusive, constitutive, and critical epistemology. It is *realist* in that it recognizes the reality of both concepts and social practices, thereby distinguishing itself from *idiographic* approaches that argue for the reality of ideas alone and *nomothetic* approaches which claim that ideas are only labels for the singular reality of human action. Following from this, political economy is *inclusive* in that it rejects essentialism, which would reduce all social practices to a single political economic explanation, in favor of an approach that views concepts as entry or starting points into a diverse social field (Resnick and Wolff, 1987, 2006). The choice of certain concepts and theories over others means that our thinking and experience warrants giving them priority. But they are not assertions of the one best, or only, way to understand social practices. Additionally, the epistemology is *constitutive* in that it recognizes the limits of causal determination, including the assumption that units of social analysis interact as fully formed wholes and in a linear fashion. Rather, it approaches social life as a set of mutually constitutive processes, acting on one another in various stages of formation, and with a direction and impact that can only be comprehended in specific research. Finally, the approach is *critical* because it sees knowledge as the product of comparisons between research findings and other bodies of knowledge as well as with social values. For example, this political economy is critical in that it regularly situates the knowledge acquired in research against alternative bodies of knowledge in, for example, neoclassical economics, pluralist political science, and cultural studies. Furthermore, it measures political economic knowledge against the values that guide our praxis, including the social democratic values of public participation and equality.

If epistemology provides a framework for understanding how we know things, then ontology gives us a foundation for understanding the nature of being. In general, ontology distinguishes between seeing things as either *structures* or as *processes*. This is important for political economy because it departs from the traditional approach to political economy, which concentrates on such structures as the business firm and government, by placing social processes and social relations in the foreground. This means that research starts from the view that social change is ubiquitous, that structures and institutions are constantly changing, and that it is therefore more useful to develop starting points that characterize processes rather than simply to identify relevant institutions. Studying media institutions is important but it follows from an analysis of a social process. Subsequent chapters describe these processes.

Guided by this principle, the remainder of Chapter 7 and the following two chapters develop a substantive map of political economy with three entry processes, starting with *commodification*, the process of transforming use to exchange value, moving on to *spatialization*, the transformation of space, or the process of institutional extension, and finally to *structuration*, the process of constituting structures with social agency. Placing these processes in the foreground does not replace structures and institutions, something that would substitute one form of essentialism for another. Rather, these are entry points that comprise a substantive theory of political economy, one preferred choice among a range of possible means to understand the social field.

Commodifying Content, Audiences, and Labor

Chapter 7 takes up commodification or the process of transforming goods and services which are valued for their use, e.g. food to satisfy hunger, stories for communication, into commodities which are valued for what they can earn in the marketplace, e.g. commercial farming to sell food, producing drama for commercial broadcasting. The process of commodification holds a dual significance for communication research. First, communication practices and technologies contribute to the general commodification process throughout society. For example, the introduction of computer communication gives all companies, not just communication companies, greater control over the entire process of production, distribution, and exchange, permitting retailers to monitor sales and inventory levels with ever-improving precision. This enables firms to produce and ship only what they know is likely to sell quickly, thereby reducing inventory requirements and unnecessary merchandise. Wal-Mart, one of the world's largest corporations, is noted for its aggressive use of information technology. It has been at the forefront of propelling the process of tracking inventory and monitoring sales using satellite and computer communications to link its corporate headquarters in the United States with its nationwide network of stores (Head, 2004). The ability to exercise deep and extensive surveillance enables the company to measure and monitor precisely what its customers buy, thereby increasing its efficiency and profitability.

Second, commodification is an entry point to understand specific communication institutions and practices. For example, the general, worldwide expansion of commodification in the 1980s, responding in part to global declines in economic growth, led to the increased commercialization of media programming, the privatization of once public media and telecommunications institutions, and the liberalization of communication markets, including in places, like the Middle East, where commodification had been limited (Khiabany, 2006; Sreberny, 2001).

The political economy of communication has been notable for its emphasis on examining the significance of institutions, especially those businesses and governments responsible for the production, distribution, and exchange of communication commodities and for the regulation of the communication marketplace. Although it has not neglected the commodity itself and the process of commodification, the tendency has been to foreground corporate and government institutions. When it has treated the commodity, political economy has tended to concentrate on media *content* and less so on media audiences and the labor involved in media production. The emphasis on media structures and content is understandable in light of the importance of global media companies and the growth in the value of media content. Tightly integrated transnational businesses, such as Time Warner, News Corp., and Sony create media products with a multiplier effect embodied, for example, in the cross-promotion of a new Hollywood film through subsidiaries of these companies that operate in television, over the Internet, and in print media. Political economy has helped to understand the many different ways that corporations and governments shape the full range of media content from news (McChesney, 2003) to pornography (Jacobs, 2007). The growth of the Internet has advanced opportunities for commodification because it deepens and extends opportunities to measure and monitor, as well as to package and repackage, communication content.

Commodification applies to *audiences* as well as to content. Political economy has paid some attention to audiences, particularly in the effort to understand the common practice whereby advertisers pay for the size and quality (propensity to consume) of an audience that a newspaper, magazine, website, radio, or television program can deliver. Years ago, this generated a vigorous debate among political economists about whether audiences, in fact, labor, sell their labor power (in effect, their attention) in return for whatever content they receive (Lebowitz, 1986; Murdock, 1978; Smythe, 1977). The debate was useful because it broadened the discussion of commodification beyond content and because it meant that communication research would have to examine all businesses that advertise and not just media companies. Recent political economy research has extended the analysis of audience research to examine audience history and the complex relationship of audiences to the producers of commercial culture (Butsch, 2000; Compton, 2004; Hagen and Wasko, 2000; Ross and Nightingale, 2003). It has also extended the debate over audience labor to the Internet, where the process of building websites, modifying software, playing online games, and participating in online communities both resembles and differs from the labor of audiences that Smythe described (Campbell, 2005; Grimes, 2006; McMillan, 1998; Meehan, 1999; Smith-Shomade, 2004; Terranova, 2000).

In addition to examining the process of commodifying media content and audiences, it is important to consider the commodification of media *labor*. Braverman's (1974) now classic work directly confronted the transformation of the labor process in capitalism. According to him, general labor is constituted out of the unity of *conception*, the power to envision, imagine, and design work, and *execution*, the power to carry it out. In the process of commodification, capital acts to *separate* conception from execution, skill from the raw ability to carry out a task, and to *concentrate* conceptual power in a managerial class that is either a part of capital or represents its interests. In the extreme, and with considerable labor resistance, this involved the application of detailed and intrusive "scientific management" practices. Braverman documented the process of labor transformation in the rise of large-scale industry, but he is particularly recognized for demonstrating the extension of this process into the service, information, and communication sectors. His work gave rise to an enormous body of empirical research and theoretical debate, the latter focusing principally on the need to address the contested nature of the process, the active agency of workers, and how the transformation of the labor process was experienced differently by industry, occupation, class, gender, and race (Berberoglu, 1993; Huws, 2003).

The labor of communication workers is also being commodified as wage labor has grown in significance throughout the media workplace. In order to cut the labor bill and expand revenue, managers replaced mechanical with electronic systems to eliminate thousands of jobs in the printing industry as electronic typesetting did away with the jobs of linotype operators. Today's digital systems allow companies to expand this process. Print reporters increasingly serve in the combined roles of editor and page producer. They not only report on a story, they also put it into a form for transmission to the printed, and increasingly, electronic page. Companies generally retain the rights to the multiplicity of repackaged forms and thereby profit from each use. Broadcast journalists carry cameras and edit tape for delivery over television or computer networks. The film and video industry demands complete control over the profits that arise when a movie or television show is distributed over the Internet and other new media. Companies now sell software well before it has been debugged on the understanding that customers will report errors, download and install updates, and figure out how to work around problems. This ability to eliminate labor, combine it to perform multiple tasks, limit payment for multiple uses, and shift labor to unpaid consumers further expands the revenue potential (McKercher and Mosco, 2007). Workers have responded to this by bringing together people from different media, including journalists, broadcast professionals, and technical specialists in the film, video, telecommunications, and computer services sectors, into trade unions and other worker organizations that represent large segments of the communications workforce (McKercher, 2002; Mosco and McKercher, 2008). This is one of several examples of resistance to commodification that are highlighted in Chapter 7.

From Commodification to Spatialization

Chapter 8 reports on the second starting point for rethinking the political economy of communication, *spatialization*, or the process of overcoming the constraints of space in social life. Political economists start from how communication content, audiences, and labor are turned in marketable commodities. But they do not reduce all communication to this single process. From the earliest development of a political economy approach, spatialization has taken its place alongside commodification. Classical political economists, such as Adam Smith and David Ricardo, found it necessary to devote considerable attention to the problems of how to value the spaces taken up by land and our built environment. Furthermore, their development of a labor theory of value was connected to the problem of how to define and measure labor time. Marx (1973) came closer to spatialization when he noted that capitalism "annihilates space with time." By this he meant that business makes use of the means of transportation and communication to diminish the time it takes to move goods, people, and messages through space, thereby saving on the costs of distribution and overall company management. Today, political economists would say that rather than annihilate space, business, aided by developments in communication and information technology, transforms space (Castells, 2001). People, products, and messages have to be located somewhere and it is this location that is undergoing significant transformation, evidenced in, for example, upheavals in the international division of labor that has seen millions of jobs relocated to low-wage regions of the world, especially to China and India.

Spatialization builds upon ideas offered by sociologists and geographers to address structural changes brought about by shifting uses of space and time. Giddens (1990) refers to the centrality of *time–space distanciation* in order to examine the decline of our dependency on time and space. He suggests that this process expands the availability of time and space as resources for those who can make use of them. Harvey (1989) identifies *time–space compression* to suggest how the effective map of the world is shrinking, again for those who can take advantage of it. Castells (2001) calls our attention to the declining importance of physical space, the space of places, and the rising significance of *the space of flows* to suggest that the world map is being redrawn according to boundaries established by flows of people, goods, services, and messages, creating what Massey (1992) refers to as a transformed "power-geometry."

Communication is central to spatialization because communication and information technologies and processes promote flexibility and control throughout industry, but particularly within the media, communication, and information sectors. Spatialization encompasses the process of *globalization*, the worldwide restructuring of industries, companies, and other institutions. Restructuring at the industry level is exemplified by the development of integrated markets based on digital technologies and, at the firm level, by the growth of the flexible or net-worked company, which makes use of communication and information systems to continuously change structure, product line, marketing, and relationships to other companies, suppliers, its own workforce, and customers.

Globalization and industrial restructuring mutually influence four major patterns of government restructuring. *Commercialization* establishes state functions, such as providing mail and telecommunications services, principally along business or revenue-generating lines. *Privatization* takes this a step further by turning these units into private businesses. *Liberalization* gives the state's approval to opening markets to widespread competition, and, finally, *internationalization* links the state to other states thereby shift-ing economic and political authority to regional authorities that bring together several countries in one geographical area. A good example of this is the alliance among the United States, Canada, and Mexico established by the North American Free Trade Agreement (NAFTA) (Mosco and Schiller, 2001). Internationalization also encompasses the growth of global authorities such as the World Trade Organization (McChesney and Schiller, 2003).

The political economy of communication has traditionally addressed spatialization as the institutional extension of corporate power in the communication industry. Political economists have typically referred to this as the problem of media concen-tration which is manifested in the sheer growth in the size of media firms, measured by assets, revenues, profit, employees, and stock value. For example, communications systems in the United States are now shaped by a handful of companies, including US-based firms General Electric (NBC), Viacom (CBS), the Walt Disney Company (ABC), Time Warner (CNN), Microsoft, and Google. There are others, including non-US-based firms such as the News Corporation (Fox) and Sony. Political economy has specifically examined growth by taking up different forms of corporate concentration (Bettig and Hall, 2003; Herman and Chomsky, 2002; McChesney, 2007). *Horizontal integration* takes place when a firm in one line of media buys a major interest in another media operation that is not directly related to the original business. The typical form of this is *cross-media* concentration or the purchase by a firm in an older line of media, say a newspaper, of a firm in a newer line, such as a television station or website. Horizontal concentration also takes place when a media company buys all or part a business entirely outside the media or when a company outside the media and communication industries buys various media or communication enterprises.

Vertical integration describes the amalgamation of firms within a line of business that extend a company's control over the process of production, as when a major Hollywood film production studio purchases a distributor of film or when a software company buys a social networking site. This is also referred to as forward integration because it expands a firm further along the production and distribution processes. Backward vertical inte-gration took place when the *New York Times* purchased paper mills in Quebec, thereby expanding the company down to the base of its production process.

In addition to demonstrating how media firms have developed into transna-tional conglomerates that now rival, in size and power, firms in any industry, political economists are addressing the development of flexible forms of corporate power evidenced in the *joint ventures, strategic alliances,* and other short-term and project-specific arrangements that bring together companies or parts of companies, including competitors. These take advantage of more flexible means of communication to unite and separate for mutual interest (Wasko, 2003).

One consequence of spatialization is the development of global labor markets. Business can now take advantage of differential wages, skills, and other important characteristics on an international scale. Much of the early political economic work in this area concentrated on the spread of the computer and communication component manufacturing (southeast Asia) and data entry (the Caribbean) businesses into the Third World, where companies were attracted by low wages and *authoritarian* rule (Heyzer, 1986; Sussman and Lent, 1998). The scope of research has expanded to address what is now called outsourcing, or business efforts to find sources of relatively low wage but skilled labor, needed in such areas as software production and call-centre sales and services in the less developed world, especially today in India (Mirchandani, 2004; Mosco and McKercher, 2008; Taylor and Bain, 2004). Spatialization of this sort also takes place within the developed world, where a prime example is the growth of US film and video production in places like Toronto, Vancouver, and other parts of Canada where lower labor costs add to business profits (Magder and Burston, 2001; Wasko and Erickson, 2008). Finally, spatialization gives rise to debates about resistance, the formation of public space, and to globalization. Chapter 8 concludes by examining the complex connections that link globalization to nationalism, terrorism, and religious fundamentalism.

Structuration: Social Structure and Human Agency

Chapter 9 examines structuration, the third entry point for a renewed political economy of communication. The process of structuration amounts to a contemporary rendering of Marx's view that people make history, but not under conditions of their own making. In other words, social action takes place within the constraints and the opportunities provided by the structures within which action happens. We can bring about social change and "make history" but only under the terms that social structures enable. Research based on structuration helps to balance a tendency in political economic analysis to concentrate on structures, typically business and governmental institutions, by incorporating the ideas of human agency, social process, and social practice. The concept was usefully explored in the work of Giddens (1984), but this chapter gives it a stronger social emphasis. A focus on social structuration is especially important in building connections between political economy and the concepts of social class, gender, and race.

Structuration calls on us to broaden the conception of social class from its structural or *categorical* sense, which defines class in terms of what some have and others do not, to incorporate both a relational and a formational sense of the term. This takes nothing away from the value of seeing social class, in part, as a designation for the differences between the "haves" and the "have nots." The political economy of communication has addressed social class in these terms by producing research that documents persistent inequalities in communication systems, particularly in access to the means of communication (Kyasny, 2006; Murdock and Golding, 2004). This has been applied to labor, particularly in research on how communication and information technology has been used to automate and deskill work, including work in the media industries (McKercher, 2002; Rodino-Colocino, 2006). It has also been used to show how the means of communication are used to measure and monitor work activity in systems of surveillance that extend managerial control over the entire labor process in precise detail (Parenti, 2003). Sophisticated electronic surveillance of the labor process has also been used to construct new forms of employee deviance exemplified in the neoliberal discourse on worker "theft of time" (Snider, 2002).

In order to enrich the categorical view of social class, Chapter 9 builds on the categorical conception with a *relational* view of class that defines it according to those practices and processes that link social class categories, the relationship between business and labor for example. In this view, the working class is not defined simply by its relative lack of access to the means of communication, but by its relationships of harmony, dependency, and conflict with the capitalist class (McKercher and Mosco, 2007). Moreover, a *formational* conception of social class views the working class as producer of its own identity in relation to capital and independently of it (Dyer-Witheford, 1999; Maxwell, 2001; Mosco and McKercher, 2008). The political economy of social class structuration aims to demonstrate how classes constitute themselves, how they make history, in the face of well-researched analysis of the conditions that constrain this history-making activity. Social class is a category defined by what some have and others do not. But classes also actively relate to one another and they also constitute or make themselves, independently of one another.

Chapter 9 also demonstrates that it is important to balance another tendency in the field. When it has given attention to agency, process, and social practice, political economy tends to emphasize social class. There are good reasons for starting from social class because class structuration is a central entry point for understanding social life and numerous studies have documented the persistence of class divisions in the political economy of communication. Nevertheless, Chapter 9 re-emphasizes the general need to avoid the essentialism that, in this case, would reduce all social relations to class relations. There are other dimensions to structuration that complement and conflict with class structuration, including *gender*, *race*, and those broadly defined *social movements*, which, along with class, make up much of the social relations of communication.

Political economy has made important strides in addressing the intersection of feminist studies and the political economy of communication while also insisting that more critical work needs to be done (Byerly, 2004; Lee, 2006; McLaughlin, 2004; Meehan and Riordan, 2002; Sarikakis and Shade, 2007). It has also taken major steps in research on information technology, gender, and the international division of labor, which addresses the double oppression that women workers face in industries such as microelectronics, where they experience the lowest wages and the most exploitive working conditions (Huws, 2003; Mosco and McKercher, 2008, especially Chapter 2; Pellow and Park, 2002).

Race also figures significantly in this analysis and more generally in the social process of structuration, as Oscar Gandy (1998, 2003), one of the central figures in the development of a political economy approach to communication, takes up in his multi-perspectival assessment of race and the media. Racial divisions are a principal constituent of the multiple hierarchies that comprise the contemporary global political economy, and race, as both category and social relationship, helps to explain access to national and global resources, including communication, media, and information technology (Green, 2001; Pellow and Park, 2002; Ya'u, 2004).

Chapter 9 concludes by demonstrating how *social movements* that intersect with class, gender, and race are significant forces in opposing mainstream media and its version of "common sense" or hegemony with alternative media that can forge a genuine counter-hegemony (Downing, 2001; Hanke, 2005; Howley, 2005; McChesney, 2007). Political economists conclude that out of the tensions and clashes within various structuration processes, the media come to be organized in mainstream, oppositional, and alternative forms.

Building Bridges: Cultural Studies, Public Choice, and Beyond

To develop a complete political economy of communication, particularly one that recognizes that it is but one way to look at social life, then it is necessary to examine and build bridges to approaches on its intellectual borders. Political economy is an important perspective, but it is not the only useful way to see the world. To address this, the final chapter of the book situates the political economy of communication opposite cultural studies, on the one side, and public choice theory on the other.

The cultural studies approach is an intellectual movement which focuses on the constitution of meaning in texts, defined broadly to include all forms of social communication (McRobbie, 2005). The approach contains numerous currents and fissures that provide for considerable ferment from within (Grossberg, 2006). Nevertheless, it can contribute to understanding and advancing political economy in several ways.

Chapter 10 describes how cultural studies has been open to a broad-based critique of positivism (the view that sensory observation is the only source of knowledge). Moreover, it has defended a more open philosophical approach that concentrates on subjectivity or on how people interpret their world, as well as on the social creation of knowledge. Cultural studies has also widened the meaning of cultural analysis by starting from the premise that culture is ordinary, produced by all social actors, rather than only by a privileged creative elite, and that the social is organized around gender, race, and nationality divisions and identities as much as by social class.

Although political economy can learn from these departures, it can also contribute to advancing cultural studies. Even as it takes on a philosophical approach that is open to subjectivity and is more broadly inclusive, political economy insists on a realist epistemology that maintains the value of historical research, of thinking in terms of concrete social totalities, with a well-grounded moral philosophy, and a commitment to overcoming the distinction between social research and social action. Political economy departs from the tendency in cultural studies to exaggerate the importance of subjectivity, as well as the inclination to reject thinking in terms of historical practices and social totalities. Political economy also maintains that cultural analysis should be accessible to those ordinary people who are responsible for creating culture. Finally, it calls on cultural studies to pay greater attention to labor and the labor process, including addressing the importance of labor in movements for social change (Denning, 1996, 2004; James and Berg, 1996; Maxwell, 2001; Mosco, 2004). Meehan (1999) argues that a more fruitful encounter between the political economy of communication and cultural studies is possible if one focuses on the critical rather the celebratory strand of cultural studies. Dialogue with critical cultural studies is not only useful for political economy, she maintains, it is also essential to understand media artifacts, audiences, and institutions. Her work signals the progress made over the last decade in building a fruitful dialogue between political economy and cultural studies (Deetz and Hegbloom, 2007; McLaughlin, 1999; Peck, 2006).

Chapter 10 also demonstrates that political economy can learn from the development of a *public choice* perspective whose political wing has tended to place the state at the center of analysis, and whose economic wing aims to extend the application of primarily neoclassical economic theory over a wide range of political, social, and cultural life (Buchanan, 1999; Posner, 1992; Stigler, 2003).

Political economy has tended to regard government as overly dependent on and determined by the specific configuration of capital dominant at the time. It would therefore benefit from an approach that takes seriously the active role of government. Moreover, political economy shares with public choice theory the interest in extending analysis over the entire social totality, with an eye to social transformation. Nevertheless, political economy departs fundamentally from the public choice tendency to a pluralist political analysis that views the state as the independent arbiter of a wide range of social forces, none of which, including business, has enough power to dominate society. Against this, political economy insists on the power of business and the process of commodification as the starting point of social analysis. Furthermore, political economy rejects the public choice tendency to build its analysis of the social totality, and of those values that should guide its transformation, on individualism and on the alleged rationality of the market. Against this, it insists on social processes, starting from social class and labor, and on setting community and public life against the market and a rationality that, from a political economy perspective, actually reproduces class power (Lewis and Miller, 2003). Building bridges can only be genuinely productive when we are clear about what distinguishes each approach.

The book concludes by looking ahead to two additional bridge-building processes. One would draw on the growth of science and technology studies and the other, a larger project, would bring together the broad program of the social sciences and the humanities, of which political economy, cultural studies, and policy studies, are a part, and the program of the sciences, mainly physics, chemistry, and biology, that claims near complete authority in intellectual life today. The divide separating these is arguably as great or greater than when the writer C.P. Snow spoke of "Two Cultures" going their separate ways over fifty years ago. Overcoming the divide is an enormous but vital challenge and the book ends with some initial thoughts on how to do so.

2

WHAT IS POLITICAL ECONOMY?
DEFINITIONS AND CHARACTERISTICS

Before taking up the political economy of communication, we need to examine the general field of political economy. After defining the approach, this chapter discusses a set of its central characteristics. The next chapter addresses the major schools of thought that have provided political economy with its richness and diversity.

Beginning with the classical political economy of Adam Smith, David Ricardo, and others, the chapter proceeds to take up the criticisms leveled by conservative and Marxist theorists. In the late nineteenth century, influenced by the drive to create a science of society modeled after developments in the hard sciences, William Jevons and Alfred Marshall, among others, established the neoclassical paradigm that continues to provide a model for mainstream economics. Choosing to concentrate on describing, preferably through a set of mathematical equations, the outcomes of different combinations of productive factors (land, labor, and capital), this school of thought eliminated most of the political from political economy.[1]

In the twentieth century, the neoclassical view became what Kuhn (1970) calls "normal science," or textbook economics. Not unlike the way Newtonian mechanics came to mean physics, the neoclassical approach came to mean economics. But the process of normalizing economics was one of continuous intellectual and political ferment that itself merits a volume on the political economy of economics (Foley, 2006). The so-called Austrian and Cambridge wings of the mainstream neoclassical school debated the centrality of markets and the role of the state. Institutional, Marxian, and corporatist approaches leveled more fundamental criticisms at the paradigm's assumptions, concepts, conclusions, and engagement (or lack of engagement) with political and social life.

---

1 This does not mean that the new science of economics lacked a political theory. The explicit choice to eliminate the word *political* reflects an important view of power and government that has carried forward in debates among neoclassical economists and between defenders of the paradigm and its critics. In essence, it states that economics is not only more important than politics; as an objective science, economics can and should be disconnected from politics.

This tension between normal science and ferment continues. On the one hand, neoclassical economics appears to have triumphed in the university and in political life. Economics journals chiefly address the puzzles that remain to be solved and the relationships that need to receive mathematical fine-tuning within the neoclassical paradigm. The ranks of government and corporate policy analysts and policy-makers are filled with some of the discipline's smartest and shrewdest practitioners. On the other hand, fundamental criticisms continue to mount about the limits of normal economics. Scholars trained in the discipline question its ability to explain even that limited sphere defined as the formal domain of economics (McCloskey, 1985, 2002; Foley, 2006). Economic policy observers complain that the traditional economic medicines do not work, or worse, make the patient sicker (Shiller, 2006). Alternatives to neoclassical orthodoxy multiply. Ranging widely over the political spectrum (from heirs to the conservative tradition of Edmund Burke, such as Michael Oakshott, to the range of institutional and neo-Marxist perspectives) and equally widely over substantive terrain (e.g. feminist, ecological, and moral economics; public choice theory applied to the family, sexuality, etc.), there is no shortage of pretenders to the throne. What all of these share is a commitment to expand the conceptual, methodological, and substantive parameters of conventional economics. It would take more than this chapter to do justice to the full weight of the debates within contemporary economics and political economy. This chapter is limited to offering a map of the territory and an analysis of the major differences between mainstream economics and the variety of political economies.

One might wonder about the appropriateness of two chapters on general political economy in a book whose focus is the political economy of communication. There are four major reasons for this. First, political economists of communication have tended to emphasize communication at the expense of political economic theory. Furthermore, an overview of political economy provides a basis from which to think about the emphases and gaps in the political economy of communication. Additionally, the chapters offer an opportunity to incorporate the thinking of those communication scholars who have reflected on the general field of political economy. Finally, an assessment of political economic theory helps us improve on the theoretical foundations of the political economy of communication.

Definitions of Political Economy

Raymond Williams suggested that when taking up a definition, one should start with basic social practices, not fully formed concepts. He called for an etymology based on social as well as intellectual history because the meaning of ideas is forged in concrete social practices (1977: 11). Offering a conceptual point of view, a dictionary of economic terms tells us that "political economy is the science of wealth" and "deals with efforts made by man [sic.] to supply wants and satisfy desires" (Eatwell, Milgate, and Newman, 1987: 907). But following Williams' socially grounded etymology, it is important to stress that before political economy became a science, before it served as the intellectual description for a system of production, distribution, and exchange, political economy meant the social custom, practice, and knowledge about how to manage, first, the household, and later, the community. Specifically, the term "economics" is rooted in the classical Greek *oikos* for house and *nomos* for law. Hence, economics initially referred to household management, a view that persisted into the work of founding influences in classical political economy, Scottish Enlightenment figures like Francis Hutcheson and, crucially, Adam Smith.[2] "Political" derives from the Greek term (*polos*) for the city-state, the fundamental unit of political organization in the classical period. Political economy therefore originated in the management of the family and political households. Writing fifteen years before Smith's *Wealth of Nations*, Steuart (1967: 2) made the connection by noting that "What economy is in a family, political economy is in a state."

It is also important to note that from the very beginning, political economy combined a sense of the descriptive and the prescriptive. As communication scholar Dallas Smythe describes its driving force or "meta-political economy," it is "the body of practice and theory offered as advice by counsellors to the leaders of social organizations of varying degrees of complexity at various times and places" (Smythe, December 4, 1991). This is in keeping with the *Dictionary of Economic Terms*, which defined the original intent of political economy as a "branch of statecraft," but which is now "regarded as a study in which moral judgments are made on particular issues" (Gilpin, 1977).

Other definitions concentrate on how the development of economics narrowed what was originally a broadly based discipline. As early as 1913, a standard economic dictionary noted that "although the name political economy is still preserved, the science, as now understood, is not strictly *political*: i.e., it is not confined to relations between the government and the governed, but deals primarily with the industrial activities of individual men" (Palgrave, 1913: 741). Similarly, in 1948, the *Dictionary of Modern Economics* defined political economy as "the theory and practice of economic affairs" and noted that:

> Originally, the term applied to broad problems of real cost, surplus, and distribution. These questions were viewed as matters of social as well as individual concerns. ... With the introduction of utility concepts in the late nineteenth century, the emphasis shifted to changes in market values and questions of equilibrium of the individual firm. Such problems no longer required a broad social outlook and there was no need to stress the political. (Horton, 1948)

At the same time, there is evidence that the transition from political economy to economics was not inevitable. This same 1948 volume notes the beginnings of a revival of interest in a more broadly defined political economy. It senses that "the emphasis is once again returning to political economy" with the "recent rise of state concern

---

2 It is hard to pass without comment on the irony that a discipline organized for two thousand years around household management must still be pressed by feminist economists to take into account the value of household labor (Bezanson and Luxton, 2006).

for public welfare." This was echoed later on in a standard book on economic terms (Eatwell, Milgate, and Newman, 1987: 906). According to it, the combination of Marxists who "never abandoned the old terminology of political economy" and "by the 1960s the radical libertarian right from Chicago and the Center for the Study of Public Choice at Virginia Polytechnic" gave a renewed life to this old discipline.

Drawing on these ways of seeing political economy, which emphasize that definitions are grounded in social practice and evolve over time in intellectual and political debate, the next sections concentrate on definitions and characteristics of the field that have influenced the political economy of communication. One can think about political economy as the study of *the social relations, particularly the power relations, that mutually constitute the production, distribution, and consumption of resources.* From this vantage point the products of communication, such as newspapers, books, videos, films, and audiences, are the primary resources. This formulation has a certain practical value for students of communication because it calls attention to fundamental forces and processes at work in the marketplace. It emphasizes how a company produces a film or a magazine, how it deals with those who distribute the product and market it, and how consumers decide about what to watch, read, or listen to. Finally, it considers how consumer decisions are fed back into the process of producing new products.

But political economy takes this a step further because it asks us to concentrate on a specific set of social relations organized around *power* or the ability to control other people, processes, and things, even in the face of resistance. This would lead the political economist of communication to look at shifting forms of control along the circuit of production, distribution, and consumption. Examples include how the shrinking number of big media companies can control the diversity of content or how international marketing firms have strengthened their power in the media business by using new technologies of surveillance and measurement to produce valuable information about consumers. It would also lead us to consider the extent to which activists can use new media tools like blogging and social networking sites to resist the concentration of power in business and government.

The primary difficulty with this definition is that it assumes we can easily recognize and distinguish among producers, distributors, and consumers. But this is not always so and particularly not in some of the more interesting cases. For example, it is useful to separate film producers, those who organize and carry out the steps necessary to create a finished product, from distributors or wholesalers who find market outlets. But film-making is not so simple. Distributors are often critical to the production process because they can guarantee the financing and marketing necessary to carry on with production. Does that make our distributor in reality a producer or a producer-distributor? Similarly, notwithstanding the common-sense value of seeing audiences as consumers of media products, there is a sense in which they are producers as well. One might say that consumers produce the symbolic value (or meaning) of media products (or texts) as they consume them. Similarly, producers consume resources in the process of production. They also distribute by virtue of their reputation as producers. This suggests that while the definition is a useful starting point, it is limited by what we miss when we apply it in a too rigidly categorical or mechanistic fashion.

A far more general and ambitious definition of political economy is *the study of control and survival in social life*. Control refers specifically to the internal organization of individual and group members, while survival takes up the means by which they produce what is needed to reproduce themselves. Control processes are broadly political in that they involve the social organization of relationships within a community. Survival processes are fundamentally economic because they concern the production of what a society needs to reproduce itself. The strength of this definition is that it gives political economy the breadth to encompass at least all of human activity and arguably all organic processes. This is in keeping with the pattern of analysis in environmental, ecological, and science studies which, among other things, aim to identify processes at work in all forms of life and to assess their differences and interrelationships (Haraway, 2003; Meadowcroft, 2005; Rosewarne, 2002). There are not many explicit examples of this view in communication and information research. James Beniger (1986: 107–9) applied information systems theory to determine fundamental processes in living systems: organization, metabolism and growth, responsiveness, adaptability, reproduction, and evolution. Addressing the complexity and social contestation of control and survival, Dallas Smythe (1991) drew on theories of complex systems or chaos theory to understand the dialectical relationship of communication and information in living systems. Gunaratne (2002a, 2002b, 2004, 2005) has made new theories of living systems which draw from chaos theory the centerpiece of his research on global systems of communication and power.

There is a great deal to be said for a definition that raises basic questions about the narrowness of both political economy and communication studies. It is hard to question the claim that these disciplines have been rooted in the study of human behavior (mainly male) in the present. The result is neglect of how humans relate to the rest of life, and a neglect of social, particularly communication, practices in human orders other than contemporary capitalism.[3] The drawback of the approach is that it can lead one to overlook what distinguishes human political economy from general processes of control and survival. These include the power of a goal-oriented consciousness and a reflexive subjectivity literally aware of its own awareness. It can also lead one to underestimate the overwhelming transformation, what amounts to an historical break, forged out of contemporary capitalism. By looking for common processes that transcend natural and historical differences, we can lose sight of how those processes have been transformed in the contemporary world to a point where the one species uniquely responsible for the transformation has the power to eliminate both nature and history for all species. Notwithstanding these limitations, the broad reading of political economy reminds us that whatever our specific entry point or focus of analysis, it is inextricably bound up with a long history and with a vast organic totality.

---

3 Communication studies suffers deeply from the view that history takes place almost exclusively in the West and began with the invention of the telegraph. This bias owes a great deal to the understandable but limiting tendency to examine the field as a set of industries (broadcasting, telecommunication, publishing) that evolved from the development of technological forms (print, broadcasting, computer communication).

Central Characteristics

Definitions are useful but they take us just so far. Another way to describe political economy is to focus on a set of central qualities that characterize the approach. These broaden the meaning of political economy beyond what is typically provided in definitions. Drawing on the work of Murdock and Golding (2005), among other scholars, this section focuses on four ideas at the cornerstone of political economy: social change and history, the social totality, moral philosophy, and praxis.

Political economy has traditionally given priority to understanding *social change and historical transformation*. For classical theorists like Adam Smith, David Ricardo, and John Stuart Mill, this meant comprehending the great capitalist revolution, the upheaval that transformed societies based primarily on agricultural labor into commercial, manufacturing, and, ultimately, industrial societies. For political economists like Karl Marx, it meant examining the dynamic forces in capitalism responsible for its growth and change. The object was to identify both cyclical patterns of short-term expansion and contraction as well as long-term transformative patterns that signal fundamental change in the system. In his introduction to the 1923 edition of John Kells Ingram's influential *History of Political Economy*, Richard Ely explains the central role of history in the mind of the political economist:

> It is now universally acknowledged that societies are subject to a process of development, which is itself not arbitrary, but regular; and that no social fact can be really understood apart from its history. Hence the 'pocket formulas' in favor with the older school, which were supposed to suit all cases and solve all problems, have lost the esteem they once enjoyed, and Economics has become *historical* in its method, the several stages of social evolution being recognized as having different features, and requiring in practice a modifying intervention which ought to vary from one stage to another. (Ingram, 1923: 4–5)

Looking back over the development of economics, sound as it was, Ely's optimism about the triumph of history in the discipline was clearly misplaced. History would remain central to political economy but the neoclassical synthesis, which became mainstream economics, set history aside or at least kept it in the background. This was chiefly because history made all the more difficult the drive to turn economics into a science.[4] Compare Ely's optimism with the view of Baran and Sweezy, who, after praising the historical sensibility of Adam Smith and his

---

4 I am indebted to Dallas Smythe for suggesting Ingram's history. Smythe notes (1991) that he read the book as a doctoral student in 1932 and that it had a significant influence on the development of his thought about the political economy of communication. The field was beginning to move away from the emphasis on history even as Ely and Ingram wrote about the triumph of historical thinking. Nevertheless, for a young economics graduate student, this book would occupy the center of a curriculum. Eric Roll's 1942 *A History of Economic Thought* appears to have played a similar part in the development of another central figure in the political economy of communication, Herbert Schiller. Today, as McCloskey (2002) notes, economic history is a marginalized subdiscipline in a field that pays more attention to building mathematically rigorous models of the present. Parker (1986) offers one of the better recent critiques of economics' (mis)treatment of history.

followers, attack contemporary economics: "Anti-historical to the core, present-day bourgeois economics scorns any effort to investigate the nature of the changes that are taking place or where they are leading" (1965: 29). For Bell, the absence of a sense of time and history is part of the general crisis in economic theory:

> And finally, economic theory has to return to time (in the logical sense) and to history (in the empirical fact) in order to be responsive to the complex new social arrangements that derive from the widening of the scales and new arenas of economic and social actions. (In Bell and Kristol, 1981: 79)

One source of renewed interest in political economy is the drive to determine whether we are in the midst of an epochal transformation similar to the one that occupied the thinking of political economy's founding figures. People experience what appears to be profound social change and wonder whether they are witnessing a fundamental rearrangement of social structures and processes that reflect the turn to one or a combination of post-industrialism, postmodernism, post-Fordism, a network society or, instead, a deepening and extension of fundamental tendencies at work since the earliest days of capitalism. The answer to this question is central to how we think about social change. Moreover, the question itself suggests a turn to the historical thinking that propelled the development of a political economy approach.[5]

With its long tradition of support for historical analysis and this renewed interest in the field, political economy is well prepared to take on central questions of our time. However, in order to do so effectively, political economy needs to pay closer attention to the relationship of history to its position on social structure and social reproduction. Political economy has tended to concentrate on the production and reproduction of invariant structures. This is understandable considering the sheer power of structures like Time-Warner, Sony, Microsoft, the News Corp., AT&T, IBM, Google, etc. However, this focus has made it difficult to integrate an historical understanding because, as Connell (1987: 44) puts it, "history enters the theory as something *added on* to the basic cycle of structural reproduction." One solution is to focus on constituting processes more than on the reproduction of structures. Again, Connell:

> For history to become organic to theory, social structure must be seen as constantly *constituted* rather than constantly reproduced. And that makes sense only if theory acknowledges the constant possibility that structure will be constituted in a different way. Groups that hold power do try to reproduce the structure that gives them their privilege. But it is always an open question whether, and how, they will succeed. (1987: 44)

---

5 It was not just mainstream economics that jettisoned a concern for history. As Frederic Jameson notes in his introduction, Jacques Attali's *Noise*, an interesting, unconventional political economy of music, is important because it is part of the renewed interest in historiography "after a period in which 'historicism' has been universally denounced (Althusser) and history and historical explanation generally stigmatized as the merely 'diachronic' (Saussure) or as sheer mythic narrative (Lévi-Strauss)" (Attali, 1985: vii).

The Canadian political economist Wallace Clement captures this theme in setting out a clear vision for history in political economy: "It is fundamentally historical and dynamic in the sense of seeking understanding of the social transformations, including the agents and forces of change" (2001: 406).

Political economy, from the time of its founders, has also maintained that the discipline should be firmly rooted in an analysis of the wider *social totality*. This means that political economy spans the range of problems that today tend to be situated in the compartments of several academic disciplines where those with an interest in social class go to sociology, those interested in government to political science, in the market to economics, and so on. From the time of Adam Smith, whose *Wealth of Nations* knew no disciplinary boundaries, political economy has been taken up with the mutual constitution and multiple determination of social life. Early in the development of political economy Mill described the necessity of a broad approach to social life:

> For practical purposes, Political Economy is inseparably intertwined with many other branches of Social Philosophy. Except on matters of mere detail, there are perhaps no practical questions which admit being decided on economical premises alone. (Stone and Harpham, 1982: 12)

Like many political economists, Mill is interested in using political economy as one means of understanding the social whole, even while acknowledging that his own approach is interconnected with the other branches of what he calls Social Philosophy. From this perspective, political economy is not just another approach. It is also a guide to understanding the relationships that prevail among numerous approaches and to the relationships among many aspects of social life. As Heilbroner (1986: 15) put it, "the great economists were no mere intellectual fusspots. They took the whole world as their subject and portrayed that world in a dozen bold attitudes – angry, desperate, hopeful."

This view prevailed for quite some time as the generally accepted goal of political economy. By 1923, even as the name was changing to economics, general texts continued to support this broad-based view of the political. Again, Richard Ely:

> As to the place of Economics in the general system of the sciences, it holds that the study of wealth cannot be isolated, except temporarily and provisionally, from the other social phenomena; that it is essential to keep in view the connections and interactions of the several sides of human life. (Ingram, 1923: 4)[6]

This concern for the social totality is reflected in otherwise fundamentally different approaches to political economy. The perspective often referred to as public choice theory (the labels positive or constitutional political economy are also used), takes its

---

6 It is also interesting that Ely would see economics as simply one part of sociology: "There is, in fact, properly speaking, but one great Science of Sociology, of which Economics forms a single chapter which must be kept in close relation to the others" (Ingram, 1923: 4). This provides a sobering reminder to those who would see the latest disciplinary status rankings, which today place economics ahead of sociology, as the last word on the subject.

inspiration from the conservative wing of economic theory (Buchanan, 2003). Setting aside for the moment the assumptions and ideas that propel this view, this branch of political economy maintains that it can and ought to be applied to all forms of social behavior. According to Brennan and Buchanan (1985: x), public choice theory or constitutional political economy marks a return to the classical tradition that viewed economics as the study of "how markets work" with markets understood so broadly as to encompass "the coordination of individual behavior through the institutional structure." For those who advance this view, the subject of political economy is the study of the rules governing the connection between the individual and the institution. Such rules are constituted, they contend, out of the choices made by "homo economicus, the rational, self-oriented maximizer of contemporary economy theory" (1985: 65). Hence, the entire social arena is the field of analysis for political economy. The choices that create rules governing markets in everything from the traditional private markets in goods and services, to the markets for votes, spouses, children, sex, communication, and so on are its subject matter.[7] One of its proponents defends this view as a necessary "economic imperialism" (Lazear, 2000).

On the other side from the conservatives, there is the political economy inspired by Marxian, socialist, and institutionalist approaches. These differ from the public choice view on almost all points except this one: notwithstanding variations among theorists, they approach political economy with an eye to understanding the social totality. This view is firmly rooted in the work of Marx and carries forward among Fabian Socialists, Western Marxists, autonomists, theorists of underdevelopment, and institutionalists who trace their lineage to Commons, Veblen, Robinson, and Galbraith. These perspectives have clashed over most central points of political economic theory, but recognize and seek to account for, in distinct ways, the relationship between the economic and the political as well as between these and the wider arena of socio-cultural institutions and practices.

First and foremost, a commitment to the social totality means understanding the connections between the political and the economic. In reaction to what were considered tendencies in Marxist theory to reduce everything to the economy, numerous works appeared in the 1970s and 1980s that aimed to correct this by arguing for the "relative autonomy" of government *vis-à-vis* the economy (Jessop, 1990). This sparked a lively debate that revived interest in the growth of the state, its relationship to social class, gender and race, and called attention to the dynamic connection between the political and the economic in political economy. The ferment is likely to continue for some time (Jessop, 2001). Nevertheless, the debate has always been about *relative*

---

7 One is struck by the near messianic zeal of the positive political economists. This is more than building a discipline; it is, in the words of Brennan and Nobel-laureate James Buchanan (1985: 150), creating a "civic religion" that will "return, in part, to the scepticism of the eighteenth century concerning politics and government." They intend to "concentrate our attention on the *rules that constrain government* rather than on innovations that justify ever expanding political intrusions into the lives of citizens. Our normative role, as social philosophers, is to shape this civic religion, surely a challenge sufficient to us all."

autonomy. Although the term "relative autonomy" is slippery and can get in the way of an informed exchange of views, none of the parties to the debate seriously called for separating political from economic analysis. Most recognized that the existing division of academic labor is seriously flawed because those who have the upper hand in determining its direction accept the formal separation of the political from the economic, the need to model economics after the physical sciences, and the view that economics can be rendered free from ideological biases by eliminating political content.

Political economists who work in the institutionalist, socialist, and Marxian traditions are also concerned to identify the links between society's political economy and the wider social and cultural field. Drawing on the work of Veblen (1934), institutional economists are interested in the relationship of acquisitiveness or greed and what he called "conspicuous consumption," or the drive for power and status which, in their view, is fuelled not by the rationality featured in mainstream economics, but by deeply buried irrational drives.

Inspired by Marxian theory, the writers of the French Regulation School looked to identify the relationship between regimes of accumulation and associated modes of social and political regulation which encompass but extend beyond the state (Aglietta, 1979; Boyer, 2000). Their influence began to wane in the 1990s, but theorists inspired by Marx and the Italian Marxist theorist of the early twentieth century, Antonio Gramsci, continued to build a bridge between political economy and broader social and cultural forces (Jessop, 2001; Sayer, 2001). In addition to bringing the state back into our understanding of the economic, they called for closer links between culture and political economy. As Sayer (2001: 697) puts it:

> One of the hallmarks and prime achievements of cultural political economy is its explorations of the "embedded" nature of economic activities – how they are set within social relations and cultural contexts that make a difference to those economic processes.

Additionally, in an effort to explain what they perceive to be transformations in the political economic order brought about by the decline of a mass production and mass consumption economy organized around large national businesses, political economists argue for the need to think about a broad social, economic, and cultural shift from a Fordist to a post-Fordist society built on the principle of flexible accumulation (Castree and Gregory, 2006; Fuchs, 2007; Harvey, 1989). Furthermore, world systems theorists led by Wallerstein (1991: 129) reject the narrowness that constrains current social science research and call for reversing the tendencies that have "pushed us away from holistic and systemic realities toward the individual (or its organizational equivalent: the firm, the family, the state) as the appropriate unit of analysis." Finally, theorists of the autonomist school argue for a political economy that examines the social totality as a set of network connections between local and global conflicts, starting not from the power of capital but from the struggles of what is called "the multitude" (Hardt and Negri, 2000, 2004).

This broadly based effort to examine the wider social totality does not receive complete intellectual support. For example, those aligned with streams of postmodernist and post-structuralist thinking reject, sometimes emphatically, the idea of a social totality. Across the range of differences within these views, one finds agreement that the term *society* is an attempt to apply a unity in discourse to something fundamentally divided, disconnected, and hence indefinable. The general tendency is to argue that there is no social totality, no individual totality, and no discursive totality. According to this view, the implosions of twentieth-century life, set off in part by the power of new communication and information technologies, have broken apart totalities, taking with them measures of time and space that ultimately used to provide some degree of unity (Lyotard, 1984). We are left with the task of understanding the local, the fragmented, the parts, of what used to be thought of as the elements in a wider whole, but which are, in reality, unconnected or loosely tied pieces. By removing the ideological glue of social unity, one can comprehend the real value of these pieces and, ultimately, celebrate them in their resistance to all totalizers – including capitalism, the state, and the producers of all metanarratives.

Chapter 9 examines the relationship of this point of view to political economy. For now, it suffices to concentrate on one particular response in political economy that acknowledges the weight of the postmodern view and yet retains an understanding of the social totality. It starts with the understanding of social totality found in the work of Adam Smith and Karl Marx (particularly evident in the early work and in *The Grundrisse* (1973)) as opposed to that of classical structuralists like the sociologists Emile Durkheim and Talcott Parsons, or, philosophical structuralists such as Louis Althusser. Smith and Marx differed fundamentally, but agreed on the need to reject the essentialist view that all is reducible to the social whole, all analysis to what Durkheim called the "social fact." Their historicity, the recognition of the contingent nature of social life, ruled out such essentialist thinking. But making use of the social totality does not require essentialism or reductionism of thought. In fact, as Marx, and his twentieth-century interpreters like Gramsci and Lukács remind us, dialectical thinking leads us to recognize that reality is comprised of both the parts and the whole, organized in the *concrete totality* of integration and contradiction that constitute social life.

David Harvey (1989), a leading proponent of this view, acknowledges the growth of a dispersed, mobile, flexible, and recombinant political economy and culture. Such developments can signal shifting identities and local resistance. But they can also mark a more tightly organized capitalism which uses its control over technologies and expertise to give it the flexibility to tolerate, resist, absorb, commodify, or ignore these resistances. Hence, the relationships among parts varies from loose to tight and the whole itself may contain numerous fissures, eruptions, and distortions. Nevertheless, according to this view, any discussion which addresses solely the parts or the whole is elliptical. This perspective rejects both the idealism of systems thinking and the positivism of conventional science that calls for direct sensory observation of each and every link in the social field. It rejects as equally essentialist, attempts to provide unassailable priority to the global or the local. Research determines the nature and extent of resistance and control, weakness and strength, etc. Defending the use of totality in the field of literary criticism, Ahmad (1992: 121) nevertheless cautions about the need "to specify and historicize the determinations which constitute any given field." Nevertheless, "with sufficient knowledge of the field, it *is* normally possible to specify the principle ideological formations and narrative forms."[8] Political economy lays the groundwork for such research with its openness to a contingent, non-essentialist social totality.

Moral philosophy provides a third characteristic of a political economy approach. Moral philosophy refers to social values and to conceptions of appropriate social practices. The goal of this particular form of analysis is to clarify and make explicit the moral positions of economic and political economic perspectives, particularly because moral viewpoints are often masked in these perspectives.

When Jeffrey Sachs, a leading architect of economic reconstruction in the former Communist world, was asked about his work in the region, he began by calling it "the greatest moral challenge of our time" (Rusk, 1991: B8). When his colleague Benjamin Friedman wrote a book (1988) attacking the excesses of Ronald Reagan's presidency, he introduced each chapter with a Biblical citation. In their overview of the political economy of communication, Golding and Murdock (1991: 18–19) maintain that what distinguishes critical political economy is that "perhaps most importantly of all, it goes beyond technical issues of efficiency to engage with basic moral questions of justice, equity and the public good." These are examples from across the spectrum of perspectives in economics and political economy that suggest some unease with what has become the customary practice of separating science from morality. Their interest in moral philosophy reflects a central concern of some of the founding figures in political economy.

Adam Smith, who was not a professor of economics but of moral philosophy, offers a vision of how to advance the social good. It is not, as he would later argue in *The Wealth of Nations*, through selfish behavior or self-interest, but by doing good in society:

> And hence it is that to feel much for others, and little for ourselves, that to restrain our selfish, and to indulge our benevolent affections, constitutes the perfection of human nature; and can alone produce among mankind that harmony of sentiments and passions in which constitutes their whole grace and propriety. (Smith, 1937, Pt. 1, Sec. 1, Chap. 5: 71)

Similarly, Thomas Malthus, son of a preacher, warns of the moral consequences of unchecked population and Karl Marx offers a political economy that would create a society based on satisfying human needs, not one founded on class power. However one responds to their specific visions and values, it is hard to deny that visions and values were central to their analyses, that the moral sphere was integral to their work. As the noted political economist Joan Robinson maintained, it would be left for later analysts to take "this branch of ethics" and turn it into a discipline "that is striving to be a science" (Robinson, 1962).

---

8 Ahmad's (1992: 121) defense of what he calls "Totality" comes in the midst of a longer argument attacking its misuse by those who refer to singular tendencies (e.g. nationalism) within "Third World Literature" based on analysis of "the few texts that become available in the metropolitan languages."

There are two central points in this plea for moral philosophy. First, the moral, cultural, or spiritual domain is itself the central subject of analysis. Adam Smith chose to write *The Theory of Moral Sentiments* before his analysis of the division of labor in the marketplace because it was essential to understand the moral basis of a commercial society on the rise in Britain in the last half of the eighteenth century. He felt that it was a better work than *The Wealth of Nations* and returned to it near the end of his life because, according to Lux (1990: 98), "there was a more serious problem with unmoderated commercial motives than he was aware of earlier." Similarly, Marx began with moral philosophical treatises that are too readily dismissed as the writings of the "young Marx," but which form the core of understanding the values of a growing industrial society.

These people were moral visionaries in another sense. They felt that an essential element of their responsibility as social philosophers was identifying visions of a morally appropriate way of life. For them, the moral vision became the feature that distinguished reason from rationality. This can be a difficult point to understand because Western culture has tended to separate science from morality. One voice speaks the language of rationality, logic, and positivism; the other, a normative language that is generally permitted to talk back but not with the other. One is customarily permitted to go only so far as Max Weber (1946), who felt that it was acceptable to be motivated by moral concerns, but that the canons of science left no room for morality in analysis. The defense of this standpoint is that moral concerns get in the way of the objectivity essential for scientific achievement and ultimately prevent science from developing the means to address the very problems that moralists raise. Defenders of moral philosophy respond by pointing to the many problems, from climate change to world poverty, that an unreflective science has helped to create.

One of the central breaks in the transition from political economy to economics was the acceptance of the Weberian view that value neutrality defined the limits of the relationship between economics and moral philosophy. Economics could study values, although in practice this meant identifying values with preferences registered by marketplace choices. Moral comment would hold little or no explicit place in the economist's explanation or assessment. Some would contend that the separation of moral philosophy from economics meant simply that the form went underground only to insinuate itself into the economists' assumptions and choices of ideas, concepts, and variables. For example, the decision to define human labor along with land and capital as merely a factor of production may very well make analytic sense, but it also reflects a certain moral vision, however implicit, that people are interchangeable with things or that lives are interchangeable with capital. The economist argues that such a view is limited to the economic domain and reflects economic practice. Critics respond that visions spill over into other areas of social life so that workers viewed as tools for the economist's research purpose come to be seen more widely as mere tools and are often treated accordingly.[9] By naturalizing specific economic practices that reduce living labor to a factor of production, economics slips a moral vision through the back door.

9 Rabinach (1990) argues that the identification of people with machinery, the productivist ethos, is one of the defining characteristics of modernism.

The debate over the separation of fact and value, analysis and prescription, economics and moral philosophy continues, but there are signs of changes in the wind. As noted at the start of this section, today's leading mainstream economists are less averse to using moral language in their economic discourse; although it is more likely that 'moral challenge' appears in speeches rather than in journal articles. They are also more likely to make use of specific moral philosophical work, particularly Rawls' theory of justice, which offers connections between moral thinking and welfare economics (Castagnera, 2002). There is certainly discomfort within the ranks of mainstream economics about the moral consequences of a system rooted in commercial values (Foley, 2006: 219–20).

Nevertheless, it is chiefly the heterodox schools of thought, rooted in political economy, that take up the moral concern. The conservative wing of public choice or constitutional political economy seeks to extend the tools of economic analysis to moral choice and aims to use economics to establish Brennan and Buchanan's (1985) civic religion. The Marxian and institutional traditions are steeped in debates over the place of moral philosophy. One of the major forms these have taken in recent years is over the challenge that structuralism, especially in the work of Althusser and Lévi-Strauss, posed to the humanistic versions of Marxian thought. Seeking to apply the logic of *Capital* to general forms of thought and action, Althusser called for eliminating the moral philosophical dimensions from the Marxian tradition. The attack continues today, although protagonists tend to take up the cause of poststructuralism and postmodernism, drawing on a Nietzschean tradition to attack the value of moral philosophy (Eagleton, 2003). Nevertheless, the moral dimension remains strong in Marxian political economy because it provides a powerful defense of democracy, equality, and the public sphere in the face of dominant private interests. This is one reason why, despite the attacks from structuralist and deconstructionist quarters, political economists of communication retain a strong position on the importance of moral philosophy (Artz, Macek, and Cloud, 2006; Murdock and Golding, 2005).

The fourth characteristic of a political economy approach is *praxis*, an idea with deep roots in the history of philosophy and one which has found several paths to communication studies, including Marxian theory, the Frankfurt School of critical thought, and the "action-research" tradition best embodied in sociology. Most generally, praxis refers to human activity and specifically to the free and creative activity by which people produce and change the world, including changing themselves. The word originates in the ancient Greek where it typically referred to the political and business activities of free men (as well as the name of a lesser known goddess of mythology). It reached some prominence in the work of Aristotle, who considered economic, political, and ethical studies as forms of practical knowledge to be distinguished from theory and poiesis. Where theory sought truth and poiesis the production of something, the goal of praxis was action. The term played a major role in debates about the division of knowledge in medieval and early modern philosophy.

Praxis came to occupy a central place in the work of the philosophers Kant, Hegel, and Marx. For Kant, praxis or practical reason takes primacy in the unity with theory that comprises full reason. Indeed, morality is defined as the "absolutely practical."

Hegel also recognized the superiority of praxis to theory, but looked to a higher unity for truth to be found in freedom where the absolute spirit realizes itself in philosophy, the arts, and religion. Marx was concerned with praxis from his earliest work, a doctoral dissertation on Greek philosophy, which insisted that philosophy be made practical. His principal interest in the term was to create an alternative to alienated labor. In Marx' view, capitalism freed labor from the alienation of necessity only to replace it with a new form of alienation – the reduction of labor power to a marketable commodity. The revolutionary goal was to transform alienated labor into praxis or free, universal, self-activity.

Gramsci and Lukács made use of praxis to attack the more deterministic forms of Marxism contained in *Capital* and in Engels' re-reading of Marx. The term entered debates in communication theory through the work of the Frankfurt School and particularly that of Marcuse and Habermas, who added weight to praxis by defining it as a general form of action, of which labor was one type. Traditionally, labor occupied a central place in economic thought because human history has been forced to live in the realm of necessity that requires human labor. As the productive forces develop and offer the first historical opportunity to overcome necessity, Frankfurt theorists turned to other forms of praxis to envision what was to constitute the realm of freedom. In his critique of Marx, Habermas (1973) argued for the distinction between work, or purposive rational action, and interaction, or communicative action. Marx was understandably taken by the first because labor was central to the transformations brought about by capitalism. For Habermas, however, social praxis was made up of both work and communicative action. The latter, based on consensual norms and constitutive symbols, offered an alternative model of social life provided that it could be freed from the distortions that restrict democratic, open communication.

Praxis is important to both the epistemological and substantive premises of political economy. In brief, praxis guides a theory of knowledge to view knowing as the ongoing product of theory and practice. It rejects as partial those epistemologies which conclude that truth can only result from contemplation. Knowledge requires more than a process of honing and purifying conceptual thought. Rather it grows out of the mutual constitution of conception and execution.[10] Praxis has also occupied an important place in the substantive development of political economy. After all, political economy began as the practical activity of household management and control of the *polis*. Aristotle placed it among the practical disciplines whose wisdom would guide the conduct of rulers. There is a notable tension in classical political economy between the desire to understand the sources of wealth and productivity and the need to advise elites on the appropriate labor, trade, and social welfare policies. Those

---

10 Marxian theory views the separation of conception from execution as a central step in the process of alienation. Braverman (1974) makes use of the distinction in pathbreaking work on the labor process in capitalism. Praxis resonates beyond Marxian theory. It is particularly prominent, in substance if not in name, in the work of the pragmatic philosophers, including Pierce, James, and Dewey. In his history of communication research, Hardt (1992) suggests that praxis can provide one bridge between Marxian and pragmatic thought.

schooled in the Marxian tradition explicitly united the role of political economist and activist in, for example, Gramsci's conception of the organic intellectual. Writing from prison, where he was incarcerated for opposition to Italian fascism, Gramsci provided a model of the intellectual schooled in both the theoretical tools of analysis and in the common sense of practical political struggle and resistance.

The tension continues in a far different part of the intellectual universe where contemporary mainstream economists struggle over the drives to purify economics with mathematical rigor and to market their advice to businesses and governments. This is not to suggest that the problems posed by praxis are identical for the wide range of thinking that encompasses political economy and economics. More importantly, however hard one might try, it is impossible to escape the problems that praxis poses for the scholar who would work in these fields. Specifically, political economy is inextricably bound to policy studies and the political economy of communication needs to address both the strengths and the pitfalls the relationship creates.

Conclusion

This chapter set the stage for the detailed examination of the political economy of communication by presenting political economy as a broad-based and variegated approach to social analysis. It started with a set of definitions that suggested how political economy developed out of practical questions of household and community management. The history of how to think about political economy is marked by differences over whether the discipline should encompass the full range of social activity or take on a narrower, scientific remit even at the price of limiting its scope to economic phenomena presented in the form of falsifiable propositions using mathematical discourse. The chapter highlighted two definitions which have been used in communications research. One concentrates on the social relations, particularly the power relations, governing the production, distribution, and exchange of resources; the other on broad problems of control and survival.

Following this presentation and assessment of definitions, the chapter took up central characteristics which mutually constitute a political economy approach. These include social change and history, the social totality, moral philosophy, and praxis. Political economy has made use of these from its roots in the thinking of eighteenth-century Scottish Enlightenment philosophy. Their meaning has shifted as they have been tested against a changing world order and challenges from alternative intellectual currents.

3

WHAT IS POLITICAL ECONOMY?
SCHOOLS OF THOUGHT

──────── **The Origins of Political Economy and the Classical Paradigm** ────────

Histories of political economic thought tend to begin with either the period of classical Greece, which allows for a start at the etymological origin of the term, or with the eighteenth-century Scottish Enlightenment moral philosophers, culminating in Adam Smith.[1] Whatever the choice, one cannot review major histories without recognizing that most build on a metanarrative that sees the discipline rooted firmly within characteristic patterns of Western white male intellectual activity. To cite one example of notable omission, histories neglect the development of social science in the Arab world that anticipated by centuries, particularly in the work of Ibn Khaldun, what we in the West call classical political economy.[2] One of the difficulties of this overview is that, in a brief space, it must balance the need to present the canonical positions, what most people are taught as economics, and heterodox views that aim to modify and transform them.[3] Keeping these aims in mind, the primary objective is to provide a general grounding in the traditions that inform most political economic analysis to prepare for the next chapter which takes up the development of a political economy of communication.

───────────

1 There is no agreement even among those who start from the modern era. Most contemporary texts begin with the work of Smith. However, some start with earlier figures such as Sir William Petty, whose 1690 book *Political Arithmetic* discussed the division of labor in the production of timepieces and implied that labor is the source of all wealth.

2 I would like to thank the communication scholar Hamid Mowlana for reminding me of this omission, my first economics professor Ibrahim Oweiss and my professor of intellectual history Hisham Sharabi, who struggled to broaden the dominant tradition at Georgetown University. See Gran (1990) for a discussion of the relationship between Western political economy and Islamic thought.

3 The editors of the *The New Palgrave* learned how difficult this balancing act can be when they were soundly criticized by Nobel laureate Robert Solow, whose review appeared in the *New*

Classical political economy was founded on two of the pillars of the Enlightenment: Descartes' vision of rationality and Bacon's approach to empiricism. In general, it sought to extend the seventeenth-century revolution in the physical sciences by applying the principles of physics to the world of eighteenth- and nineteenth-century capitalism. As Bell (Bell and Kristol, 1981) reminds us, central to the scientific project was the shift from studying concrete objects to concentrating on their abstract properties, such as mass, acceleration, and velocity. For Adam Smith, an heir of the Scottish Enlightenment, as well as for his English counterparts, David Ricardo, Robert Malthus, and John Stuart Mill, this meant determining the economic constants that constituted the stable, underlying reality for a world undergoing massive transformation. Arguably, the most important of these was anchoring the concept of value in productive labor, a marked departure from the prevailing view, defended by their adversaries, the Physiocrats, who insisted that economic wealth was literally rooted only in land.

Focusing on variables like value, price, and cost led to abstract laws, codified in a mathematical form, that described their interrelationships. Additionally, by abstracting the specific concept of value from the narrow context of gold and other precious metals, so dear to the mercantilists, and from land, the alternative offered by the Physiocrats, the classical school of political economy opened the way to the general application of their "laws" to all forms of industry and trade. The classical position was not the first school of economic thought, but it was arguably the first such system, i.e. a set of abstract variables believed to be applicable to all economic activity.[4]

According to Roll (1942), the classical view was rooted in three immediate traditions. From Locke's vision of political philosophy, it derived the ideas of self-interest, private property, and the labor theory of value. Mercantilist thought contributed the notion of exchange value, although the classical political economists would modify this in the labor theory of value. Finally, however much this also meant a rejection of the view that land was the ultimate source of value, classical theory supported the French physiocratic notion of laissez-faire, an alternative to the views of mercantilists, who supported government intervention to support the economy.

Following the Enlightenment tradition, classical theorists maintained that individuals were capable of using reason to maximize their self-interest and, by extension, the interests of society. The latter was reduced to an aggregation of individuals with no existence *sui generis* and no teleology. Institutions were natural results of

---

York Times. Objecting to what he perceived to be the book's excessive indulgence of critical views, Solow adopts a fatalistic demeanor, concluding that economics will always be "contaminated by ideology." Citing Marxism ("the most persistent") but Austrian, post-Keynesian and neo-Ricardian as well, Solow attacks *The New Palgrave* because it failed to "keep the various 'paradigms' in proportion." The editors replied with a count that totaled about 15 per cent of entries falling outside the "current professional consensus" (Amsden, 1992: 795–7). Apparently, this was too much deviance for Solow to tolerate.

4 For Smith and others, the method of abstraction was a general one, not limited to the analysis of economic activity, a point which led a commentator on Smith's assessment of the market for religion to call him the "first economic imperialist" (Anderson, 1988).

human interaction, but were to be watched with a skeptical eye because of their tendency to restrict the freedom of individual choice and social intercourse, including the free flow of ideas, commerce, and labor. Only individual freedom could maximize efficiency and therefore the wealth of nations. The institution of government bore special watchfulness because the tradition of sovereignty, which gave it the power to defend the realm, could also easily be used to create special privileges, including government enterprises that would restrain industry and trade.

Wide variations within the classical approach gave subsequent generations of political economists much to claim and to contest. The dominant view is to be found in Smith's resounding defense of self-interest over benevolence: "It is not from the benevolence of the butcher, the brewer or the baker, that we expect our dinner, but from their regard to their own interest" (1937, Bk 1, Chap. 2: 14).[5] In the extreme, this view would propel Thomas Malthus to defend the practice of permitting raw sewage to flow freely in city streets as a means of killing off the weak and thereby ensuring population control and survival of the fittest. According to this view, governments should not act to control the spread of disease because such action would only lead to more misery in the long term. Why? Because unchecked population and resources diverted to the weakest would undermine the long-term strength of society.[6] Nevertheless, for all his concern about government controls, even Smith rejected the view that the state's role should be limited to national defense alone. Recognizing the relationship between labor and culture, the man who defended the division of labor in pin making, also acknowledged that "the man whose whole life is spent in performing a few simple operations ... generally becomes as stupid and ignorant as it is possible for a human creature to become unless the government takes some pains to prevent it" (1937: 734–5). Moreover, in *The Theory of Moral Sentiments*, written in 1759, seventeen years before *The Wealth of Nations*, Smith attacked Hobbes' notion of self-interest with a call to do good for others (Smith, 1976: 71). The point is not to argue for one or the other as the real Adam Smith, but to suggest that Smith has been oversimplified by his critics, particularly those who see in his position a defense of the unbridled market.

The work of David Ricardo (1819) and John Stuart Mill (1848) departs further from the image of classical political economy as the unabashed home of free market economics. Their attention to the distributional consequences of the free market raised the specter of inequality and exploitation. Ricardo leveled his strongest criticism at landowning interests who used their control of a vital resource to attract higher rents

5 Smith's butcher, brewer, baker quote is widely repeated. Another, also from *The Wealth of Nations*, suggests that he was not entirely comfortable with the pre-eminence of self-interest: "All for ourselves, and nothing for other people, seems, in every age of the world, to have been the vile maxim of the masters of mankind" (Bk III, Chap. iv, Para. 10).

6 Malthus's consistent attack on government intervention did not extend to the Corn Laws, which permitted the government to protect British landowners with a high tariff. Malthus supported the laws by arguing that political economy, which more greatly resembled "morals and politics than mathematics," simply did not apply in this case (Lux, 1990: 41).

that hurt both workers and capitalists. Mill, at heart a pragmatist, backed off from a flirtation with socialism, calling instead for expanding education to control population and thereby to diminish want. It would be left to the Utopian Socialists, and, of course, to Marx and his followers to place systematic alternatives to the unrestricted marketplace on the intellectual agenda.

The classical political economists are important for many reasons. For all of their differences, they succeeded in focusing intellectual attention away from the prevailing emphasis on equating economic value with gold, other precious metals, and with land, by agreeing that value was determined by productive labor. They understood the power of the division of labor in the marketplace to create wealth. They also realized that the extension of this practice was transforming the world and shared the profound ambiguity of many at that time about the overall benefit of the changes they were just beginning to experience.

The classical position attracted substantial criticism from conservative and Marxian socialist positions. Before turning to these criticisms, which laid the groundwork for alternative perspectives, it is useful to consider one fundamental way in which the classical position fell short of its own fundamentals. For all of its attention to freedom and individuality, classical political economy took for granted the goal of economic nationalism. It was, for example, to explain and advance the wealth of *nations* that Smith wrote his major work and by that he meant primarily the wealth of Britain. Trade would enhance the productivity of one or more *nations*. As Joan Robinson remarked in her *Economic Philosophy*, although their position "purported to be based on universal benevolence, yet they naturally fell into the habit of talking in terms of National Income. ... Our nation, our people were quite enough to bother about" (1962: 125). So powerful was the hegemony of nationalism, that, although classical political economy successfully demystified many of the ideas entrenched in earlier schools of thought, e.g. land is the source of wealth, the conflict between national and general welfare was simply not entertained.

The Radical Critique

Utopian and Marxian socialists developed a powerful critique of the classical position, from the human devastation brought about by policies enacted in its name to the theoretical shortcomings of its presumed commitment to Enlightenment rationality. Their radical response was supported and sustained by workers' and other social movements that enlarged the intellectual critique by incorporating the democratic forces erupting in response to the industrial revolution.

Utopian critics built their arguments out of involvement with oppositional social movements struggling for democracy, such as the Levellers in Britain and the radicals of the French Revolution. Utopians like Godwin and Paine (whose attack on British colonialism helped inspire the American Revolution) chronicled the growth of exploitation accompanying the removal of what few government protections stood between the poor and starvation. Moreover, they attacked the classical view for failing to direct the

Enlightenment spirit of rationality against a cornerstone of the new economy: private property. What system (and what, in Carlyle's words, "dismal science") could be more irrational than one that would defend the practice of excluding the masses of people from the fruits of their own sweated labor? This strong moral voice and political commitment rejected the classical retort that hunger and misery cannot be avoided because population was growing and land was shrinking. Several of the later Utopians, notably Owen, Fourier, and Saint-Simon, aimed to build alternatives to what they called the anarchy of the market with an explicit commitment to planned, communal societies.

Marx built on this critique, accepting its concern to shift the terms of debate to equality and community but rejected the substitution of moral outrage, however well justified, in defense of an abstract and idealistic notion of humanity, for sustained materialist analysis. The power of his analysis has itself attracted a legion of critics but it has also won their grudging and even not-so-grudging respect.[7] This overview cannot and is not intended to do justice to the contribution of Marxian theory and to the numerous interpretations of its legacy. Rather, the goal is to describe some of the major dimensions of a Marxian political economy which grew out of a critical engagement with the classical school of thought.

Marx built on a number of the contributions in classical theory. He accepted the focus on labor as the chief source of value, although he systematically recast it to take into account divergences between the use and exchange value of labor so that he could develop a theory of exploitation. This identified the difference between the value and price of labor or the *surplus value* that accrued to capital as a result of increasing the workday (absolute exploitation) or of intensifying the work process during the workday (relative exploitation).

Marx's response came in his critique of political economy which turned, in part, on a thorough attempt to historicize the perspective and, particularly, its view of labor. The classical school was interested in the historical transition from feudalism to capitalism, but tended to limit application of its historical imagination when it examined capitalism itself, save for specific debates on the question of whether capitalism contained an inherent, natural tendency to immiseration. For Marx, capitalism was a system of unprecedented dynamism, continuously revolutionizing its productive processes with new technologies and new forms of organizing the labor process. Although capitalism faced a continuous maelstrom of conflict and struggle that

---

7 In 1942, Joseph Schumpeter, one of Marx's more luminous adversaries, put it quite well, in words that hold particular meaning in a world that celebrates "post-Marxism" and "the end of history":

> Most of the creations of the intellect or fancy pass away for good after a time that varies between an after-dinner hour and a generation. Some, however, do not. They suffer eclipses, but they come back again, not as unrecognizable elements of a cultural inheritance but in their individual garb and with their personal scars which people may see and touch. These we call the great ones – it is no disadvantage of this definition that it links greatness to vitality. Taken in this sense, this undoubtedly is the word to apply to the message of Marx. (1942: 3)

changed its practices and forms, at the end of the day no custom, ritual, or value would block the development of the market, the production of commodities, including labor, and the growth of surplus value. The capitalist tendency to continuous revolution, what Schumpeter (1942) would later appropriately call the process of "creative destruction," could only be undone by forces that capitalism alone was able to release. Included among these was the working class, defined as those who are made to sell their labor power and give up control over the means of production.

Classical theory identified the forces propelling capitalism but tended to view them as natural.[8] Marx sought to situate capitalism within the dialectical flow of history, but with a materialist vision that would break with established tendencies in historiography, epitomized in the work of Hegel, which above all valued the history of ideas, beliefs, and governments or states.[9] In fact, in addition to building on much of the Hegelian tradition, particularly Hegel's concept of the dialectic and his goal of a practical philosophy (meant to fuse theory and practice), Marx took up the challenge of revolutionizing it. He would do so by showing how people make history and themselves, albeit under conditions that are not of their own making. For Marx, history meant, above all, how people make themselves through labor.

In addition to this radical view of history, the Marxian critique of political economy developed an equally radical social conception of capitalism. Capitalism is a material system, not because of what it appears to be, i.e. a system of things (of machinery, workplaces, products, etc.), but because it contains an historically unique set of *social relations*. The appearance of naturalism masked the reorganization of social life principally along social class lines. For Marx, moreover, capitalism is not a material system because it engages in commodity production. This is important, but it is still merely the stuff of commodities. Granted, Marx makes a great deal of this stuff. Consider that he begins *Capital* (1976a), arguably his most mature work, with a chapter on "The Commodity." But as the first sentence makes clear, although the commodity is ubiquitous, it is nevertheless a ubiquity of appearances: "The wealth of societies in which the capitalist mode of production prevails appears as an

---

8 Marx stressed this in his critique of classical political economy. In *Capital*, he singled out their theoretical formulations in this way:

These formulas, which bear the unmistakable stamp of belonging to a social formation in which the process of production has mastery over man, instead of the opposite, appear to the political economist's consciousness to be as much a self-evident and nature-imposed necessity as productive labour itself. (1976a: 175)

9 Marx was stinging in his criticism of "True Socialists" who, he argued, refused to confront the material roots of conflict and change:

It is difficult to see why these true socialists mention society at all if they believe with the philosophers that all *real* cleavages are caused by *conceptual cleavages*. On the basis of the philosophical belief in the power of concepts to make or destroy the world, they can likewise imagine that some individual "abolished the cleavage of life" by "abolishing" concepts in some way or other. (1976b: 467)

immense collection of commodities" (1976a: 125). Peel back the layers of appearance and we find a set of social relations, specifically "all commodities are merely definite quantities of *congealed labour-time*" (1976a: 130).

More generally, the social relations of capitalism embody a mass of producers who do not own the means of production but have to sell their labor power to a class of owners organized in separate firms that compete in various commodity, labor, raw material, and capital markets. Competition drives these different firms to maximize surplus value by exploiting labor in order to increase capital accumulation. The Marxian literature is filled with the debate over the precise definition and consequences of the capital–labor relationship. Nevertheless, the tendency in the traditional Marxian view is to argue that the system built on the capital/wage-labor relationship leads to the growing mechanization of labor, the concentration and centralization of capital, and periodic crises, of which the tendency to overproduction is probably the most pronounced (Mandel, in Marx, 1976a: 82). One can certainly find the seeds of this view in some of the work of classical political economy, particularly in that of Ricardo and his left of center followers. However, until Marx, no one ventured an analysis of capitalism that so thoroughly sought to strip away the power of its apparent features that define a natural, taken-for-granted world, to reveal a set of socially dynamic, but fundamentally contradictory and, therefore, unstable social practices and social class relations.

Among the numerous critiques of the traditional Marxian view, one is particularly important to communications studies: Marx did not carry the social analysis of capitalism far enough. This does not refer to the widespread, but generally mistaken view, that Marx missed the rise of today's managerial capitalism and service economy. For sympathetic critics like Williams (1977), Baudrillard (1981), and Dallas Smythe (1981), these are far less consequential than what results from an essentialist and narrow view of labor. The traditional Marxian analysis places a great deal of weight on the concept of labor. In his early work, as well as in *The Grundrisse* (which connects the early Marx to the Marx of *Capital*), Marx envisions labor as a broad category encompassing the social activity by which people constitute themselves and history. Nevertheless, even here, the emphasis is on the instrumental and productive nature of labor rather than on its expressive and constitutive qualities. *Capital* takes an even more productivist view of labor, largely, according to Marx's defenders, because it is a critique of capitalism, one of whose central features is the narrowing of labor into the instrumental–productivist wage relationship, turning human beings into objects or mere factors of production. However, one consequence of a formulation that identifies labor as the essential material activity but narrows it into the wage system is that other material practices of working people are minimized. This is especially true of those which we would identify with communication, including culture, language, and social reproduction. These are rendered non-material, dependent on, and in extreme formulations, superstructural reflections of, a material base defined by labor. According to Haraway (1991: 132), although Marx and Engels recognized that labor encompassed the production of human beings themselves, they give greatest weight to the production of the means of existence and thereby offer little more than a starting point for theories of, among other things, the sex/gender division of labor.

One of the central tasks of a political economy of communication that aims to build on a critical encounter with traditional Marxian analysis is to demonstrate how communication and culture are material practices, how labor and language are mutually constituted, and how communication and information are dialectical instances of the same social activity, the social construction of meaning. Situating these tasks within a larger framework of understanding power and resistance would place communication directly into the flow of a Marxian tradition that remains alive and relevant today (Potts, 2005; Saad-Filho, 2002).

The Conservative Critique

Responding to the social and intellectual transformations that were surging across Europe in the last half of the eighteenth century, the British conservative philosopher Edmund Burke (1955: 86) pronounced: "The age of chivalry is gone. That of sophisters, economists, and calculators has succeeded, and the glory of Europe is extinguished forever." For Burke, the French Revolution not only failed as a political project, it was an intellectual disaster as well. For him, as for other conservatives, such as Thomas Carlyle, the French Revolution demonstrated the utter failure of the Enlightenment view that the universe was a grand rational machine that, much like a clock, could be understood, fixed, and changed for the better. After all, here was a revolution carried out in the name of reason, democracy, and freedom and all it brought about was terror, slaughter, and authoritarianism. According to this view, society is not a mechanism that can be taken apart and put back together, but a fragile organism bound together by tradition and wisdom (Gray, 2007).

This fundamentally anti-modernist view held little hope that the proponents of a political economy would be able to improve material or intellectual life. Carlyle, in fact, was the first to dub political economy "the dismal science," adding that it was little more than "pig philosophy." If the big clock of Galileo and Newton cannot work for society (in fact, it only added to the *hubris* that would inspire many failed revolutions), then it cannot work in those economic models inspired by it. Specifically, conservatives opposed the assumption that economic progress results from self-interested individuals rationally seeking to maximize their wealth. The self-interest of Smith's butcher, brewer, and baker might also drive them to destroy one another. Rather, wealth grows out of an organic order that produces respect for traditions offering people a clear sense of their social role and a moral grounding that motivates them to carry it out. The alternative might work in the short run (although the French Revolution proved just how short that run could be), but in the long term, rational self-interest was a weak basis for social unity.

At one extreme, the conservative view supported all defenses of hierarchy and difference, whether based on gender, race, or class. The natural order would be led by those who were male, white, and wealthy. There was no Mill, Marx, or Mary Wollstonecraft in their ranks to defend the need for equality as the basis for an ordered community. On the other hand, however, there was more support for working people among conservatives than could be found in most classical political economy. For example, Carlyle (1984) proposed giving more power to labor in order to create a greater sense of community and harmony in the workplace. He also supported government intervention to regulate health and safety in the workplace and to provide social assistance for those people the system rejects. There was no Malthus in their ranks to support free-flowing sewage as a form of population control. But neither would social utopians or Marxians find a welcome. Whatever the surface affinity in their concern for recognizing the needs of working people and of the poor, the conservative and socialist/Marxian paradigms were fundamentally at odds. Conservatives drew the line at social intervention that would ameliorate the worst consequences of social change. They rejected the Enlightenment view, pressed by social democrats and Marx, that one could intervene in social life to fundamentally alter its arrangements and bring about a more rational world. They particularly opposed giving power to the masses to carry out this social transformation.

From Political Economy to Neoclassical Economics

There is no sharp break that permits a precise designation of when classical political economy became economics. However, during roughly about the last half of the nineteenth century, several developments began to coalesce around a formulation that would eventually come to embody the neoclassical economics approach. One of the critical sources for the shift was the increasing willingness to accept Bentham's utilitarian attack on the classical defense of natural law and rights. Bentham (1907) argued that pleasure and pain, not some religious or natural code, were to be the sole determinants of ethical and moral behavior. For him, the philosopher's task is to develop a Felicific Calculus made up of precise measures of social welfare based on maximizing pleasure over pain and to recommend the necessary social changes to bring it about. Drawing explicitly from this work in his 1870 book that would rename the discipline, Jevons defined economics as the study of "the mechanics of utility and self-interest":

> to satisfy our wants to the utmost with the least effort – to procure the greatest amount of what is desirable at the expense of the least that is undesirable – in other words, to maximize pleasure, is the problem of economics. (1965: 101)[10]

---

10 Although Bentham provided an immediate influence on the development of neoclassical economics, his work is well-rooted in that of predecessors who arguably took stronger positions. Consider the philosopher David Hume's remarks on sorting out the wheat from the chaff in libraries:

> If we take in our hand any volume; of divinity or school metaphysics, for instance, let us ask, Does it contain any abstract reasoning concerning quantity or number? No. Does it contain any experimental reasoning concerning matter of fact and existence? No. Commit it then to the flames: for it can contain nothing but sophistry and illusion. (Ward, Trent, et al., 1907)

Unlike political economy, economics was not concerned with determining human needs or rights, natural or otherwise. Rather, it would be the wants expressed in preferences, the determinable and measurable choices made in the marketplace for capital, labor, and consumer goods and services, that would comprise the substance of the discipline. Moreover, economics was less interested in the absolute utility of a good than in the utility of the last available item or its *marginal utility*. In 1871, Jevons in Britain, Menger in Austria, and, a bit later on, Clark in the United States hit upon the idea that, all things being equal, the utility of any good or service declines with its increasing availability. It is the utility of the marginal unit, the last and least wanted, that sets the value for all. Furthermore, the concept of marginality could be extended from the demand for a good or service to its supply. Ricardo had demonstrated that continued pressure for agricultural production drove landowners to cultivate at the less arable margins, thereby increasing production costs. Jevons and his contemporaries noted the same tendency in manufacturing: factories incur increasing costs as they press to extract more from machinery and labor. As a result, the supply side faced the same problem of diminishing returns and utility was to be determined at the margin.

These insights would be put together by numerous successors, although Alfred Marshall is most often credited with having achieved the synthesis that makes up the neoclassical system. In simple terms, market price (for goods, services, labor, and capital) is determined at the intersection of a downward sloping demand curve (downward because of the decreasing propensity to consume at the margin) and an upward sloping supply curve (upward because of the rising costs at the margin). In his *Principles of Economics*, Marshall developed this idea into a universe of discourse that John Maynard Keynes, who in the twentieth century, produced one of the major ruptures in the neoclassical world, called "a whole Copernican system, in which all the elements of the economic universe are kept in their places by mutual counterpoise and interaction" (Heilbroner, 1986: 208).

Marshall's *Principles* (1961), which was published in 1890 with new editions appearing until 1920, was driven by two notions that continue to characterize economics as a discipline. First, following particularly on the work of Walras, economics was concerned with social order, i.e. with describing forces in equilibrium. Just as astronomers and physicists had identified the essential harmony of the physical world, the economist would locate and describe qualities of economic units and their relationships that maintained balance in the world of goods. To use Walras's term, movement consists largely of *tatonnement*, the groping advances and retreats of individuals in response to signals from an external environment. Second, as the book's motto succinctly states: *Natura non facit saltum*, nature makes no sudden changes. The economic universe, just as the Newtonian, was comprised of small, incremental changes and therefore favored an analysis that took for granted wider institutional arrangements. It takes hardly a leap to go from these ideas to the conclusion stated most clearly by Jevons that "economics, if it is to be a science at all, must be a mathematical science" (Galbraith, 1987: 125).

In the drive to become a mathematical and parsimonious science, economics shed most of the fundamental characteristics that characterize political economy. Given the interest in equilibrium states, economics would concentrate on synchronic analysis to the neglect of the traditional interest in history. Concluding that the study of institutional change and structural transformation could not be rendered with mathematical precision, economics would limit its interest in social change to small, incremental adjustments in general equilibrium patterns. The methods of economic analysis would apply across the range of historical periods. However, they were admittedly incapable of addressing the transition from one period to another, particularly when the transition was marked by disjunctions and upheavals.

Furthermore, parsimony demanded that economics give up a systematic concern for understanding the wider social totality. There was no room for the political in this new science of economics because the tools were not available and probably never would be to examine the political system with mathematical certainty.[11] Economics would also best give up the goal of understanding those social institutions, psychological forces, and cultural values that political economy argued was necessary for a complete analysis. Even Alfred Marshall, whose interests tended to roam as widely as those of his political economic predecessors and counterparts, called for the strict limitation of economics to "that part of individual and social action which is most closely connected with the attainment and with the use of the material requisites of well-being" (Clark, 1991: 92). Unlike others who saw their work taken up solely with understanding the allocation of scarce material resources to accomplish any goal, Marshall was interested in and commented on the distribution of power in the workplace and in society. Nevertheless, economic analysis would have to stand the test of mathematical rigor and scientific objectivity. This meant breaking the tie to sociology and political science, as well as to history.

It also meant breaking the connection to moral philosophy. Working in a transition period, the best of the new economists were well versed in what they were setting aside. Marshall, for example, had studied ethics and demonstrated a solid understanding of both Kantian and Hegelian approaches to moral concerns. He was genuinely concerned with environmental pollution and with the market's inability to provide for universal goods like education. Nevertheless, Marshall and his fellow neoclassicals held firmly to the view that economists should study wants expressed in preferences and not needs determined by a moral philosophy. Of course, they would admit, wants are often formed out of a moral position, but the moral standpoint is irrelevant to understanding the economic significance of wants. Therefore, although one might take an intellectual or more broadly humanistic interest in moral concerns, one would not get very far by incorporating them in economic analysis.

Finally, the paring-down process led economists to set aside an interest in social praxis. Like other disciplines, economics was increasingly institutionalized in universities

---

11 Jevons spoke for many in the neoclassical camp when he acknowledged that "About politics, I confess myself in a fog" (Heilbroner, 1986: 184). It is no wonder that he recommended the name economics replace political economy, "the old troublesome double-worded name of our science" (Clark, 1991: 32).

and subjected to the formal and informal rules governing the academic division of labor. As a consequence, it was more and more likely that academics would be separated from social movements and from the wider public outside the university. Some, like the institutional economist Thorstein Veblen, resisted this tendency with a measure of success. More typically, academics settled into the relative comfort of a university life that kept away the people and events that might prove disruptive. In sum, mathematical and scientific legitimacy came with a substantial price tag: set aside political economy and the integration of history, the social totality, moral philosophy, and praxis into the meaning of research and of intellectual life.[12]

Notwithstanding this, it is important to resist the understandable tendency to comment on the early history of a discipline as if it were simply the seed of what we observe today. Today's economists are not the inevitable result of Jevons, Menger, Clark, Walras, and Marshall. The transition from political economy to neoclassical economics took place over widespread disagreement and intellectual conflict. Consider the differences between the Austrian and Cambridge wings of neoclassical thought. The former was established in the work of Menger and Böhm-Bawerk and later in that of von Mises and Nobel-laureate Friedrich Hayek (Boettke and Storr, 2002; Chang, 2002). Sensitive to the long, slow decline of the Hapsburg empire and morally repulsed by the more proximate threat of class conflict and socialism, these economists were demanding in their insistence on the virtues of pure capitalism. Their work provides the ringing defense of neoclassical methods and the justification for exacting whatever price to achieve a pure market economy. Only a market economy could provide the discipline of supply and demand essential to guarantee the most efficient allocation of resources, including goods, services, labor, capital, and the information required for rational action. The market provided its own moral justification.

The other principal, or Cambridge, wing of neoclassical thought was less willing to completely accept an individualistic, market-centered approach. Fundamentally committed to these concepts, the heirs to Marshall's tradition, notably Pigou, Robinson, and Keynes, were nevertheless concerned about the range of market failures and externalities that justified corrective mechanisms, including government intervention. Pigou's work on externalities was used to defend taxation and subsidy policies for firms that created respectively net external costs and benefits. Finding that the marketplace fails to guarantee full employment output, Keynes recommended government fiscal intervention.

These struggles within the developing neoclassical paradigm suggest difficulties that continue to raise critical questions today (Colander, Holt, and Rosser, 2004). From

---

12 Heilbroner ruminates on the consequences of what he considers an "intellectual tragedy of the first order":

> For had the academicians paid attention to the underworld, had Alfred Marshall possessed the disturbing vision of a Hobson, or Edgeworth the sense of social wrong of a Henry George, the great catastrophe of the twentieth century might not have burst upon a world utterly unprepared for radical social change. (1986: 211–12)

within the perspective, these basic questions arise: Do we continue to trust the market as the best and perhaps even the only way to organize and distribute our resources, including communication and the media? Or should government intervene to regulate or even manage communication and the media so that everyone is ensured affordable access to a fully diverse array of content and to the full range of media?

The triumph of the neoclassical model could not easily be foreseen at the turn of the century. In fact, in the early decades, up to around 1930, neoclassical economics fell out of general favor because it appeared to be too academic, abstract, ahistorical, and incapable of addressing the growth of large, vertically integrated corporations that devoured the competition in practically all major industries. The neoclassical model saved itself by developing new tools and new responses to attacks from the right and left. The growth of statistical analysis and econometric modeling gave the approach strong tools and, of no small import, strong looking tools, with which to represent the state of the economy and to simulate the impact of changes in its major features.[13] In addition, Chamberlin's work on how one could think about monopolistic competition and Keynes' insistence on the inherent tendency to disequilibria and underemployment of resources led some of the neoclassicals to incorporate elements of the left of center critique. Furthermore, the development of a quantity theory of money firmed up the monetarist wing of neoclassical thought. These developments helped provide the groundwork for what Daniel Bell has called the "golden age of economics," roughly the period 1947–73. That these years corresponded to those of the great postwar boom suggests that economic growth also gave a shot in the arm to mainstream economics.

Today, the neoclassical paradigm occupies the center and right of center space in the political spectrum. The center reflects the vestiges of a Keynesian approach which took issue with the view that business cycles were natural products of market activity which would invariably provide the appropriate signals for making sound decisions. For Keynes and his followers, the cost of this signaling mechanism, i.e. high unemployment and deep income inequalities, was not worth the benefit. According to this view, the Great Depression of the 1930s was the inevitable consequence of economic policies that concentrated on the lack of saving, on the assumption that the latter would be *naturally* channeled into productive investment. Keynes (1964) demonstrated that in recessionary periods, this was not at all likely and the consequences of the failure to turn savings into investment would multiply throughout the economy thereby aggravating the decline. The Keynesian approach called for government fiscal policies, mainly increased spending in recessionary periods, to counter declines in consumer and business spending and eventually to stimulate investment. In the short term, this would create budget deficits in government accounts, but these would be overcome by the increase in revenues brought about by economic growth and by

---

13 The attraction that the sheer formal elegance of these tools provides should not be discounted. As the philosopher of communication Kenneth Burke (1969a: 58) once noted: "A yielding to the form prepares for assent to the matter identified with it."

controlling government spending once the expansion was underway. Numerous forms of Keynesian economics influenced both the discipline and economic policy in the post-World War II period.[14] Sustained economic growth in the 1950s led economists to see Keynesian fiscal policies as the solution to the chronic boom–bust cycles in capitalism (Heller, 1967). By far the dominant textbook, produced by Nobel laureate Paul Samuelson, made Keynesian economics the standard for macroeconomic analysis. But the global recession of the mid-1970s, bringing with it a new wrinkle, economic "stagflation" or slow growth *and* inflation, reminded people why economics was called the "dismal science" and sparked a shift in both the direction of neoclassical economics and in the economic strategies of governments.[15]

By the late 1970s, right of center economists like Milton Friedman increased their influence over the discipline and government economic policy (Klein, 2007). Contrary to the Keynesians, these monetarists held that the cornerstone of the explanatory apparatus was the money supply and their policy advice centered on controlling inflation with reduced government spending and high interest rates. Though they admitted that, in the short term, a tight money policy would lead to higher unemployment, as it certainly did, they felt that this was a price worth paying in order to control the more significant damage that inflation was inflicting on the world monetary system. By the 1980s, Western governments adopted monetarist policies and used their control over international organizations like the World Bank and the International Monetary Fund to impose them on much of the rest of the world. Today, versions of Keynesian and monetarist economics continue to contend for the neoclassical mainstream, raising questions about the state of this paradigm and its value in economic policy-making. More fundamental questions come from streams of thought outside the mainstream to which we now turn.

Varieties of Political Economy or Heterodox Economics

Contemporary economics presents this paradox: the neoclassical paradigm, for all its internal disagreements, appears to have triumphed in the profession and in public policy; nevertheless, criticism of the perspective deepens from familiar sources and new voices add to the attack. The next section explores these critical schools of thought, several of which have contributed to the foundation of research in the political economy of communication. The following section takes up what some claim to

---

14 These differences were heavily influenced by domestic political considerations. The US practiced military Keynesianism, a policy that channeled public investment mainly into the defense sector. Western European countries, particularly the nations of Scandinavia, as well as Japan, Canada, and Australia, tended to build fiscal policy around the civilian sector, favoring national companies and domestic social welfare programs such as national health insurance.

15 Many Keynesians defend their analysis and policy advice by arguing that governments ignored their prescription to cut back on spending during periods of economic growth.

be a general crisis in economics and the fundamental distinctions between modes of thought in economics and in political economy. This discussion lays the groundwork for Chapter 4 on the development of a political economy of communication.

Neoconservatism

Since mainstream economics occupies the center and right of the political spectrum, there would not appear to be much room for a conservative critique of the mainstream. Nevertheless, one can observe important responses from conservatives in two different schools of thought that often compete. One departure characterizes those who argue that mainstream economics has been excessively cautious in concentrating on economic behavior. Variously labeled public choice theory, the rational expectations school, the new or positive political economy, this approach aims to extend the principles of economic analysis to all forms of social, political, and cultural activity (Basu, 2000; Klein, 1999; Stigler, 2003). For example, Stigler (1971) and Wilson (1980) laid the groundwork for analyses of government regulatory behavior by arguing that we should view regulation as an organizational market that tends to be captured by rent-seeking civil servants who increase the amount and scope of regulation, even as they restrict access to valuable information, in order maximize their own gains. The government, not the general public, they maintain, is the primary beneficiary of regulation. One solution, popular in the 1980s, is to cut back on regulation and thereby eliminate this form of government restriction on competitive activity. From the 1990s on, it was increasingly applied to international economic affairs through regional and global trade agreements. This perspective has taken on a more adventuresome spirit in applications of the perspective to the family, gender, and sexuality (Posner, 1992). The same argument is used to explain the long delays and 'red-tape' that clog adoption agencies and the remedy is not much different. According to Judge Richard Posner, an economist elevated to the US federal bench by then-President Reagan, efficiency calls for allocating babies by establishing a market in what he calls "parental-right selling." In this view, neoclassical economics is too timid: the fundamental precepts of market behavior and marginal utility can be applied across the range of human behavior.

Another wing of the conservative critique, the *corporatist* position prominent in the work of Nisbet (1986) and Kristol (1983), takes issue with some of this vision. Although not nearly as coherent a perspective, it criticizes the neoclassical school for neglecting the *political* in political economy (Streek and Kenworthy, 2005). In essence, the conservative price paid for its scientific warrant is setting free the political for capture by liberal and socialist thought. Public choice theory is one attempt at recapture but, according to this view, it fails because of its excessive commitment to individualism and contractualism. The alternative to individualism is to see society as a collectivity of communities, with organic normative orders of which economic activity is merely one part. Rather than following rational expectations, individuals act with reference to social custom, including customs of deviant practice, often bearing no resemblance to economic logic. This form of conservative thought would build a political economy on the need to identify traditional social practice, determine the civic virtue, and intervene politically to uphold the moral value of that practice. Taking up a conservative variation on corporatism, according to this approach, the best guide to appropriate conduct is the standard established by elites across the range of social institutions. The fondness for "making markets" in public choice theory is tempered and often resisted by political conservatives, who view it as an intrusion, often a radical one, into the organic, moral order (Camerer, et al., 2003).

These two conservative positions have gotten along to the extent that they have been able to maintain the division between the economic and political worlds. The former is the place where utility reigns, the latter is the home of custom and order. The growth of the new positive political economy and of a new institutional economics (not to be confused with the "old" institutional economics described below) signals a dissatisfaction with this division and the likelihood is that these positions will clash as much with one another as with mainstream economics (Little, 2002; Furubotn and Richter, 2005). The new "Civic Religion" that Nobel-laureate James Buchanan and his followers aim to establish may not usher in a peaceable kingdom.

Institutional Political Economy

The major established heterodox positions on the left draw from the institutional and Marxian perspectives. The former departs from neoclassical economics by maintaining that the organizational structure of the economy, not the market, is the major force in the production, distribution, and exchange of goods and services. The analysis of organizational structure incorporates institutional history, the sociology of bureaucratic activity, the assessment of technological constraint and opportunity, and the influence of social custom, law, and culture on the social construction of value. By demanding an explicitly historical and holistic point of view, the institutional school sought to replace what neoclassical economics gave up to achieve parsimony, mathematical rigor, and scientific legitimacy. In its most basic form, the institutional paradigm replaced the neoclassical emphasis on markets as the measure of social worth and the solution to social problems with an understanding of the constraints imposed by social custom, social status, and social institutions on all behavior, including market behavior.

The contours of the institutional perspective were initially laid out principally by Thorstein Veblen, Charles Ayres, John R. Commons, and Wesley Mitchell. Each, but especially Veblen, described a world in which the exceptions to the neoclassical world appeared to rule. This was the late nineteenth and early twentieth centuries when the great trust companies and monopolies seemed to mock the competitive market models at the heart of the neoclassical universe. Veblen's *The Theory of the Leisure Class* (1934) drove home the point that neither rationality nor common sense informed consumer choice. Rather, consumers decided on the basis of deeply buried irrationalities that found expression in the status emulation practices we now know as conspicuous consumption. Veblen was particularly skeptical of both the working class, who would rather imitate than overthrow their bosses, and the business leader, whose "function was not to help make goods, but to cause breakdowns in the regular flow of output so that values would fluctuate and he could capitalize on the confusion to reap a profit" (Heilbroner, 1986: 236). Following a line of thought dating back to Saint-Simon, Veblen argued that the machine and the engineer would eventually triumph (Lawson, 2005; O'Hara, 2002).[16]

Commons and his followers tended to disagree with this conclusion, concentrating on understanding the relationship of technology to institutions as instruments of collective action. Nevertheless, they all more or less agreed that the neoclassical paradigm missed central features of the contemporary economy: the breakdown of competition and the growth of monopoly, the social construction of wants and of value, and the transformational consequences of technological innovation.

Contemporary institutional theory is represented in the work of John Kenneth Galbraith, Kenneth Gordon, and Walter Strassman, among others. Galbraith is still certainly the most widely read, partly because he wrote for a wider public and was skilled in peppering his prose with an acerbic wit that Veblen would appreciate.[17] Galbraith has also popularized a continental European variation on institutional theory, best exemplified in the work of Schumpeter.[18] His work extends Veblen's analysis of consumption by attacking the neoclassical assumption that wants registered in the marketplace embody consumer sovereignty. *The Affluent Society* (Galbraith, 1958) was one of the early examinations of how the advertising industry influences the social construction of wants. Perhaps more importantly, in *The New Industrial State* (1985), Galbraith returned to the traditional interests of institutional theory in technology and structure to examine what he called the corporate *technostructure*. This defined the bureaucratic combination of technical and organizational strength that enabled companies to leverage size and power to control formally free markets. Such a view took root in the political economy of communication because of concerns over the ability of large media companies, aided by technology and the bureaucratic state, to dominate markets in broadcasting, print journalism, telecommunications, and film.

Other contemporary institutionalists, like Kenneth Boulding, concentrated on one particularly powerful embodiment of the technostructure – the growth of a military–industrial complex and on structural alternatives to concentrated economic power. However, they all tend to share a characteristic that separates them from both the neoclassical and the range of Marxian perspectives. Institutionalists view the maximization of power within bureaucratic structures as a more potent

---

16 Veblen placed little faith in the ability of higher education to either understand or act on this analysis. He subtitled his book *The Higher Learning in America* (2005) "A Study in Total Depravity."

17 Here is Galbraith commenting on the prominence of individual price theory in current textbook economics: "In the future the economist who is too exclusively concerned with what anciently has been called price theory will, indeed, shrink to a public stature not above that of Keynes's dentist" (Galbraith, 1987: 289).

18 Schumpeter's legacy is claimed by numerous schools of thought. He left both a large corpus and sufficient ambiguity to defy easy categorization. Institutionalists lay claim to his view that the concentration of economic power and the growth of unwieldy bureaucracies are the logical consequences of capitalist development.

driving force, for better and for worse, than the maximization of profit (Hodgson, 2004; Rutherford, 2001).

Marxian Political Economy

There are many Marxian political economies directing criticisms at the neoclassical synthesis (Millard, 2000). On the understanding that no single overview can be exhaustive, this section examines major exemplars that owe their inspiration and influence to different elements of the Marxian legacy. Political economists like Baran, Sweezy, Mandel, and Gunder Frank developed their critique explicitly from the Marx of *Capital* (1976a). Following a largely determinist epistemology, their work takes up the labor theory of value, social class exploitation, and struggle, the concentration of economic power, imperialism, and crisis. It attacked neoclassical economics for its failure to address social change in anything more than an incremental fashion. According to them, the transition to capitalism, and within it, to monopoly capitalism or the tendency for a few large companies to dominate markets and restrict competition, represent central shifts in the economy that neoclassical economics largely ignores. It also takes the neoclassicals to task for creating a narrow, technical discipline that did not permit the examination of the wider social totality encompassing the state and social class struggle. Furthermore, traditional Marxists found a central place for both the technical and the moral analysis of a system of thought that was satisfied to have markets allocate more to advertising than to education and to ignore exploitation by companies doing business throughout the world.

The contribution of those advancing Marxian political economy in the 1950s and 1960s is important in itself and all the more remarkable because its practitioners came under constant attack from those who would silence people perceived to be on the wrong side of the Cold War. When Baran died in 1964, he was considered virtually the only Marxian economist in American academia.[19] However, social upheavals brought about by the Vietnam War, the civil rights movement, feminism, and student activism contributed to the resurgence of many neo-Marxian political economies. Just four years after Baran's death, a group of American graduate students met after the tumultuous Democratic Party convention of 1968 to form the Union for Radical Political Economics (URPE). The Union grew throughout the 1970s and sustained about 1,000 members in the conservative 1980s to become what one member (Miller, 1992: 4) calls "the oldest and largest disciplinary group of leftists in the academy." URPE continues the work of upholding a neo-Marxian political economy into the new century and it is no longer alone in the organized effort to promote heterodox research (Markusen, 2005). In fact, it has been joined

---

19 Writing at the time of Baran's passing, one friend noted that "Paul Baran's death almost completely closes the door of the professed open society whose establishment apparently cannot find it possible to tolerate in academia or elsewhere any other acknowledged Marxist theoretician" (Miller, 1992: 4).

by the Association for Heterodox Economics which promotes a diverse collection of alternative perspectives, including neo-Marxian theory (Lee, 2002).

There is not a clear-cut boundary between those who carried on the tradition of deepening and extending the application of *Capital* to the contemporary political economy and those neo-Marxists who sought to rethink *Capital* and the entire Marxian corpus in fundamental ways. In the United States, the journal *Monthly Review* and its book series tend to reflect the former. Although open, for example, to analyses of sexism and the environmental crisis, it tends to concentrate on *class analysis*, including the structure and operation of capital, the nature and consequences of social class divisions, the labor process, class struggle, and on inquiries into *imperialism and dependency*, encompassing the globalization of capital, militarism, class oppression, and struggle in the dependent world.

One bridge between this traditional Marxian viewpoint and neo-Marxian political economy is the work of the *world systems perspective*, which combines the materialist historical analysis of the *Annales* school of French historiography pioneered by Fernand Braudel (1975) and the global sociology of the American Immanuel Wallerstein (1979, 1991, 2004). Critics and supporters alike acknowledge the central place that materialist history and a comprehensive view of the social totality take in this perspective. These views are tightly interwoven: history is taken up with the development of the world economy comprising an international class system, a core/periphery hierarchy of nations and regions, a network of relationships among national, regional, and international government organizations, and a world market (Chase-Dunn, 1989). World systems theorists tend to accept essential elements of the Marxian analysis of capitalism, including generalized commodity production, private appropriation of the major means of production, and the wage system. Criticized for their early neglect of class analysis, they have come to incorporate and examine the sites of class contradictions, including in the workplace, in government, and in the core–periphery relationship (Sanderson, 2005; Wallerstein, 2004). And recent work suggests a growing interest in inserting culture, communication, and information technology into their thinking about world systems of power (Gunaratne, 2005; Wallerstein, 2001).

Debates among contemporary Marxian political economists have also addressed the significance of corporate structure and the labor process. Neoclassical economics tends to view corporate concentration as an addressable aberration. Institutionalists see it as more deeply embedded in capitalism but correctable through state intervention (e.g. anti-trust enforcement and independent regulation). In its analysis of monopoly capitalism, Marxian political economy views concentration as the logical consequence of capitalist development and an indicator of crisis. The neo-Marxian literature is less certain about the meaning of economic concentration and debates about post-Fordism, flexible accumulation, modes of regulation, and autonomy reflect considerable ferment.

These debates respond to perceived major changes in the global political economy, including transformations in production technology, industrial organization, and world markets. One response to this perception is an approach, pioneered in the work of Piore and Sabel (1984), which argued that capitalism is undergoing a profound transformation from mass production (Fordism) to craft production or *flexible specialization* (post-Fordism). This involves a transition to a production system based on the manufacture of a shifting and diverse range of products, customized to specific market segments, and produced with sophisticated ("intelligent") machinery and an adaptable, skilled labor force. Drawing on this work, Christopherson and Storper (1989) opened a debate on the implications of flexible specialization for the media industries by maintaining that this process diminishes the power of the major Hollywood film companies. This position was criticized by Marxian political economy for its failure to recognize that flexible specialization actually increased the power of big Hollywood firms because it enabled them to enjoy the benefits of flexible production but with fewer of the risks because these were absorbed by so-called independent companies that the Hollywood majors in fact controlled (Aksoy and Robins, 1992). Following Harvey's (1989) formulation, flexible specialization is better viewed as capitalism's heightened ability to achieve the flexible accumulation of wealth. Wayne (2003) has revisited what is now known as Hollywood's media industrial complex and advances this argument by calling on political economists of communication to recognize the value of discussions about flexible production. This is because flexible production within a corporation that centralizes major decisions about finance and investment but decentralizes operational or day-to-day decisions to its subdivisions and allied companies, actually strengthens the power of capitalism, especially its largest businesses.

Variations on the flexible specialization perspective aim to combine its acceptance of contingency while asserting the systemic nature of capitalism, something that tends to disappear in the flexible specialization literature. One of the more prominent is the *regulation* approach (Boyer, 2000; Lipietz, 1988), which examines successive developmental periods in capitalism that are based on combinations of regimes of accumulation and modes of regulation. Regimes of accumulation are stable and reproducible relationships between production and consumption that, though defined for the global economy, contain unique characteristics for national and regional economies, depending on their history and position in the international division of labor. There are four chief regimes identified in the history of modern capitalism: extensive accumulation, Taylorism or intensive accumulation without mass consumption, Fordism or intensive accumulation with mass consumption, and an emerging post-Fordist regime of flexible accumulation with customized consumption and precarious employment. The mode of regulation is made up of the institutional and normative apparatus that secures accommodation to the dominant regime at the individual and group level. According to this view, capitalism is undergoing a transition from monopolistic to flexible forms of regulation that make extensive use of communication and information technology to integrate people into society through control over the labor process and over patterns of consuming material and immaterial products.

Systemic alternatives to the regulation approach assert more explicitly a turn to a *post-Fordist* period. This includes work, heavily influenced by radical geography, that aims to integrate post-Fordist with *postmodernist* scholarship to produce an analysis of the transformation in the global space of flows: material, informational, and cultural (Castells, 2001; Harvey, 1989, 1999; Thrift and Crang, 2007). Alternatives also encompass research steeped in the institutional literature of political science that argues for a transition from organized to *disorganized capitalism* (Lash and Urry, 1987), which has been recently applied to understand the global culture industry (Lash and Lury, 2007). Finally, there is an attempt to understand capitalism by examining the various *long-waves* of innovation and development that take it through new periods of growth and inevitable decline largely as a result of technological innovation, the latest wave of which is powered by communication and information technologies (Freeman, 2007; Mandel, 1995).

Neo-Marxian political economy sustained the critique of neoclassical economics, often in critical encounter with Marxian theory. *Analytical Marxism* (Cohen, 2000; Tarrit, 2006), which, in its integration of political philosophy, economics, sociology, and history, is true to the spirit of political economy, attacks the neoclassical defense of capitalism not just because it contributes to inequality, but because even when capitalism can reduce labor-time, it chooses, obsessively, to opt for growth. Neoclassical economists are attacked at the heart of their values: not just because their system denies a social safety net, which it does, but because capitalism fails to guarantee free time to pursue what it most promises: freedom. This approach has been critical of traditional Marxism, especially its method of historical materialism. Nevertheless, analytical Marxism has supported the fundamental promise of a rational organization of society that permits people to control their own destinies with the fewest possible social constraints.

Neo-Marxian political economy has also been influenced by work that accepts the benefits of the marketplace without accepting capitalism. Nove (1983) and Miller (1989) have pursued the vision of *market socialism* as a form of social organization that abolishes the distinction between capital and labor – a class of owners facing workers who give up control over the means of production – and replaces it with a market system based on worker-owned firms. The rise of market economies in formerly socialist societies, especially China, has led to renewed interest in the equitable distribution of income and public (not government) ownership within a competitive market economy (Milonakis, 2003).

There is great diversity in the Marxist approach to political economy. But it is the case that much of this tradition has sought to understand capitalism, business, and the power of a dominant class. There is less explicit attention in political economy to the Marxian ideas of class struggle, class conflict, and the independent activity of the working class and the poor. One stream of thought that has sought to remedy this is that of the *autonomous* school or *autonomous Marxism*. Building on a long tradition of Italian social theory, Hardt and Negri gave this autonomist perspective wide circulation in their 2000 book *Empire* and the 2004 *Multitude* (see also Dyer-Witheford, 1999; Lazzarato, 1997; Terranova, 2004), and it has been the subject of critical reflection from established Marxian scholars (Sayers, 2007). One of the most important North American autonomists, Harry Cleaver, gained prominence by addressing its relationship to Marxist theory, and to labor and gender as well. In a 1993 interview with the Italian journal *vis-à-vis*, he took up these themes. For Cleaver ('Interview with Harry Cleaver', 1993), "autonomist" refers to the power of workers to define themselves autonomously "from capital, from their official organizations (e.g. the trade unions, the political parties) and, indeed, the power of particular groups of workers to act autonomously from other groups (e.g. women from men)." The term also represents a recognition of people's right to struggle against their reduction to "mere worker." Says Cleaver, "Precisely because capital seeks to intervene and shape all of life, all of life's rebels, each nook and cranny of it becomes a site of insurgency against this subordination. Housewives go on strike in the home or march out of it collectively into the streets." Gender takes a central place in this vision not only because the home becomes a site of resistance. Autonomy also means a refusal and a reconstitution, for "much of the revolt of women can be seen as a refusal of their traditional roles in the social factory: as procreators and recreators of labor power accompanied by demands for new kinds of gender and other social relations."

The Marxian tradition continues to inspire a wide variety of positions in political economy. In spite of numerous differences, they are generally alike in their commitment to history, the social totality, moral philosophy, and praxis. The final two perspectives in this overview, feminist and environmental political economy, contain strong affinities to the Marxian tradition, but are sufficiently different from it to merit distinct treatment. Both grow out of arguably the most important social movements of our time. Both provide substantial critical assessments of the neoclassical school.

Feminist Political Economy

Early in the twentieth century, Charlotte Perkins Gilman attacked the neoclassical view, what she called "the infant science of political economy" as "naïvely masculine":

> They assume as unquestionable that "the economic man" will never do anything unless he has to; will only do it to escape pain or attain pleasure; and will, inevitably, take all he can get and do all he can to outwit, overcome, and, if necessary destroy his antagonist. (1966: 235–6)

A feminist political economy has grown over the years partly because little has changed in the basic view of mainstream economics. The feminist perspective on the field has sprung from activism, from specific issues such as the lack of attention to domestic labor and household maintenance, and from the pressing need to broaden the field of economics and political economy to take into account feminist thought.

Activism certainly propelled a great deal of feminist rethinking of economics. For example, Marilyn Waring started in social movement work that propelled her into the New Zealand Parliament where she had the responsibility of evaluating a proposal to adopt the United Nations System of National Accounts (UNSNA).[20] It did not take her long to recognize that since UNSNA is based on market and exchange value principles, it "supports and formalizes the invisibility of women's labour, environmental values, and the like" (Waring, 1988: xx). For example, the UNSNA counted institutional

---

20 For his role in creating this accounting system, Sir Richard Stone won a Noble Prize in 1974.

childcare, the use of energy fuels purchased in the marketplace, the processing or manufacture of foodstuffs in a factory, tap-delivered water, and a meal taken at a restaurant or laundry. But when a Zambian woman does all of this by herself as housework, it does not count. Waring also found that the UN International Labor Organization counted the work of a man in the eight hour a day workforce as an "active labourer" but not his wife who puts in eleven hours in and around home. She is simply "helping the head of the household in his occupation" (Waring, 1988: 29–30).

Conceptual and methodological problems are typically cited as reasons for ignoring household labor. But, feminist critics point out, more energy is spent on solving the conceptual and methodological problems posed by the underground economy of crime, the drug trade, and prostitution than on how to include housework and childrearing. In her 1934 work on household labor, Margaret Reid offered a guiding principle to account for household labor: any activity that results in a service or product that one can buy or hire someone else to do is an economic activity whether or not a financial transaction takes place. Nevertheless, economic practice and the policies of governments worldwide continue to reflect the view offered in this entry on "The Labour Force – Definitions and Measurement" provided in the 1968 edition of the *International Encyclopedia of the Social Sciences*:

> Housewives are excluded from what is measured as the working force because such work is outside the characteristic system of work organization or production. Moreover their inclusion in the working force would not help policy makers to solve the significant economic problems of American society.

As a result, feminist activists and theorists continue to call for taking domestic labor into account:

> By defining the economy as comprising firms and markets, conventional economics fails to recognize – to value – domestic work, the care of children and other household members, shopping, and home maintenance (Meaghar and Nelson, 2004: 109; see also Huws, 2003; Jefferson and King, 2001).

In addition to fighting to include domestic and associated labor in both mainstream economics, with not much success, and into political economy, with some, feminists have argued for the need to use the condition of women as the basis for rethinking fundamental elements of economic thought. This includes using feminist insights to redefine the field:

> One proposal is to think about economics as the study of how humans organize themselves to provide for the sustaining and flourishing of life. Such a definition encompasses both choice behavior and behavior strongly shaped by habit and social institutions, and both market and non-market activities. (Meaghar and Nelson, 2004: 110)

Not only do scholars call for using feminist thought to reinvigorate economics and political economy, they also call on feminists, whose work has been taken up mainly with cultural concerns, to pay closer attention to the issues that especially political economists have addressed. These include the changing global division of labor, the privatization of public services, the loss of welfare state benefits, as well as racism and social class exploitation (Bezanson and Luxton, 2006; Peterson, 2005; Vosko, 2002). Some of the most interesting work in this area has come from scholars working on the study of media, communication, and information technology (Huws, 2003; Lee, 2006; Sarikakis and Shade, 2007). As a result, considerable progress has been made over the last ten years in the integration of feminist and political economic thought (Baker, 2005; Peterson, 2005).

Environmental Political Economy

Feminist political economy addresses irrationalities in a mode of analysis that literally cannot figure how to count the work of most of the world's women. Environmental political economy identifies the irrationalities in a paradigm that assigns economic growth to a massive oil spill because the clean-up increases spending on labor and capital equipment. There is nothing new in the view that ecological matters are important to economic analysis. Classical political economy, particularly the work of Malthus and Ricardo, was especially concerned with the carrying capacity of land in the face of growing human populations.

The climate change issue has accelerated research in environmental economics and political economy (Rosewarne, 2002; Wall, 2006). Mainstream environmentalists, not unlike mainstream economists, aim to save capitalism from its own self-destructive tendencies either by moderating marketplace excesses or by creating markets that would ostensibly make the value of the environment more transparent. Putting a price on emissions, it is felt, would make it more likely that the economy would take better financial account of socially damaging environmental activities. Public choice theorists, following their belief that practically anything can be addressed by the market, have proposed markets for pollution that would enable companies to trade pollution credits. Under this system, which some jurisdictions have put into practice, the government sets a cap on the amount of pollution permitted and organizations that pollute can trade pollution credits among themselves provided the total amount does not exceed the cap.

Traditionally, a strong environmentalist position, reflected principally in "Green economics," attacks both neoclassical and Marxian traditions because "both are dedicated to industrial growth, to the expansion of the means of production, to a materialist ethic as the best means of meeting people's needs, and to unimpeded technological development" (Porritt, 1984: 52). However, in recent years, an interconnected network of perspectives, that often aim to accommodate Marxian and feminist political economy, has addressed the need for strong action on climate change. Initially given prominence in the journal *Capitalism Nature Socialism* (see also Benton, 1989), this position started from a commitment to both socialism and environmentalism, claiming that only the collectivist and participatory decision-making characteristic of democratic socialism can produce a healthy ecology. Furthermore, it argued that building an alliance among socialists, feminists, and environmentalists was necessary to correct the Marxian tendency "which in arguing the dominance of social over natural factors literally spirits the biological out of existence altogether" (Soper, in J. O'Connor, 1991: 10).

Marxian political economists have responded with their own vision of a critical political economy of the environment that addresses nature and economic value, the consequences of treating nature as capital, and the concept of sustainable development (Burkett, 2006; Foster, 2002). So too have feminists who emphasize "the theoretical and material links between biophysical reproduction and social reproduction and the importance of each of these processes to the economy" (Perkins and Kuiper, 2005: 108) as well as "the links between the marginalization and exploitation of the natural world and women's labour" (Mellor, 2005: 122). Finally, institutional political economy has set out its own synthesis that would combine the economics of the environment with an appreciation for what institutions do to advance and retard forms of governing the natural environment (Paavola and Adger, 2005).

In general, an environmental approach advances political economy's interest in the idea of the social totality by incorporating the natural totality of organic life. Concomitantly, it broadens political economy's concern for moral philosophy by expanding the moral vision beyond human life to all life processes. As the feminist political economist Mary Mellor (2005: 125) insists, "all human activities have to take account of natural conditions, limits, and uncertainties because humans are immanent rather than transcendent in relation to the natural world." Humans are a part of the world and grow out of it; they are not above it. Nevertheless, even as we recognize that humans are embedded in the world, we also must acknowledge that humans are the sole moral actors and therefore the only beings capable of uniting conception and execution in democratic praxis.

The growth of communication and information technologies has raised environmental concerns with special attention directed to the gap between the perception that these are clean technologies and the growing evidence of their threat to human health because of their toxicity. Indeed, the icon of high-tech development, Silicon Valley, contains some of the worst hazardous waste sites in the world, as do regions of China where the world's discarded digital devices are taken and dumped (Grossman, 2006; Pellow and Park, 2002; Smith, Sonnenfeld, and Pellow, 2006).

Conclusion: The Limits of Economics or Why We Need Political Economy

This chapter addressed the development of major schools of thought in political economy, suggesting how the discipline evolved initially out of the tensions between a classical approach established in the work of Adam Smith and his followers and challenges from conservative and Marxian perspectives. In the last half of the nineteenth century, this struggle grew into the differences between an increasingly orthodox economics that traded the broad characteristics of political economy for utilitarian principles and a positivist method and heterodox approaches that covered a range of conservative, institutional, and Marxian perspectives. These have leveled a wide-ranging critique at what has come to be called the neoclassical approach, a loose synthesis of characteristics that contains its own internal ferment. Recently, perspectives marked by the growth of feminism and environmentalism have joined the major heterodox approaches.

The wide range of conservative, institutional, Marxian, feminist, and environmentalist critiques of mainstream neoclassical economics describe a discipline in ferment, if not crisis (McCloskey, 2002; Radziki, 2003). This contrasts sharply with the triumphant bearing economics brings to the tables of social science and public policy. The chapter concludes by bringing together the various critiques of economics described above and by defining the specific points of difference that help to specify the alternative in political economy.

Economics prefers to describe static models that are resolved in equilibrium. It is limited to taking up incremental change within one given set of institutional relations. Actual economic practice, like the wider social and physical world, is not so easily constrained. Equilibrium is only one outcome; incremental change is only one form; the given set of institutional relations is only one among many possible arrangements.

Economics does not take into account many of the significant socio-economic determinants of productivity, including corporate structure and ownership, access to information, education and training, and social background. It tends to ignore the relationship of power to wealth and thereby neglects the power of institutions to control markets (Rothschild, 2002). Sounding like an early astronomer who, in spite of all the evidence, persists in believing that the sun revolves around the earth, the economist persists in the view that market competition makes it unnecessary to consider power. Just as the followers of the astronomer Ptolemy chose to adjust the mathematics rather than give up an earth-centered universe, the economist persists in believing that monopoly and oligopoly are exceptional practices, requiring a few mathematical adjustments to incorporate them within the competitive model. Critics, including some from within the profession (Davis, 2006), insist that the growth of concentrated economic power has forced the model to the breaking point.

Economics assumes that information flows freely to consumers who register their wants in the marketplace. It contends that the distinction between human needs, which are common to everyone, and human wants, which are idiosyncratic, psychological, and subject to external pressures, can be eliminated so that all needs can be treated as wants. According to its critics, the discipline provides at best a primitive theory of how wants are created, at worst a circular argument that defines wants as whatever people choose in the market. Economics excludes the complex interactions among production, marketing, and desire. These structure the flows of information, diverting them into specific directions. Economics underestimates both the power of marketing to construct wants and the complexity of human desire. The latter is left unexplained (desire is what desire chooses) or when desire is taken up, it is reduced to rational choice. According to Bell (Bell and Kristol, 1981: 71), the conclusion that all we do is seek pleasure and avoid pain "is itself the most narrowly culturally-bound interpretation of human behavior, ignoring the large areas of traditionalism on the one hand and moral reflection on the other." This is important because both tradition and morality, bound up with need and desire, create their own calculus which rests uncomfortably and often simply refuses the constraints of a calculus of wants. For Bell (1976: 223), the economist's universal market is really one very specific form of economic activity. It is not universal but rather a "bourgeois economy," whose ends of production are individual and not collective and whose motives for the acquisition of goods are wants and not needs.

Economics tends to view markets as natural products of individual interaction rather than one among several sites of social activity. Markets are abstracted from class, race, and gender, as well as other forms of social division, that provide the vast social system of supports for market activity, including a flexible supply of low-wage labor, unpaid household labor, and a social system of desire that connects needs to wants in a form amenable to market transactions. Consequently, market success, the smooth operation of a market system, is viewed as social success, even if the consequences deepen social class, race, and gender divisions, or ruin the physical environment (Sayer, 2001). Those who oppose these consequences are seen to be acting out of irrational motives that are themselves best corrected by the discipline of the marketplace.

Heterodox views, in spite of other differences, agree that the substantive weakness of economics can be traced to a fundamentally inadequate understanding of the social. Economics is based on the view that one can eliminate what cannot be rendered scientific without giving up what is fundamental to understanding the economy. Alternatives to the mainstream contend that it is a hollow science indeed that would try to comprehend economic behavior without understanding the complexities of power, social structure, organizational behavior, and cultural practice. Where economics begins with the individual, naturalized across time and space, political economy starts with the socially constituted individual, engaged in a social process of production (Jessop and Sum, 2001; Sayer, 2001).

Some would take this substantive critique to a still deeper level; as Bell (Bell and Kristol, 1981: 47) puts it, "in short, there is the question not only of whether there is a crisis *in* economic theory but also a crisis of economic theory itself." According to this view, there is a crisis *in* economic theory because economics rests on a naïve and simplistic social theory: society is the sum of individuals; human action is predominantly rational; information flows freely to everyone; and markets disperse power, signal human wants, and, most importantly, register genuine social needs. But in addition to these shortcomings, there is the deeper crisis *of* economic theory that stems from its positivist roots, the belief that the only reality worth examining is what is observable, measurable, and quantifiable.

McCloskey provides a detailed critique of economic positivism in *The Rhetoric of Economics* (1985). Trained as a conventional economist who fears that many economists are "crippled" by a set of epistemological and methodological demands more appropriate to a religious system, McCloskey (1985: 4) concludes that:

> The faith consists of scientism, behaviorism, operationalism, positive economics, and other quantifying enthusiasms of the 1930s. In the way of crusading faiths, these doctrines have hardened into ceremony, and now support many nuns, bishops and cathedrals.

The positivist faith system includes numerous commandments: prediction and control is the point of science; only observable implications of a theory matter to its truth; observability is defined by objective, reproducible experiments; a theory is false if and only if an experimental implication proves false, etc. Moreover, positivism treasures objectivity, the separation of fact from value, and the language of mathematics. According to McCloskey, this regimen stultifies the minds of economists who, as a result, tend to be bored by history, condescending when not downright disdainful of social scientists, and wilfully ignorant of what lies outside the narrow confines of their field (McCloskey, 2002). A major consequence of what this renegade economist considers the fetishistic commitment to a rule-bound methodology and a slavish devotion to observable fact is that much of the richness of description and explanation is lost.

Admittedly, McCloskey tends to get carried away with her own rhetoric. More importantly, her interest in derailing economic positivism by uncovering fundamental philosophical shortcomings leads her to neglect the vital connection between the discipline of economics and systems of political and economic power. Conventional economics does not succeed only because economists agree on a set of narrow rules about research and discourse. Mainstream economics also succeeds because it serves power by providing information, advice, and policies to strengthen capitalism. Important as it is to see economic orthodoxy as a system of rhetoric, it is at least as important to see it as a system of power. To understand that system and to propose ways to change it, now, more than ever, we need political economy.

4

THE DEVELOPMENT OF A POLITICAL
ECONOMY OF COMMUNICATION

Chapter 4 starts by defining communication and proceeds to consider the social and intellectual context that gave rise to a political economy of communication. Chapters 5 and 6 describe and analyze research in the political economy of communication, making use of the growing body of literature in the field, discussions with many of its key figures, and over three decades of my own encounter with the political economy of communication.

One of the major conclusions from this assessment is that the political economy tradition, spanning principally Marxian and institutional approaches, has produced a substantial research record, well out of proportion to the organizational support it has received. Although the number of people making use of the perspective has grown over the years, especially over the last decade, they continue to work largely as isolated individuals. It is hard to speak of research centers, since collaborative work is largely the product of mutual interests among individuals generally in the face of, at best, tepid institutional support and often outright opposition.

──────────────── **The Concept of Communication** ────────────────

One of the challenges facing any discipline is the understandable tendency to *essentialism*, that is, an inclination to reduce reality to the discipline's central constituents. In taking up the characteristics of political economy, Chapter 2 addressed the need to avoid reducing social reality to political economy by seeing the latter as one among several ways of understanding social life. One can certainly appreciate the pressures toward essentialism. The sheer explanatory power of Marx's *Capital*, Marshall's *Principles*, and Keynes' *General Theory* offer compelling grounds for reducing social reality to a political economic or even to just an economic logic. Nevertheless, there are important epistemological, theoretical, and substantive grounds for resisting this tendency. Mindful of these, I view political economy as an entry point in social analysis, one important opening to the social field, but not one to which all approaches should be reduced.

Similarly, while it is very important to be clear about its meaning, it is also necessary to avoid communication essentialism. Again, the pressures in this direction are strong, particularly in the current intellectual climate. These include calls for reconstituting epistemology by shifting from analytical methods that have guided science for three hundred years to a range of communication-based approaches centering on rhetoric and a set of standards to be found in rules of discourse (Burke, 1969a, 1969b; Latour, 1999; McCloskey, 2002; Rorty, 1979). From this point of view, the rhetoric of conversation, as much as the logic of inquiry, should provide the standards of science. Specifically, it maintains that understanding is not a process by which one person observes and reports on reality by using language that reveals that reality. Rather, understanding takes place when two or more people exchange observations and ideas, and express them in language that does not just reveal reality, but which helps to constitute reality.

Moreover, the development of a cultural studies approach has given weight to organizing analysis around elements of communication content such as text and discourse. As a result, scholars are inclined to reduce epistemology, how we know things, and social analysis to communication. Specifically, this means viewing both the act of knowing and the object of knowledge primarily, or only, as discourse accomplished by reading texts. By focusing on how this approach can provide powerful tools for unmasking the universalistic claims of, among other forms of knowledge, science and economics, the emphasis on communication and discourse opens an important alternative. Nevertheless, this power can overwhelm even the most skilled of users, who effectively universalize conversational epistemologies and discourse analysis. The approach taken here is to acknowledge both the strength of this perspective and the danger of creating a new essentialism that takes with it a reductionist view of communication.

Political economy offers another reason for taking care to avoid communication essentialism. Although there is understandable tension over this, political economists of communication have sought to *decenter the media of communication* even as they have concentrated on investigating its economic, political, and other material constituents. Decentering the media means viewing systems of communication as integral to fundamental economic, political, social, and cultural processes in society. There are several ways to accomplish this, including, for example, starting from constituents of capitalism, such as capital accumulation, wage-labor, etc., and situating the media within the framework of production and reproduction set out by these basic elements. According to this view, the media, in its economic, political, social, and cultural dimensions parallels education, the family, religion, and other foci of institutional activity. One distinguishes them because each is exceptional in some respects, but since all are mutually constituted in capitalism, one avoids exceptionalism, of the media, or of any other institutional activity. The point is that the political economy approach to communication places its subject within a wider social totality and therefore tends to be especially concerned with avoiding essentialism in communication research.

With these cautions in mind, it is useful to move on to the meaning of communication. One of the first things to notice in doing background research on how to define communication is that virtually every academic discipline, from the physical sciences to the variety of the social sciences and the arts and humanities, has its own definition of communication. These tend to fall into two types: those that concentrate on the transmission of information and those emphasizing the constitution of meaning. For example, biology sees it as "an interaction between two organisms in which information is conveyed from one to the other" (*A Dictionary of Biology*, 2004; see also Breed, 1999), and likewise computer science sees it as the conveyance of information (Losse, 1999; Walton, 2000).

This transmission model made its way into communication research through the now classic work of Shannon and Weaver (1949). Although they begin with the rather ethereal view of communication as the ways one mind can affect another, the authors concentrate on the process by which a communicator or encoder sends a message or signal through a transmitter in such a way as to minimize noise and reach a recipient or decoder. Like the economist who narrowed the mandate of political economy in order to make it a mathematical science, Shannon and Weaver sought to create a mathematically grounded science of communication (they called their model "mathematical"). What was a big gain for the mathematician or the engineer was a loss for those who saw information as something more than the binary choice: noise or not noise. While the binary opened the door through which walked engineers who would code computer systems in the familiar ones and zeros, it closed the door on those who would find complexity and nuance in communication. These numbered a considerable range of approaches. Hence, the sociologist sees communication as a "process of establishing meaning" (Scott and Marshall, 2005), the social systems theorist as "the interactions between speakers and receivers which are determined by social and cognitive rules" (Klüver and Stoica, 2005: 877), and the marketing expert "a transactional process between two or more parties whereby meaning is exchanged through the intentional use of symbols" (Holom, 2006: 27).

My conception of communication follows from a general interest to place social process and social relations in the foreground of research. It therefore begins with the idea that *communication is a social process of exchange, whose product is the mark or embodiment of a social relationship.*[1] Broadly speaking, communication and society are mutually constituted. The tendency within political economy and forms of institutional analysis is to concentrate on how communication is socially constructed, on the social forces that contribute to the formation of channels of communication, and on the range of messages transmitted through these channels. This has contributed to an important body of research on how business, government, and other structural forces have influenced communication practices. Moreover, it has helped to situate these structures and practices within the wider realm of capitalism, trade, and the international division of labor. Nevertheless, it is also important to recognize that the social process does not end by structuring communication practices.

Communication is not simply an effect of social practices, not just the description of a cultural landscape that can only be genuinely explained by economics,

---

1 This appears to get at what Smythe meant when he refers to the dialectical relationship between communication and information.

political science, and sociology. Because it has tended to practice this form of essentialism, social science in general and political economy specifically have neglected communication and some of the substantial changes that transformations in communication are helping to bring about in the world. It is therefore equally important to think about how communication practices, including communicators and the tools they use, construct a social and cultural world that includes myth and symbol. For example, communication about new media like the Internet is not just shaped by the big companies who profit most from it. It is also molded by people whose aspirations lead them to construct grand visions or myths from the technology (e.g. create a new world that breaks through the constraints of space, time, and politics; realize genuine equality and democracy) (Flichy, 2007; Mosco, 2004).

Communication is not just the transmission of information; it is also the social construction of meaning. The latter includes but is not limited to those social rituals that bring people together (Hodgetts, Bolam, and Stephens, 2005). We use communication to share experience but also to contrast it; we use communication to bring our values together *and* to demonstrate their differences. Communication encompasses the two people in conversation and the broadcast of the Super Bowl in high definition. It includes a phone call with your mother and the AT&T network. It is watching children performing a play, the *New York Times* delivering "all the news that's fit to print," and Fox broadcasting its "fair and balanced" reports. It includes conversation, print, broadcasting, telecommunications, and the Internet. But perhaps most importantly of all for the political economist, it is not just about cooperation in networks; it is also about power in hierarchies.

Hence, it is important to resist seeing the political economic as the realm of structure, institution, and material activity while communication occupies culture, meaning, and subjectivity. Both political economy and communication are mutually constituted out of social and cultural practices. Both refer to processes of exchange which differ, but which are also multiply determined by shared social and cultural practices.

Social and Intellectual Influences on the Political Economy of Communication

The remainder of this chapter takes up the social and intellectual influences that propelled the development of this tradition. There is no simple way to examine the wider influences on a field that spans at least five generations, with researchers scattered around the world, some of whom do not explicitly identify with the political economy approach. This is especially challenging today because the field is no longer confined to a small set of universities mainly in North America and Europe. As Chapter 6 describes, the political economy of communication is now global, in both its physical and intellectual geography. Nevertheless, it is useful to begin with those broad social forces that contributed to the development of a political economy approach and then take up specific influences on individuals when we move into a more detailed treatment in the next chapters.

Social Forces

One of the chief influences on the development of a political economy approach was the transformation of the press, electronic media, and telecommunications from modest, often individual or family-owned enterprises, into the large, multidivisional organizations that marked the twentieth-century industrial order. The process of change has not been an inevitable one, nor necessarily linear. Some of the major media companies remain in family hands and are famously run by cantankerous moguls such as Rupert Murdoch, who presides over the News Corporation, parent of the Fox television networks and film companies. What we have learned is that the person who sits on top matters less than the application of strict industrial models to media production and strict financial accounting that puts the interests of revenue, profit, and stock value over all other considerations. It took a while but the development of industrial and corporate management activities familiar to most modern businesses, including the application of production, marketing, finance, and accounting practices, has extended to the full range of media businesses.

Some of the early political economy work took up the task of describing the structure and operations of large communication enterprises and addressed concerns about the use of power in such large enterprises. Danielian's (1939) research on the largest such company, AT&T, exemplifies this tendency, as did Smythe's (1957) on the structure of the American media industry. This tradition has continued in later generations of research, although this research has also moved on to reflect the tendency to corporate integration across media industry divisions and throughout manufacturing and, even more so, service industry lines (Artz and Kamalipour, 2003; Schiller, 2007a; Thomas and Nain, 2004). Much of this work involved "catching up" with historical patterns that occupied classical political economy, such as the transition to capitalism (how did the public interest principle in broadcasting give way to full commercialism?) and the creation of wage labor (how did media professionals become waged employees?). It also included key concerns of Marxian political economy, such as the transition to monopoly capitalism (how did one or a few media firms come to dominate markets?) and the creation of a labor process that separates conception from execution (how did media management get control over media labor?) The catch-up results from the persistence of craft traditions in the media industry, the strength of trade unionism in the media, and problems with commodifying these industries, as well as the relatively recent introduction of technological innovation to advance the application of market practices (McKercher and Mosco, 2007).

Current political economy research is played out against the background of debates on social and cultural forces called post-Fordism and postmodernism. For example, political economists now recognize that it is important to understand the changes to the industrial or Fordist economy. The media are organized along industrial lines and most media labor works for a wage, not unlike factory workers. However, media companies are now organized more flexibly in loosely connected divisions, or through alliances with independent companies in co-production arrangements that frequently cross national borders. Workers are full-time, part-time, contractual, or outsourced globally. One of the major contributions of current political economy is to respond to those who see this as evidence that media companies are not as powerful as we might think. Political economy maintains that these arguments miss a deeper level of concentration in global media conglomerates which are now powerful enough to control circuits of accumulation without needing to retain the risks of outright ownership. Flexible accumulation strengthens global media power (Baltruschat, 2008; Wayne, 2003).

The political economy approach began by concentrating primarily on the production side of the communication process by examining the growth of the communication industry and its links to the wider political economy. Nevertheless, the development of a mass consumption economy impelled political economists to take up the complete process of realizing value, including the social relations and organization of consumption. They addressed consumption by examining its growth as a *structural* response to the economic crisis of overproduction and as a *social* response to the political crisis of democracy, each arising from the mass organization of the working classes in North America and Europe (Ewen, 2001). How would capitalism respond to the challenge of getting people to buy the growing stream of goods it could produce without empowering those people to demand more of a say in the economy and in government? The growth of a mass circulation press, the spread of national telecommunications systems, and, more importantly, the development of radio and television broadcasting, were central elements that made up specific forms of mass consumption. But this was a mixed blessing for the political economy approach. The intimate connection between mass consumption and mass communication, linked from the start, meant that a political economy of communication would be centrally placed to examine one of the critical developments of the twentieth century. On the other hand, mass consumption and mass communication brought with them concepts and activities that differed in some fundamental ways from the range of political economy traditions. Political economy was ill-prepared to address activities organized around the household rather than business, and equally challenged by the use of a new language that spoke of audiences who participate in the accumulation process by listening, reading, and viewing, as well as by shopping.[2]

---

2 Once again, consider the irony of a discipline founded to examine household labor, struggling over two millennia later with new processes of accumulation organized around the household as a fundamental site of productive activity. Is this only consumption? Production and consumption? Something entirely different? Additionally, the reorganization of the basic circuit of economic activity brought with it a painful effort to literally come to "terms." What are the fundamental units of analysis: Classes? Gendered households? Audiences? Debates within political economy such as that inspired by Smythe's (1977) work on the audience as a commodity are partly a result of this understandably difficult process.

These issues are now compounded by the debate over post-Fordism and postmodernism because these theories contain conflicting views about the significance of tendencies to flexible and specialized consumption (Harvey, 1989). One of the major issues confronting political economic research today is the significance of the tendency to organize production around customized or niche, rather than mass, markets. Applied to consumption, the post-Fordist idea of flexible specialization suggests a substantial restructuring directed at the continuous production of specialized or customized products for particular markets. This issue is particularly important for communication studies because communication is implicated in every part of this transformed circuit. Communication systems are central to customizing production lines, critical to marketing these lines to customers, and vital to the rapid response times necessary to translate actual purchases into new production decisions. Finally, the proliferation of channel capacity for communication and information transactions suggests that specialized and customized media products for increasingly fragmented audiences are one concrete consequence of the process. These developments lead contemporary political economy to reflect on their pervasiveness (do they constitute the elements of a new epochal transformation?) and their wider significance (what are the implications for power relations in the global political economy?).

Political economy studies also grew in response to the expansion of government as a producer, distributor, consumer, and regulator of communication. Much of this activity arose from the pressures to manage the conflicting demands of growing domestic and international business. The Great Depression of the 1930s demonstrated that Big Capitalism needed Big Government. And if anyone needed further convincing, World War II provided an even stronger answer. The results can be found in the expansion of government intelligence, information gathering, propaganda, broadcasting, and telecommunications systems. In particular, the relationship between the military and the media, telecommunications, and computers has occupied several generations of political economists (Der Derian, 2001; Dyer-Witheford and Sharman, 2005; Mosco, 1989a; Roach, 1993; Schiller, 1992; Smythe, in Guback, 1993: Chapters 7–9; Winseck and Pike, 2007). In addition, the state's communication sector has grown with systems of regulation and policy-making that mediate business rivalries, respond to struggles emanating from class, gender, race, and social movement pressures, and coordinate long-range planning among leading fractions of capital. Political economy has taken up the role of the state in the construction of national telecommunication, broadcasting, and information systems, and assessed the consequences of a range of public and market-based approaches (Chakravartty and Sarikakis, 2006; Garnham, 1979, 1990; Schiller, 2007a; Smythe, 1957). Early in the development of a political economy approach to communication, the chief preoccupation was with supporting social movements for public access and control over these systems. The global pressures to privatization then led political economy to address the instrumental and structural roots of the process. More recently, particularly in response to the tendency of privatization to create disparities in access and changes in content that reflect largely market pressures, political economy has revived interest in exploring a wide range of alternative forms of the public sphere, civil society, and community communication (Hackett and Zhao, 2005; McChesney, 2007). Much of this research responds to the growing interest to use new media to resist and create alternatives to the dominant world of private media supported by national governments and most international government bodies (Abbott, 2001; Hanke, 2005; Howley, 2005; Stengrim, 2005).

The growth of business and the state contributed to global upheavals as both projected their power from the Western core nations into the rest of the world. The result was a body of political economic research that sparked a widespread debate on the issue of media imperialism. The transnationalization of what had been the US-based communication industry took place concurrently with the massive process of decolonization during the first two decades after World War II. It was this process of transnationalization, which is too often referred to more blandly and less clearly as globalization, that triggered powerful political responses, and arguably the most important in the communication sphere was the call for a New World Information and Communication Order (NWICO). This was a genuine social resistance movement which developed during the 1960s and 1970s out of the Non-Aligned Movement formed by Asian, African, and Latin American states that proclaimed a commitment to national self-determination. This movement, a genuine call for global communication democracy, including universal access to communication media, control over decisions about the production and distribution of communication, and the basic human right to communicate, gave a political purpose to a dynamic new research agenda for the political economy of communication. The field would address the role of communication in the US-led postwar reorganization of global capitalism. In addition, it would examine just how communication and culture were implicated in the renewal of domination over formally independent nations. Moreover, this new research program would assess what steps might succeed in overcoming global inequalities in communication, including establishing policy mechanisms to promote democratic communication.

Joined by communication scholars from North America, including the Canadian Dallas Smythe, and from Europe and the global South, with Armand Mattelart a notable representative of both regions, political economists such as Herbert I. Schiller responded by developing a powerful critique of mainstream theory.[3] Modernization or developmentalist theory originated in Western, particularly American, attempts to incorporate communication into an explanatory perspective

---

3 This research is taken up in greater detail in the discussion of the growth in political economy across different regions. Among the representative work is that of Schiller on Western imperialism (1992, 1993); Atwood and McAnany (1986), Beltrán and Fox de Cardona (1980), Dorfman and Mattelart (1975), and Freire (1974) on Latin America; Smythe (1981) on Canada; Ibrahim (1981) on Africa; and Tran van Dinh (1987) on Asia. For collections containing the work of international scholars, see Mowlana, Gerbner, and Schiller (1992), Nordenstreng and Schiller (1979 and 1993), Roach (1993), and Sussman and Lent (1991).

on development congenial to dominant academic and political interests. The developmentalist thesis held that the media were resources which would, along with urbanization, education, and other social forces, mutually stimulate economic, social, and cultural modernization in the less developed world. As a result, media growth was viewed as an index of development. Drawing on several streams of international neo-Marxian political economy, including world systems and dependency theory, political economists challenged the fundamental premises of the developmentalist model. In particular, they attacked its technological determinism and the omission of practically any interest in the power relations that shape the terms of relationships between rich and poor nations and the multilayered social class relations between and within them (Pendakur 2003; Thomas and Nain; 2004; Zhao 2008).

In place of modernization theory, political economists helped to elaborate a theory of cultural imperialism. This theory identified an array of structures and practices that functioned as instruments of transnational corporate and state power. The undermining of domestically produced news and entertainment in emerging and poor nations, via the dumping of US-made films and television programs at below market prices, underlay a one-way flow of culture and information from center to periphery. One of central goals of transnationalized companies and their government supporters was to press for the introduction of commercial media systems to permit advertising and programming that would cultivate consumerism. This drive supplanted development priorities that would favor universal access to adequate food, water, health care, and education. Moreover, in its own right, consumerism generated damaging environmental and cultural effects.

Furthermore, national sovereignty was undermined as US-based transnational corporations, the US government, and their comprador elites in the global South used new technologies like the undersea cable and the communication satellite to extend their control. Global data networks using emerging computer-communications systems gave a further advantage to big corporations over national authorities. As a result, audiences throughout the world viewed distorted images of poor nations, and foreigners who came to study in the United States were schooled in the built-in US assumption that private, advertiser-supported media should dominate over all forms of public communication. Charting the growth and power of transnational communications corporations, and their close interlocks with the US state, became a significant and enduring focus of the political economy of communication.

At their own conferences and before the United Nations, the Non-Aligned Movement pressed for the NWICO and brought together most of the scholars active in the political economy of communication around the world who produced basic research (Nordenstreng and Varis, 1974), policy analyses (Somavia, 1979, 1981), and assessments of the movement itself, including how Western media worked to undermine it (Preston, Herman, and Schiller, 1989). This wide-ranging effort to integrate academic research with political activity exemplified the commitment to the political economy ideal of praxis. Neo-conservative governments of the 1980s, with near complete support from mainstream media, slammed the door on all but a few token efforts to implement the UN's own report on the subject (UNESCO, 1979).[4] Nevertheless, political economists continued to press for the NWICO's goals, principally through the MacBride Roundtable, an organization committed to carrying on the work of decolonizing the media and documenting the continued need for a new world order in communication and information (Roach, 1993; Traber and Nordenstreng, 1992).

Indeed, the explanatory power of the many critiques of cultural imperialism, and their increasing use as a touchstone in international debate, soon triggered a counter-reaction. Under President Ronald Reagan, the United States ended its financial support to UNESCO, around which debates over NWICO had often centered. Beginning early in the 1980s, modernization theorists searched for revised models which, they claimed, offered novel insights by recentering around telecommunication and new computer technologies. University researchers found support from multilateral institutions such as the World Bank, as they insisted that information and communications technologies (ICTs) would ameliorate global poverty and inequality.

Political economists based in different parts of the world have responded by addressing the power of ICTs to reintegrate the global division of labor. At first, researchers saw the division largely in territorial terms. Unskilled labor was concentrated in the poorest nations, semi-skilled and more complex assembly labor in semi-peripheral societies, and research, development, and strategic planning limited to first-world corporate headquarters to where the bulk of profit would flow. More recent research acknowledges that class divisions cut across territorial lines. It also emphasizes the flexibility enjoyed by transnational companies because of their control over new communication technologies that overcome traditional time and space constraints (McKercher and Mosco, 2007; Pellow and Park 2002; Schiller 1999a; Sussman and Lent 1998).

These shifts in the division of labor (and in the labor process) constitute one component of a wider transformation: the rise of communication and information to a central position within overall global capital investment and profit-making (Schiller 2007a). The growing economic importance of communication and information has engendered a new cycle of debate and intellectual ferment. Building on their earlier research, political economists of communication began to document the integration of communication institutions, mainly businesses and state policy authorities, within the wider capitalist economy, and the central role of new information and communications systems in the neo-conservative agenda for promoting commercialization, liberalization, and privatization.

---

4 One sign of just how powerful the reaction against popular national sovereignty became was the appearance of work in the mainstream elite press supporting a return to colonialism. In one example, Paul Johnson (1993), author of the widely read history *Modern Times*, wrote in *The New York Times* that "Colonialism's Back – and Not a Moment Too Soon: Let's face it – Some Countries are just not fit to govern themselves." He called on the "civilized world" to return to the colonial trusteeship system that would seize control of countries it deems unfit to govern themselves. The 2003 invasion of Iraq is the direct outcome of this view.

Along with the growth of the transnational corporation, the expanding role of government, and the struggles over a New World Information and Communication Order, the putative emergence of an "Information Society" stimulated research in the political economy of communication. In the narrowest use of the term, it describes the simple acknowledgement that the production, distribution, and exchange of information and communication has come to occupy relatively more economic activity than either agriculture or manufacturing, which dominated production for most of human history. This development has attracted enormous attention because many have argued that it signals a revolutionary transformation in society with the potential to expand political democracy, create social equality, and accelerate cultural diversity, as well as signal a radical rupture in time, space, and social relations (Flichy, 2007; Mosco, 2004).

Most political economists have tended to argue that the nature and dynamics of capitalism have not changed in any fundamental way. The production of exchange value from use value, and the organization of the economy to maximize surplus value, remain central to the global political economy. Communication and information technology contribute to capitalism by expanding the size of the market for products and labor, but do not call into question the fundamental nature of capitalism. Borrowing a phrase from Dan Schiller (1999a), one might describe the economics of the information society as "digital capitalism," but it is capitalism first and foremost.

Sparking debate, others who are at least sympathetic to the political economy of communication have claimed that the terms "information age" or "information society" represent a new form of capitalism, simultaneously strengthening some of the fundamental tendencies of the system by expanding markets while also challenging them. In this respect, information society is more than just a description of a type of capitalist society, one with relatively more economic activity bound up with information. Rather, it refers to a society whose activity raises major questions about the viability of capitalism because it opens new forms of production, both within and outside the system and its legal structure. Perhaps the best current example of work that straddles the fence between a focus on capitalism and on a fundamental break with capitalism is that of Manuel Castells (2001). The fact that Castells switches back and forth between calling it "informational capitalism" and a "network society" reveals a genuine concern that, while elements of traditional capitalism persist, one needs to be open to the view that we are experiencing the creation of a fundamentally new type of society. The importance of making the most profitable use of the means of production, including labor, continues, and the social relations of production, if increasingly organized around communication and information, remain distinctly capitalist. However, the enormous and accelerating capacity to create communication and information networks challenges capitalism's ability to manage and contain them. The volume of information and communication that falls out of the orbit of value extraction – from the simple act of downloading material free of charge, to sending a video message to the world on YouTube, to carrying out criminal activities like money laundering under the cover of cyberspace – threatens the singular dominance of the capitalist mode of production. Open source and hacker networks challenge property rights in the digital world. Criminals and terrorists use digital technology to hide, and thereby expand, their activities. For Castells and others, who question the continued dominance of traditional capitalism, the network begins to replace the commodity as the central axis of social development. We live in a changed world, marked by the tension between information that wants to be free and a capitalism that wants to use it for the singular purpose of creating surplus value.

Castells openly moves between both views, and his work embodies the tensions in the scholarly community and among political economists, over the significance of an information society. Others, like Hardt and Negri (2004) and Terranova (2004), take a more explicit position that the information society – from its networks that blur the lines between real and virtual, to its labor that blurs the distinction between material and immaterial – is transforming capitalism into something fundamentally new. One consequence is that political economy needs to rethink some of its fundamental tenets. Why? Incapable of containing the process of value creation within the confines of capitalist processes and institutions, capitalism morphs into an information society, whose rules and relationships are increasingly up for grabs. According to this view, a society built around information networks erases the once-clear demarcations between work and home, labor and leisure, economic value and social value, and in so doing, begins to become a new kind of society. Myth-making aside, it is certainly not a utopian world; the reliance on massive surveillance alone challenges that claim. But the growth in the multiplicity and intensity of challenges to traditional capitalism, according to this view, begins to raise fundamental questions that lead some to find answers in a new type of society, an information society.

Although not an exhaustive treatment, these are some of the prominent general social forces that motivated the development of a political economy approach. In addition, there are significant intellectual influences.

Intellectual Currents

Every generation of political economists has been influenced by the perceived need to create alternatives to orthodox economics and, following from this, to develop media policies based on these alternatives. For the reasons discussed in Chapter 2, political economists reject the neoclassical synthesis that created mainstream economics. Political economists of communication have consistently argued that the approach is particularly unsuited to the analysis of the communication industry because most of its fundamental characteristics occupy the area that neoclassical economics reserves for exceptional cases. Throughout the last century and continuing into the new millennium, the media business has been highly concentrated with one or a few large firms controlling markets for production and distribution. Moreover, outside the United States, mass media and telecommunications networks have been organized in government-owned monopolies. Even in the United States, where only the postal service remained in government hands, the telecommunications and broadcasting networks were placed under government regulation from their early years. Furthermore, there was considerable ambiguity about the nature of what exactly was produced by these industries.

Although a radio news broadcast delivered through commercial sponsorship appeared to be a standard commodity, it retained certain unique characteristics (e.g. it was not used up in consumption) that made its treatment under orthodox economic approaches ambiguous. Moreover, while it is the case that Smythe sparked an intellectual debate about the nature of the audience commodity, the industry, as Smythe himself recognized, understood quite clearly that it operated in both the market for programming as well as in the market for audiences. The point is that there was enough uncertainty about the nature of the primary commodity in the communication industry to prompt consideration of alternatives to standard economic approaches. In sum, while many critics argued that much of the Western economy does not easily fit the models that neoclassical economics provides, this lack of fit appeared to be particularly pronounced in the communication industry. The drive to deregulate and privatize the communications sector diminished some of the arguments about its distinctiveness, but there remain significant non-commercial and regulated elements. Perhaps more importantly, the industry is further away than ever before from the competitive market model of mainstream economics (McChesney, 2007).

Following on this interest in substitutes for mainstream thought, over the generations, political economy has constructed alternatives to orthodox communication policy. For example, Dallas Smythe, one of the founding figures in the field, pursued a career that combined academic analysis, policy research, and activism. He began it in 1937 as an economic policy analyst with the US Department of Agriculture and followed this with a stint at the Department of Labor where he worked with trade unions representing newspaper, postal, and telegraph industry workers. In 1943 he was appointed the first chief economist at the Federal Communications Commission, where he addressed the many broadcasting and telecommunications issues that had been put off during the war. After entering an academic career, Smythe's policy work continued to advance public interest concerns, including support for public broadcasting, for public control over the communications satellite network, for the development of a New World Information and Communication Order, and for the demilitarization of global communications systems.

Similarly, a younger generation of political economists, led by Herbert Schiller and Kaarle Nordenstreng, provided assistance on the development of national communication policies in Latin America, Asia, and Africa. Thomas Guback, a student of Smythe's, applied political economy to the global film industry and carried out policy research on the industry during the heyday of UNESCO's interest in democratic communication. William Melody, a close colleague of Smythe's, trained in institutional political economy, has been active in the critique of policies inspired by neoclassical economics across North America and worked for major policy centers in the UK and Australia. His student, Robin Mansell, has carried on this work for policy centers in France and Great Britain. Nicholas Garnham was a trade union activist in the British communication industry and later joined with Graham Murdock, Peter Golding, Kevin Robins, and other British political economists who attacked the deregulation and privatization of that country's broadcasting and telecommunications systems.

One can find similar policy applications of the political economy perspective in the work of Robin Andersen, Andrew Calabrese, John Downing, Oscar Gandy, Robert

Hackett, Edward Herman, Robert McChesney, Eileen Meehan, Manjunath Pendakur, Dan Schiller, Gerald Sussman, Janet Wasko, and myself, among others in the United States and Canada. In recent years, Ronald Bettig, Nick Dyer-Witheford, Patricia Mazepa, Andrew Reddick, Vanda Rideout, Ellen Riordan, Ben Scott, Leslie Regan Shade, Dwayne Winseck, and Yuezhi Zhao have combined a strong commitment to political economic analysis with policy research and activism. McChesney especially has made an enormous contribution to activism in the United States by taking a leading role in the surge of media reform activity across the country.

Furthermore, Armand Mattelart, who built a well-earned reputation as a leading scholar and policy activist on communication issues confronting the developing world, in the 1980s turned his attention to the communication policy ferment in Europe. The model of the activist scholar working in political economy and public policy extends to many others with roots in the global South. These include Alhassan Amin, Indrajit Bannerjee, Paula Chakravartty, Wan-Wen Day, Wayne Hope, Yahya Kamalipour, Jyotsna Kapur, Keval Kumar, John Lent, Guillermo Mastrini, Zaharom Nain, Pradip Thomas, Keyan Tomaselli, and Y.Z. Ya'u.

This is simply a sampling of examples that are taken up in the more detailed analysis of political economic work below. The point is that five generations or so of people whose work has been guided by a range of political economic perspectives have used that work to engage the major policy issues in communication.

In addition to this consistent critique of orthodox economics and policy research, the development of a political economy approach responded to intellectual concerns that run deeper. The first generations of political economists tended to react against the *behaviorist* paradigm within which orthodox economics, as well as political science, psychology, sociology, et al., were situated.[5] It is based on the view that the job of a scholar is to create a science of the social by examining only those behaviors that the senses can directly observe and measure, and preferably describe in the language of mathematics. There was no room for a critical view based on moral philosophical considerations and certainly no room for praxis. Although debates between political economy and cultural studies receive a great deal of attention, it is absolutely vital to consider first the relationship to behaviorism.

The political economy of communication started against the intellectual backdrop of a multidisciplinary movement to apply the epistemology and methods of the physical sciences to the social sciences. This included the goal of using empirical observation to

---

5 This point was brought home to me in an interview with Dallas Smythe (December, 1991). Smythe was taken aback by my question regarding the tension between political economic and culturalist approaches to communication. Referring to the major intellectual divides that occupied his thinking, beginning with his graduate training in the 1920s, Smythe saw political economic and cultural analysis as close partners in the critique of behaviorism. In his view, it was the latter that presumed to limit research to positivist methods of empirical observation. Political economic and culturalist approaches opened research to questions of meaning, dialectics, and critique. This view of behaviorism as the principal intellectual adversary for early political economy was confirmed in interviews with Herbert Schiller (January, 1992) and James Halloran (April, 1992).

build systems of law-like theories whose constituents were falsifiable propositions. Propositions or hypotheses would be continually tested against additional empirical evidence in an ongoing process of refinement. In essence, the scientific method that appeared to serve the physical sciences so well would realize the goal of creating a science of the social (Nagel, 1957).[6] Applied to the social sciences, this positivist approach to investigation was commonly known as *behaviorism*. Its exemplars can be counted across psychology (the conditioning theories of Pavlov and Skinner), sociology (the analysis of group behavior in Homans), and political science (the public opinion work of Key). Behaviorism made its way into communication studies through several routes, prominent among them the work of Lazarsfeld and Cantril, who sought to create a social science of mass communication by examining behavioral responses to mediated messages. The point here is not to retell the history of behavioral communications research, a story that has received some interesting treatments (Buxton, 1994; Gitlin, 1979; Morrison, 1978; Park and Pooley, 2008). Rather, it is to situate the first generations of political economy opposite their principal intellectual adversary.

Early work in the political economy of communication never opposed empirical investigation or the gathering of material evidence, both quantitative and qualitative, to advance an argument.[7] Rather, political economy distanced itself from *empiricism* or the reduction of all intellectual activity to the production of falsifiable statements about observed behavior. The goal was to replace this with a broad analysis based on the dialectical relationship (what I call the mutual constitution) between theory and observed behavior. Moreover, political economy aimed to situate theory about mass mediated activity within the wider framework of political economic, particularly Marxian, theory. Political economy also argued for a critical approach that examines empirical findings in the light of a critical purpose, such as the need to advance democratic communication by building public systems of communication. For the political economist, empirical results neither arose out of a black box nor spoke to one. They grew out of a dialectical relationship with theoretical formulations and spoke to a broadly defined political interest. Finally, political economy identified the researcher as an active participant in the social process under investigation. Denying the possibility of a "free-floating intellectual," political economy sought to account for the relationship of the researcher to the research subject. In this respect, as Smythe noted (Interview, December, 1991), this placed political economy within the range of the hermeneutic approach that was more fully developed in anthropology and, specifically, in the critical cultural studies research of the Frankfurt School. In essence, as Dan Schiller (1996) has

---

6 I use the word "appeared" because an extensive body of research has called into question just how faithful the physical sciences have lived up to the strictures of the scientific method (Haraway, 2003; Latour, 1999; Sokal, 2008).

7 Dallas Smythe carried out one of the first content analyses of commercial television in order to make the case for a public network. This work caught the eye of *Time Magazine*, which wrote a story about it. He was also involved in an attempt to secure Ford Foundation funding for a content analysis of the popular television program *The Mickey Mouse Club* (Interview, December, 1991).

described in perceptive detail, the first generation or two of the political economy of communication, making allowances for variation within specific work, was *allied* with cultural approaches against what they both perceived to be the essentialist account proffered by behaviorism.

Subsequent generations of political economy continue to distinguish themselves from behaviorism. However, what was once an affinity with culturalist approaches against positivist accounts turned adversarial in the 1990s (*Critical Studies in Mass Communication*, 1995). Recently, the tensions between the two approaches have abated significantly as scholars associated with each come to appreciate and make extensive use of the other (Meehan, 2005; Miller, 2007; Ross, 2004; Wasko, 2001). Nevertheless, it is useful to refer to it here because one way to comprehend current developments in political economic research is by setting it within the context of a shift from stressing differences with behaviorism, which it still addresses, to its differences with cultural studies.

Political economists raised several concerns about cultural studies, including giving near essentialist warrant to the subjective, the local, and the particular; privileging speech, conceptual or naming activities over all others; and resisting the development of explanatory schemes that unify a range of activities. Recalling the behaviorist effort to write a metanarrative of positivist social science, political economists raise concerns about the metanarrative, however ironic in light of its professed opposition to forms of totalizing thought, contained within the culturalist project. According to Garnham (1990), this tendency grew out of literary and film studies, extending into the range of structuralist, post-structuralist, and postmodern thought. In the course of its development, he concludes:

> It took with it the bacillus of romanticism and its longing to escape the determining material and social constraints of human life, from what is seen as the alienation of human essence, into a world of unanchored, non-referential signification and the free play of desire. (Garnham, 1990: 1–2)

Strong language is not limited to one side of the divide. Proponents of cultural studies tended to reject political economic approaches as economistic, totalizing, or simply derivative of the "outmoded" Marxism of *Capital* (*Critical Studies in Mass Communication*, 1995). Moreover, the heat is not limited to communication and cultural studies. Just about every discipline has been occupied with concerns raised on either side (Sokal, 2008).[8] Nevertheless, as Chapter 10 demonstrates, the new century has brought with it some evidence that the divide between political economy and

---

8 Consider this analysis of the linguistic turn in history. After acknowledging that "this is not an entirely pernicious development," social historian Bryan Palmer concludes:

> What I question, what I refuse, what I mark out as my own differentiation from the linguistic turn, is all that is lost in the tendency to reify language, objectifying it as unmediated discourse, placing it beyond social, economic, and political relations, and in the process displacing essential structures and formations to the historical sidelines. (1990: 5)

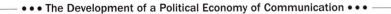

cultural studies is diminishing (Miller, 2004; Mosco, 2004; Philips, and Meehan, 2006; Pratt, 2004; Ross, 2004; Wasko).

Conclusion

This chapter began the task of examining the political economy of communication. It started by defining communication as a social process of exchange whose outcome is the measure or mark of a social relationship. In keeping with the broad approach to the field, the definition includes both the transmission of information and the social constitution of meaning and includes face-to-face and mediated communication in all of its many forms, from the printed page to Facebook.

The political economy of communication developed in response to several social and intellectual challenges. The former included the growth of the media as a business, particularly in the form of the transnational corporation. It also encompassed the growth of government and debates about the need for a New World Information and Communication Order to redress global disparities. Finally, political economy has developed in part to address the putative rise of an Information Society. The political economy of communication also emerged in debates with leading intellectual traditions, including mainstream economics and the policies it supports, such as the promotion of a commercial media system supported by government with minimal oversight. The chapter concluded by explaining that the behaviorist tradition, actually an intellectual metanarrative, provided a formative challenge to the political economy of communication in its early years. Beginning in the 1990s, cultural studies posed the major challenge. However, the new millennium brought with it closer ties, if not a *rapprochement*, between political economy and cultural studies. We now turn to the first of two chapters that map the political economy of communication.

5

THE POLITICAL ECONOMY OF COMMUNICATION: BUILDING A FOUNDATION

The foundation for a political economy of communication was established from the years immediately following World War II to about 1980. This chapter tells the story of this early development, beginning with key figures and ideas from North America and Europe. The chapter concludes by addressing the political economy of communication in the rest of the world, particularly in those societies that comprised what we once called the Third World. Given the numerous difficulties with that term, particularly since the fall of the Soviet Union, once the anchor of a Second World, it is more useful to simply refer to the developing world.

North American Origins

There are many potential starting points for this analysis. For example, Dan Schiller (1999b) has written about the work of Robert A. Brady (1901–63), who is among the early critics of business power and one of the first to call for media democracy. However, we start with Dallas Smythe and Herbert Schiller, the two North Americans who arguably have exerted the most significant influence on the field.[1]

Dallas W. Smythe began the study of the political economy of communication in the United States. He taught the first course in the field and several of his junior colleagues and students have gone on to do prominent work. Like others who work in political economy, Smythe was influenced substantially by engagement with central political issues and social forces. For him, these were principally the Great Depression and the rise of fascism in the 1930s. Specifically, Smythe cites three turning points that helped to transform him from someone who cast a 1928 vote

---

1 This section draws on the written record, on interviews with Smythe (December, 1991) and Schiller (January, 1992), and on my relationship with them from the late 1970s.

for the successful Republican presidential candidate Herbert Hoover into a person who pursued radical ideas and political activism.

These include his observation of clashes between National Guard troops and striking dockworkers, interviews with impoverished migrant farm workers that formed the basis of a graduate school project on agricultural assistance programs, and his contact with people who supported and fought with the anti-fascist forces during the Spanish Civil War.[2] He concludes that his own version of political economy grew first from the practical experience of political struggles and only later from intellectual encounters.

Trained as an economist at the University of California, Berkeley, Smythe benefited from the wider range of viewpoints then admissible in the economic canon. Although the neoclassical perspective was achieving some closure by the 1930s, challenges from institutional and Marxian sources, sustained by horrendous economic conditions, were important components of graduate education at that time. Specifically, Smythe read economic history and theory from people like M.M. Knight, who accepted institutionalists such as Veblen and American interpreters of Marx into the economic corpus. Moreover, Smythe placed substantial emphasis on his immersion in government reports and documents that provided concrete analyses of political economic conditions. These included extensive government hearings on the economic collapse of the 1890s and research on the history of the transportation industry that would form the basis of his doctoral thesis.

If the Great Depression helped to shape Smythe's thinking, the New Deal response influenced the course of his career. After being awarded the PhD in 1937, Smythe went to on work for the federal Department of Agriculture and later the Department of Labor, where his associations with politically progressive civil servants and trade unionists strengthened his critical thinking. Smythe's work on the media began with his job at the Department of Labor, where part of his responsibility was tracking the media and telecommunication industries, their labor practices, and trade unions. He observed first hand the struggles between supporters of radical and company unions battling for the support of workers at the telephone giant AT&T and its counterpart in the telegraph industry, Western Union. This work also brought him into close contact with the details of a changing labor process in the communications industry as skilled radio and telephone operators began to feel the effects of new technologies which were automating work and eroding skills.

Smythe left the Department of Labor in 1943 to become the first economist to work at the Federal Communications Commission (FCC). His job was to follow labor relations and to provide advice on rate hearings. Smythe also participated in one of the busiest periods of radio spectrum allocation as the agency took up the backlog of license requests, the issue of allocating new FM frequencies and, arguably the most important, channel allocation for television. Smythe's future work was indelibly

---

2 His support for the anti-Franco side would place him among those the US government called a "premature anti-fascist," a label that would ill-serve Smythe in the 1950s.

marked by the lessons he learned from the mobilization of commercial interests to defend private control over radio and television.[3]

Smythe left the FCC in 1948 to begin an academic career at the University of Illinois, where Wilbur Schramm had started the Institute for Communication Research. Opening the first PhD program in communication studies, the Institute became a crossroads for several people who would leave their mark on the field, including several who worked in critical media studies and in political economy. These include the communication psychologist Charles Osgood and, later on, George Gerbner, for a brief time Theodor Adorno, and Herbert Schiller. In the Cold War climate and with communication research so sensitive to the increasingly powerful mass media, Smythe began cautiously with a course on the economics of communication before developing one specifically about the political economy of communication. This period is also marked by Smythe's research on the need for public broadcasting, publication of the first political economy of the electronic media (1957), and the beginnings of his theoretical work on the audience as a commodity.[4]

The scourge of McCarthyism did not end with the senator's demise and, as university life in America became more politically repressive, Smythe decided to return to his native Saskatchewan, Canada, where he established a communication program at the University of Regina. He had met Herbert Schiller at the University of Illinois and, when Smythe left, Schiller was brought into the Institute from economics to teach the political economy of communication. Smythe spent a decade at Regina where, with William Livant, he further advanced the idea that the audience was the principal commodity in the mass media. In 1974 Smythe joined the faculty at Simon Fraser University in British Columbia, where he worked with the institutional political economist William Melody. Here, Smythe concentrated on telecommunication policy (the antitrust case against AT&T was a central concern), on the audience commodity paper, and on his major academic work *Dependency Road*, a dialectical analysis of monopoly capitalism anchored in the case of US domination over Canada's economy and media. During this time he traveled widely, carrying out research on the reforms Salvatore Allende's Popular Unity government was bringing about in Chile, and on communication practices and policies in China, Japan, the UK, and Eastern Europe. At Illinois, his major student had been Thomas Guback, who would go on to become a leading figure in the political economy tradition. At Simon Fraser, his work in political economy and public policy influenced an even greater number of future political economists. In addition to Melody, these included Robert Babe, Manjunath Pendakur, William Leiss, Sut Jhally, Robin Mansell, and Rohan Samarajiva.

---

3 Under the influence of pro-market Commissioners, the FCC voted to protect the largest commercial AM radio broadcasters (whose "clear channel" stations covered half of the United States in nighttime hours) against the challenges from the advocates of FM and public broadcasting. The Commission also limited its allocation of the first television channels to commercial interests, most of which were also powers in the radio industry (Mosco, 1979).

4 Smythe gave the first formal presentation of the audience commodity idea at a 1951 talk to a meeting of the Consumers Union Institute at Vassar College.

Smythe left Simon Fraser in 1980 to take a position at Temple University where, for a short time, he joined Janet Wasko, who had been a student of Guback's at Illinois, Dan Schiller, and myself. Smythe continued to work in a series of visiting appointments, eventually returning to British Columbia, where he died in 1992. A Festschrift volume (Wasko, Mosco, and Pendakur, 1993) gives some evidence of his impact on four generations of political economists around the world. So too does the annual Smythe Lecture at Simon Fraser and a prize awarded in his name by the International Association for Media and Communication Research, the organization that has given the most attention to political economy over the years, thanks in part to Smythe's work.

Like Smythe, Herbert I. Schiller attributed his political and intellectual development to the experience of transformation in the American and global political economies. For Schiller, about a half-generation removed from Smythe, this meant entering his high school and university years during the Great Depression and serving in World War II. He attended the City College of New York, which provided a free education to the city's working class in what most accounts conclude was a highly politicized atmosphere (Maxwell, 2003). Although his interests ran to the literary, he chose to study economics, for him "a Depression induced choice," which was more likely than a concentration in English Literature to lead to a job. As with many people living through this economic cataclysm, Schiller was left with an intense sense that something was fundamentally wrong with the Western political economy.

The other substantial formative influence was his service in the war and his work for the US military government in Germany immediately thereafter. The latter was particularly important because it gave Schiller the opportunity to observe first hand the imposed transformation of a nation's political economy compressed into a very short period. Among intellectual influences, Schiller emphasized the research carried out by US government bodies in the 1930s on the structure of the American economy and on the causes of the Depression. For him, these detailed political economic studies provided concrete, systemic evidence of how business power works.

The war, economic necessity, and his own uncertainties about the academic world delayed the start of Schiller's academic career.[5] He spent ten years as an overworked sessional instructor, before receiving the doctorate from New York University in 1960 with a thesis on the political economy of postwar relief efforts. He started with a visiting position at the University of Illinois Bureau of Economic and Business Research where his interests in resource allocation led eventually to research on the radio spectrum as a natural resource. Although remaining at the

---

5 Though accused, as he puts it, of having "an animus against business," Columbia University awarded Schiller the master's degree in 1941. He was not impressed with this center of elite intellectual life:

It was a revelation because I came to realize how totally inadequate the graduate process was. The textbooks used in those days were just appalling, conservative concoctions that were presented in ways that were desiccated and abstracted from reality. Not to say anything of the theories they presented. (Interview with author)

Bureau throughout his time in Illinois, Schiller attracted the attention of the Institute for Communication Research, where he met Smythe and took over the political economy course when his Canadian colleague left for Regina. His *Mass Communication and American Empire* appeared in 1969 to widespread attention that included growing pressure from conservatives at Illinois who did not appreciate the book's criticism of capitalism and the author's outspoken opposition to the war in Vietnam. These factors and the attractiveness of a proposed alternative college at the University of California, San Diego, where the Frankfurt School theorist Herbert Marcuse had settled, led to a move in 1970.

At San Diego, Schiller produced a series of books that helped to define the political economy of communication in the United States and had enormous influence on the development of critical perspectives worldwide. Schiller's work has consistently aimed to situate communication studies in the wider political economic context. His second book, *The Mind Managers* (1973), offered the first sustained critique of the information society idea by documenting the growing integration and transnationalization of the information and cultural industries and the broad political and cultural power of major exemplars, such as the Gallop polling company, *Reader's Digest Magazine*, and the *National Geographic*.[6] Following this, his *Communication and Cultural Domination* (1976) addressed the question of cultural imperialism and his first-hand observation of Chile's effort to build an alternative under Salvatore Allende. In *National Sovereignty and International Communication* (1979), Schiller teamed up with Kaarle Nordenstreng to produce a collection that addressed central issues in the New World Information and Communication Order debate.[7]

Schiller returned to issues of information control in his next two books, *Who Knows* (1981) and *Information and the Crisis Economy* (1984). These examined the vital significance of information and communication systems for the general operation of transnational capital and, particularly in the second book, the role of these systems in overcoming the crisis of accumulation that continues to bedevil capitalism.

In *Culture, Inc.* (1989), Schiller revisited the cultural industries and departed from his previous work by addressing trends in academic disciplines, specifically his concerns over the turn to cultural studies. Schiller was committed to media research because he knew that culture was critical to democracy. In the last decade of his life he assessed its importance for communities by examining culture in city streets and parks, billboard advertising, museums, libraries, and a host of other places which

---

6 The book was published in the same year as Daniel Bell's *The Coming of a Postindustrial Society*, a work that shaped the agenda for the debate on the "information society" and one year before Harry Braverman's *Labor and Monopoly Capital*, now a classic in the study of "information labour." Schiller attracted particular attention when an excerpt on polling appeared in the popular magazine *Psychology Today*, whose editors gave what Schiller calls the "inflammatory" title "Polls are Prostitutes for the Status Quo."

7 This book is also notable because it was the first communication volume published by Ablex which, under the editorship of Melvin Voigt, produced many of the major works in political economy into the early 1990s.

demonstrated for him that "a community's economic life cannot be separated from its symbolic content" and that "speech, dance, drama, music and the visual and plastic arts have been vital, indeed necessary, features of human experience from the earliest times" (Schiller, 1989: 31). Schiller focused a critical eye on culture, not as a superstructural derivative of an economic base, but to demonstrate that the symbolic is not only inextricably bound to the material, it *is* material. His concern with academic cultural studies was based on the fear that it diminished the cultural by removing it from the arena where it was most important in mutually constituting economic, political, and social life.

Schiller returned to his longstanding interest in the transformation of international communication with *Hope and Folly* (1989), a book written with William Preston, Jr. and Edward Herman, that documents the demise of the call for a new information order, and a second collection with Kaarle Nordenstreng, *Beyond National Sovereignty* (1993). Along with Hamid Mowlana and George Gerbner, Schiller provided a global perspective on the Gulf War with a collection of papers from international media scholars.[8]

In Schiller's final two books he returned to a focus on the United States and its deepening troubles. In *Information Inequality* (1996), he wrote about the growing gap in access to communication, anticipating the soon to be hot topic of a "digital divide." But unlike those who would see the gap as merely a matter of providing people with technology, Schiller saw it as a symptom of ongoing social class and racial divides in the United States that create gaps in economic and political resources as well. Finally, in a book he continued to work on until he died in 2000, *Living in the Number One Country*, Schiller provides an analytical and personal account of what it meant to be a critical scholar based at the center of a world empire.

Schiller was a model of the activist scholar. In addition to his enormous research contribution, with editions published in most major languages, he spoke out on cultural and information issues before many local, national, and international organizations. His remarkable record of speaking out throughout the developing world, before international organizations like UNESCO, and in the First World, where he starred in the indymedia classic Paper Tiger's "Herb Schiller Reads The New York Times," demonstrated his belief that it was essential to oppose the

---

8 *Hope and Folly* documents the triumph of US-led conservative forces at UNESCO. It was initially commissioned by UNESCO during a period when the organization supported many of the concerns raised by NWICO proponents. But by the time the report was completed, the agency was so concerned to transform itself, in hopes of bringing back US and British membership, that it refused to release it. The University of Minnesota Press published the book, but with a printed disclaimer that completely disassociates UNESCO from its contents. According to Nordenstreng (1993: 253), this is not the first example of "anti-intellectual repression" by the UN agency. In 1973, it dropped Dallas Smythe from a Panel of Experts formed to establish the UNESCO communication research program. This took place after Smythe presented two papers critical of mainstream international communication policy and its infatuation with new technologies. Finally, it refused to publish a paper commissioned from Schiller in a 1982 collection.

global media industries and produce an alternative to commercial culture. His work provided one of the principal inspirations for the new world information order idea. He was one of the leading figures in the International Association for Media and Communication Research. And although the vision of an alternative college at the University of California, San Diego fell victim to neo-conservatism, Schiller left his mark on many students there, as well as on his and subsequent generations of communication research.

As work in Europe developed in the late 1960s into the mid-1970s, North American research in the political economy approach remained primarily based on the work of Schiller and Smythe, until Smythe's student Thomas Guback took a position at the University of Illinois, Urbana-Champaign and began to attract graduate students influenced by the political and social upheavals of the time. By the end of the 1970s the time was ripe for a significant upward turn for political economy in North America.

One meeting cannot alone be responsible for the emergence of a field. However, if there was one key event in the development of a political economy of communication in North America, it took place in March 1979 at a conference held at the University of Illinois, Urbana-Champaign. It brought together students of Smythe and Schiller as well as others who knew their work and were interested in advancing a political economy perspective. Thomas Guback, a pioneer in the political economy of the film industry, took the lead, along with several of Guback's students, including Janet Wasko (film), Eileen Meehan (audience studies), Jennifer Slack (technology), and Fred Fejes (imperialism and Latin America). Addressing critical communication, the conference gathered numerous people who would go on to make a substantial contribution to a political economy of communication. In addition to these, it included Dallas Smythe himself, who came from Simon Fraser University with a current graduate student Manjunath Pendakur (film and Indian media), as well as Oscar Gandy (technology, race), Carolyn Marvin (the history of technology), Timothy Haight (communication activism and policy), and myself (sociology and policy), then a professor of sociology at Georgetown University.

The meeting was significant for several reasons. It was the first to collect three generations of political economy scholars, including Smythe, his student Guback, and several of Guback's students, as well as Smythe's student Manjunath Pendakur. Furthermore, it signaled a major step in the formation of a network of political economy scholars, a major advance for an approach that had been largely limited, in North America at least, to the work of Smythe and Schiller. Moreover, the conference demonstrated that the field was beginning to attract a number of women into what had been a perspective dominated by men, and the presence of Gandy meant that the field would not be limited to Caucasians. Finally, the conference was a major step toward the formation of the Union for Democratic Communications, the organization that for close to thirty years has best represented political economy and activist approaches to communication studies in North America.

At about this same time several other scholars began to establish significant careers in political economy research in North America. Stuart Ewen's research on advertising, Dan Schiller on the history of journalism, Gerald Sussman on Asian media and political communication, and Emile McAnany on Latin American media and development communication are representative examples.

The Emergence of Political Economy in
European Communication Research

The emergence of a political economy tradition in Europe is not as clearly associated with key figures like Smythe and Schiller. Nevertheless, it is useful to begin with such early figures as James Halloran in Britain and Kaarle Nordenstreng in Finland, who helped to develop the tradition in their own regions and, perhaps more importantly, called attention to political economy by virtue of their international work.

James Halloran was a leading figure in the development of communications studies in Britain. For over two decades he headed the Centre for Mass Communication Research at the University of Leicester, where Peter Golding and Graham Murdock produced work that helped set the research agenda for the political economy of communication. Moreover, Halloran influenced the development of communication studies worldwide with close to two decades of service as President of the International Association for Media and Communication Research (IAMCR) (Hamelink and Linné, 1994; Hamelink and Nordenstreng, 2007). Although the long-time head of the international professional association most closely identified with political economy research, Halloran did not identify with the approach, choosing to situate his work and that of the Centre within the tradition of critical sociology and social psychology (Interview, April, 1992). He notes that the Centre was initiated in response to concerns raised by the Home Secretary in 1961 about problems of juvenile delinquency and the interest in assessing television's impact. Although he acknowledged the importance of political and economic research, his main scholarly and programmatic interest was focused on developing a critical sociological approach (Centre for Mass Communication Research, 1984: 8). Halloran distinguished this from the work of mainstream pioneers in communication research whose positivist approach put data gathering ahead of "asking the right questions" (Halloran, 1981: 23).

During Halloran's tenure as Director, the Centre maintained a steady flow of research reports, several by scholars, particularly Graham Murdock and Peter Golding, who made important contributions to the political economy of communication. Nevertheless, as Halloran, Murdock, and Golding all agreed, the overwhelming number take up specific social problems from a sociological or social psychological perspective. Although certainly wide-ranging, the emphasis is on problems facing young people, families, and communities, including the sociological concerns and communication needs of ethnic and racial minorities. In fact, Murdock observed that the Centre received few grants for political economy research. Most of these, such as Philip Harris's work on news agencies, Peter Hartmann's on the New World Information Order, and Murdock's on the advertising industry, incorporated several approaches along with political economy. Moreover, all of this work appeared in the 1970s and early 1980s. Sociological, social psychological, and policy research occupied practically all of the Centre's reports from 1984 on (Interviews with Halloran, Murdock, and Golding, April, 1992; Centre for Mass Communication Research, 1991). Almost all of the research and publication in political economy that people have associated with the Centre were produced outside the auspices of the Centre itself. Affirming this point, Golding concludes that there never was a "Leicester School" of political economy in nearly the sense that one can speak of a Birmingham School of Cultural Studies under Richard Hoggart and Stuart Hall, or even comparable to a School of Political Communication under Jay Blumler and Dennis McQuail at Leeds. Following a pattern common throughout the field of political economy, what appears to be an institutionalized program of research is actually a collection of individuals, in this case Graham Murdock and Peter Golding, who, along with Philip Elliott and from time to time others, pursued political economy research (Golding, Murdock, and Schlesinger, 1986). They did so in a setting congenial to critical social research, but not one that gave particular attention to political economy.

Halloran is not alone in his generation of European communication scholars who have played a role that supported, if not directly shaped, the political economy approach. For example, Dieter Prokop produced studies on the political economy of the media that connected the business of communication to concerns raised by the Frankfurt School (Prokop, 1973, 1974, 1983). Enzensberger's "Constituents of a Theory of the Media" (in Enzensberger, 1974) offered one of the early attempts to fill what he argues is one of the "empty categories" of Marxist thought by developing a theory of media that accentuates class relations, conflict, and the contradictory and subversive qualities of media. The point is that, although one can identify examples of the political economy of communication in Schiller's, if not Smythe's, generation of European scholars, the influence on subsequent political economy work in Europe is not nearly as evident as the influence of Smythe and Schiller on the development of a political economy approach in North America. Sustained research from this perspective begins with subsequent generations of communication scholars.

For many years Kaarle Nordenstreng of Finland has played a leading role in the development of international communication studies and in the political debate over the NWICO. From the 1960s, he has taken critical issue with the positivism and technological utopianism in Western communication research (1968). Nordenstreng is best known for his work on the dynamics of global communication and specifically on the effort to redress imbalances and otherwise democratize the mass media (Nordenstreng, 1984; Traber and Nordenstreng, 1992). He has combined a strong research record in the field with persistent political activism at the national and international levels in the effort to bring about the NWICO and in the drive to extend it to the Internet and to other new media in the process known as WSIS or the World Summit on the Information Society (Mansell and Nordenstreng, 2006; Nordenstreng and Padovani, 2005). Nordenstreng has been particularly important for his ability to bring together scholars, including political economists and policy activists from around the world. There are few parts of the globe that have not felt the influence of his organizational acumen.

Nordenstreng's collaborations with Schiller (1979, 1993) produced major collections in international communication that exhibit a strong political economic influence.

Nevertheless, one cannot identify Nordenstreng with a political economy approach as easily as one can Smythe and Schiller. This is not because Nordenstreng lacked interest in theoretical matters of major concern to political economists. He has made the case for a disciplinary framework that certainly overlaps both Schiller's and Smythe's (Nordenstreng, 2004). Nevertheless, although certainly sharing values and evaluations congenial to a political economy perspective, Nordenstreng has not taken as strong a research interest in the economic dimensions of mass media and communication. Whereas Halloran chose *critical sociology* as a focus of attention, Nordenstreng concentrates on a *critical politics* of communication, particularly in its international and ethical manifestations. This has provided him with a grounding for his long-standing commitment to policy research and intervention. In this fashion, Nordenstreng has influenced numerous communication scholars and activists, including political economists. However, the influence has not been as direct on the latter as that of Smythe and Schiller because Nordenstreng has not taken as sustained a research interest in the economic aspects of the political economy of communication. Choosing to concentrate on explicitly political fora, he has had less to say about the business of media and the commodification of culture and communication.

Dallas Smythe and Herbert Schiller established a program of research in the political economy of communication that influenced the shape of the field internationally, particularly in the United States and Canada. James Halloran and Kaarle Nordenstreng provided an important bridge for that research to Europe and, through Halloran's work for the IAMCR and Nordenstreng's work in a number of international fora, to the rest of the world. However, the sustained development of a political economy approach in Europe emerged with the appearance between 1974 and 1982 of a set of theoretical and programmatic pieces that contributed substantially to placing the field on the European intellectual map. The core works include Murdock and Golding's (1973) "For a Political Economy of Mass Communications," their (1979) "Capitalism, Communication, and Class Relations," Garnham's (1979) "Contribution to a Political Economy of Mass Communication," and the near book-length introductions that Armand Mattelart produced for the two-volume work he edited with Seth Siegelaub, *Communication and Class Struggle: Capitalism, Imperialism* (1979) and *Communication and Class Struggle: Liberation, Socialism* (1983). These works are given particular attention because they set out programmatic positions that have significantly influenced political economy research.[9]

————————————

9 This was an important period for the development of a political economy of communication in Europe. In additions to these works, several others sought to bring together political economy, Marxian theory, and the particular problems posed by communication practices (de la Haye, 1980; Hund and Kirchoff-Hund, 1985; Prokop, 1983). It is also important to mention the influence of a political economy group in Italy, including Giovanni Cesareo, Roberto Grandi, and Giuseppi Richeri, whose publication *IKON* influenced the development of political economy in Europe and North America. In Spain, a group including Madrid scholar Enrique Bustamente developed the journal *Telos*, which produced political economic and policy analyses on communication and new technology issues.

Trained in economics and sociology at the London School of Economics, Graham Murdock began his career by applying this background to understand cultural life. Specifically, in the late 1960s at the University of Sussex, he wrote about the rise of New York and the decline of Paris in the elite art market. His interest in popular and youth culture took him to Leicester where, for two decades, he worked at the Centre for Mass Communication Research in the sociology and political economy of culture and communication. In the mid-1990s he left Leicester to rejoin Peter Golding, who had moved to the University of Loughborough after spending most of his career at Leicester. Golding's training is also in sociology, although he has taken a stronger interest in the social policy dimensions of communications research. Garnham came to communication research from a background in film. A founding editor of *Media, Culture and Society*, he spent his academic career at the University of Westminster.[10]

Belgian-born Armand Mattelart received his doctoral training in law and political economy from the University of Louvain and a postgraduate degree in sociology from the Sorbonne. He was a professor at the University of Chile from 1962 until the 1973 US-backed military *coup d'état* ended the government of Salvatore Allende which had been elected on a platform of democratic reform. During his years in Latin America, Mattelart was influenced by and helped to shape the course of research in that region. It also brought him into contact with Smythe and Schiller, who spent time in the region examining the impact of American media (see Schiller, 1976). Mattelart also recognizes the influence of a French "cultural industries" approach developed by the sociologist Edgar Morin. Since leaving Chile he has been a professor at the University of Paris.

Although differing in some respects, the early work of these scholars shares an explicit interest in making critical use of Marxian theory, in its different readings, to understand communication, the mass media, and cultural practices. Murdock and Golding's 1973 work is a ground-breaking exercise because it sets out a conceptual map for a political economic analysis of the media where none had existed in the British literature.[11] Using the British media as a case study, they examine the process of consolidation and concentration at work in publishing, the press, broadcasting, cinema, and recording. In addition to addressing what have become accepted dimensions of media concentration – integration and diversification – they also take on what for that time was a new development, the internationalization of British media. Finally, they assess the wider implications, including restricted choice in entertainment and information. Although providing one of the early

---

10 Garnham emphasizes two primary influences on his development. The first is the tradition of British cultural studies and social history that grew out of the work of Hoggart, Leavis, Thompson, and Williams. This led him into the cultural industries where he worked on documentary films in the 1960s, including a television program with Raymond Williams. The second is his involvement in debates on the development of British television and the role of the BBC.

11 They note (1973: 205) that the media, unlike the study of education, "has gone largely unexamined" and cite a 1973 collection of writing on *Power in Britain* (Urry and Wakeford, 1973) which not only lacked a chapter on the media, but contained no reference to the media in its index.

systematic analyses of the commercial power of the mass media, they are also careful to qualify their conclusions by situating them within an inclusive position:

> To describe and explicate these interests is not to suggest a deterministic relationship, but to map the limits within which the production of mediated culture can operate. Cultural production retains a real autonomy derived from tradition, occupational ideologies and the genuine tolerance of the liberal consensus. (Murdock and Golding, 1974: 226–7)[12]

Murdock and Golding's 1979 work provides an even more explicitly theoretical effort to place the political economy approach within the wider framework of critical theory. It demonstrates that, for them, a critical reading of the Frankfurt School's analysis of the cultural industries offers one of the primary links between the Marxian legacy and their application of it to communication studies. For example, Murdock and Golding begin their overview of Marxian approaches to cultural analysis by noting the contribution of Horkheimer and Marcuse at the Institute for Social Research, singling out Adorno's work on the music industry. They conclude that: "Adorno's insistence that the process of cultural domination has its roots in the economic dynamics of the 'culture industry' is an indispensable starting point for any Marxist analysis" (1979: 18).

Nevertheless, they insist that "it is only a starting point" and proceed to criticize as "not sufficient simply to assert that the capitalist base of the 'culture industry' necessarily results in cultural forms which are consonant with the dominant ideology" (1979: 18).[13] Similarly, in his article of the same year, Garnham applauds the particular way the original Frankfurt School position addressed the relationship of base and superstructure in contrast to post-Althusserian tendencies. He credits the Frankfurt School with recognizing that "under monopoly capitalism the superstructure becomes precisely industrialized; it is invaded by the base and the base/superstructure distinction breaks down via a collapse into the base." He contrasts this with the alternative position, taken up in cultural studies, which concludes that we are observing the "transformation of the base into another autonomous superstructural discourse" (Garnham, 1979: 130). Nevertheless, like Murdock and Golding, he takes issue with the Frankfurt tradition on this point:

> the real weakness of the Frankfurt School's original position was not their failure to realize the importance of the base or the economic, but insufficiently to take account of the economically contradictory nature of the process they observed and thus to see the industrialization of culture as unproblematic and irresistible. (Garnham, 1979: 131)

---

12 It is interesting to observe this caution in one of the earliest attempts to situate the political economy of the media in a wider theoretical framework. It suggests that right from the start the approach steered clear of "economism."

13 In an interview (April, 1992), Murdock refers to a more immediate link to the Frankfurt tradition in the early 1970s work of Dieter Prokop.

Starting from the more explicitly anti-imperialist Marxian literature, Mattelart is not as concerned to connect his approach to the Western Marxism of the Frankfurt School. This undoubtedly results in part from what he acknowledges to be a central problem in French communication research. Little of the theoretical work developed by French intellectuals like Althusser and Barthes, which influenced Stuart Hall at Birmingham, was taught in the primary media research schools of France. The failure to produce French editions of Habermas's work until the 1980s also contributed to the lack of a connection to Western Marxism (Mattelart and Mattelart, 1992). Nevertheless, like his British counterparts, Mattelart steers clear of seeing power as a singularity and looks beyond it to fundamental contradictions, thereby setting aside the more rigid Althusserian structuralist approaches to ideology from the start.[14]

This interest in rooting communication studies in the Marxian tradition led these writers and their counterparts to an inevitable decentering of the media.[15] True to a Marxian political economy, this meant placing in the foreground the analysis of capitalism, including the development of the forces and relations of production, commodification and the production of surplus value, social class divisions and struggles, contradictions and oppositional movements. Decentering the media actually raised the stature of media studies by moving it from an isolated, marginalized and largely untheorized area of activity to one that is fundamental to processes of production and reproduction within the wider capitalist system. Murdock and Golding (1979) discuss this specifically with respect to the "double vacuum" in media studies and sociology. Whereas media studies typically approached the social realm with a laundry list: the media and class, the media and youth, the media and women, etc., which suggests a loosely articulated pluralism, sociological theory tended simply to ignore the media.

Sharing the view that communication needs to be situated in a wider theoretical framework, Garnham argues (1979: 202) for placing the political economy of culture within an overall analysis of capitalism with "a political economy of mass-communication taking its subsidiary place within that wider framework as the analysis

---

14 As he puts it:

One of the most misleading tendencies of Althusserian ideological theory is that its monolithic and vertical concept of how the dominant ideological apparatuses function does not conceive of them as being subject to class contradictions. The most concrete effect of this approach is that its field of observation marginalizes the resistance practices of the dominated classes against the dominant ideology, as well as it marginalizes the internal incoherencies which characterize the operation of these ideological apparatuses. (Mattelart and Siegelaub, 1979: 29)

15 It is not possible to discuss every one of their counterparts. Nevertheless, it is important to mention Seth Siegelaub, who worked closely with Mattelart on several projects, including co-editing the two-volume *Communication and Class Struggle* and editing issues of the multi-volume bibliography *Marxism and the Mass Media*. He also founded the International Mass Media Research Center and directed the publishing enterprise International General, which was responsible for these and other volumes of critical media research. Siegelaub's principal education was as a political activist and a manual laborer.

of an important, but historically specific mode of the wider process of cultural production and reproduction." Much of Garnham's interest in this area grows out of his reading of and involvement in central policy debates about the course of the mass media and telecommunication in the UK.[16] It also flowed out of his association with Raymond Williams, who aimed to secure a place for popular culture as democratic, resistant, and alternative, in contrast to the market-driven effort to align popular with mass consumption (Interview, November, 1993).[17] Similarly, for Mattelart, "the manner in which the communication apparatus functions, which determines the elaboration and exchange of messages, corresponds to the general mechanisms of production and exchange conditioning all human activity in capitalist society" (Mattelart and Siegelaub, 1979: 36).

This process of decentering the media placed in the foreground the concepts of capital, class, contradiction, conflict, and oppositional struggles. The analysis of capital is, for Murdock and Golding (1973), "the obvious starting point for a political economy of communications." Specifically, this means, "the recognition that the mass media are first and foremost industrial and commercial organizations which produce and distribute commodities" (Murdock and Golding, 1973: 205–6). Challenging what he refers to as the theorization of social formations into relatively autonomous levels, Garnham argues for seeing the mass media "first as economic entities with both a direct economic role as creators of surplus value through commodity production and exchange and an indirect role, through advertising, in the creation of surplus value within other sectors of commodity production" (1979: 132). Rather than relative autonomy, the result is a "close inter-weaving within concrete institutions and within their specific commodity forms of the economic, the political and the ideological" (1979: 132). All of these are embodied in the generalizing and abstracting drive to reduce everything to exchange value, which Garnham perceives to be Marx's central insight into the capitalist mode of production. Drawing on *Capital*, which he argues is "the most mature work," Mattelart draws out specific dimensions of the mode of production of communications: (1) production instruments (machines used to transmit information); (2) working methods (genre specific practices, codes, etc.); and (3) relations of production (property relations, transmitter–receiver relations, division of labor, organizational forms and practices).

In their view, social class relations are central to political economic analysis, although they all see the articulation of class relations as a set of complex and contradictory processes. These involve principally the relationship between communication entrepreneurs and the wider capitalist class, the relationship between media industry leaders and the concrete activities of those who actually make media

───────────

16 One of the more important expressions of this is his 1973 monograph (revised in 1978) on political economic and public policy issues in the UK television industry (Garnham, 1978).

17 Garnham emphasizes that the political economy of communication is itself part of a wider process of popular cultural activity, i.e. it is one academic wing of a wider intellectual *and* popular movement for democratic action (Interview, November, 1993).

products (the specific form of the labor process),[18] and the dynamics of reception, i.e. how people adopt, reconstitute, and resist the range of meanings embodied, however tightly or loosely, in cultural commodities.

Notwithstanding capital's power, each of these moments in the valorization of capital is marked by contradictions. As a result, while acknowledging the power of capital to absorb social, including communication, practices into the logic of exchange value, they reject correspondence theories that unequivocally align capital logic with cultural production. Noting the tendency to see the imposition of this logic as non-contradictory, Garnham concludes that:

> One must stress at the outset that this is not so. Because capital controls the means of cultural production ... it does not follow that these cultural commodities will necessarily support, either in their explicit content or in their mode of cultural appropriation, the dominant ideology. (1979: 136)

Not only can such products be, in Garnham's words, "profoundly subversive," they must be seen as the product of struggles between distinct capitalist and non-capitalist social formations, and among classes within and between these formations. For example, one can see artisan or craft production of books and films as congruent with a capital logic as long as capital controls mass reproduction and distribution. Artisan production provides capital with diversity and absorbs much of the risk. Nevertheless, this form of production has also been the site of struggles against the economic logic of capitalism in defense of customized, craft production for use over mass production solely for profit.

Mattelart extends this research by situating contradiction and conflict within a global context. His early work is particularly revealing for the number of ideas that would later be taken up by political economists and communication scholars generally. He offers a highly nuanced perspective on cultural imperialism that, in addition to comprehending patterns of communication power, takes into account complex forms of "secondary imperialism," for example in Mexico, India, Egypt, and Italy, the manifold social practices that these cultural imperialisms take, e.g. sports, tourism, etc., and various ways to conceptualize contradictory and conflictual relations of production and reception, including mass, popular, and national cultures.[19] By the beginning of the 1980s, the political economy of communication was ready to develop as a collective enterprise in North America and Europe. This

---

18 Although they praise Adorno for his work on the influence of capitalism on the music industry, Murdock and Golding (1979: 18) take him to task for neglecting the "concrete activities of the people who actually make the products the 'culture industry' sells."

19 These ideas are presented in the 1979 volume and developed more fully in the 1983 collection. As Mattelart notes (Mattelart and Siegelaub, 1979: 56), Michèle Mattelart (1977) provided a clear sense of the distinction between mass and popular culture. The latter is not a formal substitute for mass culture but "a qualitatively different practice, embodying the experience of a people who *become the active subject of a cultural experience linked to their own project for liberation.*"

chapter concludes by identifying one additional pillar of this foundation, the growth of a political economy perspective in and about the rest of the world.

Steps toward a Global Political Economy of Communication

The political economy of communication built a foundation in much of the world, including other developed regions like Australia (Graham, 2000), New Zealand (Hope, 2006), and Japan (Morris-Suzuki, 1988, 2005). Some of this work is taken up in subsequent chapters, but the focus of the remainder of this chapter is the emergence of a political economy approach to communication in the developing world.

The struggle for a New World Information and Communication Order (NWICO), which developed during the 1960s and 1970s out of the Non-Aligned Movement formed by Asian, African, and Latin American states that proclaimed a commitment to national self-determination, imparted both political purpose and a dynamic new research agenda to the political economy of communication. What role did communication play in the US-led postwar reorganization of global capitalism? How were communication and culture implicated in the renewal of domination over formally independent nations? What measures could be taken to redress international communication disparities?

Developing world research departed from its counterpart in the developed world because it was largely forged out of a series of social struggles defined in a variety of ways in different regions of the world. Variously identified as anti-colonial, national liberation, or socialist struggles, these eruptions of the post-World War II era helped to create an intellectual and research agenda. In fact, it was those who played a leading role in revolutionary activity, people like Mao Zedong, Ho Chi Minh, Amilcar Cabral, and Che Guevara, who were also its leading intellectuals. These leaders of the period's liberation movements are also notable in that they explicitly recognized the importance of controlling the means of communication, including radio and other electronic means, to build support for revolution. Intellectual leaders, such as Frantz Fanon (1965) in Algeria and the Brazilian Paulo Freire (1974) throughout Latin America, wrote specifically on the mass media and literacy as tools of revolutionary activity. Although a concern for communication, public opinion, and ideology had marked earlier variations on Marxian and critical thought, their work provided a departure from economistic tendencies.

Forged in the "hot wars" of the 1950s and early 1960s, developing world research took off in two related directions. First, it forged a critique of modernization approaches, the major response of the former colonial powers to the political and military successes of anti-imperialist struggles. Second, it presented a spectrum of perspectives, best known as dependency theory, that constituted its own framework for understanding transformations in the global political economy. The approach known as developmentalism or modernization theory was also forged in struggle. In this case, it was the recognition of the developed West, particularly the United States, that the victory over fascism left little time for triumphalism because Communism, and what the West perceived to be its many manifestations in wars of socialist and national liberation, stood in the way of global capitalist expansion. In order to overcome these impediments, to win the "Third World" War, i.e. to defeat Communism and pacify the developing world, the West mounted an unprecedented global military, political, economic, and ideological campaign.

Developmentalism, one of its leading intellectual inspirations, brought together an elite corps of academics based in leading universities and research centers to determine how to safely secure the developing world within capitalism. Since its core notions have been subjected to a withering criticism that helped hone the intellectual strength of developing world scholars and their colleagues in the developed and socialist worlds, modernization theory is easy to dismiss as a simplistic apologia for capitalist hegemony. But that would be a mistake. There is no doubting the use of the perspective as a vehicle to defend the image of the United States as a different world power, one that helps nations beyond its shores, including those it conquered in warfare, to join the modern world. However, in addition to this, modernization theory, particularly as a theory of communication, contained a sophisticated set of tools that responded to changing military, political, and intellectual conditions in order to construct a hegemony.

Modernization theory arose out of a fundamental problem facing the United States, and to a lesser degree its Western allies, in the aftermath of World War II. The West confronted decolonization movements across Africa and Asia, and political upheavals in Latin America. Only the United States was in a position to manage these developments and bring the many newly independent nations within the evolving stratified hierarchy of the postwar circuits of capitalism. Much has been made of modernization theory as an outgrowth of classic sociological models, developed most explicitly by Tönnies, that distinguished traditional from modern, rural from urban, *gemeinschaft* from *gessellschaft* (Mattelart and Mattelart, 1992: 171–2). The problem with this view is the implication that modernization proponents were unsophisticated social scientists trying to apply simplistic, textbook sociology. People like Lerner, Pool, and other modernization theorists not only read their Tönnies, they understood just how the conception of "modern" had changed from his turn-of-the-century view.

The theory of modernization meant a reconstitution of the international division of labor, amalgamating the non-Western world into the emerging international structural hierarchy. One element of this was "nation-building," a process of creating national elites that could effectively substitute nationalism for the alternative models of socialism on offer from the Soviet Union and, soon after the end of the war, China. Under the banner of national identity, these elite class fractions would incorporate the remaining social structural forces necessary to fend off the challenge of revolution and socialism that threatened to transcend national differences and organize the range of excluded classes and strata against the growing power of transnational business and an increasingly militarized US government. Although it repeatedly attempted to do so, the United States could not achieve this goal by military means alone, nor would its own domestic pressures permit matching the post-World War II massive assistance program known as the Marshall Plan with a similar program for the underdeveloped world.[20] Along with military and economic weaponry, the United States made use of those communication and intelligence tools that its media and information industries had begun to hone before the war and which paid significant dividends throughout the conflict.[21]

In the early years, as Samarajiva (1985) and others (Mattelart and Mattelart, 1992; Sussman and Lent, 1991) have documented, this meant applying the methods of psychological warfare to, in the words of one of its leading figures Harold Laswell, "clarify the identity of genuine allies and enemies" in the struggle with the Soviet Union. Daniel Lerner's book *Sykewar* (1949) became the model for his classic work in the field, *The Passing of Traditional Society* (1958). The latter used extensive interviews to map the range of attitudes and values that would support or retard modernization, understood in numerous ways, but particularly as support for those national and international forces whose goal it was to construct a market economy. Later on, particularly in the work of Schramm (1964), modernization theorists turned directly to the mass media as a vehicle to achieve this goal. In fact, the level of media development became one of the principal indicators of general societal development. Following directly from this premise, Rogers (1971) took on the task of examining the general propensity to innovation and social change, including the introduction of modern means of communication. This was crucial because improving the general receptiveness to media technologies and media messages was vital to the wider aims of development, including the social need to change extended family structures, the economic need to create a market economy, and the political need to build a supportive class of national and local leaders. Charting the diffusion of innovation was another means to map a target, in this case a target of opportunity for the Western way of life, including its mass media.

The communication research program inspired by the modernization thesis was very influential. It provided enormous quantities of information on the behavior, attitudes, and values of developing world people and helped to shape university communication programs and research centers. Speaking about Latin America, McAnany (1986: 29) concluded that the first generation or two of indigenous communication scholars were trained in the American functionalist tradition from which modernization theory descended. In a region with scant resources, this meant that most schools, journals,

---

20 Proposals for a developing world equivalent to the Marshall Plan received little serious attention and when they did, as with President Kennedy's proposed Alliance for Progress in Latin America, the actual dollars never matched the rhetoric. It is also important to note that although the Marshall Plan involved a real economic commitment, the commitment was most important to US businesses understandably eager to win access to European markets unimpeded by socialist or communist threats.

21 There is research on the links between wartime intelligence activity and the American developmentalist strategy (Samarajiva, 1985; Sussman and Lent, 1991). But the communication strategy was not only forged in action against the enemy. In fact, some of the most significant strides in survey and intelligence research were carried out on the most substantial "captive audience" ever marshaled in American history, its armed forces (see Stouffer, 1949).

and texts were funded and organized with US government assistance and led by proponents of the modernization thesis. Nevertheless, however powerful the impact on all of these levels, modernization could do little to improve the real economic conditions of developing world people. The yawning gap between prescription and accomplishment was filled by a growing number of critics, some of whom sharpened their skills in the political economy of the mass media by dissecting the modernization thesis. This was particularly the case in Latin America, partly because this region was arguably the most important target of the developmentalist project. The general problem of sharing the hemisphere with nations in poverty and social upheaval was compounded for the United States following the 1959 victory of the Cuban revolution.

Partly as a result of the "special treatment" that the modernization program brought to Latin America, critical scholarship developed relatively early there with the 1960s work of Mattelart in Chile, Freire in Brazil, Pasquali (1967) in Venezuela, and Veron (1967) in Argentina.[22] These were among the first to examine the consequences of media development programs. In their studies of literacy, mass culture, journalism, and television, they showed how Western media companies were the chief beneficiaries of modernization programs. For the people of Latin America, these programs were either a waste of money or the instrument to deepen inequalities between rich and poor within developed countries and dependencies on the rich West.

In the late 1960s and throughout the 1970s, the critique mounted as research expanded over the range of mass media and received significant theoretical grounding with the emergence of dependency theory (Beltrán, 1976). Political economy research received a significant boost in 1976 with the establishment in Mexico City of the Instituto Latinamericano de Estudios (ILET). ILET originally comprised a group of scholars led by Fernando Reyes Matta, Rafael Roncagliolo, Herbert Schmucler, and Diego Portales. Its principal interest was the study of transnational business, particularly the impact of media companies. ILET's impact was most strongly felt in international policy debates, particularly through the work of Juan Somavia, a member of the UN's McBride Commission on the need to redress imbalances in the global production and distribution of information (Marques de Melo, 1991: 59–73). According to Roncagliolo (1986: 79), the ILET media research agenda addressed three central questions that political economists continue to face:

1. What is the place of culture in the transnationalization process and of communication within cultural processes?

---

22 The work of Antonio Pasquali and Eliseo Veron is less well known in North America. The former made use of his training in existentialist philosophy to critique the mechanistic formulations of modernization theorists who, he contended, were not interested in communication at all but rather with using information and technology as the means to build a mass society in Latin America. Veron was a Marxist, influenced by the structuralist work of Lévi-Strauss and Barthes, whose principal interest was the critique of ideology, including the ideological apparatus of Western "modernization." For an overview of the emergence of cultural studies in Latin America, see A. O'Connor (1991).

2. What does the transnationalization of consumption consist of, if it signifies something more than the homogenization of demand at the international level?
3. Is there such a thing as a "transnational culture," or are there simply internationalized patterns of behavior? (See today's version in Chakravartty and Zhao, 2008.)

This conceptual scheme situated media within cultural production and consumption and the latter within the general process of transnationalization. Moreover, it placed at the center of its research agenda the relationship among transnationalization, internationalization, and homogenization.[23] In addition to documenting the negative consequences of media modernization projects for the people of Latin America, ILET and others contributed to, and benefited from, the development of an alternative theoretical framework generally referred to as dependency theory.

Among other centers of communication research, the Institute for Latin America (IPAL), founded in Lima, Peru in 1983, stands out as a major source of research in political economy. Under the direction of its founder Rafael Roncagliolo, IPAL carried political economic research in two directions that are increasingly important to the approach today. Going beyond the study of print and electronic media, IPAL was particularly interested in the social relations of new communication and information technologies. This placed it at the center of debates over the next phase of modernization theory, i.e. the establishment of market-based telecommunication and telematics systems across the developing world. Furthermore, IPAL was interested in the culture of social resistance and in alternative social practices organized around popular culture and communication.

The political economy of communication was also a prominent feature in Cuban research, led by Enrique Gonzalez-Manet at the University of Havana. Gonzalez-Manet (1988) was particularly active in providing the political economic groundwork, with thorough analyses of media systems across Latin America, for developing a socialist version of a New World Information and Communication Order.

Forged in practice, the political economy of communication in the developing world was nevertheless animated by the theoretical formulation known as dependency theory (Amin, 1976; Baran, 1957; Cardoso and Faletto, 1979; Dos Santos, 1970; Emmanuel, 1972; Gunder Frank, 1969). Although there have been enough disagreements about the meaning of dependency to warrant some caution in any brief on the perspective, there appears to be most agreement on a handful of key ideas. These include the view that transnational businesses based in core countries, with the support of their respective states, exercise control over countries outside the core by setting the terms for market transactions over resources, production, and labor. By controlling the terms of exchange and the structure of markets, transnational capital establishes the conditions of economic activity in the hinterland, including the extent of development. At best, the outcome is dependent development, at worst the development of underdevelopment. As its

---

23 This approach is significant because it suggests that Latin American media scholars recognized early on that the relationship between political economy and culture is not only important but problematic and complex as well.

critics have not been hesitant to point out, the dependency approach concentrates on how external forces set the conditions for the form of social and economic development, paying less attention to the contribution made by local forces and relations of production, including the indigenous class structure.

One version of the dependency approach shifted the terms of debate to the cultural domain, as scholars whose interest was primarily in media and culture examined dependency on circuits of production, distribution, and reception controlled by transnational media firms and the state. Here was more than an empirical assessment of how well modernization theorists met their development goals. Dependency theory offered an alternative explanation that situated the practices described by modernization theorists within the wider context of transnational power and dependency, including an admittedly functional observation that modernization was an instrument to develop underdevelopment.

Dependency theory enjoyed widespread influence and equally widespread criticism. It was criticized for concentrating on the impact of transnational business on development to the neglect of internal class and power relations. Dependency theorists responded by examining the roles of comprador elites in these societies, and the impact of the richer semi-peripheral societies on specific regions, each of which played a substantial role in the core–hinterland circuit of value creation. Criticism was also directed at economistic tendencies within the perspective. Specifically, critics maintained that dependency theory tended to rest on the logic of transnational capital that appeared to capture the state, turning government into little more than an instrument to manage the accumulation process. One response was to broaden the dependency approach by incorporating a more activist reading of the state, one which recognized the need to develop transnational state structures on the order of the European Community (EC), the World Bank, and the G-8, to harmonize conflicting economic, political, and social policies, and to respond to the conflicting demands of social classes, movements, and interests. Moreover, the critique of dependency theory provided additional room for the analysis of culture, a longstanding interest of critical communication research in the developing world, but an interest that had fit uneasily within the overall economic thrust of the dependency approach. Specifically, a more mature dependency theory provided some room for those who would make the case for cultural imperialism, particularly to advance an examination of the full political economic circuit and of the processes and struggles that made up the reception and constitution of culture (Mattelart, 1986).

Nevertheless, criticism of dependency theory contributed to the deeper attacks on political economic analysis developing in various strands of post-structuralist thought. This view rejects the value of talking about circuits of capital and linkages between political economic processes and cultural practices. Maintaining that such analysis mistakenly constructs social totalities out of at best loosely articulated, discrete, local practices, post-structuralism would do away with dependency theory as simply another attempt to create a metanarrative, a totalizing discourse unwarranted by social and cultural practices (Featherstone, 1990; Tomlinson, 1991). Such attacks deepened the divide between a global political economy of communication and the emergence of a global cultural studies. It was left to new scholarship, particularly emerging outside the Western core, to face up to this divide and attempt to overcome it. For some of the results, we turn in Chapter 6 to current trends in the political economy of communication.

Conclusion

This chapter described the first decades of sustained research in the political economy of communication. It grew out of concerns with the shortcomings of mainstream research, especially with the dominant behaviorist paradigm, and with the policies that protected large media businesses from the development of a more democratic media system. In the less developed world, concrete political struggles over the shape of the postcolonial world played a large role in the growth of a political economy approach. Embodied in dependency theory, political economists contended with modernization theory and then with post-structuralism in debates about the most useful way to understand communication and culture outside the Western core. These produced the first steps toward a global transcultural political economy of communication.

6

THE POLITICAL ECONOMY OF
COMMUNICATION TODAY

Chapter 4 addressed the social and intellectual influences on political economy research and Chapter 5 took up the process of building a foundation. This chapter addresses five trends in current research.

One of the most significant developments in the last decade or so of political economy research in communication is the sheer volume of material. When I wrote the first edition of this book in 1996, it was possible to map out the field in a few chapters. That is no longer possible because the quantity of good research has expanded substantially. A complete accounting today cannot be contained within the pages of one book. It calls for something more like an encyclopedia. However, it is possible to examine central trends in contemporary research that provide a useful guide to the political economy of communication today. So before turning to Chapters 7–9, which offer my own theoretical perspective on the political economy of communication, let's consider five major tendencies in current research. These include the globalization of the field, the expansion of an enduring emphasis on historical research, the growth of research from alternative standpoints, especially feminism and labor, the shift from an emphasis on old to new media, and the growth of activism connected to the political economy tradition. None of these are brand new tendencies but rather build on existing tendencies which were often submerged beneath dominant trends in the field.

The Globalization of Political Economy

The political economy of communication has always contained an important international dimension. For example, two founding figures, Dallas Smythe and Herbert Schiller, joined Armand Mattelart to assist the Chilean government of Salvatore Allende to create a democratic media system. Moreover, research outside the developed core began as a response to what was perceived to be media imperialism in the West. Nevertheless, on balance, most of the research in political economy had nationalist tendencies and distinct regional emphases. For example, the bulk of

Smythe's major book *Dependency Road* (1981) addresses Canada's dependence on US media and asks why the Canadian nation state permitted it to continue for so long. From this perspective, nationalism became an alternative to US media imperialism. Similarly, resistance to Western media domination over the developing world was met with calls for national resistance along the lines of the national liberation movements that had won independence for many nations after World War II.

In addition to the tendency to focus on nationalist resistance to globalizing media, political economy developed specific regional tendencies that distinguished North America from Europe and both from research in the developing world. As the previous chapter described, research in the United States and Canada tended to address systemic and specific problems in the communication industries, including the deepening concentration of media power and the growth of supportive national governments. These helped to establish a military–industrial–media complex that threatened democracy and freedom for citizens of those countries and elsewhere. European research was more self-consciously theoretical, concerned about how to integrate the study of communication into the overall body of political economy and, more specifically, Marxian theory. Finally, research on and from the developing world supported the social movement for a New World Information and Communication Order. It would do this largely by countering the modernization theories of the West with national and regional applications of dependency theory. There were certainly exceptions to these tendencies, but they were sufficiently strong that when I wrote the first edition of this book, I could confidently map the political economy of communication in the mid-1990s along these regional emphases. But that is no longer possible because these regional differences have substantially diminished. Political economists from different regions are working together on common projects (Calabrese and Sparks, 2004; Murdock and Wasko, 2007) and it is no longer unusual to see research from one region taking up themes that were once prominent in another (Artz, Macek, and Cloud, 2006; Mansell, 2004).

North American scholars have made substantial contributions to political economic theory, including research on the integration of digital technologies into a capitalist economy (Schiller, 1999a), the relevance of Marxian theory to communication scholarship (Artz, Macek, and Cloud, 2006), and the application of autonomist theory to social movements that make use of new media (Dyer-Witheford, 1999). It is also just as likely that one would find concrete studies of media problems such as the commercialization of media and the decline of public media in European scholarship (Mansell, 2002; Sparks, 2007). Finally, while it is the case that scholars from developing societies are involved in the successor movement to the NWICO, the World Summit on the Information Society (WSIS), there is just as much evidence that scholarship in the former Third World has taken a strong interest in the growth of political economic theory (Chakravartty and Zhao, 2008; Liu, 2006; *Review of African Political Economy*, 2004).

The process of globalizing political economy research is proceeding rapidly. Some of this is the result of the sheer movement of scholars, a development that has sped up over the last two decades. For example, the Canadian political economist Robin Mansell established a base for institutional political economy at the London School of Economics. Yuezhi Zhao, who has provided the foundation for a political economy of China's media and telecommunications system, moved from that country to the United States and from there to Canada, establishing important connections among scholars in all three countries.[1] One of her students A.J.M. Shafiul Alam Bhuiyan came to Canada from Bangladesh and has produced important work on political economy from the perspective of a postcolonial subject (2008). The Korean political economist Dal Yong Jin moved to the University of Illinois, Urbana, and worked with Dan Schiller to complete a dissertation on the political economy of telecommunications in South Korea. He has since joined Yuezhi Zhao and Robert Hackett to continue the historically strong presence of a political economy perspective at Simon Fraser University in Canada.

In addition to formal and informal movements of scholars across regions, universities with a strong political economy orientation have established an institutional base concentrating on international research. For example, the University of Westminster, where Nicholas Garnham helped to found the political economy perspective, has established, under the leadership of political economist Colin Sparks, a major global research program with particular strength in the study of communication systems in the Middle East and in China. Similarly, the political economist John Downing, who was once based in the UK, has led the Global Media Research Center at Southern Illinois University.

At a more formal level, scholarly associations have been active in their support of global research. The International Association for Media and Communication Research (IAMCR) was founded in 1957 and, for many years, was the only global academic society that supported political economy research, making the political economy of communication one of its major sections. The organization continues to grow and to support political economic research with an international orientation. Under the leadership of its recent President Robin Mansell and through the hard work of political economy sections heads, including Janet Wasko, Graham Murdock, and Helena Sousa, the IAMCR provides a genuine home to political economists worldwide. The establishment of the Herbert Schiller and Dallas Smythe awards to recognize the work of young scholars offers the kind of recognition and incentive for continuing the political economy tradition that these founding figures were so instrumental in developing.[2]

---

1 One fruit of her labors is the development of a book series that makes important work in the political economy of communication available in Chinese translation through Peking University Press. This resulted from a collaboration between her, Jin Cao from Fudan University, Zhou Lijin of Peking University Press, Dan Schiller, and me. Another is the production of a two-volume collection of major work in the political economy of communication completed with Jin Cao and distributed in China (Cao and Zhao, 2007).

2 Awards in the name of Dallas Smythe are also given at the regular conference of the Union for Democratic Communications and annually at Simon Fraser University. Both honor political economists who have made significant contributions to the field.

The general growth of academic journals has assisted the process of globalization but specific examples have been especially helpful to political economy. Founded in 2002 by the political economist Yahya Kamalipour of Purdue University in the United States, *The Global Media Journal* (http://lass.calumet.purdue.edu/cca/gmj/gmj_about_us.htm) is an online scholarly publication that features critical, especially political economic, research. By early 2008, the journal appeared in eleven different editions, including African, Arabic, Australian, Canadian, Chinese, Indian, Mediterranean, Pakistani, Persian, Polish, Spanish, and Turkish. In addition to content from practically everywhere in the world, the linguistic range assures a genuinely global character.[3] Additionally, the Union for Democratic Communications, a US-based organization of critical scholars and media practitioners, has established *The Democratic Communiqué*, a journal that strongly supports political economic research.

One might reasonably wonder what this means for the content of research in political economy. Aside from more research, has this process of global expansion made a difference for what political economists have to say? After all, from its earliest days, the political economy approach to communication has been interested in global issues such as media imperialism, modernization theory, the call for a New World Information and Communication Order, and its own preferred theoretical approaches such as world systems and dependency theory. The primary difference is that current research addresses the profound integration of the global political economy and its media systems. Heretofore the focus was on how one (the United States) or even a handful of nation states (the United States plus the European Union) and their own corporations dominated weaker states and their nascent economies, in the process of producing little more than dependency and underdevelopment. Today the emphasis is on the integration of corporations, states, and classes across national, regional, and even developmental divides (Mosco and Schiller, 2001). In the view of Chakravartty and Zhao (2008), this involves the creation of a "transcultural political economy," which they document in a book containing contributions from primarily non-Western scholars.

Where once, corporations, including those in the communication industry, were based in one country and moved through the world as an external force, today they are increasingly integrated into the fabric of societies to the point where it is often difficult to determine their national origin. Operating as owners, partners, and in strategic alliances with companies based in the host country, they have led political economists to shift from talking about the power of multinational corporations to addressing the rise of a worldwide transnational economy. Many of these companies originate in the West but the growth of other economies, especially the Chinese and Indian economies, render simplistic many of the standard models of Western domination. India, for example, which has traditionally been portrayed, quite accurately,

---

3 I have contributed to three of the editions, including an article mapping the political economy of communication completed with one of my graduate students and translated into Farsi for Iranian scholars (Mosco and Lavin, 2007).

as the victim of British and then general Western imperialism, now contains its own transnational firms that have integrated into Western economies, including those of North America. Conglomerates like Tata, Infosys, WiPro, and ICICI have strong bases in North America, employing hundreds of thousands of workers, some of whom are dismissed because, after training their own replacements, their jobs are outsourced back to India. They also train North American students as interns and operate their own outsourcing ventures throughout Latin America (Mosco and McKercher, 2008).

Political economic research has also documented the restructuring of public authorities, including nation states, regional blocs, and global governance organizations, and it has described their integration into the commercial sector to produce hybrids that blur the distinction between public and private at every level of government activity. Again, it is no longer just a question of demonstrating how a large corporation "captures" a government by getting it to steer policies and resources to big business. Rather, we are witnessing the thorough integration of both forms of power in a transnationalization of political authority (Braman, 2007). As a result, intra-national social class divisions, which once occupied the bulk of social class analysis in political economy are now less significant than transnational class divisions that restructure networks of power across nations to link newly wealthy people in China, India, and Russia to their counterparts in the United States and Europe. Indeed, any examination of the media elite may need to start with those who run large companies in the United States, but is increasingly incomplete and downright inadequate without reference to those who wield media power in numerous other nations. This would now include, for example, the Chinese executives who own and operate Lenovo, what was once the personal computer arm of IBM, an icon of US dominance in the high-tech sector.

Much of this activity is aimed at establishing a new international division of labor with the communication industry in the forefront. By creating global labor markets and by making extensive use of communication technologies to carry out the restructuring process, transnational business gains the flexibility to make the most effective, least costly, and therefore most profitable use of labor. Students of culture have spent a great deal of time charting the transnationalization of culture (Lash and Lury, 2007; Tomlinson, 1999). Much of this work has enriched what we know about the social production of meaning worldwide. But political economists and some students of culture are making up for a yawning gap in that research: the transnationalization of the labor that produces culture as well as the other material and immaterial products of contemporary society.

The global integration of corporate, government, and social class structures is a work in progress. It is fraught with risks, tensions, and contradictions. There is also considerable opposition, evidenced in the rise of social movements that have protested this development at meetings of international agencies like the World Trade Organization and other international bodies, like the World Summit on the Information Society (WSIS), which aims to extend this process into the communication industry. Political economists have not only examined these developments, they have also taken praxis seriously and participated at the political and policy levels. In doing so, they acknowledge the importance of the trend to transnationalize the political economy of communication. They also recognize the need to create transnational democracy and a genuine cosmopolitan citizenship.

A Political Economy Approach to the History of Communication

The first trend documented an expansion in the spatial vision of political economy, from, for example, a national to a transnational orientation. There has also been an expansion in the temporal view with substantial growth in historical research. True to a central characteristic of the general theory of political economy, communication research making use of this perspective has always been sensitive to history. For example, beginning in the 1980s, historical research on the political economy of electronic media focused on the relationship between centers of political power and centers of media power. This included Herbert Schiller's (1981, 1992) research on the development of a global and heavily militarized electronic media system and Smythe's work (1981) on the evolution of Canadian dependency across publishing, broadcasting, and telecommunications. Subsequent generations of scholars further developed and reworked several of their prominent themes, greatly emphasizing the relationship between government and corporate power. These include studies of American broadcasting (Kellner, 1990; Winston, 1986) and telecommunications (McChesney, 1993; Mosco, 1982; Schiller, 1982) as well as their counterparts in Canadian broadcasting (Raboy, 1990) and telecommunications (Babe, 1990; Martin, 1991) history. Dan Schiller's work is particularly important because it identified the development of powerful forces in the telecommunications industry that had begun to flex considerable muscle. These were well-organized, large business users of telecommunications services and their emergence signaled a significant shift in the industry power structure. Raboy's book challenged the idea that public broadcasting necessarily contributes to political democracy by documenting the ways state control of the public system have silenced the voices of community and civil society groups.

Recent years have brought about significant growth in the amount of historical research and important departures from earlier work. Indeed, this expansion of research has led a leading political economist to call for shifting critical attention from political economy to history because the latter provides better guidance for the media reform movement, including those committed to advancing democratic communication (McChesney, 2007). One can understand this view if only because historical research, particularly in the area of building a more democratic media system, is one of critical scholarship's major contributions. This is particularly because, beginning in the late 1980s, scholars developed a strong interest in examining communication power from a grass-roots historical perspective that features the role of labor and social movement organizations. For example, Montgomery (1989) took up the history of the media reform movement in the United States across the political spectrum, McChesney (1992) addressed the struggles to establish labor radio broadcasting, and Winseck (1993) considered the history of labor involvement in the development of telecommunication policy in the advanced industrial societies. And, as we shall see, this specific area of interest has grown in recent years. However, there are good reasons to maintain the important link between history and political economy. History, along with a commitment to study the social totality, to moral philosophy, and to praxis, is one of the pillars of political economic theory. One simply cannot do good political economy without an historical dimension. It is also the case that the broad collection of people active in creating democratic communication mainly comprises scholars who emphasize political economy and history. To suggest an emphasis on one over the other would diminish the solidarity that has generally characterized social intervention in the political economy of communication.

Research from the mid-1990s to the present has continued the important trend to pursue historical analysis from a political economy perspective. More importantly, it has departed from more traditional forms of historical analysis in communication studies. These have tended to emphasize personalities, such as media moguls like Rupert Murdoch who, it is often maintained, drive the development of media. This version of the old "Great Man" theory of media history may be entertaining but it is as wanting today as it was in the time of William Randolf Hearst. It was good for movies like *Citizen Kane*, but bad for understanding the media. More sophisticated approaches to media history focused on the arc of technological development, equating communication history with the history of a specific medium like radio or television. However, this approach tends to reify technology, giving it a life of its own, out of proportion to the ways social and political forces shape the development of technology. When historical research has turned to the social and political, it has tended to be a top-down study of the policies and politics crafted by elites in government and business. Such a perspective is more useful than one that enshrines either a media mogul or a specific technology and, at its best, provides insights into the clashes between elites who share a general political inclination (Hills, 2007; Winseck and Pike, 2007). But it generally neglects to account for resistance outside elite circles and specifically how communication history is a more widely contested terrain.

Such a recognition characterizes today's historical analyses that adopt a political economy perspective. Specifically, they demonstrate that media systems in place today are the result of a deeply contested history, involving not just dueling capitalists and their allies in government, but labor unions, citizens groups, consumer cooperatives, religious enthusiasts, and social justice organizations of all stripes. McChesney (1993) firmly established the importance of this approach in his analysis of the battle for control over radio in the United States. Neither above politics, nor the privileged policy domain of a handful of elites, radio broadcasting was recognized early on as crucial to democracy and numerous social movement organizations used what power they had to democratize radio. They did this by fighting for stations that trade unions, local communities, and public interest organizations of all types could control for themselves. They fought for citizen access to the airwaves to counter the dominant corporate control of broadcasting. And they fought to democratize the policy process by making the case for popular control over regulations that gave and took away licenses, that assigned spectrum to services, and that established rules for the fair use of the medium. In essence, the struggle for radio was the struggle for democracy. More than the instrument of a handful of pioneers, or the esoteric magical diviner of the air, radio was embedded in the most significant political battles of the twentieth century, pitting supporters of the New Deal against the dominant conservative forces which generally held the upper hand in American politics.

Radio was a central instrument of what Denning also calls "the cultural front," a movement extending from the late 1920s to the early 1950s in the United States which provided the cultural energy for attempts to establish alternatives to America's traditional power structure led by big business. In addition to New Deal liberals, it included social democrats, socialists, and some communists. It gained strength in the Great Depression and withered in the 1950s when business marshaled a massive counter-attack, including the reactionary movement known as McCarthyism. Communication scholars writing history today from a political economic perspective are explicitly and implicitly telling the detailed story of the media's role in the cultural front. Some have continued to enrich the story of radio. For example, Nathan Godfried (1997) examines the history of a Chicago radio station that was established and run by a labor federation representing unions in that city. Providing a voice for labor in a sea of commercial broadcasting was no easy task, particularly since many of the unions, whose members were also big fans of commercial stations, struggled to define a labor alternative. In the face of enormous commercial and business pressures, WCFL (for Chicago Federation of Labor) was able to retain its unique character through the 1940s, providing both news and entertainment from a labor standpoint. Returning to WCFL, Elizabeth Fones-Wolf (2006) describes the broader role of radio in the effort to build a democratic Left in twentieth-century America. She not only tells the story of several alternatives to commercial radio; Fones-Wolf describes the political battles that pitted labor and its allies against business in some of the central policy debates of the time. These included decisions about granting and renewing broadcast licenses, determining the limits of station ownership, setting rules about acceptable content, and deciding precisely what should be the requirements to air diverse perspectives (see also Fones-Wolf and Fones-Wolf, 2007).

Political economy has also addressed the historical trajectories of other media, especially print journalism. For example, Tracy (2006) has written about the crucial role of the International Typographical Workers Union in battles to control the labor process and the introduction of new technologies in the printing industry. They culminated in a 1964 strike that shut down the newspaper business in New York City for four months. Drawing on interviews with the leader of the labor action, Tracy documents labor's once powerful voice in the media industry and assesses its strengths and also the weaknesses, such as hanging on to a narrow craft ideology that ultimately contributed to muting that voice. My research with Catherine McKercher extends this view by telling the story of the battles between craft and class among communication workers throughout the history of American media (see also Mosco and McKercher, 2008).

As political economists who study media concentration have demonstrated, one of the ways business was able to defeat those calling for more democratic communication and press for a singular commercial form of media was through cross-ownership or the purchase of multiple media located in a single community or region. But that also met with strong opposition from coalitions of citizen and labor organizations (Fones-Wolf and Fones-Wolf, 2007). The battle for control over Hearst-dominated media in San Francisco provides a stunning example of a company that refused to tolerate the slightest deviation from a conservative viewpoint in either print or broadcast media.

One can also find major recent examples that document the history of resistance in the telecommunications and computer industries. Countering the traditional great inventor, technicist, and pro-corporate readings of AT&T's story, Venus Green (2001) examines the significant interplay of race, gender, and class in the company's history. Dan Schiller (2007b) recounts the struggles in the workplace and in policy-making circles that challenged business efforts to control the postal and telephone system. Pellow and Park (2002) take the analysis into Silicon Valley by telling the story of the struggles first of indigenous people, then of agricultural workers, and now those of immigrant women who do the dirty hardware work and of more privileged but often exploited young software workers.

This is not just an American tale. Political economists north of the US border have also worked in this heterodox form of history. It is one of the truisms in countries with a national broadcaster like the BBC or the Canadian Broadcasting Corporation (CBC), that such institutions provide a public defense against universal commercialism. But in her groundbreaking research on media history in Canada, Patricia Mazepa (2003, 2007) demonstrates that the story is significantly more complex. And unlike academic complexity which often does not appear to matter, hers makes a difference for how we think about public media and for what we do about it. Drawing on archival sources, she shows that the CBC developed not just to defend against commercial broadcasting crossing the border from the United States, but also to protect against alternative definitions of "public" embodied in the media produced by immigrant, socialist, and labor organizations in Canada, which the national broadcaster generally ignored. In Canada, public broadcasting came to be associated with white settler media, mainly English, and a largely elite French version based principally in the province of Quebec. As a result, community and regional media developed by organizations outside the mainstream was not deemed fit for the CBC. Immigrant, socialist, and labor media went up against both commercial media and the state. And the state often demonstrated far less tolerance and considerable eagerness to use its policy powers to undermine media emerging from outside the CBC and outside big private broadcasting. Mazepa's work not only uncovers the largely ignored story of media production and resistance from below. It also calls on scholars, especially those involved in the process of making broadcasting policy, to question the meaning of "public" in public broadcasting. As well, it broadens that definition to incorporate genuine democratic alternatives and not just those that represent a white settler vision of Canada.

Writing about the history of journalism in Canada, McKercher (2002) charts the conflicts that erupted over control of the labor process, the use of technology, and the shape of the news. These were not simply established by those who owned the presses, nor imposed by the changing technologies in the workplace, but arose from strikes and other labor actions as well. Several of these opened spaces for workers and for those who wanted or needed a more diverse press. Many of them fell far short of success. But her historical work, like those of other political economists described in this section, offers a genuine alternative to the standard stories and, in doing so, gives back to social activists and workers the agency that is rightfully theirs.

Standpoints of Resistance

Historical research in the political economy of communication has begun to emphasize resistance and not just the admittedly important story of how the powerful dominate. The emphasis on resistance is increasingly generalized in research on the contemporary political economy, marking a shift in the central standpoint from a focus on capital, dominant corporations, and elites to alternatives that draw from feminist and labor research. This marks a departure from a trend that has been a hallmark of political economy from the start: focus on media concentration and on the erosion of content diversity (Bagdikian, 1992; Green, 1973; Herman and Chomsky, 2002).

The political economy of communication has been especially concerned with the tendency for fewer and fewer companies that grow ever larger to control more of the media market than every before. Such concentration takes place within media, as fewer newspaper companies control more of the newspaper market. It takes place across media, as owners of newspapers buy broadcasting outlets and other media properties, a process known as cross-ownership concentration. This often grows into conglomerate concentration as transnational corporations built in non-media businesses buy up media properties. The General Electric Corporation's purchase of the NBC network is a good example. Political economists have identified the leading companies, dissected their structures, and examined the impact on content diversity. As a result, we now know a great deal about who owns the media. The list of the most important does shift but the outstanding ones include the News Corporation (Fox), Viacom (CBS), Disney (ABC), General Electric (NBC), Time Warner (CNN, AOL), and Sony. Adding telecommunications and new media to the mix expands the list to include AT&T, Microsoft, and Google (McChesney, 2007; Schiller, 2007a; Wasko, 2003). Each of these companies acts to influence the global marketplace. Political economists have also demonstrated the widespread pattern of media concentration outside the United States. For example, four companies have a dominant influence in the Canadian media business. They are led by Bell Canada Enterprises (BCE), which adds control over the largest private broadcaster and the largest national newspaper to its dominance in the telecommunications market. The others include CanWest, Rogers, and, with the greatest influence in the French Quebec marketplace, the firm Quebecor (Winseck, 2008).

The emphasis in this literature does vary, with some focusing on media concentration (Kunz, 2006) and others on the combined power of media capitalism as a structural force (Artz and Kamalipour, 2003). The difference can have significant implications. Those focusing on media concentration are likely to call for breaking up big media firms in favor of several smaller-sized companies that would compete with each other more vigorously than they do today. Those placing the emphasis on the combined power of capital would see less value in breaking up media giants. For them, big or small, the problem isn't so much the number or size of firms; it is that they share an interest in maximizing profit by selling audiences to advertisers and using all other means to create networks and content that serve their business interests. They may all agree with the now classic work of Baran and Sweezy (1966) which concluded that the problem was monopoly capitalism. It is just that some would focus on monopoly and others on capital.

Recent research in the political economy of communication recognizes the importance of this research but argues in favor of a departure. There is nothing entirely new about departing from the focus on media concentration or capital as the central problems. After all, the long tradition of examining class struggle in the Marxian tradition produced now classic research such as E.P. Thompson's monumental study *The Making of the English Working Class* (1963). This work started from the standpoint of the working class and defined capitalism not as the dominance of capital but as the antagonism and subsequent struggle between classes. This certainly has its embodiments in the political economy of communication, where the work of Mattelart and Garnham made class struggle a focal point. However, research since the mid-1990s has accelerated the interest in finding alternatives to capital as the dominant standpoint.

One of the models for this type of thinking is feminist standpoint theory which maintains that social science needs to be practiced and society needs to be understood from the standpoint of women's rather than men's experience, as has been the case for so much of what has passed for general social science. Developed by Hartsock (1999) in the early 1980s, feminist standpoint theory has flourished in the work of Harding (2003), Haraway (2003), and others who maintain that women's subordination provides a uniquely important basis for understanding a wide array of issues from the most general philosophical questions of epistemology and ontology to such practical issues as the appropriate social science techniques to deploy in research. The perspective has faced charges of relativism from inside and outside feminist scholarship (Haraway, 2003), but it counters with the view that feminist standpoint theory offers a genuine alternative to the equation of science and universalism with research by and about men, as well as the reduction of feminist research to work that only documents the exploitation of women.

Feminist standpoint thinking has begun to influence research in the political economy of communication. Feminism began to enter discussions about the media and power in the 1980s. One of the leading figures in putting it on the table of political economy was the Irish scholar Margaret Gallagher (1980, 1984, 1985, 1992), who provided a general critique of leading political economy approaches and proceeded to map the terrain of a gendered political economy of the mass media. The constituents of such an approach included the positions that women have historically occupied in circuits of cultural production. Although the market for literate middle-class women has been strong almost since the invention of the printing press, that market has subordinated women in significant ways. For example, Gallagher documents the four-fold subordination of women in the social relations of fiction writing in the nineteenth century. Women novelists were tolerated as artisans, provided their work did not disturb their primary household duties. Moreover, women were subordinated with unskilled labor in the printing trade (along with child labor). Furthermore, the exploitation of women in domestic service freed up middle-class women to read and sometimes to write. Finally, novels were saturated with content to structure and appeal to the female as consumer: romance, femininity, domesticity, and motherhood. Gallagher builds on this historical argument with an analysis that connects the structural position of women in the cultural industries, i.e. underrepresentation save for certain highly visible positions, with the depiction of women across the cultural industries. This combination of historical, social structural, and cultural analysis linking social class and gender offered an important model for rethinking the political economic approach to the cultural industries.

In addition to Gallagher, Colleen Roach (1993) offered a gendered assessment of the political economy of the peace movement and of the NWICO. Steeves (1989) set out an agenda of "global gender issues." Her account included the transnational corporation as an instrument of both capitalism and patriarchy, the relationship of advertising to editorial and entertainment content promoting ideas and images of class and gender, and the presence and absence of women in media organizations and in the process of media production. She concluded by addressing forms of resistance to both social class and gender divisions, and the problems and opportunities presented by new information and communication technologies.[4] For Steeves and others, an approach based on the duality of patriarchy and capitalism has the advantage of providing a broad field of analysis because it permits one to concentrate on a specific grounding without ignoring the other, as in studies of capitalist patriarchy or patriarchal capitalism. But the approach faced some of the same challenges of any framework based on the mutual constitution of two elements, such as how to characterize the field they occupy – patriarchal or capitalist, which is adjective and which is noun, and how to describe the nature of their interaction.

Contemporary feminist research has built on this work by examining media and power from a feminist standpoint. One of the first major attempts to do so is contained in a collection by Eileen Meehan and Ellen Riordan. Meehan has made extensive contributions to political economy, most notably by extending the work of Dallas Smythe on the question of how the audience is made into a marketable commodity. In 2002 Meehan and Riordan produced *Sex and Money*, which gathered the work of leading feminists and political economists to address the relationships

---

4 In another article, Steeves (1987) offered a critical evaluation of liberal, radical, and socialist feminist perspectives on the media. She concluded that liberal perspectives tend to "speak only to white, heterosexual, middle and upper class women." Radical, including structuralist, perspectives tend to concentrate on texts, to the neglect of the wider social framework. Socialist feminism is most promising, because it is capable of addressing the linkages between the economic and cultural positions of women, i.e. the mutual constitution of class and gender, work and consumption.

between these perspectives. Specifically, it describes how both political economic and feminist standpoints contribute to understanding capitalism at many different levels, including the personal, experiential, institutional, and structural. For example, Balka's chapter on women's work in the telecommunications industry starts from the lived experience of women as they understand what she calls "the invisibility of the everyday." This includes how women experience the detailed measurement and monitoring of their work as well as their attempts to gain some control over it. Her description of this process is connected to a political economic analysis of the industry which, in the region of Atlantic Canada which she studied, is undergoing intense change. Specifically, the shift from regulation in the public interest to a more intense commercial model leads companies to eliminate jobs and, using advanced technologies, impose tighter controls on those that remain. This gendering of political economy offers a rich reading of an experience that is all too often simplistically described as the inevitable consequence of technological change and global imperatives. Chapters such as this enable Meehan and Riordan to provide the empirical detail that carries out a genuine integration of feminist and political economic theory.

In their 2007 book, *Feminist Interventions in International Communication*, Sarikakis and Shade take a further step to advance a feminist standpoint. This volume engages with central issues that political economists address but from a more explicitly feminist starting point. Like many political economic analyses, the book addresses power, technology, labor, and policy, but it views them from the entry point of gender. So, for example, the globalization of media industries is tightly connected to women's employment in media and new technology. In using a feminist standpoint, they enable us to rethink the study of international communication. Yes, traditional issues such as flows of news between rich and poor nations, do matter. But international communication is also about policies for women's development, media production of pornography, media representations of HIV/AIDS, and global campaigns to bring an end to this plague. It is about the locations of women in the new international division of labor, especially media and high-tech labor, and what women are doing about workplace exploitation. In essence, Sarikakis and Shade demonstrate that international communication is not gender blind; nor is it a field that simply describes a set of impacts on women. Rather, they and the contributors to their volume demonstrate how women can shape international communication, from production through employment to policy, and their book takes an important step by seeing all of these as women's issues.

There is a strong and growing literature that has taken off from the issues addressed in these two books. The work of Micky Lee (2006, 2007) and McLaughlin and Johnson (2007), among others, clear an enormous amount of ground in addressing political economic power from a feminist standpoint. Their work ranges from media, through telecommunications, and on to information technology, from consumption to production, and from home to office (see also Huws, 2003; and Mosco and McKercher, 2008: Chapter 2). There is also interesting work on feminist standpoint theory that spans political economy and cultural studies by examining how audience performances can be viewed as performances of power that defend or resist a dominant ideology (Atkinson, 2005).

Chapter 9 will revisit the relationship between feminist research and political economy. This section concludes by taking up new departures in political economy research from a labor standpoint. Communication studies in general has done a more thorough job of addressing media content and audiences than it has communication labor. In the 1980s and 1990s political economy literature took some steps to address this blindspot, particularly by examining the introduction of new communication and information technologies into the workplace (Mosco and Wasko, 1983). Research started to address the transformation of work, including patterns of employment and the changing nature of labor in the media and telecommunications industry. Decrying the absence of a labor perspective in journalism history, Hardt (1990) connected what is primarily a political economic perspective with a cultural history of the newsroom that focuses on the introduction of new technologies deployed to carry out work. This extended the pioneering research of political economists working outside communication studies who have examined the labor process in the newsroom (Zimbalist, 1979).[5]

Relatedly, research addressed the application of new technologies to reduce employment in the industry and to restructure the work of editors by implementing electronic page layout and by transforming reporters' jobs with electronic news gathering (Russial, 1989). These provided specific applications of the labor process view that points to the use of communication and information technologies to shift the balance of power in conceptual activity from professional newsworkers, with some control over their means of communication, to managerially controlled technological systems. Similar work began to address the transformation of the labor process in film (Nielsen, 1990), broadcasting (Wasko, 1983), telecommunications (Mosco and Zureik, 1987), and the information industries (Kraft and Dubnoff, 1986).

A start was also made on political economic work that addressed the international division of labor and labor internationalism. The former resulted from the pressures to rationalize production and the opportunities that technologies, particularly in computers and telecommunication, provided to overcome space and time constraints that once set limits on business. This research began to probe the formation of global labor markets which enabled business go take advantage of differential wages, skills, and other important characteristics on an international scale. Much of the early political economic work in this area concentrated on the spread of the hardware (southeast Asia) and data entry (the Caribbean) businesses into the developing world where companies were attracted by low wages and authoritarian rule (Mosco, 1989b; Sussman,

---

5 Following a useful overview that situates current conflicts over electronic news production technologies in the context of over one hundred years of struggle in which "newsrooms, like factory floors, have been a laboratory for technological innovations and a battleground of economic and social interests," Hardt offers a political economic perspective to explain the neglect of labor: "under prevailing historical conditions that privilege dominant visions of the press, press histories ignored working-class issues and questions of labour practices (reflecting the anti-labour attitudes of publishers)" (Hardt, 1990: 355).

1984). The growth of the international division of labor in communication sparked an interest in labor internationalism. Specifically, this involved making use of the means of communication, including new technologies, to forge close links among working-class and trade union interests across borders (Waterman, 1990, 2001).

The research on labor internationalism expanded in subsequent years and a genuine labor standpoint has begun to emerge. My work with Catherine McKercher demonstrates different dimensions of this expansion (McKercher and Mosco, 2006, 2007; Mosco and McKercher, 2008). For us, while it is important to understand how corporate power, new technology, and conservative governments are changing labor, it is equally important to determine what labor is doing about this. We identify two important developments. The first is the creation of labor convergence, which brings together trade unions from separate areas of the communication industries into one large union representing journalists, broadcasters, technicians, telephone workers, and those employed in the high-tech world. Two major examples are the Communications Workers of America (CWA) and its Canadian counterpart the Communications, Energy and Paperworkers Union. The development of integrated unions that span the converging media and information technology industries provides the resources to better face the power of transnational business. The CWA demonstrated this by carrying out an effective action against the Canadian Broadcasting Corporation when the national broadcaster locked out its workforce because it had refused to accept a shift to part-time labor and contracting-out. Believing that a union which brought together high-paid performers and lower-paid technicians would not remain unified, especially one led by a union from the United States, the CBC locked out its workers, anticipating a rapid decline in solidarity. Using its financial resources and international networks, the CWA provided the support needed to carry on and the workers not only demonstrated their solidarity across occupational and social class lines, they were able to enlist audiences to their side. After seven weeks, the CBC backed down. Other cases have not been so successful but enough success has been achieved to see some promise in the return of a One Big Union movement, this time in the communication industry.

A second labor strategy is the formation of worker associations which emerge out of social movements that aim to address a significant problem. In his book *Cyber-Marx* (1999), Nick Dyer-Witheford takes a social movement standpoint to address opposition to capitalism around the world today (see also Hackett and Carroll, 2006). He is especially focused on how social movements use new media to counter the transnational political economy. In this respect, the growth of what Marx called the General Intellect lives on in information-rich and media-savvy movements that resist and demonstrate alternatives to the status quo. McKercher and I have given attention to this among workers who develop new movements and organizations in the world of informational or knowledge labor. We pay particular attention to workers on either side of a major divide in the communication industry: technical employees, such as those who produce software like new codes for computer systems, and cultural workers, primarily those who produce media content. The Washington Alliance of Technology Workers, or WashTech, has built a movement of contract computer workers that has achieved some success at Microsoft and has also been in the forefront of efforts to address the problem of outsourcing high-tech jobs to India and other foreign locations (see also Brophy, 2006; and Rodino-Colocino, 2007). Moreover, the Freelancers Union in the United States has grown rapidly from a movement of people who work on a short-time, contract basis for media companies that pay low wages and provide few, if any, benefits.

Organizations like these are redefining the nature of the labor movement by rethinking trade unionism and by connecting its activities to wider political and social issues. For political economy, they demonstrate the importance of taking a labor standpoint (see also Kumar, 2007). Focusing on worker self-organization captures an enormous range of activities and problems that are simply not addressed in traditional research that concentrates on how capital exploits workers. Both are important, but it is time to restore the balance by describing the active agency of communication workers. This has political implications because one of the central issues of our time is determining whether those technical and cultural workers can come together. More broadly, it is not just about what will be the next new thing (i.e. the latest technological gadget), but rather, whether communication workers of the world will unite.

The Transition from Old to New Media

While understandably skeptical about research that focuses exclusively on technology, political economy made important contributions to the understanding of traditional media including advertising and public relations (Ewen, 1996, 2001); journalism (Chomsky, 1999; Curran, 1979; Herman and Chomsky, 2002; Sparks, 1985), radio (McChesney, 1993), television (Kunz, 2006), film (Guback, 1969; Pendakur, 1990, 2003; Wasko, 1982, 2003), music (Attali, 1985), and telecommunications (Babe, 1990; Garnham, 1990; Martin, 1991; Schiller, 1982; Sussman, 1984; Winseck, 1998). They have also addressed what was considered new media at the time. Smythe (1957) wrote about television when it was new, Mattelart and Siegelaub (1979, 1983) about cable television, and I wrote about videotex, which anticipated the Internet by about fifteen years (Mosco, 1982). While by no means setting aside older media, political economy has since made the transition to a focus on new media, especially the Internet and the new media forms that it has stimulated.

Some political economists have responded by emphasizing continuities between old and new media. For them, old media issues endure in the world of new media. For others, the emphasis is on discontinuities or the new connections that the networked media make possible. Still others have focused a skeptical eye on the promises that new media experts and gurus promote, while some concentrate on newer issues that today's media raise. To understand how political economists approach the shift from older to newer media, it is useful to consider each of these points.

Political economy has tended to give considerable attention to describing and analyzing capitalism, a system which, in short, turns resources like workers, raw materials, land, and information into marketable commodities that earn a profit for those who invest capital into the system. Political economists of communication have focused on media, information, and audiences as resources and charted the ways they are packaged into products for sale. Many who make the shift from the study of old to new media emphasize the continuities between old and new media capitalism. For them, new media deepen and extend tendencies within earlier forms of capitalism by opening new possibilities to turn media and audiences into saleable commodities. As a result, media concentration, commercialism, rich nation dominance over the global economy, divisions between information rich and poor, and militarism persist and grow (McChesney, 2007; Murdock and Golding, 2000, 2004; Schiller, 1999a, 2007a; Sparks, 2007; Wasko, 2003). To paraphrase the title of one of Dan Schiller's books, new media may lead us to call it "digital capitalism," but it is still capitalism and there is no doubt about which is the more important term.

Within such a framework, social and technological change does take place, as new technologies expand the market and global governance becomes necessary, but it also creates problems for capitalism. What was once a largely national market for film and video products and audiences is now a global one, posing serious challenges for coordination. In such markets, what was once a largely national system of governance and government regulation has proven to be inadequate. Global systems of governance are necessary if only to insure the coordination of something as complex as the Internet address system. As a result, we have a new alphabet soup of international organizations, such as the ICANN (Internet Corporation for Assigned Names and Numbers), which provides Internet addresses. However, such solutions create new problems as the United States tries to protect its interests by controlling the ICANN and many of the world's nations protest because they view it as little more than an extension of American power. Nevertheless, amid the changes, contradictions, opposition, and conflict, there is a consistency in the central tendency to deepen and expand the capitalist market system.

For other political economists, the emphasis is on discontinuity and departure from these tendencies in capitalism. Hardt and Negri (2000, 2004), Lazzarato (1997), and Dyer-Witheford (1999) remain political economists because they are concerned about the power relations that mutually constitute the production, distribution, and exchange of resources. However, as a result of the growth of new media, they view those power relations differently from those who focus on continuity in capitalist relations. Their autonomist perspective, so named because it starts from the autonomy of the working class, maintains that capitalism is propelled by the energy and activity of those who work within it. From this perspective, the focus needs to be on the self-activity and self-organization of what Hardt and Negri refer to as "the mass," the vast majority of people typically viewed as exploited from other critical perspectives. Furthermore, the growth of communication and information technology does not just serve capitalism, it significantly disrupts it. There are three major ways this happens.

Capitalism is based on the market and a system of private property and these require legal controls that set limits on what people can do. Copyright, trademark, and patent law constrain people's use of information and ideas that others own. Markets establish the value of products, including the information products that are increasingly prominent today. According to autonomists, the widespread availability of information and communication technology makes it very difficult for capitalism to preserve the legal regime of private property that historically limited flows of communication and information. It is now more difficult than ever to figure out what capitalism is doing when technologies challenge traditional ideas of production and consumption, use and exchange value. The ease of freely downloading music and video, of sharing files containing data, audio, and video, and of copying material of all sorts, challenges the ability of capitalism to maintain and police its property and market regimes. Like the common lands that were once widely available to all until capitalism made them private property, cyberspace was once available to all. But in order to make money it too needs to be turned into property, in this case the intellectual property of Microsoft, Google, Disney, and the other commercial giants (Terranova, 2000). But unlike the commons of old, cyberspace is difficult to fence in because it is a fundamentally immaterial resource.

For the autonomists, capitalism faces a second challenge. Although communication and information technologies provide it with the tools to manage and control large numbers of people from anywhere on the globe, these tools are also available to the masses of people and at relatively low cost too. For the autonomist, not only does technology challenge property and market rules, it enables people to disrupt the system just at a time when capitalism requires careful global coordination. For example, electronic social networking permits social movements to mobilize and coordinate as never before. The vast expansion in the number of people skilled at producing disruptive software, who can hack and crack open seemingly secure programs, creates critical problems for private property, markets, and the overall ability of capitalism to maintain authority.

Finally, the autonomist concludes that the very immaterial labor that capitalism requires to carry out more and more of its work presents serious problems for maintaining control and discipline. Capitalism needs a highly educated workforce but such a workforce is less likely to cede control over thought and ideas to management than did its blue-collar predecessors. Whether employed in developing software or working at a call centre, knowledge workers are less likely to submit to rigid time and motion controls. And the very attempts to loosen rules and introduce a more playful atmosphere into the workplace lead to more questioning of the need for any rules, including those that determine who profits from labor. How do you manage a "no-collar" workforce (Ross, 2004)?

In addition to approaches emphasizing continuity and disjunction, the political economy of communication has responded to new media in a third way, by taking a skeptical view of the enthusiasm that inevitably accompanies it. This has been particularly important in historical work which demonstrates that much of what is considered new and revolutionary in new media was actually associated with every communication technology when old media were new. For example, Winseck and Pike (2007) address the concept of convergence which has become a popular notion in contemporary discussions of what's new about computer communication. Convergence denotes the technological integration that powers new media technologies (Jenkins,

2006). It also refers to the integration of big companies that make use of new media. In essence, interconnected technologies and large integrated companies create the convergence it takes to make a revolution. Skeptical of the view that convergence is unique to new media, Pike and Winseck demonstrate that convergence is as old as the telegraph and that the promises and challenges we associate with the Internet were anticipated by that mid-nineteenth-century technology (see also Standage, 1998).

It is not just the social relations of capitalism that retain continuity; there is also nothing new about the hyperbole or mythologies that accompany today's media. Martin (1991) has described the promises associated with the telephone in much the same way. Whereas the telegraph was expected to bring about world peace, she documents the expectation that the telephone would end the exploitation of women because it would permit them to run a household *and* participate fully in society. Similar research has examined the Internet. Flichy's work on *l'internet imaginaire* (2007) views the Internet as more than just a tool or a social force. It also embodies a myth, by which he means a narrative containing both utopian visions of alternative realities and ideological discourses about how we should conduct our lives and organize society in a time influenced by proliferating computer and communication networks.

This work is also important because it reflects a stepped-up interest among political economists to demonstrate the continuity between old and new media by engaging with culture, something that I called for in the first edition of this book and which was exemplified in *The Digital Sublime* (Mosco, 2004). Drawing on the work of Martin and others, *The Digital Sublime* demonstrates that the same promises made about the Internet have been made when old technologies, like the telegraph, telephone, radio, and television, were new. World peace, gender equality, online education, racial harmony – all of these were once viewed as the inevitable consequences of these once new media. For believers, the Internet will realize all of these promises and more, including, in the work of MIT professor Raymond Kurzweil, an end to death as we know it. Ultimately, digital technologies imagine the end of history, the end of geography, and the end of politics. Those who advance these views, I maintain, are doing something prominent throughout the history of "new" media. They are invoking technology as an opportunity to achieve the sublime or the experience of transcending the constraints of everyday life (including time, space, and social relations) to achieve a utopia beyond language. Once the province of art and literature (the sublime painting or poem), and of nature (e.g. the sublime Grand Canyon), the sublime is now to be achieved through technology and, increasingly, through communication technology.

Demonstrating continuity and a link to culture are important. But it is also important to return to political economy and document how all of this matters for the study of power. First, those who have made important contributions to studying the sublime do not give enough attention to the connections between constructing the sublime and marketing, whether selling the latest computer, video game, or political candidate. Visions of transcendence make for great advertising. Second, connecting new media to the end of history, geography, and politics freezes into near inevitability and permanence the current political economy. The message is simple and powerful:

There is no sense struggling over the control of transnational capital if there is no likelihood of ever creating an alternative. Finally, the sublime can mask the often banal world of everyday politics. New York's World Trade Center was to embody the sublime new world of informational capitalism that transcended old political relations founded in an industrial era, until the cataclysm of 9/11 when history returned with a vengeance. The seductive lure of the sublime can blind its seekers from the banal and terrible politics that lurk just around the corner.

The fourth response of political economy to new media is to address problem areas that are particularly significant in this cycle of development in communication and information technology. One should be hesitant to call them new issues because there are really no significant problems that political economy has neglected to address. Rather, there are issues that are particularly important today and, among the major ones, copyright/intellectual property issues, surveillance, and the tendency toward what some call a network economy are worth some comment.

From the time of Charles Dickens, who railed against what he considered the failure of the United States to pay royalties for his novels when they were distributed in the United States in the nineteenth century, copyright has been a hot topic in debates around media. For media scholars today, including political economists, the debate has stepped up because new media make it easier to copy and share work under copyright. Bettig (1996; see also Bettig and Hall, 2003) has written about how business uses copyright to tighten its control, and Schiller (2007a) and Zhao (2008) have studied the intellectual property challenge from China and other developing nations. "Who will control intellectual property?" is one of the central questions facing political economy today.

So too is the threat of electronic surveillance. As Lyon (2003) and others have demonstrated, new media make it possible for governments and companies to monitor our activities on an unprecedented scale. The so-called war on terror has accelerated the spread of surveillance and legitimized activities that were once considered unacceptable violations of personal privacy. Political economists have addressed the extent of the problem and have also begun to document what can be done about it (Kiss and Mosco, 2005).

Finally, as the work of the autonomists demonstrates, new media call into question traditional economic categories and the capacities of capitalist economies to control them. But political economists outside the autonomist orbit are also wondering about the challenge of new media to the understanding of economics. Specifically, should we begin to think about the emergence of a network economy and the need for a network economics to address it? Network economics argues that the value of goods shift in a world of electronic networks. In particular, the value of a product or service increases when others buy the same good or service, especially when the purchase connects people in a network (Mansell, 2004; Melody, 2007). New media are based on networks of cell phone users, Internet users, participants in social networking sites, etc. Traditional economics, it is argued, undervalues additions to the network because it does not take into account the geometrical expansion in the number of potential transactions that an addition to the network makes. The question for political economists is what does this do to its conception of power? In other words, is network economics also political economy?

Media Activism

Praxis, or the unity of research and action, is a fundamental characteristic of a political economy approach. Most political economists of communication have been activists as well as scholars, involved in media democracy, development communication, independent media, and universal access work, as well as involved with labor, feminist, and anti-racist movements. The Union for Democratic Communications, which was created in the early 1980s, continues to bring together activist-scholars and media practitioners. The International Association for Media and Communication Research provides a global forum for political economists, including those active in public policy work, such as its recent President Robin Mansell. Where once political economists like Herbert Schiller and Armand Mattelart worked to make UNESCO a focal point to build a New World Information and Communication Order, politically active scholars are concentrating on democratizing the Internet through the international project known as the World Summit on the Information Society.

Important as these developments are, one of the most significant advances in political activity has been the creation in 2002 of the Free Press by the political economist Robert W. McChesney (McChesney, 2007). The organization has been a focal point for the remarkably resurgent media reform movement in the United States that has brought together a diverse collection of public interest groups, including the Consumers Union, the Center for Digital Democracy, the Media Access Project, and the Consumer Federation of America. These have joined with independent media organizations, such as Democracy Now!, a daily, national, independent news program hosted by journalists Amy Goodman and Juan Gonzalez. Free Press has attracted enormous attention, including the support of well-known people like Bill Moyers, Jane Fonda, and the Reverend Jesse Jackson. It has sponsored an annual conference on media reform that has attracted literally thousands of people, including scholars, media activists, politicians, and trade unionists. In the past such meetings might bring together at most hundreds of people, suggesting that we are observing a populist upheaval around the issue of media reform.

The upswell in the media reform movement can be attributed to the widespread view that the elimination of rules restricting media ownership, providing for some measure of content diversity, and limiting the prices that major cable, satellite, and other media firms can charge consumers, has threatened what remains of media democracy, media quality, and universal access to essential services. The loss of nearly 200,000 media jobs, out of about 1.1 million in the United States over the past five years, demonstrates for many that media concentration is an enormous labor-saving project that is eroding the quality of journalism and what remains of its independence. To counter these tendencies, Free Press mobilizes activists, lobbies politicians, and makes use of the media (including Bill Moyers' own public television show) to press for alternatives. These include ending the concentration of old and new media in the hands of a few giant transnational firms, supporting content diversity and vigorous debate, and creating social policies that guarantee universal access to essential telecommunications and Internet services.

Of particular importance is the fight to preserve "network neutrality." As pressure mounts on large media firms to increase profits, companies are tempted to restructure their networks to make more money. Specifically, they would like to create a system of faster and slower "lanes" on the information highway, reserving the faster lanes for higher paying content providers, such as certain advertisers, or for those linked to the network service provider, such as its own subsidiaries. Traffic would move more slowly for those paying less and for competitors. One important consequence is that the websites of companies outside the mainstream, including alternative media sites, which do not have the funding to pay the premium for a fast lane, would only be available in lesser quality. Responding to this threat, the media reform movement has fought for legislation and regulations that would preserve what has been the standard practice, with a few exceptions, of treating all content equally – with what amounts to one highway at one speed, delivering one standard of quality. Whatever the outcome of these specific struggles, it is evident that political economists have made a significant contribution to the overall resurgence of activism around major communication issues.

Conclusion

This chapter has addressed major trends in the contemporary political economy of communication. These include the globalization of research. The field is no longer characterized, as it once was, by specific regional tendencies, nor is it simply dominated by North American and European research. Political economy research is now global in that it is carried out by scholars from all over the world who are increasingly interested in addressing global issues.

The field has also expanded its commitment to the history of communication, especially the history of resistance to dominant powers in industry and government. In doing so, it has uncovered the unexamined stories of efforts to build alternatives to the dominant commercial system that fed into wider oppositional movements. Political economy has also departed from its traditional focus on examining dominant powers and processes of exploitation to address standpoints of resistance. These include especially feminist and labor perspectives on media and communication.

Furthermore, political economy has begun to make the transition from its established strength in examining how power operates in older media to a variety of approaches to new media, especially the Internet. In addition to accounting for continuities between old and new media, including describing how dominant powers use both to make money, political economists have also addressed discontinuities in the challenges that new media pose for traditional patterns of capitalist development. Moreover, they have documented the connections between promises made about old and new media and, more importantly, linked these efforts to reach the sublime, from the time of the telegraph to the Internet, to systems of power in society. Political economists are also taking on social issues that new media make especially prominent, including control over intellectual property, electronic surveillance, and the significance of a network economy.

The final trend in political economy research is an upsurge in political activism. This includes the growth of established organizations such as the Union for Democratic Communications and the International Association for Media and Communication Research. But it is also energized by the experience of new national (Free Press) and international (the World Summit on the Information Society) movements.

The next three chapters describe and analyze a specific theory to guide the political economy of communication. Following a section that describes the philosophical foundation of the theoretical approach, I turn to its primary dimensions: the processes of commodification, spatialization, and structuration.

7

COMMODIFICATION: CONTENT, AUDIENCES, LABOR

---------------------- **Introduction to Chapters 7–9** ----------------------

Having examined the political economy approach, the concept of communication, and the development of a political economy of communication, the book now draws on this work to offer a general theory to guide our understanding. Specifically, this chapter is the first of three to provide a conceptual framework for the political economy of communication. It starts with a philosophical foundation and proceeds to address the core ideas for thinking about the field.

We begin by considering the philosophical foundation in non-technical language and then move to a more formal presentation. The political economy of communication calls for an approach to understanding that accepts as real both the abstract ideas that guide thinking as well as concrete observations or what our senses perceive. It thereby rejects the view, prominent in some theories, that only our ideas or only our observations, but not both, are real. Political economy also rejects the position that there is no reality, that neither ideas nor observations are in any important sense real. Moreover, this philosophy means that reality is made up of many elements and cannot be reduced to one essence. Neither economics (e.g. money alone drives the media) nor culture (e.g. people's values shape the media) provide the magic key to unlock our understanding of communication. This philosophical foundation also brings to the forefront the ideas of social change, social process, and social relations which require re-evaluating the emphasis that political economy has traditionally placed on social institutions, like media businesses, or on seeing social class as a structure rather than as a social relationship.

Putting these ideas into practice, this and subsequent chapters move to identify three processes that make up the main starting points for political economy research, thereby guiding us on how to apply political economy to the world of communication. *Commodification* is the process of transforming things valued for their use into marketable products that are valued for what they can bring in exchange. A good example is the process of turning a story that friends enjoy into a film or novel to be sold in the marketplace. How does the human act of communication become a product produced for a profit? *Spatialization* is the process by which mass media and communication technology overcome the constraints of geographical space. For example, television overcomes distance by bringing images of events on the globe to every part of the world. Moreover, companies increasingly use computer communication to organize business on a worldwide basis, thereby allowing them greater access to consumers, workers, technology, and capital. It also provides them with the flexibility to move rapidly when the need arises, e.g. the availability of low-cost or better skilled labor elsewhere. What happens when communications goes global and when businesses make use of communication to create and manufacture their products worldwide? The third key concept is *structuration* or the process of creating social relations, mainly those organized around social class, gender, and race. For example, political economy describes how access to the mass media and new communication technologies is influenced by social class inequalities that divide people according to income and wealth, enabling some to afford access and leaving out others.

In more formal terms, the political economy of communications is grounded in specific *epistemological* and *ontological* principles. An epistemology is an approach to understanding how we know things. The political economy of communication is based on a realist, inclusive, constitutive, and critical epistemology. It is *realist* in the strong sense that it recognizes the reality of both concepts and social practices (see Latour, 1999: Chapter 1; Shimony and Malin, 2006). In this respect, it is to be distinguished from *idiographic* approaches that argue for the reality of ideas alone and *nomothetic* approaches which maintain that ideas are only labels for the singular reality of human action. Following from this, political economy is also *inclusive* in that it rejects essentialism, or the tendency to reduce all social practices to a single political economic explanation, in favor of an approach that views concepts as starting or entry points into a diverse social field (Resnick and Wolff, 1987, 2006). To understand social reality you need to choose concepts and theories. The choice of one concept or theory over another is made because you conclude that the concept or theory is more valuable than the alternatives. However, such choices are not meant to be assertions of the one best, or only, way to understand social practices.

Additionally, the epistemology is *constitutive* because it acknowledges the limits of causal determination, including the assumption in causal analysis that units interact as fully formed wholes and in a linear fashion. Rather, political economy approaches social life as a set of mutually constitutive processes, whose units act on one another in various stages of formation, and with a direction and impact that can only be described in specific research. Finally, this approach to political economy is *critical* because it sees knowledge as the product of comparisons with other bodies of knowledge and with social values. For example, my political economy is critical in that it regularly compares the knowledge acquired in research against alternative bodies of knowledge in, for example, neoclassical economics, pluralist political science, and cultural studies. Furthermore, this approach measures the knowledge gathered in political economic research against the social values that have guided much of it over the years, including democracy and its components, civic participation, and social equality.

In contrast to epistemology, which provides a framework for understanding how we know things, ontology describes a framework for understand the nature of being.

Specifically, ontology distinguishes seeing things as *structures* or as *processes*. Is the river a thing or a flow? It is both, but which one is emphasized? Traditionally, political economy has emphasized things or structures such a multinational media firms and the governments that oversee them. My theoretical framework calls for a departure from this traditional approach to political economy by placing social processes and social relations in the foreground. This means that research starts from the view that social change is ubiquitous, that structures and institutions are constantly changing, and that it is therefore more useful to develop entry points that characterize processes rather than simply to identify relevant institutions. According to this view, studying media institutions is important but it follows from an analysis of a social process, e.g. turning stories into films and other marketable products.

Guided by this principle, the remainder of this chapter and the following two develop a substantive map of political economy with three starting processes, beginning with *commodification*, the process of transforming use to exchange value, moving on to *spatialization*, the transformation of space with communication, and finally to *structuration*, the process of building structures with social agency. Placing these processes in the foreground does not replace structures and institutions, something that would substitute one form of essentialism for another. Rather, these are entry points that comprise a substantive theory of political economy, one preferred choice among a range of possible ways to explain social reality.

What is Commodification?

Adam Smith and classical political economy distinguished between products whose value derives from the satisfaction of a specific human want or need, i.e. use value, and those whose value is based on what the product can command in exchange, i.e. exchange value. The commodity is the particular form that products take when their production is principally organized through the process of exchange. *Commodification is the process of transforming use values into exchange values.*

Marx began *Capital* with an analysis of the commodity because he found it to be the most visible form, the most explicit representation, of capitalist production. Capitalism literally *appears* as an immense collection of commodities. Although this appearance did not go unnoticed in classical political economy, the tendency was to naturalize it, a point that marked a critical departure in Marx. What for Smith and his followers was "a self-evident and nature-imposed necessity" was instead for Marx the product of "a social formation in which the process of production has mastery over man, instead of the opposite" (Marx, 1976a: 175). One of the keys to Marxian analysis is to deconstruct the commodity to determine what the appearance means, to uncover the social relations congealed in the commodity form. As Jhally (1990) has documented, in one of the few sustained analyses of the commodity form in the communication literature, Marx took a broad view of both the commodity and the meaning of use value. For Marx (1976a: 125), commodities ensue from a wide range of needs, both physical and cultural ("from the stomach, or the imagination, makes no difference") and whose use can be defined "in various ways." The commodity might arise from a range of social needs – including satisfying physical hunger and meeting or contravening the status codes of a particular social group. Moreover, contrary to some interpretations, use value is not limited to meeting survival needs but extends to the range of socially constituted uses.

Some critics have not been satisfied with this formulation, arguing that the distinction between use and exchange value obscures more than it illuminates. For example, according to Sahlins (1976: 15), Marx acknowledges the social character of all value but tends to *naturalize use value*, "to trade away the social determination of use-values for the biological fact that they satisfy 'human wants'." Baudrillard (1981) extends this critique by maintaining that use value is ultimately left outside the sets of structures and codes that constitute specific exchange values. This critique reminds us that Marx's chief aim was to interrogate capital and, given the primacy of this interest, he neglected detailed treatment of ideas that embody the fundamental negation of capitalism, including use value and the social contours of a socialist or Communist society. Nevertheless, the cultural critique also defines a boundary that political economy will not cross because the critique aims to do more than suggest gaps. It also substitutes an idealist relativism that defines value as whatever the cultural code specifies and, as suggested in the variability of human cultural practice, this can amount to practically anything. Political economy admits to variability, but bounds it by the understanding that uses are conditioned (in Marx's language) or limited (in the language of Raymond Williams) by the structural properties of the commodity and take their existence from them. Drawing on Rubin, Jhally (1990) suggests the language of "partial necessity" to deal with Marx's recognition that "usefulness does not dangle in mid-air." Alternatively, one might suggest the mutual constitution of use values and retain the distinction between socially constituted use values and values which arise from a specific set of social arrangements, such as the market, which produce exchange values.

Peeling back what Marx called the "onion skin" of the commodity's appearance reveals a system of production. There are two general dimensions of significance in the relationship of commodification to communication. First, *communication processes and technologies contribute to the general process of commodification in the economy as a whole.* For example, improving the channels of communication in the clothing business, particularly with the introduction of global computer and telecommunication technologies, expands information about the entire circuit of production, distribution, and sales. This improves inventory controls, thereby saving on space and increasing the likelihood that stores stock only what customers want. Second, *commodification processes at work in the society as a whole penetrate communication processes and institutions, so that improvements and contradictions in the societal commodification process influence communication as a social practice.* For example, the international tendencies to liberalization and privatization of enterprises, which picked up steam in the 1980s, transformed public and state-run media and telecommunications institutions throughout the world into private enterprises. This turned public service communication with social commitments to universal access and content that reflects the broad range of society into commercial communication that provides access to those who can afford it and content that delivers audiences to advertisers.

Given the interest in situating communication within a general political economic analysis, it is useful to start from the general process of commodification and examine how it relates to communication. From the point of view of capital, the production process begins with the capitalist's purchase of the commodities *labor power* and *the means of production*. The total output is sold for more than originally invested and the addition is called *surplus value*, which may itself be invested to expand the accumulation of capital. In essence, capital is value that expands through processes of production and exchange. Marxian theory takes this analysis one step further by concluding that these are *exploitative* processes because the expansion of capitalist control eliminates alternative systems of production and forces labor into a social relationship wherein it takes on the status of a commodity, or a factor of production, along with land and raw materials, and is made to give up its control over the means of production. As a result, workers are made to exchange their labor power for a wage that does not compensate fully for the labor they sell. The commodity labor is reproduced through processes of absolute exploitation (extending the working day) and relative exploitation (intensification of the labor process) that deepen the extraction of surplus value. Exploitation is a *sine qua non* of the capitalist labor process, but the degree of exploitation depends on the state of class struggle. For example, when workers organize a union or otherwise resist exploitation, capital has to make adjustments in the labor process. Thus, the commodity whose appearance fills the markets of capitalism is also a congealed set of social relations that connect capital to the commodity labor in a struggle for control over the value generated from production and exchange. For example, the DVD of a Hollywood film that appears in a video store is also a set of social relations that links Hollywood producers to screen actors, directors, and writers, who struggle over who will profit from the value generated from sales in stores and from distribution over the Internet.

In the Marxian view, the commodity objectifies exploitative social relations by presenting them in a congealed form that makes them seem natural. Hence a computer appears to us as a commodity with a defined set of use values and a specific exchange value marked by its price. Its value in use and in exchange tends to mystify the ability to comprehend the computer as the embodiment of an international division of labor that stratifies productive relations along class, gender, national, and spatial dimensions. A deeper level of mystification is revealed in Marx's analysis of *commodity fetishism*, according to which the commodity not only congeals social relations and hides the struggle over value, but takes on a life and a power of its own, over that of both its producers and consumers. For Marx, such fetishism was once limited to religion:

In order, therefore, to find an analogy we must take flight into the misty realm of religion. There the products of the human brain appear as autonomous figures endowed with a life of their own, which enter into relations both with each other and with the human race. So it is in the world of commodities with the products of men's hands. I call this the fetishism which attaches itself to the products of labour as soon as they are produced as commodities and is therefore inseparable from the production of commodities. (1976a: 165)

In fact, for Marx, the commodity fetish is more powerful than its counterpart in religion because commodities have a material embodiment that presents itself directly to the senses in ways that religious beliefs do not.[1] In this view, the commodity contains a double mystification. First, it naturalizes the social relationship between capital and labor. It is the computer that appears and not a struggle at the point of production over, for example, how much workers who produce computers will earn. Second, the commodity is reified, i.e. it takes on a life of its own that stands against the individual and society and comes to shape both. We turn the computer into a mystical icon, the embodiment of what I have called "the digital sublime" (Mosco, 2004). The first point sees the commodity as the natural outcome of a production process, rather than the social consequence of a fundamental social struggle; the second point completely cuts the tie to a production process and situates the commodity in its own social realm. The computer appears as a power over people, as the force that shapes, determines, constrains, or otherwise controls social development. The outcome of this double mystification is that the product of a social process is given an existence of its own and the power to mold social life (Free and Hughson, 2006; Hope and Rosser, 2004).

Commodification refers to the process of turning use values into exchange values, of transforming products whose value is determined by their ability to meet individual and social needs into products whose value is set by their market price. Owing in part to the emphasis on structures and objects over processes and relations in much of political economic thought, the term commodification has not received substantial explicit treatment. Nevertheless, it is implicit in discussions of the process of capitalist expansion, including the global extension of the market (Fürsich and Roushanzamir, 2004; Murdock and Wasko, 2007), the privatization of public space (Gibson, 2003; Schiller, 1989), and the growth of exchange value in interpersonal life (Ewen and Ewen, 2006) and in sexuality (Mayer, 2005).

It is important to distinguish commodification from commercialization and objectification, processes with which it tends to be associated. Commercialization is a narrower process that specifically refers to the creation of a relationship between an audience and an advertiser. For example, the commercialization of the airwaves means the growth of broadcast advertising and the development of programming to deliver audiences to advertisers. Since the market encompasses more than commercialization, e.g. the commodification of labor, we view commodification as a broader process. Objectification is a still broader notion that is often confused with commodification. For example, in his work on reification, Lukács (1971) describes the process whereby the relations between people "take on the character of a thing and thus acquire a phantom objectivity." Commodification is

---

1 One might dispute this contention as an unwarranted conflation of the real and the material. A spiritual being can be real without being material. Nevertheless, the argument for commodity fetishism does not rest on agreeing that the commodity is somehow more real than religious faith.

a specific form of this process whereby the "thing" that acquires phantom objectivity is a commodity, that is, an object whose value is established in the marketplace. Objectification is a general process that refers to the many different ways dehumanization takes place. Political economy focuses on one important manifestation of this, the process of commodification.

The Commodity Form in Communication

The political economy of communication has been notable for its emphasis on describing and examining the significance of organizational structures responsible for the production, distribution, and exchange of communication commodities and for the regulation of these structures, principally by governments. Although it has not neglected the commodity itself and the process of commodification, political economy has tended to foreground corporate and state structures and institutions. When it has treated the commodity, political economy has tended to concentrate on media content and, to a lesser extent, on media audiences. It has paid considerably less attention to the commodification of labor in the communication industries.

The emphasis on media institutions is understandable because today's global media conglomerates are very powerful. They are able to extend that power by creating content that brings in revenue each time it is used and reused by audiences around the world. Companies then deepen that revenue stream when they take that same content and repackage it for use and reuse by subsidiaries that extend across the print, video, film, and new media sectors (Broe, 2004).

Notwithstanding the importance of institutions, emphasis on their activities has meant less than adequate attention to the commodity form of the mass media and, particularly, to the commodification of audiences and of labor.

The Commodification of Content

When political economists think about the commodity form in communication, they have tended to start with media content. Specifically, from this point of view, the process of commodification in communication involves transforming messages, ranging from bits of data to systems of meaningful thought, into marketable products. For example, consider a newspaper reporter whose job it is to apply professional skills to produce stories that contain many different use values. The history of newspaper production in capitalist society has involved numerous processes, including commodification, which make the story teller a wage laborer who sells her labor power, or the ability to write stories, for a wage. Capital turns that labor power into a newspaper article or column which, along with other stories and advertising, forms a packaged product. It sells the newspaper package in the marketplace and, if it is successful, earns a profit or surplus value, which it can then invest by expanding its newspaper business or by investing in any other venture that promises additions to capital. Marxian political economy views this as the realization of surplus value because the control that capital wields over the means of production (ownership of presses, offices, etc.) enables it to earn in profit more than it pays out in wages.

The extent of surplus value realization depends on numerous factors in labor, consumer, and capital markets. With respect to labor, Marxian political economy has examined the process of creating absolute and relative surplus value. The former involves extending the working day for the same wage; the latter to intensifying the labor process through greater control over the use of work time, including measurement and monitoring systems to get more labor out of a unit of work time. The success of these strategies depends on the ability of labor to resist, something that rests on the strength of its own organizations, and on more general social conditions, such as capital's ability to replace the workforce with new workers and new technologies. Specifically, how powerful are the trade unions representing news workers? How easy is it to outsource newspaper labor and get machines to do its work? It also depends on the extent to which government sides with capital or labor in law and public policy.

Capital also aims to control consumer markets through a range of tactics that amount to achieving the status of the "natural" or taken-for-granted provider of a product. These include building a market monopoly or controlling an oligopoly arrangement, using advertising to create brand identification with the company, and diversifying its product line to achieve the flexibility to overcome changes in market demand. The ability to realize surplus value also depends on the extent to which consumers are able to resist, a consideration that depends on its history of collective action and the general social conditions that enable or retard the ability of consumers to substitute products and services. Again, it also depends on the extent to which government sides with capital or with consumers. Finally, the realization of surplus value depends on the state of capital markets, specifically, on the cost of capital which permits the replacement of labor with capital and also allows for the expansion of the commodity form (from, for example, the newspaper format to an all-news pay cable channel, or to an online service).

This brief description suggests that the process of creating exchange value in the content of communication draws an entire complex of social relations into the orbit of commodification, including labor, consumers, and capital. The general tendency in communication research has been to concentrate on the content as commodity and, by extension, to identify the connections between the commodity status of the content and its meaning. As a result, communication is taken to be a special and particularly powerful commodity because, in addition to its ability to produce surplus value (thereby behaving like all other commodities), it contains symbols and images whose meaning helps to shape consciousness. Numerous studies have documented the value of this approach and its conclusion that the mass media in capitalist society have expanded the process of commodity production by, among other things, producing messages that reflect the interests of capital. Through however circuitous, contradictory, and contested a process, these messages advance support for the interests of capital as a whole as well as for specific segments of capital (Bettig and Hall, 2003; McChesney, 2004; Meyer, 2006; Murdock and Wasko, 2007).

Although they concurred in general terms with this conclusion, some political economists, notably Garnham and Smythe, suggested alternative formulations. Both raised concerns about the tendency to emphasize the meaning or ideological dimension of media production. Throughout his career, Garnham has directed his strongest salvos against those who would, in effect, jettison the economic for the analysis of "autonomous discourses."[2] Nevertheless, he is also concerned about the tendency within political economy to address the message, its meaning and ideology, to, as Jhally puts it, adopt a "consumer model of communications," without adequately addressing the mass media as "economic entities with both a direct economic role as creators of surplus value through commodity production and exchange and an indirect role, through advertising, in the creation of surplus value within other sectors of commodity production" (Garnham, 1979: 132). In this reading, the mass media are important because they are the immediate site of commodity production *and* because they play an important, if indirect, role, through advertising media, in the process of commodification throughout the economy. The point is not that the ideological is insignificant; rather that it is thoroughly integrated within a process of production that is too often treated as instrumental to ideology (in some political economy) or autonomous from it (in some cultural theory).

New media expand opportunities to commodify content because they are fundamentally grounded in the process of digitization, which refers specifically to the transformation of communication, including data, words, images, motion pictures, and sound, into a common language. Digitization provides enormous gains in transmission speed and flexibility over earlier forms of electronic communication which were largely reliant on analog techniques (Longstaff, 2002). This has advanced to the point that a single electronic communication can now be broken up into packets and sent down different pathways along telecommunication networks to be recombined at the destination, thereby ensuring the most efficient use of networks.

Digitization expands the commodification of communication content by extending the range of opportunities to measure and monitor, package and repackage, information and entertainment. The packaging of material in the paper and ink form of a newspaper

---

2 In his influential 1979 "Contribution to a Political Economy of Mass Communication," Garnham wrote:

> Thus economism, the concern for immediate physical survival and reproduction within the dominant relations of exchange, is an immediate and rational response to the determinants of social being. What E.P. Thompson has recently dubbed "lumped bourgeois intellectuals" too easily forget this, both because their material conditions of existence are often less immediately determinant and also because of a guilty conscience concerning the subjective relationship of exploitation in which they stand *vis-à-vis* productive material labour. (1979: 126)

And in his *Capitalism and Communication*, Garnham attacks first "the tendency which privileged the text," (structuralism and post-structuralism), for its unanchored romanticism (a "bacillus"), a view "perfectly designed as an ideology of intellectuals or cultural workers for it privileges their special field of activity, the symbolic, and provides for cheap research opportunities, since the only evidence required is the unsubstantiated views of the individual analyst" (Garnham, 1990: 1–2).

or book has provided a flexible, but limited, means to measure the commodity and monitor purchases. Challenges to the commodification of communication arose when what political economist Bernard Miège calls flow type communication systems arose, most importantly television (Miège, 1989; see also McAllister and Giglo, 2004). How does one package a television program for sale to a viewer? Initially, commodification was based on an inflexible system of delivering a batch of broadcast channels into the home with viewers paying for the receiver and for a markup or increase in the retail price of products advertised over the air. This system did not account for differential use of the medium or make any clear connection between viewing and purchasing. It amounted to a system of delivering generic programming to a mass audience which was marketed to advertisers for a price per thousand viewers.

Each step toward the digitization of television has refined the commodification of content, allowing for the flow to be captured or, more precisely, for the commodity to be measured, monitored, and packaged in ever more specific or customized ways. Early cable television improved on broadcast systems of commodification by charging per month for a set of channels. As this medium has become digitized, companies can now offer many more channels and package them in many different ways, including selling content on a per view basis. Material delivered over television, the Internet or some combination of these and other new wired and wireless systems can now be flexibly packaged and then repackaged for sale in some related form with the transaction measured and monitored by the same digital system.

The sheer ability to expand the commodification process does not guarantee its success. Internet entrepreneurs learned the hard way that charging for content can be a risky business indeed. Technical, management, marketing, and consumer demand problems can often get in the way. Nevertheless, the growth of pay-per-view television, satellite-delivered subscription radio, video delivered over the Internet, web cams, and the rise of the iTunes pay-per-song system, which has made Apple the largest commercial distributor of music, demonstrate that new media commodification has made substantial progress (Lynch, 2004; Murray, 2003; Thrift, 2006). This progress has been assisted by intellectual property laws that permit content owners, increasingly large enterprises, to control the use of content and even the formats through which content is delivered. So a company can now control not only the entertainment delivered in the television program *American Idol*, it can profit by licensing the format for the program to companies in other countries who produce, for example, *Canadian Idol* (Baltruschat, 2008).

The Audience Commodity

Nicholas Garnham has examined two principal dimensions of media commodification: the direct production of media products and the use of media advertising to perfect the process of commodification in the entire economy. Dallas Smythe (1977) took these ideas in a different direction by advancing the claim that the audience is the primary commodity of the mass media. According to him, the mass media are constituted out of a process which sees media companies producing audiences and delivering them to advertisers. Media programming is used to attract audiences; for

Smythe, it was little more than the "free lunch" that bars once used to entice customers to drink. From this vantage point, audience labor or its labor power is the chief product of the mass media.

New media amplify the elements of Smythe's argument (Shimpach, 2005). In addition to expanding the commodification of communication content, the recursive nature of digital systems expands the commodification of the entire communication process. Digital systems which measure and monitor precisely each information transaction are now used to refine the process of delivering audiences of viewers, listeners, readers, movie fans, telephone and computer users, to advertisers. In essence, companies can package and repackage customers in forms that specifically reflect both their actual purchases and their demographic characteristics. These packages, for example, of 18–25 year old men who order martial arts films on pay-per-view television, can be sold to companies, which spend more for this information because they want to market their products to this specific sector with as little advertising spilling over to people who would not be interested or able to buy. This is a major refinement in the commodification of viewers over the earlier system of delivering mass audiences and it has been applied to practically every communication medium today, including the Internet, where social networking sites like Facebook provide detailed information on users.

Smythe's analysis provoked one of the more interesting and well-examined exchanges in the political economy literature (Livant, 1979; Murdock, 1978; Smythe, 1978). Rather than review the debates on the primacy of the audience as commodity and as labor, exchanges that have been detailed more than once (Jhally, 1990), it is more useful to take up the wider significance of Smythe's argument. Neglected in the debate about whether the audience labors or whether it is the sole media commodity, is arguably the central contribution that Smythe made to our understanding of the media commodification process. For him, the process brought together a triad that linked media companies, audiences, and advertisers in a set of reciprocal relationships. Media firms use their programming to construct audiences; advertisers pay media companies for access to these audiences; audiences are thereby delivered to advertisers. Such an argument broadens the space within which media commodification takes place beyond the immediate process whereby media companies produce newspapers, radio broadcasts, televisions programs and films, and websites to include advertisers or capital in general. The process of commodification thoroughly integrates the media industries into the total capitalist economy not primarily by creating ideologically saturated products but by producing audiences, *en masse* and in specific demographically desirable forms, for advertisers. Smythe thereby aimed to rescue the materialist analysis of the media by demonstrating that it is the production of audiences for the general capitalist economy that is central to the commodification process rather than the production of ideology.

Putting aside the contentious and doubtfully productive argument about whether audiences constitute labor, Smythe's deployment of the labor process concept is useful as metaphor or analogy because it offers a way to think about the triad of media company–audience–advertiser without submitting to the mechanistic thinking that such a structural argument invites. Bracketing the question of whether audiences work in the traditional sense of the term (with all of the questions it raises about the labor theory of value), it is useful to think about analogies between audience activity and the labor process because the latter is a dynamic activity involving complicity and contestation between capital and labor over control of the process and of the product. This is considerably more valuable than addressing the audience as the inert mass that so-called mass society theorists dating from Ortega y Gasset (1957) have conjured or, alternatively, as the co-producers of media products, the view on offer from pluralists like Fiske (1989) and Ang (1991), who responded to traditional criticism of a passive mass society by going to the other extreme and describing an active audience of co-producers. The latter are correct in pointing to the co- or mutual constitution of media products, *but* they neglect to situate this process within a structure of decision-making that places in the hands of capital most, though not all, of the levers on the control over decision-making about what gets produced, how it is distributed, and what it costs.

Capital, in its own manifold and contested manifestations, must actively construct audiences as it constructs labor, but even as it does so, both audiences and labor construct themselves by deciding, within a social field whose terms of engagement are primarily set by capital, how to activate their audience and their labor power. For the audience, this means a range of alternatives: attending or watching as capital would like, interpreting programming in oppositional or alternative ways, or simply not watching at all. The new media field of computer gaming offers important insights into the concept of audience labor (Grimes, 2006). As with traditional labor, which the literature on work demonstrates brings a wide range of responses to the point of production, from full compliance to withholding labor power, the audience exercises power, but also like labor, it is power circumscribed within terms largely set by capital.

Political economy extends the analogy further by examining how the relationship between capital and the audience at the point of media reception is carried on over the expansion of commercial broadcasting at the expense of non-commercial public and community broadcasting. It also does so by addressing the use of new technologies to expand the process of measuring and monitoring audience activity, and the introduction of pay-per channel, per-view, and per-song services. Moreover, political economy examines how audiences respond and resist with file sharing, blogging, social networking, and other forms of media use that aim to counter the prevailing commercial system. These activities have sparked important new work in the political economy of the audience (Andrejevic, 2003a, 2003b; Arvidsson, 2004; Carlson, 2006; Grimes, 2006; Hope and Johnson, 2004; Morris, 2005; Shimpach, 2005; Thrift, 2006).

The Commodification of Labor

In the interest of examining the commodification of content and audiences, there has been a tendency to neglect the labor commodity and the process that takes place at the point of production. Braverman's (1974) work gave rise to an intellectual drive to end this marginal status by directly confronting the transformation of the labor process in capitalism.[3] According to him, labor is constituted out of the unity of *conception*, or the power to envision, imagine, and design work, and *execution*, or the power to carry it out.[4] In the process of commodification, capital acts to *separate* conception from execution, skill from the raw ability to carry out a task. It also *concentrates* conceptual power in a managerial class that is either a part of capital or represents its interests. Finally, capital *reconstitutes* the labor process to correspond to this new distribution of skills and power at the point of production. In the extreme, this was done through the application of so-called scientific management practices, pioneered by Frederick Winslow Taylor.[5] These amounted to the precise measurement of the time and the amount of labor it takes to accomplish tasks most efficiently, i.e. to permit the maximum return on investment. In the process, management became the scientific brains of an enterprise and workers, who once possessed the craft skill to control the labor process, were turned into appendages of the machinery. Braverman documented the process of labor transformation in the rise of large-scale industry, but he is particularly recognized for producing one of the first sustained examinations demonstrating the extension of this process into the service and information sectors. Braverman's work gave rise to an enormous body of empirical examination and theoretical debate, the latter focusing principally on the need to address the contested nature of the process and the active agency of workers and of the trade union movement (Burawoy, 1979; Edwards, 1979). Much of this work constituted what the philosopher Thomas Kuhn (1970) would call "normal science," i.e. working through and expanding upon the wide range of problems and implications contained in Braverman's contribution. This included mapping the contested terrain at the point of production, documenting its history, and demonstrating how the transformation of the labor process was experienced differently by industry, occupation, class, gender, and race. Recent work, including scholarly assessments and business press accounts, has tended to incorporate an interest in how the means of communication, sharpened by steady improvements in technological proficiency, have enhanced the commodification of the general labor process (Baldoz, Koeber, and Kraft, 2001; Huws, 2003; Mosco and McKercher, 2008).

Despite a strong political economy tradition and a broad interest among economists and policy-makers in the cultural industries, communication studies has tended to situate its object within the sphere of consumption and this has

---

3 Braverman's work was especially timely in that it appeared in 1974 at the start of the economic decline following the sustained postwar boom. It also corresponded with the start of intense use of computer communications systems to control the factory and the office.

4 The distinction between conception and execution corresponds to Marx's view that it is the potential to conceive or imagine and not just carry out or execute what our genes dictate that distinguishes the human architect from the bee. Both can produce great structures but only one can unite conception with execution.

5 In the hands of Lilian Gilbreth (whose husband, a follower of Taylor, developed the unit of worktime measurement, the "therblig") this process of Taylorization was applied to the home, thereby enabling mainly women to manage the household "scientifically."

contributed to a focus on the relationship of audiences to texts more than on the media labor process. Political economists of communication have paid considerable attention to the institutional control over media production and to the impact of this control on audiences, including the concept of audience labor. Although this is changing, arguably more attention has been directed to the labor of audiences than to the traditionally understood labor process in the media industries. Moreover, work in the media industries carries strong craft, professional, and artisan traditions that continue, even as the labor process is transformed (Deuze, 2007). The image of the crusading professional journalist or the high-tech entrepreneur overwhelms the less romantic reality of a media and high-tech world, most of whose workers toil under conditions that industrial workers of the past would recognize. There is an understandable tendency to emphasize the individual creative dimensions of media production which distinguish this sector from the many occupational sectors that share the characteristics of industrial production. Authors write books, some directors are the *auteurs* of film, stars make movies or television programs, etc. There are substantial grounds for this view, principally based on the relatively high level of conceptual thought that this industry requires. This is the chief reason why print workers and their trade unions have historically occupied a privileged position in the workforce. But the emphasis on individual creativity only obscures a complex process of production, one that, however unevenly, has come to look more like the labor process in the general economy.

Organizational communication and sociology have provided some of the better insights into the bureaucratic structure and production processes in the media industries. The work of Tuchman (1978), Fishman (1980), and Gans (1979), and more recently Deuze (2007) among others, has examined the system of bureaucratic controls that manage the complex process of, principally, news production. Their work highlights those simplifying routines such as beat reporting, a detailed division of labor, and regularized features that establish a template for what is potentially an open-ended production process. This body of research demonstrates that a substantial amount of organizational planning and pre-processing are used to gather, package, and distribute news and information on a routine basis. This line of research is important for a political economy that addresses the labor process because it describes in rich empirical detail the socio-technical processes that help to constitute the work of producing media even as it turns labor into a marketable commodity. Nevertheless, although this work gestures to political and economic influences, these are left untheorized in favor of a framework based on theories of bureaucracy and organization that foreground abstract administrative needs and functions. Notwithstanding nods to power and profit, this approach concentrates on how the structural pressures of bureaucracy, following on a literature originating in the work of Max Weber and Robert Michels, rationalize production in the cultural industries, just as they do throughout an economy managed by complex bureaucracies.

From a political economic perspective, the organizational literature contributes rich empirical detail but rests on an idealist foundation that substitutes an administrative essentialism for what it perceives to be the economic essentialism of the market. It places, as the sociologist Max Weber suggested, the determining influence of the *means of administration* over that of the means of production. The challenge that the organizational literature poses to political economy is to develop a position that examines the process of production foregrounding political and economic power, specifically the commodification of labor. This would constitute an important link between institutional and textual analysis that retains the materialist strength of a political economic approach. The point is not to reclaim ground lost to one essentialism by restoring another, but to theorize the commodification of labor in the process of media production. As Chapter 6 described, the political economy literature has taken some steps in this direction, but considerable work remains to be done (Huws, 2003; Kumar, 2007; Martin, 2004; McKercher and Mosco, 2006, 2007; Mosco and McKercher, 2008; Wasko, 2003).

Immanent Commodification

Thus far we have considered three major products of the commodification process in communication: content, audiences, and labor. The chapter now turns to consider two more dimensions of commodification: how commodities produce their own new commodities, or immanent commodification, and how new commodities are produced through the associations among different commodities.

We begin by returning to the audience commodity where the political economist Eileen Meehan offers an alternative way to think about it which centers on the audience ratings services. Since "neither messages nor audiences are exchanged: only ratings," she maintains (1984: 223) that these reports on audience size, composition, and patterns of media usage constitute the primary commodity in the media system. Meehan's research makes a significant contribution to several dimensions of political economic analysis, including the materialist history of an industry which the A.C. Nielsen Company made famous and the social construction of a statistic, the rating, whose exchange value barely resembles its use as an empirical marker for actual audience characteristics. For the purpose of this analysis, her research is particularly valuable because, when combined with research in other areas, it points to the recursive nature of the commodification process. Audience ratings are a commodity produced by another commodity. In this case, a commodity is born directly out of the process of creating another. We call this an immanent process because one commodity gives rise directly to another.

Commodification demands the use of measurement procedures to produce commodities and monitoring techniques to keep track of production, distribution, exchange, and consumption. An example of the former is the precise length of an advertisement or the amount of commercial time produced for sale to advertisers. Monitoring is exemplified by a range of practices, including traditional business accounting, marketing studies, capital cost assessments, wage and benefit studies, customer surveys, and more recent innovations like data matching systems that link a credit or debit card purchase to demographic and attitudinal information. These practices are part of the commodification process because the information they produce is used in the production of commodities, like newspapers, television situation comedies, and social networking websites. They are immanent because the outcome of the information production process is the production of a new commodity. In this respect, ratings are immanent commodities because they are constituted as commodities in the process of contributing to commodity production. Specifically, they are produced as an important element in the commodification of content and of audiences and are themselves the central commodity of the ratings industry. This makes the ratings services important not because they are *the* media commodity, but because they represent one rather advanced stage in the general process of media commodification. They are part of a family of such commodities that grow out of the development of generalized monitoring and surveillance procedures that make use of advanced communication and information technology (Campbell, 2005; Campbell and Carlson, 2002; Carlson, 2006).[6] In this respect, audience ratings are as important, though not inherently more so, than commodities produced and marketed from data automatically gathered on consumer purchases. Both are immanent commodities containing a secondary order of exchange value that depends on a first order.

Back in 1992 the prescient head of a major company which marketed such immanent commodities recognized their significance. For DeSimone (1992), they build on the original commodification process by shifting

> from the value that is *intrinsic* in the product to values associated with the knowledge of who needs it, who supplies it and what it does. You buy a magazine and pay for it with a credit card. A simple transaction? Hardly. The *information* about who you are and what magazines you prefer – recorded by a computer – is worth as much as the return on the sale of the magazine. The information can be variously packaged. It can be marketed to others. Moreover, all the internal processes are affected by your decision – from marketing to purchase to finance. Today, all organizations are in the information business.

---

6 Giddens' work has been undoubtedly valuable in calling our attention to the development of institutional surveillance systems. Nevertheless, by locating surveillance in an institutional realm occupied with the "control of information and social supervision" and separate from capitalism, which he describes as primarily taken up with "accumulation in the context of competitive labour and product markets," he and many other social theorists miss the central contribution that the accumulation process makes to the development of surveillance systems and the necessity of these systems for the expansion of capital accumulation. Giddens does speak of interpenetration, but accumulation and surveillance remain separate realms, their boundary reinforced in his *identification of surveillance with the nation state*. The latter is certainly implicated in the constitution of surveillance, but, by locating surveillance in the state, Giddens foregoes the point that surveillance, in the form of rationalizing production, distribution, and consumption, is integral to and propelled by business corporations in the commodification process (see, *inter alia*, Giddens, 1990: 55–63). For a thorough analysis of corporate and state forms of measuring and monitoring transactions, see Andrejevic (2003a, 2003b) and Lyon (2006, 2007).

Notwithstanding the need to discount for the hyperbole that typically accompanies emanations from the corporate center of the information industries, one is left with the view that it is essential to move beyond the notion of finding *the* commodity in the media. It is more significant to foreground a process of commodification that connects a range of practices in a spiral of expanding exchange value that, as DeSimone concludes, draws all organizations into the orbit of the information business that produces immanent commodities. It is within this general framework of commodification that it becomes useful to examine the application of new measurement and surveillance technologies to expand the production of media commodities. Internet cookies, digital television recording devices, "smart" cards, etc., produce new products, in the form of reports on viewing and shopping, containing demographic details that are linked to numerous databases. But these new products are more than discrete units. They are part of a commodification process that connects them in a structured hierarchy. The implications for privacy are powerful. According to one analyst:

> The driving force behind this prying is commerce. The big growth area in online advertising right now is "behavioral targeting." Web sites can charge a premium if they are able to tell the maker of an expensive sports car that its ads will appear on Web pages clicked on by upper-income, middle-aged men.

> The information, however, gets a lot more specific than age and gender – and more sensitive. Tech companies can keep track of when a particular Internet user looks up Alcoholics Anonymous meetings, visits adult Web sites, buys cancer drugs online or participates in anti-government discussion groups (Cohen, 2008).

Immanent commodification not only produces new commodities; it creates powerful surveillance tools that threaten privacy.

Externalizing Commodification

One can also observe a process of expansion that extends commodification to areas that, for a range of social, political, cultural, and economic reasons, were historically left outside the process or only lightly affected by it. These include numerous information and cultural areas that have been taken up prominently in communication and cultural studies (Murdock and Wasko, 2007), geography (Graham, 2002), urban studies (Gibson and Lowes, 2006), development studies (McDonald and Ruiters, 2005), and environmental studies (Dorsey, Steeves, and Porras, 2004). This work describes how the process of commodification has been extended to institutional areas that were once resources available to all irrespective of market power. These include media and telecommunications, but also water, education, streets, playgrounds, museums, libraries, and other objects, locations, and services that were certainly created out of a range of contested forces and motives, but which nevertheless had preserved principles of use value and universal access irrespective of one's ability to pay.

The manifestation of extensive commodification takes many notable forms, though this is not the place for a detailed discussion of each. Declines in economic growth and the rightward shift in political power have prompted funding cutbacks for public information institutions, such as libraries and public schools (Monahan, 2004; Tracy and Hayashi, 2007). We have also witnessed the broad-based privatization and commercialization of public information, postal, broadcasting, and telecommunications systems and the introduction of the neoclassical economic logic of "cost-based" pricing or what amounts to governance in the interests of those with market power. Extensive commodification also includes the transformation of common spaces, from public parks to privately governed shopping malls, and the increasing reliance on commercial sponsorship of museums, sports, and festivals (Gibson, 2003; Gibson and Lowes, 2006; Gittings, 1998; Negra, 2001). The growing power of branding and the tendency for people to wear corporate logos and other advertising commercializes the body and personal identity (Arvidsson, 2005; Klein, 2002; Rajagopal and Bojin, 2004; Riordan, 2001). We are also seeing the commodification of privacy itself, as people are required to pay to maintain anonymity (Deery, 2004a, 2004b). These developments suggest that the process of commodification has extended into places and practices that once tended to be organized according to a different social logic, one based on universality, equality, social participation, and citizenship, which, for all of its well-chronicled shortcomings, broadened the grounds of social action that is now increasingly reduced to a market logic that equates rights with market power.

One of the important contributions of a political economy perspective has been to document the process by which government and corporate power extend commodification. What this perspective needs to address more substantially than it has is how the process is linked to what takes place, as it were, at *the point of extension*. The use of political and economic power holds considerable explanatory value for understanding the success of commodification. The process reduces the resources, the time, and the space available to alternatives, so that commodification is perceived not as a process of power but as the natural order, common-sense, taken-for-granted reality of social life. This is an important argument, but the process of arriving at it foregoes an important step that takes us to the border of political economy and cultural studies. Institutional power, promoting one logic and eliminating alternatives, is central to the construction of a dominant view or *hegemony*. But there is also the question of the link between institutional power and the power that works on the multilayered relationship between use value and exchange value. Exchange value expands not only by undermining use or non-commodity values, but also by using these values to enhance its own attraction and, in the process, by transforming use to exchange values.

Consider how Crawford (1992) describes this process at work in a shopping mall. Research based in political economy documents the use of institutional power to change transportation, land use, investment, media, and other institutional policies to reconstruct patterns of shopping and, more generally, of social interaction around the shopping mall. Crawford gestures to this literature but concentrates on how the process of commodification works *inside* the mall. She offers an example from a shop window display that sets an ordinary pot in a Moroccan harem scene. This, she argues, decontextualizes the pot, thereby turning it into something unanticipated, exotic, and hence, stimulating. As she puts it:

> This logic of association allows noncommodified values to enhance commodities, but it also imposes the reverse process – previously noncommodified entities become part of the marketplace. Once this exchange of attributes is absorbed into the already open-ended and indeterminate exchange between commodities and needs, associations can resonate infinitely. (Crawford, 1992: 15)

The reference to infinite resonance exaggerates by turning an interactive process into runaway feedback. Numerous processes, including the recollection of our mundane experience with pots, can short-circuit this one. Moreover, the description of the process as "retail magic" idealizes something that is mutually constituted out of material use and images of association. Nevertheless, Crawford's description gives texture and nuance to the process of commodification by suggesting how it takes place at the point of extension where use value meets exchange value. It provides one means to deepen the analysis of a process whose general structure has been well described by political economists.

If Crawford's example provides a useful broadening at the boundary of political economy and cultural studies, two other tendencies are less productive. Since these bear directly on the process of commodification, it is useful to address them here rather than wait until Chapter 10 which takes up general challenges at political economy's borders. One unproductive tendency is to conflate commodification with universal tendencies to social reciprocity. The latter refers to a generalized sociality that binds people in exchange relationships. Proponents of this view (Davis, 1992; Schudson, 1984) tend to reference the anthropological literature on gift exchange rituals, such as the Potlatch, which suggests that the construction of markets and the development of exchange value are deeply rooted in more general processes of social group formation, i.e. the market is natural. From this vantage point, rather than a principal entry point for comprehending the social field, commodification is merely one among many expressions of a universal tendency to social exchange. This view is valuable in that it directs attention to the layers of ritual that adhere to social processes and contributes to their constitution (Davis, 1992).

In political economy, Veblen (1934/1899) put this approach to use in what are best appreciated as the anthropological insights of an ethnographer among the leisure and business classes. But Veblen recognized and steered clear of the temptation to conflate the general tendency to ritual exchange with its specific manifestation in the commodification process. He recognized that the former is an idealist trap, suggesting, in its abstract universality, that the dynamic processes of social transformation, which gave rise to capitalism, are less important than the general similarities among tribal, feudal, and capitalist societies. Veblen would appreciate this powerful irony: today academics aim to de-historicize exchange, diminish the concrete significance of the transformation to capitalism by referencing tribal practices in societies that capitalism has all but eliminated. Political economy acknowledges that the process of commodification involves ritual practices that can serve to tighten or loosen social bonds. Indeed, one of its primary criticisms against orthodox economics is the tendency to eliminate the power of custom and morality in economic life. However, political economy also aims to avoid idealism by focusing on the power contained in the historically specific substance and form that the process takes in mutual constitution with a capitalist society (Rucinski, 1991).

Another problematic tendency does the reverse by arguing for the universality of commodification in a form that replaces its traditional connection to the transformation of use to exchange value and the production of goods with the production of codes and the hegemony of sign value (Baudrillard, 1981). Offering the converse of an approach that would fold commodification into tribal ritual, Baudrillard proposes a radical mitosis in which objects and the labor process that gave rise to them break off and dissolve before the free-floating power of the sign. All is absorbed within a transformed process of commodification. He could not be more emphatic:

> The super-ideology of the sign and the general operation of the signifier – everywhere sanctioned today by the new master disciplines of structural linguistics, semiology, information theory and cybernetics – has replaced political economy as the theoretical basis of the system. (Baudrillard, 1975: 122)

This is not the place to examine the widespread debate over Baudrillard's position (see Gane, 2006; Kellner, 1989). Rather, it is more useful to consider the implications for the specific process of commodification. Here Baudrillard appears to support the view that the commodity has swept aside alternatives to its universal power and won out – a view that is shared by political economists of communication. However, political economists take issue with two fundamental dimensions of the argument. First, whether framed in the modernist discourse of universal contamination or the triumphalism of post-structuralist thought, the argument for the emergence of commodification suggests that there are no alternatives to this all-encompassing process. Commodification is everything, so make the best of it. Such an argument lacks a sense of the contradictions that emerge in the process of commodification and of alternative processes. Moreover, it is not clear just what the victory of the commodity actually means because the sense of the term changes fundamentally in Baudrillard's analysis. Particularly in his later work, Baudrillard replaces the process of using commodified wage labor to turn use into exchange value with a generalized social process that creates sign value. But to the extent that it holds a specific meaning, sign value is limited to the needs of capital to produce a dense, hierarchical system of meanings, of status identifications, in order to cement its power. However warranted as one reading of political economy, it purchases this warrant by eliminating two fundamental considerations of political economy – the existence of human needs, which emerge in use values and which constitute the standpoint of political economy from the viewpoint of the working class, and an institutional system organized around transforming use into exchange value for the purpose of producing surplus value or political economy from the standpoint of capital.

Consider, once again, Veblen, whose influence Baudrillard acknowledges but whose analysis of status he treats as an independent ground of social organization without what Veblen saw as its fundamental foundation – the existence of human need and an institutionalized political economy that supports and subverts it. In Baudrillard, the process of commodification is reduced to the free-floating circulation of symbols, an outcome obscured by the misappropriation of political economy's conceptual apparatus, itself reduced to a set of free-floating terms, torn from their historically constituted and specific meanings, to add weight to an otherwise light argument. Instead of escaping into the hopeless conclusion that commodification is everything, it is more useful for political economy to firmly establish its understanding that the commodity is not everything, that genuine alternatives exist and that they should be pursued.

Alternative Processes in Private and Public Life

Critics of political economy, including those who resist its use in communication studies, have consistently raised concerns that it has tendencies to essentialism. The argument is put in many ways, but, with respect to communication research, it rejects the idea that one can reduce all communication and cultural practices to an underlying or more fundamental political economic reality which encompasses the process of commodification (*Critical Studies in Mass Communication*, 1995). Earlier chapters offered evidence that this view is overstated. Both general political economy and its application in communication contain rich, diverse, and comprehensive bodies of research that are not at all reducible to simple categorizations or simplistic charges. Specifically, commodification transforms media content, but does not reduce it to a singularity that would allow one to interpret media content directly from the commodification process. By beginning with commodification, this chapter has established a theoretical frame of reference, even as it recognizes the multiple determination and mutual constitution of all processes. The chapter now proceeds to identify additional processes and their accompanying structures that are made up of alternative and oppositional practices.

One of the more valuable theoretical suggestions in this area addresses the role of the state in what Offe calls the process of "administrative recommodification." For Offe, a period of laissez-faire, which emphasized the market as the solution to most problems, is inevitably followed by *decommodification* or the "socialization" of political economic life. This takes place in response to instabilities and conflicts brought about by failures in the overwhelming reliance on the market mechanism. The collapse of banks and investment firms which succumbed to the crisis in housing and lending in 2007–08 led to government intervention to nationalize or otherwise assist failing financial institutions like Northern Rock in the UK and Bear Stearns in the United States. It also included assistance to homeowners unable to meet mortgage payments. Decommodification involves the creation of social policies and programs to protect the economic existence of social actors, in the ranks of both capital and labor, including those who are by and large incapable or unable to participate in commodification. However, the transfer payments and other sources of income that prevent these people from "dropping out" of the process prove to be fiscally unsustainable in the longer term. Moreover, Offe maintains, the process proves to be politically unsustainable because it is practically impossible to politically regulate the economy without materially politicizing it (Offe, 1984: 35–64). As a result, Offe sees capital responding with *recommodification*, that is, "to solve the problem of the commodity form by politically creating conditions under which legal and economic subjects can function as commodities" (Offe, 1984: 124).

Specifically, this calls for a set of programs intended to enhance the market value of labor, integrate and concentrate transnational capital, support those with the propensity to consume, and permit the exclusion of those who fail the market test. However, according to him, these are only partially successful because the state is caught up in trying to use non-market means to advance the market and must pay, however indirectly, the price of exclusionary practices, e.g. crime control and prison expansion. Moreover, as critiques of bureaucratization dating back to Max Weber have demonstrated, the result is often that non-market mechanisms, initiated as a means, become ends in themselves and undermine the recommodification process. This brings about its own government response, particularly prominent in the 1990s and the early years of this century, that amounts to the application of market principles to the state in the expectation that if the state took on the look of a market enterprise, it would advance market principles. The problem, one that Offe returns to time and time again, is that although the state can be made to *look* like a market enterprise, there are fundamental limits on its ability to *act* like one, primarily because the state is ruled out of direct accumulation. In other words, when the state succeeds as a capitalist, i.e. by making money, capitalism pressures the state to cease competing with private enterprise.

Offe's arguments, echoed in others (Jessop, 2001), take a step toward correcting the essentialism inherent in the assertion of a simple, deterministic process of commodification. Nevertheless, it is limited to the demonstration that social change comes about from the limits of commodification and the limits on genuine social change in a capitalist society always lead back to commodification. Are there genuine alternatives to commodification in private and in public life?

Social Process in Private Life

The remainder of this chapter draws out tendencies in contemporary social thought and communication scholarship that point to alternatives to commodification. They suggest that commodification, although powerful and pervasive, is not a singularity. These alternatives are each generally linked to use value and specifically to what we typically call private and public life. Private life refers specifically to the process of face-to-face interaction, what Habermas (1989) calls the domain of the life-world (*lebenswelt*) or, in phenomenological sociology, the realm of intersubjectivity. Processes based in private life are typically affective ones that center around identity formation, friendship, and kinship. The emphasis is placed on how people and objects, both material and symbolic, are valued as ends in themselves and not for their market value. Those that emanate from public life tend to be civic processes that bring people together to exchange ideas, govern themselves, support, resist, oppose, and attempt to create alternatives to what Habermas (1989) calls the organization of power and money in the "system" world. One of the central alternatives to the process of commodification in the private sphere is the constitution of friendship and kinship; in the public sphere, it is citizenship.

One of the challenges facing the attempt to address the relationship between commodification and social processes at work in private and public life is overcoming the inclination to mechanized thinking embodied most powerfully in the general tendency to reduce the discussion simply to the dichotomy between private and public. One of the major problems with this is that the term private has taken on the burden of including both the most intimate of human experience and the market behavior of the transnational business system. Both are part of the private sphere. It is easy for the idea to collapse under such weight and it seriously constrains the ability to comprehend the wider implications of commodification. We would be much better off to eliminate the term "private sector" and reserve private for the sphere of intimacy and identify business with the "market sector" or something similar. The division among private, public, and market spheres is not perfect but is certainly an improvement over the private–public dichotomy. But given the power and the inertia of popular usage, it is not easy to be optimistic about remedying the problems associated with the term private and with the mechanical dichotomy between private and public life. Consider this one small step in the direction of doing so.

The structure of communication studies, reflecting divisions within the social sciences, makes it particularly difficult to conceptualize the relationship between private processes and commodification, as well as those that mark public life. This is because the discipline tends to be organized along levels of social complexity which set apart interpersonal from organizational and institutional communication. Although there are exceptions, it is generally the case that interpersonal communication, like microsociology, is set apart as the sphere within which one can examine affect and intimacy. Affect and intimacy gradually lose their significance as one leaves the interpersonal level of analysis. By the time one reaches political economy, located at the upper levels of social complexity, the issues taken up at the micro or interpersonal level virtually disappear. This is significant for the broadest conception of political economy's mission because it restricts both theoretical comprehensiveness and social praxis (Eagleton, 2003). Without a direct encounter with the interpersonal, political economy has little to say about that realm of experience, the realm of affect, and therefore little to say about the consequences for action among people who experience an enormous gap between what takes place at the institutional levels of power, the traditionally central focus of political economy, and their daily existence as a series of encounters in small groups, with mediated presentations of word and image, and with themselves.

Over the years, the concern over mediating the institutional and the personal has taken up considerable theoretical reflection. Back in 1959, the sociologist C. Wright Mills began one of the classic works in sociology by identifying as a central problem in modern society the inability of people to connect private well-being and problems with "historical change and institutional contradiction ... the big ups and downs of the societies in which they live." It is hard, he went on, to live up to our potential to change history when we are unable to connect our lives to it (Mills, 1959: 3). To remedy this problem, we continue to observe the growth of work within social science on identity, including the politics of identity and self-identity (Calhoun, 1994; Castells, 2004; Giddens, 1991; Hall, 1989; Van Galen and Noblit, 2007; Woodward, 2004). There are numerous reasons for this, including a tendency which Hall (1989: 12) observes, that "the great social collectivities which used to stabilize our identities – the great stable collectivities of class, race, gender, and nation – have been, in our times, deeply undermined by social and political developments." Globalization is frequently cited as the major socio-political development propelling this destabilization. Moreover, the rise of feminism, especially the political and intellectual drive to overcome the prominent division in social thought under patriarchy which separates the personal from the political, has played a leading role in the ensuing ferment over these developments and the process and possibility of reconstitution. Finally, the growth of new media which enables the creation of virtual worlds in cyberspace makes possible the development of many persona situated throughout virtual communities.

There is considerable room to debate the issues raised by this literature. For example, given globalization, the feminist movement, and the digital media, one can understand how Hall was correct to call attention to the destabilization of subjective identities. But it is also the case, as political economy has demonstrated, that *capitalism has always destabilized identities* and that, in terms of education, income, power, and general life chances, social class, race, and gender matter now as much or even more than they ever have.

Conservative and liberal thinkers have offered their own specific solutions to the problem of the divided self (Bell, 1976). The former call for a return to traditions that historically provided moral anchors for the self in private life. The latter tend to argue for more communication, viewing participation in networks of flows, including the social networking sites that form digital communities today, as improvements on the more rigid and absolutist ties that bound people in the past (Castells, 2001; Jenkins, 2006). Since the 1970s, more radical forms of thinking, embodied in the movements called postmodernism and post-structuralism, have addressed the problems of private life by accepting the inevitability of fracture, division, and deconstruction and, instead of attacking these with old values or new communication, they value the freedom it provides. This includes the freedom from the need to construct and maintain a single identity (McGowan, 1991; Newman, 2007).

Political economy has struggled with these issues. Better equipped to examine commodification's assault on private life than to figure out how to resist and create alternatives, it has suffered the consequences of being left out of an important debate. When it has engaged these issues, it has been to chide the varieties of cultural theory for choosing to focus so intensely on how everything solid seems to melt into air, on how all grand narratives are dissolving, that they tend to miss the 800-pound gorilla in the room, capitalism, which is more alive than ever as a solid global force and as a grand narrative.

A more positive alternative would be for political economy to return to the anchors of critical social thought by creating alternatives to commodification in a lived experience that includes the moral, the libidinal, and the aesthetic. These interact with more distinctly social forms like social class, race, ethnicity, gender, and the social movements with which we might identify. Provided that we view these not as rigid categories given to us but as social relationships that we create to make both history and ourselves, they can help us to make the connection between the personal and the political (Eagleton, 2003: 222). This would enable political economy to speak of a contested terrain in which the processes at work in private life meet commodification in a contested terrain of ongoing tension. Furthermore, one can push beyond the mapping of this tension to the point of resistance, which O'Connor describes in this way:

> This moment of crisis is precisely when transformation into a social individuality becomes possible. ... At this moment, one can externalize the internal struggle, or know and feel that the ways in which one suffers are also the ways in which others suffer, grasp suffering as a social process, externalizing suffering through social and political struggle. (1987: 181–2)

Two significant problems continue to confront the political economist of communication regarding this resistance. How is it organized and how is it expressed? For this we turn from private to public life.

Social Process in Public Life

Social theory and communication research have taken up public life as a set of processes that advance fundamental characteristics of democracy, i.e. social equality and the fullest possible participation in the decisions that affect our lives. It is thereby a form of resistance to commodification and provides guidance on the development of alternative social practices. The work of Habermas (1989) on the public sphere is particularly important because it has examined the idea critically and has provided the conceptual tools that help to restore an historic debate on public life and citizenship. His work attracts the attention of communication scholars partly because he maintains that communication, or the "ideal speech situation," provides the foundation for a flourishing public sphere. He also concludes that the contemporary commodified mass media, along with the general expansion of consumerism and of the bureaucratic state, are root causes of its decline. Habermas began a debate on the public sphere and others have improved on the idea by incorporating women, the non-Western world, and other features that would give it a more universal or cosmopolitan scope (Crossley and Roberts, 2004; Negt and Kluge, 1972; Peiss, 1991). But not all are satisfied with this. Some would discard the notion as hopelessly compromised, reduced as Derrida (see Keenan, 1993) says of public opinion to the "silhouette of a phantom." Another attempt to critically advance the idea views the public sphere as a set of principles, including democracy, equality, participation, and citizenship, that point to an alternative to the set of practices bound up with commodification. The latter has been the most prominent position taken in communication research, particular by those with an interest in political economy (Calabrese and Burgelman, 1999; Calabrese and Sparks, 2004; McChesney, 2007). This work addresses the use of the press and new media, as well as systems of regulation and policy, to create oppositional spaces for the development of a public sphere. Communication research has also been interested in the concept of the *public interest*, a term with roots in the law governing regulation of the communication industries. The notion has received extensive treatment, including criticism for ambiguity, particularly when set against the seemingly clearer test of the marketplace. The public interest idea nevertheless survives in law, though the process of commodification has weakened its standing. It also survives in research as an extension of the public sphere notion to refer to those interests that transcend commercial gain and consumerism.

The debate on the public sphere is undeniably one of the more significant intellectual currents in social thought today. This is partly because it constitutes a widespread movement to develop substantial alternatives in social life to the market and the process of commodification. But it is also an exasperating debate because the public sphere umbrella covers the widest range of definitions and positionings. For some, it opposes both the state and the market; for others, it is aligned with one or the other. For example, Herbert Schiller (1989) offered a powerful critique of the state, but also pointed to the value of government-operated public institutions, such as public libraries and public schools and universities, that have suffered from the attacks of commercialism. On the other hand, Andrew Ross (1993) made the case for viewing the market as an oppositional force to repressive forms of regulation. Depending on the theorist, the public sphere encompasses civil society, is encompassed by it, or is distinct from it. It can occupy physical space, institutional space, or electronic cyberspace. It includes the widest range of social behavior from debate on central public issues to shopping and music videos. Notwithstanding these problems, the alternative, scrapping the idea altogether, is less appealing.

The problem is how to address whatever *it* is. Or, since it is popular to think of it as a sphere, *where* it is. My view is that the latter question raises a critical problem with the notion of a public sphere. The tendency is to think of it as an object that occupies a specifiable space, whether physical, social, electronic, or mythical. Defenders of the public sphere sound like they are protecting a territory from a powerful, hostile invader whose goal is conquest. The analogy works to help one comprehend how the market and the public are opposed. But it suffers when it leads one to think of the market and the public as objects that occupy specific places, that are themselves difficult, if not impossible, to pin down. As a result of this difficulty, positions change about what is in or out of the public sphere. The term "public" is far from unambiguous, but the problem appears to be less with it than with the idea of a sphere, however it is specified.

One way to address the problem is to define the public sphere as a set of social processes that carry out democracy, namely advancing equality and the fullest possible participation in the complete range of economic, political, social, and cultural decision-making. These processes are distinct from those centered in private life, which promote interpersonal intimacy, and from those of the marketplace, which advance the creation of exchange and surplus value. The value of thinking in process terms is that, while there may be a greater likelihood that equality and participation adhere to some institutional forms and spaces rather than others, it does not rule out, by definition, any structural embodiment or location. The latter are better viewed as contested terrains, whether the state, the marketplace, or those structures, such as social movements, that manage to distance themselves from both state and market, in which the processes of commodification and democracy contend. All can be sites of the struggle between one's identity as, for example, a consumer and as a citizen.

Thinking in terms of a public process is difficult because the alternatives, clearly distinguished institutions and structures, give a concrete sense to what can otherwise be viewed as an idealist abstraction. More than that, they provide a road-map which, however often it needs to be revised, offers guidance on getting from one point to the next, suggesting what course to follow and what to avoid. Nevertheless, institutions and structures can also offer false security. It is now fashionable to argue that the state in advanced capitalist societies, to which many once turned for alternatives to commodification, is hopelessly compromised, if not thoroughly market-contaminated and bureaucratized beyond any likelihood of realizing anything more than formal democracy. And, as the US presidential elections of 2000 and 2004 demonstrated, even the formal democracy of voting in elections appears compromised. As a result, the search for oppositional and alternative forms, including media and culture, must be found outside, in places that have managed to maintain some distance from both state and market. There is considerable substance to the charge against the state and much to be said about finding uncontaminated spaces. Depending on how you define free, i.e. how much contamination can be absorbed before free space turns into market or state space, the free spaces in communication include traditional forms, such as the alternative press, public service (as opposed to state controlled) broadcasting, as well as new forms, like public access cable channels and computer networks that open an electronic meeting place through blogging and social networking. The problem with seeing these as embodiments of free space is that, in non-trivial ways, they are neither free nor spaces. The alternative press may be the most free but, depending on state practice, makes use of mail subsidies and direct government grants, as well as market support mechanisms that include subscription fees, advertising, and commodified labor processes and distribution networks. Again, depending on the jurisdiction, public service broadcasting depends on user fees, government grants, commercial advertising, and government appointment of major management personnel, who are often required to demonstrate their ability to meet either political or market criteria of success. Public access cable channels produce demonstrably more diverse content, but they are limited to those who can afford a cable subscription fee and, again, depending on the jurisdiction, are subject to the oversight of both the cable operating company and government regulators. Interactive computer networks are particularly constrained by market and class considerations. They require access to computers and to telecommunications, and either the ability to pay for communication charges or the privileged access of the university professor whose charges are underwritten by the state, by universities (which are the recipients of considerable state support), or by companies trying to create a market in new forms of communication.

It is important to emphasize that these media provide major forms of alternative and oppositional communication. Nevertheless, by looking at them as free spaces, we tend to miss the significant ways in which the unequal structure of representation, of hierarchies organized according to class, gender, and race, are replicated, admittedly with specific variations, within each of these media forms. Additionally, it also draws attention away from struggles that take place over resistance to commodification in both state and market. Here is where the contributions of political economists are so telling because they have addressed media, communication, and information issues in the contested terrain at the heart of state activities, including public education, public libraries, government information, and the social welfare system. Furthermore, research on commercial speech and design describe the contested nature of the commodification process within the innermost regions of the market. It is, above all, research that starts from the lived experiences of people who today confront the clash of opposing processes in schools, in shopping malls, in social service agencies, and on the job, as much as they do in alternative media and computer networks. Moreover, one of the central lessons of this work is that the market, the state, and the public are, in a real sense, located everywhere and therefore have no fixed coordinates. This should discourage the tendency to think about finding free space, or about looking for that ideal social form, whether located in a privileged class, or in a new social movement, that might represent a particularly stronger or purer manifestation of social opposition.

This should also encourage thinking about social processes, those vectors of social action that form different relationships in different dimensions of social life. The public sphere is more usefully conceptualized as a set of processes constituted out of the agency of people organized and identified as citizens, and which promotes equality and participation, the core of democracy. These processes exist only in relationship to a social field whose primary entry point, commodification, gives it pattern and initial shape, but a relationship that is nevertheless continuously reconstituted out of the interaction between commodification and social processes in public and private life. It is a social field from the standpoint of commodification, but a standpoint that is mutually constituted by private and public life. What we call the public media is public, not because it occupies a separate space, relatively free from market considerations, but because it is constituted out of a particular patterning of processes that privilege the democratic over commodification. To the extent that it does not, the expression *public media* diminishes in value.

Whereas resistance to commodification in private life is founded on building alternatives based on intimacy and personal relationships, like friendship, resistance to commodification in public life is founded on democracy and citizenship. Democracy is another complex notion, one that is also often conflated with technology. The more people use the Internet or the cell phone, the story goes, the more likely they are to participate more actively in social life. In addition, the definition of democracy is often narrowed to a particular practice, voting, that is merely one embodiment of democracy. We need to approach democracy, as we approached communication, as socially grounded and profoundly broader than the act of voting. Specifically, this means seeing democracy as the fullest possible public participation in the decisions that affect our lives. This includes the political arena, but it also means the fullest possible participation in the economy, in society, and in culture. Certainly, the act of voting is an important social assertion of political democracy, but its ability to bring about democracy is limited when wealth is concentrated in the hands of a few. In other words, concentrated market power diminishes the popular power that voting is supposed to bring about. Similarly, when cultural power is concentrated in the hands of a few, as is the case when a handful of companies own a nation's major newspapers, broadcasting, telecommunication, and computer companies, voting is also distinctly limited in what it can accomplish. This means ideological hegemony is perpetuated and defended by the same power brokers who control the most substantial means of communication. For democracy to flourish, society needs to create the conditions for relative equality and civic participation across the political, economic, and cultural spheres. Extremes of wealth and deep divides in power make full public participation in decision-making nearly impossible, including participation in worker organizations and trade unions. But even when relative equality applies, societies face a risk that democracy will stagnate without the institutions and traditions that make widespread participation possible.

Democracy is mutually constituted with citizenship. T.H. Marshall (1964) made what has become the standard contribution here and political economy has built upon it. He noted that citizenship began as a legal notion that conveyed certain rights, including such fundamental ones as habeas corpus, due process under the law, the presumption of innocence, and the right to a trial by a jury of one's peers. Over time and much social struggle, these legal rights were extended into the political arena, with the right to vote and to participate in political life. Today, the struggles center on extending these rights to new areas, such as the economic, to include ideas like the right to a job, to membership in an organization that represents the interests of workers, and to a standard of living that meets basic needs. These struggles are also addressed to expanding social citizenship, which includes the right to community and to the existence and use of public space. Finally, trade unions and social movements have connected citizenship to a set of communication rights, including the right to communicate (not just to receive information) and to those services that make the right to communicate possible, such as the right to education and to the means of communication, including universal public postal services, universal access to the telephone, and now to the Internet. It is worth noting that citizenship may also be used as an exclusive concept, not just an inclusive one: in other words, as a way of dividing "us" from "them." This can be done positively, in order to build internal solidarity, or negatively as a means to exclude people from the benefits of membership in a collective. However, on balance, the struggle over citizenship in the political, economic, and social realm more often represents a struggle for inclusion, focused on the effort to extend the right to fully participate in all areas of society.

Conclusion

The political economy of communication accepts the reality of the abstract ideas that guide our thinking, as well as the concrete observations that we perceive with our senses. It declines to accept the position, prominent in some theories, that only our ideas or only our observations, but not both, are real. Political economy also rejects the view that there is no reality, that neither ideas nor empirical observations are, in any important sense, real. Moreover, this philosophy means that reality is comprised of many elements and cannot be reduced to one essence. Neither economics (e.g. money controls the media) nor culture (e.g. people's values shape the media) contains the only key to unlock our understanding of communication. This philosophical foundation also places in the foreground the ideas of social change, social process, and social relations. Doing so requires re-evaluating the emphasis that political economy has historically placed on social institutions, like media businesses, or on seeeing social class as a thing or structure, rather than as a social relationship.

Commodification is the entry point from which to begin to theorize the political economy of communication. Commodification is defined as the process of transforming goods and services, including communication, which are valued for their use, into commodities which are valued for what they will bring in the marketplace. There are three types of commodification that are important to communication: the commodification of content, of audiences, and of labor. Commodities give rise to new commodities, in what is called immanent commodification, and they are created in association with non-commodified goods and services, in what is called external commodification. There are alternatives to commodification in private life through the cultivation of intimacy, friendship, and kinship and in public life through the development of democracy and citizenship. Building on this foundation, the next chapter takes up a second entry point, the process of spatialization.

8

SPATIALIZATION: SPACE, TIME, AND COMMUNICATION

Commodification is the starting or entry point for the political economy of communication. As such, it opens a field of analysis that includes processes emanating from private and public life which relate to one another and to commodification. This chapter takes up the entry point of spatialization, a term introduced by the social theorist Henri Lefebvre (1979) to denote *the process of overcoming the constraints of space and time in social life*. Spatialization holds special significance for the political economist of communication because communication is one of the primary means of bringing about spatialization throughout society and, because of this, spatialization makes the communication industries especially significant.

Although there is probably more interest in spatialization now than there has been in the past, social scientists, including political economists, have paid attention to it for some time. The question of how to measure the value of land and labor time, as well as how to understand the relationship between the spatial extension of markets and the division of labor, were central issues for Adam Smith, David Ricardo, and other classical political economists. We find a closer approximation to the concept of spatialization in Karl Marx, who, in *The Grundrisse* (1973) remarked on the tendency of capitalism to "annihilate space with time." This refers to the growing power of capitalism to use and improve on the means of transportation and communication, to shrink the time it takes to move goods, people, and messages over space, thereby diminishing the significance of spatial distance as a constraint on the expansion of capital. Among political economists who developed this theme, the Canadian political economist Harold Innis (1972) stands out for his sustained effort to establish the connections among forms of media, time, and space, and structures of power. Contemporary political economy (Harvey, 2006) has amended the Marxian view by suggesting that rather than annihilate space, capital transforms it, by restructuring the spatial relationships among people, goods, and messages. In the process of restructuring, capitalism transforms itself.[1]

---

1 We should not make too much of Marx's reference to *annihilating* space. He recognized that in practice this meant a shift in the balance of attention that capital would direct to different spaces, specifically to new markets:

The use of the term spatialization draws on concepts and arguments that social scientists with an interest in the global political economy, and especially in communication, have taken up over the past two decades. For example, the sociologist Anthony Giddens (1990) made use of the term *time–space distanciation* in order to examine how time and space have diminished as a controlling influence in the world. The ease of emailing someone halfway around the world suggests that time and space are better viewed as flexible resources (Giddens, 2000; Hutton and Giddens, 2000). The geographer David Harvey's description (1989) of *time–space compression* strikes a similar chord, but with a stronger interest in the political economic implications, such as for an international banking system that, among other things, manages trillions of dollars, euros yen, and yuan, moving over electronic highways that know few of the limitations of time and space. The social theorist of information technology, Manuel Castells (1989, 2002), has drawn attention to the declining significance of physical space relative to what he calls *the space of flows* which enable organizations to build local and global networks that are not dependent on any specific locale. Once the movement of goods required bodies of water for their flow, and while cargo continues to flow down the Mississippi river to the port of New Orleans, such specific locations are no longer central to the flows that constitute today's political economy. The feminist geographer Doreen Massey (1992, 2005) refers to space in relational terms, comprising sets of dynamic social relations organized in a "power-geometry." She has noted how this conception differs from the traditional gendered conception of space as simply the absence of time, "the slice through time, Mother Earth dependent on time's dynamism for its ability to change." Finally, the political economist of space Saskia Sassen (2007) has mapped the new networks of finance capital, global cities, as well as movements to resist the spread of a business-led form of globalization in favor of a more democratic vision.

—— Communication and Concentration: Space as Institutional Extension ——

In general terms, spatialization research has addressed the geographic and institutional extension of organizational activity. The political economy of communication has specifically taken up spatialization, chiefly in terms of *the institutional extension of corporate power in the communication industry*. This is manifested in the sheer growth in the size of media firms, measured by assets, revenues, profit, employees, and the value of their shares in financial markets. Political economy placed the most emphasis on studying different forms of *corporate concentration* or the ways companies strengthen their organization to dominate markets. The primary reason for this focus is to better understand how power works in the communication industry and because corporate concentration has significant consequences for society. Corporate concentration permits companies to better control the production, distribution, and

---

the opportunities created by the development of transport and communication facilities make it imperative, conversely, to work for evermore remote markets, in a word – for the world market. (In *Grundrisse*, de la Haye, 1980: 156)

exchange of communication, and also limits competition and therefore the diversity of information and entertainment available in society. Although both growth and concentration are central features of the contemporary communication map, concern about the social consequences of these developments is not new. For example, over a century ago, Honoré de Balzac criticized the Charles Havas monopoly on French wire service copy because it led to a decline in information sources.

The simplest form of concentration takes place when a media firm buys a controlling interest in a company operating principally in the same business.[2] The *New York Times* purchase of the *Boston Globe* newspaper is a prime example of this basic form. Traditional thinking examines the major different types of concentration according to their *horizontal* and *vertical* forms. Nevertheless, although these terms are used widely, it is important to underscore the point that there is less than complete agreement on concepts, definitions, and applications in this area. This is partly due to the underdeveloped state of research on media concentration, which, in some measure, results from the media industry's ability to influence the research agenda, leaving us with more studies on how to market products than on the nature and implications of media concentration. The lack of conceptual agreement is also partly the consequence of a rapidly changing industry. Changes in industry structure, technology, services, as well as in state policy and regulation (which typically lags these changes), have made it difficult to provide a generally agreed upon language for mapping media concentration.

Taking into account the limited agreement on terminology, we can consider some of the major ways people have thought about media concentration. Horizontal concentration takes place when a firm in one line of media buys a major interest in another media operation, not directly related to the original business, or when it takes a major stake in a company entirely outside the media.[3] The typical example of the first or *cross-media* concentration is the purchase by a firm in an older media line, say a newspaper, of a firm in a newer one, such as a radio or television station. This is one way an industry like newspaper publishing is able to remain profitable in the face of newer media forms, exemplified in the purchase of the Twentieth Century Fox Film Corporation and the social networking site MySpace by Rupert Murdoch's News Corporation. Horizontal concentration also takes place when a media firm moves on a company entirely outside the media business or when a media firm is swallowed up by a non-media business. For example, in 2007 Google acquired Panoramio, a company that enables digital photographers to geolocate, store, and organize their photographs, an acquisition that better enabled Google to use images in Google Earth and Google Maps. An example of a non-media takeover occurred when the General Electric Company, an electronics firm and a major defense contractor, purchased the Radio Corporation of

---

2 The definition of a controlling interest or major stake varies widely, from as little as 2 per cent in a company with widely dispersed shareholders to 51 per cent or more, which gives a company majority control of stock and consequently of the board of directors.

3 The phrase "not directly related" is significant for more than definitional reasons because the purchase of a related firm could diminish the degree of competition in one or more markets. Conversely, one could argue that the purchase of a related firm is more likely to increase market efficiency because it would enable the purchaser to rationalize operations.

America (RCA), a company it actually once owned in the 1920s. This form of horizontal concentration results in the creation or expansion of *conglomerate* ownership, a product of the amalgamation of firms in different lines of business.

Vertical integration describes the concentration of firms within a line of business that extend a company's control over the process of production. Time-Warner's purchase of CNN gave the former greater opportunities to distribute its news product. Similarly, the purchase by the ABC television network of the ESPN collection of sports television and radio networks expanded opportunities and cost savings in sports programming. This is also referred to as forward integration because it expands a firm further along the circuit required for the realization of value. Backward vertical integration took place when the *Washington Post* purchased paper mills in Nova Scotia, Canada, thereby expanding the company's control down to the base of the production process. Depending on its ability to manage the flows among stages in production, a company can gain a competitive advantage from the opportunities that vertical integration offers to rationalize its operations. By owning program production companies, television networks are guaranteed a supply of product at prices that offer few surprises. This holds as well for telephone companies that own equipment suppliers, for film companies whose control over exhibitors provides a guaranteed outlet for their products, and for computer companies that own websites.

These forms of integration are essentially a means of controlling uncertainties that arise when a company has to rely on external markets to complete the circuit of production (Wayne, 2003). Business historians have long recognized the significance of this process in the development of, depending on the interpretation, corporate, managerial, organized, or monopoly capitalism. For example, Chandler (1977) has documented management strategies that produced integrated companies, such as DuPont, General Motors, and Sears, which succeeded in dominating industries over several decades. According to him, what stands out in an examination of their success was a management strategy to seal off the company from many external market uncertainties produced by, for example, several strong competitors along the circuit of production. They also created markets within this protected environment by requiring competition among product line divisions. General Motors succeeded where others failed, in part, because vertical and horizontal integration protected it from competition *and* because it created an internal market in which its Oldsmobile, Pontiac, Chevrolet, and Cadillac divisions competed as independent product lines responsible for meeting individual growth targets. The Executive Committee of the corporate board served as the manager and banker to this integrated multidivisional corporate form, assessing success and shifting resources accordingly.[4] According to Chandler,

---

4 Chandler contrasts successful firms which tended to make the shift to a multidivisional quasi-market arrangement with those firms, such as Ford, which were less successful, in spite of a significant measure of integration. In his view, the latter neglected the internal market by retaining a functional corporate structure divided according to traditional finance, marketing, production, and accounting lines, which precluded, or made much more difficult, intracorporate competition.

companies that instituted this structure enjoyed many of the benefits of internal market competition even as they reduced the uncertainties of hostile competition from outside the corporation. Chandler, along with other business historians (see also Brunn and Leinbach, 1991; Yates, 1989, 2005), also acknowledges that communication and information technology, as well as transportation systems, have been central to these processes, because they have given management the tools to control the speed and the form of integration. Rapid and efficient communication systems are essential for a company to manage the multiplicity of exchanges that flow within an integrated, multidivisional corporation whose success depends on timely assessments of relative performance, e.g. which division has the best return on capital and why.

The postwar acceleration in *multinational* enterprises introduced another form of media industry growth that increasingly occupies communication scholars. As Smith (1991), Tunstall (1977), and Winseck and Pike (2007) have demonstrated, transnational media enterprises are as old as the mass media itself. The production and distribution of news in the nineteenth century was controlled in large measure by three international press conglomerates – the British Reuters, the French Havas, and the German Wolf – which divided the world's markets into monopoly zones that, for a considerable time, kept out the competition.[5] This tendency has expanded in recent decades as communication firms seek out new markets for products, low-cost labour, and areas with minimal government oversight and regulation. The media industries have been particularly important to the general process of transnationalization because media, directly through advertising, but indirectly as well in all forms of media, call attention to products in general, in addition to the specific media product for sale. Moreover, the means of communication, including new technologies such as communication satellites and high-capacity cables, have made it cost-effective and easier for firms, including most of the communication industry, to operate efficiently across several borders. It remains the case that the largest transnational media firms retain a base in one generally identified nation. Nevertheless, they are increasingly able to use the genuine multinational dimensions of their product, marketing, labor, and financing to transcend the legal, regulatory, cultural, and financial constraints of their home base.

One obvious consequence is the rise of massively large global corporations that operate in many different areas of media, communication, and information. These include Time Warner, Bertelsman, News Corporation, Walt Disney, Sony, Google, Microsoft, General Electric, and Viacom, among others. Firms like these integrate vertically by securing control over production, distribution, and exhibition; horizontally across a range of media products, including hardware and software; and globally

---

5 The United States chafed the most under the worldwide press cartel, demanding, as many of the world's poor nations would demand decades later of the United States, that size and assets alone should not be permitted to determine who controlled the production and distribution of information (Schiller, 1976: 26–9; see also Cooper, 1942).

by taking advantage of an international division of labor that makes possible the flexible and cost-effective use of labor, capital, research, and development. They embody enormous concentrated economic power. Nevertheless, the conglomerate form is not the only or even the most effective form of corporate response to global restructuring. The integrated conglomerate benefits from competition within, as it flexes its market power without. But it does so at a price. Big mergers often mean taking on big debt. Moreover, although the conglomerate form provides for enormous flexibility, it can also develop bureaucratic tendencies that restrict more innovative units, as the conglomerate ITT learned in the 1970s, IBM in the 1980s, Microsoft in the 1990s, and Time Warner in the new century.

Political economists have been interested in many different forms of concentration. Nevertheless, there has been an overwhelming interest in *ownership* as the primary defining element in media concentration. This is chiefly because of the concern that ownership concentration can restrict the flow of communication and information by limiting the diversity of producers and distributors. Hence, research on the variety of vertical, horizontal, and transnational forms of concentration tends to emanate from debate on the consequences of ownership concentration. There are, however, significant differences in the measurement of concentration and in the assessment of its significance. One can focus on how much of the market a firm controls, the size of the firm, or the diversity of the products in the marketplace. Nevertheless, the unit of analysis in all of these measures is the firm, under ownership that is discernibly different from that of other firms in the market. For example, in a newspaper market, a daily owned by Murdoch's News Corporation and one under the Gannett banner would be considered competitors; two Gannett papers would not. Although the market is foregrounded, the unit that provides the test of concentration remains the firm.

A broader conception of concentration takes into account the market, but shifts attention to the degree of ownership concentration that enables firms to make use of resources based on operations in a *range of markets*. Moreover, it shifts the focus from the sheer multiplicity of products (how many of the same product) to their *diversity* (how different are they). For example, this approach weighs more heavily the ability of *The Wall Street Journal*, a unit of the News Corporation, to draw on the resources of the parent and its divisions for product, financing, and political lobbying power. *The Wall Street Journal* is thereby a fundamentally different firm from one without these connections. Yet, for the purpose of a market-specific analysis, it is treated like any other discretely owned entity.

Moreover, the broader form of concentration analysis shifts attention from the sheer number of conduits into a market, to the diversity of content provided by whatever number of channels. It follows from this view that one cable television firm with an ownership monopoly in a market, but also with a wide range of different voices reflected in its various channels, constitutes less concentration than a market with several newspapers that, although under different ownership, offer essentially the same point of view. It is more difficult to measure such forms of concentration (what constitutes the same or a different point of view?), but the more narrow view, with its indices of market share, provides a mechanistic and inadequate barometer of concentration.[6]

However differently approached, the narrow and broad views of concentration share a primary focus on ownership as the central measure of concentration. One major exception to this tendency is the broader view's interest in the analysis of *corporate boards of directors*. Rather than examine who owns the media, the goal of this approach is to map relationships among members of the body holding primary responsibility for corporate performance. Although the law governing what corporate boards of directors must do varies from jurisdiction to jurisdiction, most boards select the highest level of management, including the chief executive officer, and decide on major budget allocations, such as capital outlays and retrenchments. The latter includes decisions to build or to close plants and offices. Boards are formally selected by shareholders, but, in practice, it is the board itself that generally succeeds in determining its own composition. Board size varies with the size and diversity of the company, with a range of ten to forty members common. The chief distinction within the board of directors is between *inside* members, who are part of management, and *outside* directors, who are generally executives with other firms, though this category might also include token representation from civil society groups.

For example, the board of directors of Time Warner as of January 1, 2008 included the following people:

Richard D. Parsons, Chairman of the Board, Time Warner Inc.
James L. Barksdale, Chairman and President, Barksdale Management Corporation
Jeffrey L. Bewkes, President and Chief Executive Officer, Time Warner Inc.
Stephen F. Bollenbach, Co-Chairman and Chief Executive Officer of Hilton Hotels Corporation – 2004–07
Frank J. Caufield, Co-Founder and Partner, Kleiner Perkins Caufield & Byers
Robert C. Clark, Distinguished Service Professor, Harvard University
Mathias Döpfner, Chairman, Chief Executive Officer and Head of the Newspapers Division, Axel Springer AG
Jessica P. Einhorn, Dean, Paul H. Nitze School of Advanced International Studies (SAIS), Johns Hopkins University
Reuben Mark, Chairman, Colgate-Palmolive Company
Michael A. Miles, Special Limited Partner, Forstmann Little & Company
Kenneth J. Novack, Senior Counsel, Mintz, Levin, Cohn, Ferris, Glovsky and Popeo, PC
Francis T. Vincent, Jr., Chairman, Vincent Enterprises

---

6 Orthodox economists explain their reluctance to address the broader view of diversity, whatever its merits, because it cannot be measured empirically. They tend to equate program diversity with the number of competitors and production quality with the size of program budgets (Noam, 2008).

Deborah C. Wright, Chairman, President and Chief Executive Officer, Carver
  Bancorp, Inc. and Carver Federal Savings Bank
(www.timewarner.com/corp/management/board_directors/index.html)

As is typically the case, the board contains inside directors from the senior ranks of
the corporation, and outside directors, primarily from other corporations. It also drew
a few from the non-corporate sector. As is also common, the board at Time Warner
contains only two women and no one from the ranks of labor or from any of the
many citizens' movement organizations active today.

Studies of corporate boards examine the ties that connect board members to a
common fiduciary responsibility, or the obligation to maximize return on the investment of shareholders. Analysts distinguish between *direct* interlocks, which link two
firms through the membership of an executive from one company on the board of
another, and *indirect* interlocks, that connect two companies through common membership on a third board. Colgate-Palmolive and Axel Springer AG are each directly
connected to Time Warner through the common responsibility that their representatives on the board have for the performance of Time Warner. Colgate-Palmolive
and Axel Springer AG are also indirectly linked to each other through their common
membership on the Time Warner board. Moreover, corporate directors tend to serve
on more than one board. For example, Frank Caulfield also served on the board of
the Council on Foreign Relations, one of the more important research and policy
organizations with considerable influence in Washington, DC. Stephen Bollenback
also served as Chairman of the Board of KB Home, and as Director of Harrah's
Entertainment, Inc. and Macy's, Inc. Concentration is thereby extended through the
shared responsibilities for performance among companies that compete in some
markets. The analysis of company boards developed with some rigor through the
application of common statistical measures, network analysis, and matrix algebra
(Burt, 1992; Scott, 1991). The central point of the analysis is that overlapping board
structures provide not just the opportunity but the responsibility for close cooperation among the representatives of firms, some of which are competitors.

There are many other places that afford opportunities for elite corporate interaction and planning. These include private clubs, associations, and professional organizations which serve as nodes in networks of class power. The annual meeting of
global elites at Davos, Switzerland, provides one major example. Nevertheless, the
corporate board stands out among these venues because of the added legal, fiduciary
responsibility demanded of its members. The Time Warner board offered more than
just the opportunity for people from different corporations to meet and discuss common concerns. Board members have a legal responsibility to act on behalf of Time
Warner and, according to those who argue for the significance of indirect interlocks,
for one another. It is through this process that concentration achieves a texture comprising both the opportunity and the responsibility for cooperation and planning
that overcomes differences and tempers competition. This texture, made up of the
many daily occasions for contact and interaction, gives concentration the quality of
hegemony, a taken-for-granted belief in the right to use power.

There are also important opportunities for companies to work together, and thereby add to concentrated power without actually merging. These forms encompass a range of "teaming arrangements," including *corporate partnerships* or *strategic alliances* for specific projects such as media co-productions or for the development of new technologies (Fuchs, 2007). They also include *merchandising arrangements* that link media companies with marketing and merchandising firms.[7] These practices are not new to corporations, including media firms, but they have grown more common in recent years. This is partly because the process of spatialization enables companies to restructure internal operations and their external relationships for a specific period of time, such as the duration of one project, without incurring organizational disruptions that often ruled out these arrangements in the past. Whether or not the project succeeds, companies can reconstitute to carry out their major businesses. Moreover, they can cooperate and compete at the same time.

One caveat for understanding these developments is that the language used to describe them, for example "synergy," is formulated for its public relations, as much as for its analytical, value. As a result, terms like strategic alliance and synergy, which offer rhetorical weight, also carry different meanings.[8] In the pure sense, a strategic alliance brings together two or more firms, or specific units of these firms, for one or more projects, without any change in ownership or investment of one in the other. Alliances may involve the creation of a new company, though this is not essential. Media co-production arrangements constitute a good case of the pure form. Prompted by compelling economics that often deliver lower production costs, this form of alliance has grown to dominate video and film production in Europe. International alliances are also influencing significantly the once insular American production industry. Such activities have also brought companies together in the area of new communication technologies where, for example, two fierce competitors, IBM and Apple, formed an alliance to develop specific new generation components, such as the Power PC computer system. Since IBM gave up most of its hardware business (the once venerable IBM PC is now owned by Lenovo and is based in China), Apple has now teamed up with Intel, which provides the processors for the company's computer line.

Alliances bring companies together for many reasons, including the need to agree on a technical standard for high-definition television or for a new generation of digital video players. They also come together to lobby governments, for assistance to fight off what they perceive to be unfair competition, the theft of their intellectual property, or the need to import more low-cost foreign workers.

---

7 Merchandising, as Wasko notes (1994), is formally the mechanical act of creating and selling a product based on a copyrightable product. Licensing is the legal mechanism by which a copyright trademark holder receives a royalty for the use of a name, a likeness, or an image.

8 For Herbert Schiller (1989), synergy is a glossy term for corporate control over the entirety of consumer images and products. Drawing on Meehan's concept of the "cultural fund," Wasko (1994) refers to cultural synergy as the set of overlapping cultural images produced by these companies.

A major reason for the recent wave of mergers and alliances across media is that companies are eager to take advantage of converging hardware and software systems that enable them to control major pieces of the entire circuit of production, distribution, and exhibition or display. Specifically, companies want to be indispensable participants in the reconstitution of entertainment and information networks. That is why the News Corporation purchased the social networking site MySpace and why Microsoft pressed so hard to purchase Yahoo!. These developments have raised the specter of monopolization to a new order of magnitude as one integrated conglomerate might hold the potential to substantially control the production and flows of communication, information, and entertainment. Nevertheless, there continue to be great uncertainties about what specific combination of companies and technologies will be most successful, particularly in an environment of rapid technological change. Should a company try to challenge Apple's dominant position as the major distributor of music in the United States by introducing a new player and downloading system? Or should it focus on mining and marketing the data gathered from surveillance of social networking sites? Very large companies can spread the risk by investing in many areas because they can afford to lose out in a few. But Google was once a very small company that grew astronomically because it was able to focus on meeting a very specific need that Microsoft did not meet because Bill Gates' company was spreading its investments widely.

Networks of corporate power are also constituted out of product placement and merchandising agreements which connect companies that market a specific media product, such as a feature film or an athlete. The watershed moment here was the decision to include the candy Reese's Pieces in the film ET after the candy maker M&M turned down producer Stephen Spielberg's request to use what was then the more popular product. After the movie brought enormous gains in Reese's sales, product makers flocked to have their brands placed in Hollywood films. Not everyone supports the use of product placement deals. In the United States, both the Writers Guild and the Screen Actors Guild, which represent those who work in the Hollywood media industry, have waged protest campaigns because they feel that product placement practices demean their artistic integrity and because they do not benefit financially from such placements. Merchandising deals differ from product placement arrangements. Here the media company, a Hollywood studio, for example, licenses to a third-party manufacturer the right to use the names and likenesses of the movie characters for spin-off products such as clothes, toys, and media products. Merchandising deals have become so lucrative that many animation productions today expect more revenue generated from merchandising than from ticket sales. Nevertheless, it is still a risky business because many films fail. Sport is one of the fastest-growing merchandising sectors. Here, athletes, linked through contractual agreements with their league and a major advertising/management consulting company, use images that are carefully cultivated across the range of media to create a lucrative business, the entirety of which now supports a market of over $100 billion worldwide, surpassing $25 billion in the United States alone. Again, however, lucrative as this business has become, one bad bet on an athlete whose reputation has been tarnished adds risk to this business.

The pure form of strategic alliance, involving contractual arrangements to cooperate without a complete or partial ownership takeover breaks some new ground in corporate practice. But there is nothing new in communication industry alliances that bring about a new entity or which result in one company taking a position in another. Nor is there anything new in alliances that cut across industry sectors or technologies. It was a strategic alliance that brought about the creation of one of the most powerful companies in electronic media history, the Radio Corporation of America (RCA). In the 1920s, RCA was founded out of a strategic alliance among major corporate forces in the early development of electronic media: AT&T, Westinghouse, General Electric, and the United Fruit Company (which invested heavily in radio to build a communication grid for its US and Latin American operations). In the 1960s, the US Communication Satellite Corporation, Comsat, the institution responsible for creating a US-led global satellite system, was formed out of a strategic alliance among AT&T, RCA, and the International Telephone and Telegraph Company. These are far from exceptional examples of alliances among leading forces in different segments of the communications industry that built corporate success stories out of some of the same, and some very different, communication technologies. The RCA and Comsat cases are powerful reminders that there is nothing particularly new about the dynamism of capitalism. Today's alliances, as Vernon (1992: 16) suggests, are not all that much different in function from jointly owned oilfields and mines that competing refiners and marketers, such as ARAMCO in Saudi Arabia, Southern Peru Copper, now Southern Copper still based in Peru, and HALCO Mining in Guinea, once shared. Change, including structural transformation in business, has always been a constant.

Nevertheless, there are several dimensions of the current wave of restructuring that mark a departure from the established pattern. First, it is arguably accelerating in both time and space. The pace of corporate restructuring, the process of formal and informal coupling and decoupling, has speeded up and become more unstable. Furthermore, the spatial agglomeration of such activity knows fewer constraints. Whereas alliances once would only rarely cross national borders, today such developments are commonplace. These include co-productions and contractual agreements to work together on a common project, as well as various forms of ownership, ranging from the creation of a new company to taking a position in another, or to a complete takeover.

In addition to these considerations, the role of government has changed substantially. This is a subject to be taken up at greater length below, but it is important to highlight here the significant alteration in state activity. Although this has varied by nation and historical circumstances, the state used to occupy a considerably different role in the process of structural transformation in the communication industries. This is because, unlike many other economic sectors, the communication industry was owned outright by the state or, if not completely a part of the state apparatus, was closely integrated into wider state functions through processes of budgetary allocation, policy oversight, and regulation. To return to the RCA example, the strategic alliance that constituted the company did so with complete US government participation, as the next best alternative to government ownership of radio, and at the price of government participation at the board and management levels. Similarly, the alliance that formed Comsat came together at the specific request of government, under the threat of outright government control over the company, and the outcome was an organization subject not only to government regulation, but also to its direct representation on the company's board. Admittedly, it is still the case that states own some communication facilities and continue to provide services, particularly telecommunications and broadcasting, in much of the world, but this role is diminishing. Moreover, although states still play a role in cross-border alliances, such as the regulation of co-production agreements, this too is changing. It is more typically the case for the companies themselves to negotiate deals directly, whether within a country or across borders. States may intervene to assess antitrust or trade implications, but today they are more likely to take the lead in encouraging such arrangements, rather than regulate them or take an ownership stake. Strategic alliances, which were once more likely the result of an effort to create what have been called *chosen instruments* of government policy, are now typically the result of corporate policy to expand into new areas with partners who are willing to pool expertise and risk.

Furthermore, the current form of alliances exhibits a greater tendency to include the best organized among the major *users* of communication. Again, as the United Fruit Company's participation in the RCA alliance suggests, there is precedent for this in communication history. However, the recent involvement of users, particularly banks, investment companies, and other large corporate communication customers, suggests that a common practice has grown from what was once an occasional one. Recognizing the importance of communication and information technology for growth and control, companies outside the formal boundaries of the industry use their individual and combined power, in large user associations, to steer the development of the communication industry to meet their interests in the creation of high-quality and low-cost networks and services. The growing involvement of large users in the spatialization of the communication industry suggests an important power shift that brings to the center of the industry a new set of participants to join the traditional companies that produce and distribute hardware and services. In addition to marking an important power shift, this development points to the remapping of the communication industry from a highly differentiated sector, whose boundary with the rest of the economy was easily delineated, to one that is so increasingly integrated into the wider economy that it is becoming difficult to identify clear boundary distinctions. Private data networks, in-house video services, and just-in-time inventory control systems are just a few of the rapidly growing business sectors that have turned consumers of services into major producers. In essence, traditional categories and the legal, regulatory, and policy apparatus that came with them are eroding. What separates an American from a Japanese company, or a telephone from a cable or from a computer company, or a producer from a consumer? All of these differences are tending to disappear as we move into a global *electronic services marketplace.*[9] These developments are part of a wider process in which

---

9 It may be the case that much of the heat coming out of the battles among media firms results from an understandable tendency to cling to old categories, as they puzzle over how to think about this new reality.

companies adopt *new organizational structures* that combine the power to command resources and the flexibility to respond to changing markets. Economic restructuring sometimes leads to the conglomerate, but this is not essential to success. It is more important to develop flexible structures that can take on new forms rapidly to meet changing demands.

In conclusion, political economy recognizes that, though important, corporate size and concentration are just starting points for understanding the transformation of the communications business. Global restructuring offers numerous opportunities to expand control from the conglomerate form to the range of flexible alternatives. The chief requirements include controlling central points in the production, distribution, and exchange process (outright ownership is one among numerous alternatives) and remaining flexible to respond to changing markets and technologies.

Spatial Agglomeration: Remapping Corporate Space

The growth of strategic alliances and other forms of corporate linkages that do not require ownership changes, or even a significant investment, suggest the need to build on traditional concentration research. Firm size and market control remain important indicators of concentration. But corporate restructuring also creates forms of concentration based on dense networks of connections among producers, suppliers, and customers. So in addition to the traditional hierarchies of power that concentration research has focused upon, we now observe the growth of network hierarchies.

In addition to corporate restructuring, changes in the spatial patterning of business activity create another form of business concentration. Specifically, and contrary to forecasts that telecommunications would necessarily decentralize business activity, the concentration of business activity in New York, London, Tokyo, and other international cities, provides grounds for thinking about spatial agglomeration as a major form of business activity. Economic restructuring and spatial agglomeration are central features of a resurgence of interest in the discipline of geography. Although these developments have been taken up across the social sciences, they have had the most pronounced influence on geography, which now addresses central issues in political economy, including the relationship of spatial structures to capital accumulation, class, gender, and race (Bruff, 2005; Graham, 2002; Harvey, 2001; Vertova, 2006).

Transportation and Geography

For most of human history, transportation was slow and inefficient and the cost of overcoming geography prohibitively high. By the end of the eighteenth century, with the exception of a few stagecoaches and ships, vehicles could not move faster than a person could walk. Geographers have documented the changes brought about by technological innovation over the last two centuries. The nineteenth century saw the application of steam power as a means of propulsion and the use of iron and steel for ocean-going vessels, trains, and track. The twentieth century introduced the gasoline-powered internal combustion engine which made truck and automobile travel widely available. Large, ocean-going "superfreighters," containerization, and commercial jet aircraft reduced travel times further (Dicken, 1986).[10]

In their attempt to comprehend the significance of transportation-based changes, Malone and Rockart (1991) identify three orders of effects. A first-order substitutes new technologies for old, as people ride trains and cars, rather than horses and horse-drawn carriages. Improvements in technology lead to the emergence of a second-order effect, i.e. people travel more, whether to work each day, to visit distant friends, or to attend business meetings. Finally, a third-order effect is marked by the rise of new transportation-intensive social patterns. These include principally suburbanization, shopping malls, and, more recently, the vast exurbs that bring people into semi-rural areas beyond the suburbs.

One way to understand the radical shift in the geography we now experience is to consider what is called time–space convergence (Brunn and Leinbach, 1991). For example, assuming a foot speed of three miles per hour, until the sixteenth century, the effective distance between Portland, Maine and San Diego was two years. Horseback reduced this distance to eight months by the seventeenth century. By the mid-nineteenth century the stagecoach and wagon halved the distance to four months and, at the turn of the next century, trains could make the trip in four days. By 1950, air travel reduced it to ten hours and today to five. In the experience of someone living before the sixteenth century, San Diego is, in effect, now fifteen miles from Portland. Alternatively, in terms of transcontinental or intermetropolitan area travel time, the United States is now as large as the state of Maryland and New York is now closer to Tokyo than it was to Philadelphia in colonial times (Woytinsky and Woytinsky, 1955). Similarly, innovations in vehicle and road technologies reduced the distance between London and Edinburgh from 20,000 minutes by stagecoach in 1658, down to 2,500 by the modernized stage of 1840, to 800 minutes by rail in 1850 (400 in 1950), and down to 200 by air in 1970. This marks an annual rate of convergence between the two cities of about 29 minutes a year, though, with each innovation in transportation, locations converge at a decreasing rate. Since 1840 when the best average speed of horse-drawn coaches and sailing ships was ten miles per hour, the speed of transportation has increased seventy times for jet passenger aircraft.[11]

---

10 Lawrence (1983) reminds us that it was not simply the speed of travel that overcame geographical constraints, but the regularity of service. For example, the development of a packet ship service between New York and Liverpool was significant because it regularized service, including a message distribution service, between the two points.

11 It is hard to question the declining price–performance ratio of transportation technologies. Nevertheless, the curve does not travel in one direction for everyone who would travel. For example, the state of small towns in the United States has fluctuated drastically depending on the rise and fall of the bus service (Schwieterman, 2007).

Communication and Geography

Until electronics brought us the telegraph in the nineteenth century, transportation and communication were effectively united because information could only move as fast as transportation systems could take it. Pred (1973) has documented and mapped the time it took for information to circulate within the United States and between it and foreign centers in the pre-telegraph era. Although he notes significant advances, these depended entirely on improvements in transportation technologies. For example, the Postal Act of 1836, which supported "express" mail routes, coupled with the growth of steamboat traffic, decreased the public information time lag between Cincinnati and New York from nineteen to seven days.

Although the semaphore, bonfire, and smoke signals offered transport-independent means of communication, it was the telegraph and the submarine cable that were most responsible for severing the link between transport and communication, with significant consequences for geography. Telegraphy enabled a message to move instantly across the country; undersea cable took it across oceans. Communication and transportation systems worked together to lay the groundwork for the modern American business system (Chandler, 1977). The telegraph extended the reach of timely price information and the railroad sped the product to market (DuBoff, 1984, 1989). Along with them came organizational innovation required to run railroad companies, and new "transaction" jobs, e.g. commodity dealer, wholesale jobber, retailer, which tied together networks formed out of the extended reach of new transport–communication systems (Beniger, 1986). Today, transportation and communication systems are integrated with intelligent highway and geographic information systems that expand the distributional flexibility of large organizations.

Since communication has trivialized, if not entirely flattened, most graphs of time against distance, geographers have turned to more interesting dimensions of the measure, such as *cost–space convergence*, which refers to the cost of moving a message over a given distance (Knowles, 2006). For example, while the time–space convergence of a telephone call is solely dependent on the presence of telephones anywhere on the earth, the cost–space convergence differs from location to location and this has an influence on how corporations shape their global operations.

Drawing on the classic research of Malone and Rockart (1991), Hua Lee (2007) deepens their research on three stages in the application of communication to spatialize business. A first-order impact of reducing communication costs is the *substitution* of information technology for human coordination, as when computer systems eliminate clerks in the back offices of banks and insurance firms, and directory assistance operators from telephone companies. Declining communication costs have the second-order effect of increasing the *scale* of communication used to manage activities. As a result, travel agents and websites can more easily provide more diversity in travel options for customers and airlines can offer a wider range of fares. Third-order effects emerge with a *structural* shift to communication-intensive structures. These include intrafirm structures where salespeople record all sales of each item on hand-held electronic devices, as they deliver products to customers. Each night the information is summarized for senior executives who can make quick price, product, and marketing adjustments. Communication-intensive structures also cut across firms to link the chain of, for example, textile suppliers, manufacturers, and retailers in an interfirm network committed to reducing inventory and responding to changing fashions.

Researchers have also developed measures of *social space* to denote the number of social contacts over a specific territory, one variation of which measures the probability of communication against the distance between communicators (Abler, Adam, and Gould, 1971; Hagerstrand, 1968). Measures of social space are used most in research on patterns of innovation and diffusion to measure the time it takes, for example, for a new technology to move from one area to another.

In addition to these objective measures of time–space convergence, geographers take into account the *perceptual* or cultural dimension of convergence. In fact, Abler, et al. (1975: 53) suggest that:

> What people *think* about distance and space is more important in the long run than the "real" nature of space and distance. Even if ... convergence succeed[s] in producing a functionally dimensionless world, people will continue to have strong feelings about places and what they perceive to be distance.

It is also the case that convergence measures vary by the individual's place within society. Although it is clearly the case that time–space and cost–space convergence demonstrate that places are moving closer together, Abler suggested that "for those possessing lesser means, time–space convergence may be negligible. In fact, there is reason to believe that convergence contributes to the polarization of the 'haves' and 'have nots'" (Abler, et al., 1975: 9). For example, he cites research suggesting that, in large US cities, the average distance between home and work decreased for whites but increased for African Americans.

The research literature offers a number of general conclusions. The declining price–performance ratio of transportation and communication technologies has contributed to spatial convergence. The extent of the convergence is widespread but varies by cultural, social, and political conditions. Cultural conditions include the values embedded in specific places and in the distances between them. For example, a person based in Akron, Ohio, headed for New York City has a different perception of New York and the distance from Akron depending on whether the trip is viewed as a chance to visit the center of cosmopolitan culture or a descent into barbarism. Social variations include an individual's place in various economic, educational, and social status hierarchies which would make convergence a taken-for-granted reality or, at the other extreme, practically unthinkable. Finally, political economic decisions about transportation (do airline carriers fly the route? Non-stop? How often? For how much?) and communication (what is the quality and cost of communication between the two cities?) influence the nature of convergence. Not so much "the end of geography," research suggests that convergence *transforms* geography by increasing the spatial flexibility of those who can take advantage of computer communication technology and by underscoring the significance of non-technical factors that can enhance or impede convergence. What Abler, et al. described before the computer era applies today: "A world without distance will not be an undifferentiated, isotropic sphere; because it would allow preference free reign, such a world would be immensely varied and differentiated" (1975: 53). The only amendment that a political economist would make is that this world is also immensely political.

Location: Dispersal and Concentration

Research on the significance of geography for organizations has been guided by location or logistics theory, a set of ideas systematized first in the 1909 work of Alfred Weber (Chapman and Walker, 1987; Hoover, 1937; Isard, 1956).[12] Weber and his followers developed a normative approach that aimed to help businesses determine the least cost location for their plants and offices. Their work calculated transportation, manufacturing – particularly labor – and marketing costs and used these to identify the least expensive site. Weber contributed the notion of *agglomeration economies* to locational studies, a term denoting the value of concentrating plants and offices in one location. This has become especially important in recent years as the agglomeration of information technology companies in one area came to be viewed as a key to economic growth (Saxenian, 2006). Research on the actual locational practices of firms confirmed what Weberians considered to be considerable "suboptimalities," including the influence of "personal consideration" in locational decision-making. This gave rise to a behavioral approach to locational choice that extrapolated from the actual locational practices of successful and unsuccessful firms. The concepts and ideas informing this perspective drew heavily from the work of Herbert Simon, particularly from his thoughts about the temporal constraints on information processing, which led to the notions of bounded rationality and satisficing, as opposed to optimizing, behavior. According to this view, time imposes constraints on all sorts of spatial decisions and so there are constraints on rational decision-making and therefore limits on how well people or organizations can process information.

In addition to the costs of making and moving goods, which occupied normative theorists, behaviorists took into account the costs of making and moving information about the business, including information about where to locate. Behaviorists maintained that the optimal choice of the normative theorist was often only optimal (and rarely chosen) because it neglected the real costs of producing, processing, and distributing timely information relevant to the locational choice. Aiming to correct the "information blindspot" in the normative approach, Pred (1973) created a "behavioral matrix" which factored into the locational assessment both information and the firm's ability to use it.

By examining the actual process of locational decision-making, and by taking information into account as a variable in the decision-making process, behaviorists acknowledged the complexity of the subject. Research has slowly turned to the role of

---

12 Weber's work did not appear in English until 1929.

communication, particularly computer communication, in locational decisions. Studies typically elaborate on the general conclusion that technology increases the number of locational opportunities because it overcomes the need to be physically near information resources. Transportation and power technologies once eliminated the need to locate near bodies of water. Now, the near ubiquity of computer communication networks diminishes the need for a company to choose a specific location because of its proximity to telecommunications networks. Locational decisions are increasingly premised on the view that you can communicate reasonably well from anywhere to anywhere. Therefore decisions are based on the opportunities and constraints that remain, such as a labor force, customers, and environmental considerations.

Advances in transportation, and especially in communication, make it easier for firms to operate at a distance and thereby take advantage of benefits enjoyed in locations that were once not cost-effective. In fact, centralization and dispersal are part of the same process that makes up the structural transformations of contemporary economic geography. It is therefore important to examine spatial agglomeration because it has practical consequences for cities and towns and for the people who live in them. It is especially vital to view spatial agglomeration from a political economy perspective because there are significant implications for how power operates in the process of creating new spaces (Gibson, 2003; Gibson and Lowes, 2006). Specifically, spatial agglomeration enforces new hierarchies that concentrate wealth and power in some cities while others decline. It also establishes hierarchies that concentrate wealth and power in some parts of cities while other parts decline. These regional disparities go together with growing social class disparities. That New York grows and Detroit declines has direct consequences for the lives and the life chances of the people who live within and around these places. So does the transformation of Manhattan into a power center at the expense of New York's outer boroughs which, with some exceptions, fall into decline.

This line of spatialization research further suggests the value of breaking new ground in the analysis of media concentration. Spatial agglomeration, as well as ownership agglomeration, is a significant form of business concentration. It brings together companies, whether connected or unconnected by ownership ties, in dense networks of producers, suppliers, and customers whose mutual dependence, consolidated geographically in global cities and dispersed electronically across the globe, creates significant forms of concentrated economic power (Sassen, 2001). This development is especially important for the communication and information industries because they are central to the producer services sector, which is primarily responsible for spatial agglomeration today. In essence, communication and information processes, and the industries in which they are organized, contribute fundamentally to a principal form of economic restructuring in the global political economy: the rise of concentrated economic power in the spatial agglomerations of business. But it is also important to emphasize that the integration of all sorts of media, telecommunications, and computer devices into the corporation puts practically all companies in the communication business.

No company has understood this better than Wal-Mart, which is primarily in the business of selling merchandise, but could not have risen to its position as the most powerful company in the world today without mastering communication and information technologies. These enable the company to coordinate its network of suppliers, which are based everywhere in the world but primarily in China, and distributors, which transport merchandise to its retail stores. The close coordination of decisions about what to buy, from whom, how much, and at what price enables the company to maintain dominance in its business. Questionable labor practices, ruthless elimination of the competition, and powerful lobbying efforts in Washington, Beijing, and in other world power centers also play a significant role in the company's success. But the ability to extract value from practically every bit of information the company collects on customers, workers, suppliers, distributors, and so on, and to communicate that information to the people best positioned to act on it also counts for a great deal (Bianco, 2006; Fishman, 2006). Furthermore, as the second largest distributor of recorded music in the United States, Wal-Mart is also one of the largest media companies in the world.

Research on spatial agglomeration shares with the more traditional forms of media concentration research an interest in providing ways of seeing a dynamic industry within a dynamic economy. Both are necessary to provide a complete picture of spatialization in the global political economy. But both also need to deepen their vision of government.

The State

There is certainly ample evidence to support the view that the contemporary state has reacted to changes in corporate and industry structure, as well as to changes in technologies and services. Nevertheless, there is also support for the view that these changes have come about with the active legal, regulatory, and policy direction of the state. In fact, there is enough support for the latter to warrant the conclusion that political economy would benefit from a greater emphasis on the *political*, calling attention to the *constitutive* as well as the reactive role of the state in the communication industry. This has been difficult to accomplish because, with few exceptions (Braman, 2007), much of the literature on the role of the state in the communication industries provides narrow descriptions based on the language of policy-makers. The tendency is understandable because mastering legal, regulatory, and policy processes, and their various languages, is difficult. The problem for political economy is that explaining the role of the state and situating the state–media relationship in the wider political economy requires a transition from focusing on the day-to-day world of policy action to that of political economy.

The problem, and the significance of addressing it, are exemplified in the concept of *regulation*. There is an extensive literature on regulating the communication industries and, though some variation exists, one finds consistency in the view that regulation is a government reaction to market problems. Explanations certainly range widely, including the presence of natural monopoly conditions, industry pressures on the political apparatus, public interest pressures from citizen groups, etc. The definition of the problem *is* significant, but each tends to be couched within a conception of regulation as something governments do in reaction to perceived problems. As a result, when policy-makers and academic analysts review industry regulation, they tend to examine government practice and contend over whether more or less regulation is needed. Hence, debate on the role of the state in the communication industries frequently comes down to the choice between regulation and deregulation.

A political economy approach, particularly one that reflects fully on its constituent terms, sees this quite differently. Political economy takes the entire social field, including the pattern of industry activity, as a form of regulation.[13] For example, a social field primarily influenced by industry decisions, rather than by state intervention, can be characterized as a form of *market regulation*, as opposed to *state regulation*, which takes place when government plays the prominent role.[14] From a political economy perspective, the policy debate over deregulation is disingenuous at best, because deregulation is not an alternative. Rather, the debate comes down to the choice among a mix of forms that foreground the market, the state, or interests that lie outside both. Eliminating government regulation is not deregulation but rather the expansion of market regulation.

Political economy avoids the language trap, concentrating on assessing the merits of different forms of regulation, such as market and state, for different groups in society. This reassessment of regulation is necessary to consider the constitutive role of the state, which the policy concept of deregulation masks. It suggests another step in the political economy approach to the state, namely, how it actively constructs forms of regulation. One starting point is to consider four processes characterizing current state constitutive activity that emanate from both spatialization and commodification. The first, *commercialization*, takes place when the state replaces forms of regulation based on public interest, public service, and related standards, such as universality, with market standards that establish market regulation. In communications, this has meant greater emphasis on market position and profitability, even among state and public service broadcasting and telecommunications firms. Specifically, it leads to greater emphasis in broadcasting on audience size, advertising revenue, producing programming that anticipates an international market and linkages to other revenue-generating media. In telecommunication, commercialization means building and

---

13 The so-called Regulation School has taken the lead, though other political economy approaches have also developed this formulation. According to Lipietz (1988), one of the leading advocates of the Regulation School position, regulation is an adjustment of contradictory tendencies within a social field.

14 Depending on the market structure, several types of regulation exist within the market form. These range from monopoly through oligopoly to fully competitive forms of regulation. What tends to be called "expanding competition" in the communication sector actually means the addition of one or more companies that permits a shift from monopoly to duopoly or oligopoly regulation. This hardly justifies the policy conclusion that "expanding competition" warrents a decline in government oversight.

organizing networks and services with a greater concern for those customers, principally business, likely to increase revenue, even if that means greater attention to linking metropolitan centers in global networks, rather than to extending networks into rural and generally underserved regions. Commercialization has led government communications authorities to separate telecommunications, Internet, and other revenue-generating activities from postal and other services, which are mandated by constitution or legislation. Defenders of commercialization argue that it does not preclude and may even enhance public service goals, such as universality (Noam, 2008). Conversely, opponents contend that it is a means of transforming the space of communication flows which, in a world of limited resources, inevitably means supporting one class of users over others (McChesney, 2007).

Second, *liberalization* is a process of state intervention to expand the number of participants in the market, typically by creating, or easing the creation of, competing providers of communication services. This typically involves the creation of a private competitor in a state or private monopoly marketplace. Unlike commercialization, which aims to make business practices the standard for the communication industry, with or without competition, liberalization aims specifically to increase the number of companies in the market. Over the past thirty years, governments have changed the communication industry in most parts of the world by introducing private competitors over a range of broadcasting and television services. Supporters contend that liberalization lowers prices, expands services, and generally speeds up the process of innovation (International Chamber of Commerce, 2007). Critics counter that it substitutes private oligopoly regulation for state regulation, carrying out price, service, and innovation mandates that advance the interests of an oligopoly cartel and its more privileged customers (Schiller, 2007a).

Third, *privatization* is a process of state intervention that literally sells off a state enterprise such as a public broadcaster or a state telephone company. Privatization takes many forms, depending on the percentage of shares to be sold off, the extent to which any foreign ownership is permitted, the length, if any, of a phase-in period, and the specific form of continuing state involvement, typically constituted in a regulatory body, in the aftermath of privatization. This process has accelerated for several reasons, including the rise of governments ideologically committed to private control over economic activity, the attraction, if for one time only, of fresh revenues for government coffers, and the pressures of transnational businesses and governmental organizations, such as the International Monetary Fund, the World Bank, and the World Trade Organization. For its supporters, privatization is necessary because commercialization is, at best, an inadequate first step toward market control (Vickers and Yarrow, 1991). Critics see in privatization the elimination of the primary alternative to complete market regulation, the loss of sovereignty for nations selling off to foreign firms, and the consequent loss of local control over national policy (Aubrey, Kingstone, and Young, 2004).

Finally, governments have created their own regional and global organizations that integrate them in different degrees of *internationalization*. These include regional trade alliances, such as the North American Free Trade Agreement, that brings together the United States, Mexico, and Canada. On a global scale, there is the World Trade Organization, which manages relations among the most developed nations and negotiates the terms of development (and underdevelopment) in the rest of the world. This process has been particularly important in the communication arena because the transnationalization of communication networks requires some degree of interstate coordination. Again, this is not new to the industry – the International Telecommunication Union (ITU) began to bring together governments to coordinate telegraph policy in the 1860s. In recent years, states have developed new arrangements that enable the richest nations to exert tighter control over global communications policy. These have brought about significant changes in international policy-making, including the decline of UNESCO, site of the major support for the New World Information and Communication Order (NWICO), and the opening of the ITU to considerably greater private sector participation.

As these organizations have declined in power, short-term, function- or technology-specific sites for meeting and planning have increased their influence, especially those that bring together government and corporate decision-makers who, largely outside the formal and publicly accessible sites of regulatory activity, coordinate technologies, services, and pricing. In the Internet era, formal regulatory authority for overseeing the important global domain name system has been given to a private corporation, the Internet Corporation for Assigned Names and Numbers, based in California, which operates under the authority of the US government. The attempt to build a more democratic process grounded in genuinely global governance, through what is called the World Summit on the Information Society, has served as a platform for different perspectives, but has not changed any of the decision-making power over the Internet.

Commercialization, liberalization, privatization, and internationalization are among the more significant examples of the state's constitutive role. More importantly, they suggest the value of a political economy approach which starts from the mutual constitution of the industry and the state in the creation of regulatory forms. These reflect the needs and interests of capital and the nature of opposition at a particular historical period. This does not mean that the industry and the state are therefore *equally* responsible for the resulting structure and practice of communication, just as it does not suggest that different industry forces are equally responsible. Rather, historical practice leads a political economic analysis to conclude that both the industry and the state are primary forces in the development of communications, that their relationship is mutually constitutive and variable. Furthermore, political economy argues against an analysis that concentrates solely on one or the other. Both industry and state are central to a political economy analysis, specifically important for creating the form of regulation that governs the industry and the social field, including oppositional forces with a relationship to the industry. Finally, the active state cannot guarantee its own success. In fact, the sheer growth in the number of participants in the communication arena and the rise of *ad hoc*, flexible mechanisms to manage this growth, create significant problems of coordination and control that make success far from guaranteed. This is partly because the recent expansion in state activity has not included any growth; in fact, it has come about along with a noticeable decline in the direct participation of the state in the process of capital accumulation. This accentuates a long-term problem in capitalism: the state is necessary to manage the multiplicity of short-term specific interests of capital, but is not permitted to participate fully in the process of capital accumulation itself.

Globalization and its Antimonies

From a political economic perspective, globalization refers to the spatial agglomeration of capital, led by transnational business and the state, that transforms the spaces through which flow resources and commodities, including communication and information. The outcome is a literal transformation in the geography of communication and information that accentuates certain spaces and the relationships among them. For example, the New York–London–Tokyo axis anchors a map of communication and information services, which extends secondary connections to Frankfurt, Shanghai, and Los Angeles, and so on, to form a network grid of worldwide linkages. Like any map, it cannot be drawn with absolute precision (Jessop, 2000). New York's place on the grid does not extend to the entirety of the city but includes lower Manhattan, the center for financial services, mid-Manhattan, where we find the headquarters of communication and entertainment conglomerates, and parts of the outer boroughs and suburbs. Communication and information technology expand the range of locations that can link people to the wealthy core of the city, but they also intensify the importance of the core because, at the center, one not only has direct access to the technology, but also to the principal people and organizations that have the power to constitute the network of flows. According to Agnew (2001: 52–3), the world has become "a complex mosaic of inter-linked global city-regions, prosperous rural areas, resource sites, and 'dead lands' increasingly cut off from time–space compression." These transformations create hierarchies of control over which the term globalization can serve as a mystifying gloss. In other words, the practice of globalization creates new hierarchical networks of power. But the myth of globalization submerges these unpleasant realities beneath utopian visions of a flat world, a network society, and, most utopian of all, the end of geography (Mosco, 2004).

This mythology grows partly out of a deep resistance to the view that space, and not just time, is dynamic, that what we map, whether physical space, political space, or the space of human communication flows, is constantly changing (Massey, 1992; Winseck and Pike, 2007). The choice of the term spatialization is precisely intended to underscore the process of constant spatial change, which geography has documented over the range of configurations of absolute space, time–space, cost–space, social space, and cultural space. The process, popularly referred to as globalization, identifies today's patterning of spatial change. It does not signal a flat world or the end of geography. The departure which fuels the mythology is the real expansion in the ability of those people and organizations with the power to command political economic resources to make greater use of time and space as resources by altering the space of flows to their benefit.

It starts from the political economy of capitalism, which constitutes the process of re-zoning spaces, in part, by stratifying and concentrating the power to do so along class, race, and gender lines. As Fuchs (2007: 74) puts it, "These spaces are not inclusive, open and participatory, but segmented, exclusive, centralized and hierarchic. To speak of the network society is an ideological construct that obscures capitalist relations and structural inequalities that shape contemporary society."

The vision of globalization, suggesting (with Disney) that "it's a small world after all," makes it difficult to face up to the antimonies of spatialization. But it is essential do so to fully understand the changes that spatialization is bringing about in the world today. As the world came to experience beginning in 2007, spatialization can extend the reach of capitalism beyond the ability of its managers to maintain political economic stability. For example, enticed by the seemingly limitless potential of communication and information technology to expand the instruments of capitalist expansion, businesses in the investment and banking industries created entirely new forms of credit to market around the globe. Specifically, banks that hold mortgages on homes gather these together and sell them on global markets, hoping to spread the risk in the event of problems. Along with the expectation that governments will bail them out in the event of a crisis, banks are emboldened to provide loans to riskier customers who are enticed to take out mortgages they cannot possibly repay on the expectation that when that point arises they can get out from under their problem by selling the property. When the inevitable crash in the housing market hit in 2007, the effects were felt not only in the United States, where most such loans originated, but around the world, where banks and investment firms collapsed because they had joined this global market. As a result, numerous governments rushed to save the global financial system by injecting enormous amounts of cash. This is but one example of how the world economy can be rocked by the sheer opportunity to inject local and national economic practices into global networks without knowing what to anticipate, let alone how to manage it. Globalization can easily get far ahead of its capacity to operate effectively because spatialization promotes the view that anything is possible.

Moreover, it is not only the legitimate financial system that extends its reach in globalization. Spatialization provides enormous opportunities for networks of criminal activities to operate on a global scale because communication and information technology can move money swiftly and surreptitiously. This supports international networks of illegal gambling, drug and weapons trafficking, the sale of stolen property, and, worst of all, the smuggling of people across borders for cheap labor and worse. One analyst estimates that global organized crime, including cybercrime, accounts for 20 per cent of global production (Glenny, 2008). Much attention has been directed at one piece of this story, namely the growing capacity of terrorism to attack central nodes in global networks and create enormous damage at little cost. Given the dramatic power and political upheaval that terrorist attacks can unleash, embodied most dramatically in the events of 9/11, the attention is understandable. However, in all of the focus on the lightning strike of terrorism, one can easily forget the damage brought about by international crime organizations which rely on communication networks that mirror the systems essential for the daily operation of legitimate business.

Globalization is also founded on a reductionist view of spatialization. Understandably taken by the spatial transformations that make up the process of redrawing the map to take into account the space of flows, proponents tend to miss other related processes, including oppositional ones. One of the chief reasons for this is the tendency to treat contemporary capitalism as a distinct set of relations among the advanced societies *alone*, rather than as a set of *hierarchical* political economic and cultural relations articulated and disarticulated within and across all nations. The tendency is understandable because the capitalist core has assumed enormous power over the global political economy and culture. But it has not abolished class, imperialism, or nation, in all of their varied forms. These are arguably more vital than ever in the global political economy. Moreover, although the world of "actually existing" socialisms hardly exists, the principles of socialism, of democratic control over production, distribution, exchange, and use, live on in a wide range of political economic, social, and cultural movements. Finally, the tools of globalization also assist the work of those who would create alternatives to its current form. Opposed to a system felt to be too dependent on private markets that distribute benefits to the few at the expense of the many, and which create environmental devastation, social movements are making use of communication and information technology to fight back. Global networks that work for the poor and the exploited, for democracy and environmental sustainability add another significant dimension to the process of spatialization (Della Porta, et al., 2006; Hardt and Negri, 2000, 2004; Tarrow, 2006). As Jessop (2000: 356) concludes, globalization "is a contradictory, conflictual, contested, and complex resultant of a multi-scalar, multi-temporal, multi-centric process that develops unevenly in time and space, and, indeed, exploits and intensifies differences as much as, if not more than, it produces new complementarities and uniformities."

Globalization is central to the forces that promote division and conflict in the world today. Specifically, nationalism, terrorism, and religious fundamentalism, three alleged enemies of globalization, are intimately connected to globalization and make full use of the instruments of communication that propel it. As a result, intrinsic to globalization today are the forces that would divide the world.

Nationalism is often set apart from globalization because it represents the old order of modernity based on competing and often warring states that resisted the inexorable pull of global markets and global culture. Indeed, nationalism remains a tool of the anti-globalization movement as national sovereignty is upheld against the challenges to national companies, national trade unions, national public broadcasters, and national systems of social welfare. But nationalism has now become a critical force in the spread of globalization as countries use national identity and all of the emotional sentiments it conjures to better compete in the global marketplace. Consider China, with its massive mobilization of nationalism in the service of winning in global competition for markets. In this respect, globalization does not undermine nationalism; rather, it sharpens nationalism, turning it into a tool to more effectively promote the interests of nations in global competition. There is nothing terribly new here. After all, in the name of nationalism, nineteenth-century America refused to protect the legal copyrights of authors whose works were printed outside the United States, much to the chagrin of world famous writers like Charles Dickens, who railed against copyright piracy in the United States. Like China today, the United States was simply using nationalism to better position itself in the early days of globalization. Once it became a net exporter of intellectual property, the United States joined the world of global copyright protection and now echoes Dickens in attacking intellectual property pirates. But the United States still claims the national right to go to war to protect its power in global competition for oil. As the geographer Neil Smith (2005: 16) puts it, "nationalism infuses the arteries of a globalizing capitalism."

If nationalism is typically set apart from globalization, then terrorism, embodied in organizations like al-Qaeda is considered its absolute antithesis. And yet, what recent success the al-Qaeda network has enjoyed is based on following principles honed by some of the strongest supporters of globalization. As the head of the Rand Corporation's Washington office put it:

> Indeed, what bin Laden has done is to implement for al-Qaeda the same type of effective organizational framework or management approach adapted by many corporate executives throughout much of the industrialized world over the past decade. Just as large, multi-national business conglomerates moved during the 1990s to more linear, flatter and networked structures, bin Laden did the same with al-Qaeda. (Hoffman, 2004: 32)

Like many modern corporations, al-Qaeda is a network-based organization that eschews the centralization and rigid hierarchy of the old order in favor of an agile collection of cells and individuals who connect and disconnect as necessary. Moreover, like most such organizations, al-Qaeda makes use of the most advanced forms of communication essential in any global operation today. Websites are critical. Indeed, several of the terrorists who drove planes into the World Trade Center booked their tickets on the website Travelocity.com.

Finally, globalization goes hand in hand with religious fundamentalism, one of the most significant developments in the world today, including the United States. That alone is an extraordinary fact to consider. The richest nation in the world, which has built a global empire based on the most rational economic strategies, now identifies one-third of its citizens as born-again Christians who believe in the literal interpretation of the Bible. Indeed, a principal reason for the power of religious fundamentalism is the development of global networks that make use of advanced computer communication technologies to distribute their messages. The Christian Broadcasting Network is now the envy of public and private broadcasters worldwide. Churches that virulently oppose modern science, including the theory of evolution, now use the most advanced technologies to spread their archaic messages to audiences around the world. Now that is closer to the genuine spirit of globalization. It is a conflict-ridden contradictory process that does not stand above or against the ancient forces of nationalism, tribalism, and religious fundamentalism. It advances them and they use it. Or to put it another way, yes, Marx may have been right when he described the great power of capitalism to overcome everything in its way (or, as he put it, to make all that is solid melt into air). But Marx was also wrong because what melts tends to solidify again into strange hybrid forms, remixes of nationalism, tribalism, religious fundamentalism, and the globe-spanning networks that accelerate the contradictions of spatialization.

Conclusion

Chapter 7 introduced a theory of political economy to guide communication studies that began with the entry point of commodification. Chapter 8 added a second entry point, spatialization, which addresses the process of overcoming the constraints of space and time in social life. The chapter described the use of the term across the social sciences, including sociology, geography, and new media studies. Drawing on this work, it proceeded to examine the use of spatialization in communication research primarily to address how organizations use communication to extend their power through various forms of concentration. This enables successful organizations to succeed in markets that now, with the aid of communication and information technologies, extend around the globe. The chapter also addressed additional forms of market power embodied in the interlocks of corporate boards, strategic alliances among firms, and such popular practices as merchandising agreements and product placements that extend the reach of companies across the economy.

Building close ties between political economy and geography, the chapter addressed the idea of spatial agglomerations or the concentration of businesses in a specific physical location. The study of geography has documented the many ways transportation and communication technologies have overcome the constraints of physical space. But this does not end the significance of geography because companies benefit from the opportunities to interact that locations like Silicon Valley provide. The prominence of regional centers like this, and all of its many offshoots, suggests that the globe is not becoming even figuratively flatter. Rather, it is comprised of hierarchies of places that feature powerful agglomerations of businesses which enable these regions to tower over others. Such hierarchies persist across regions and within cities. The gap between rich and poor in Silicon Valley and in New York's Manhattan is as great as it is between those places and poorer regions of the world. Communication and information technology is more likely to deepen global divisions than it is to overcome them.

Such divisions mean that governments continue to play a significant role in the global political economy. Some would look to government to bring fairness to the divisions that current forms of spatialization create. But given the power of business today, the tendency has been to make government look and act more like business. Hence, the major processes at work have included commercialization, which replaces public interest regulation with letting the market regulate business, and liberalization, which introduces competition into markets. It also includes privatization, which turns government-run organizations into private businesses, and internationalization, which establishes regional and global governance organizations that bring together government and business to manage international trade and eliminate the constraints on business that social welfare programs and public interest standards once imposed. These developments provide short-term gains for business. But their long-run efficacy is questionable because scaling back government ultimately makes it more difficult to manage increasingly complex global problems.

The chapter built on these ideas by examining the concept of globalization as a utopian myth, as a system for enabling capitalist businesses to flourish, and as a set of contradictory forces that globalization tries to incorporate even as these same forces challenge the very nature of a global political economy. These include the tendency for faith in communication and information technology to lead companies to extend their global reach beyond the ability to control their own practices. The resulting financial crises challenge the smooth functioning of globalization. So too does the global spread of organized crime, global terrorism, nationalism, and religious fundamentalism, as well as social movements based on the need to expand democracy. It is therefore best to view globalization as a conflict-ridden process that would use the tools of communication and information technology to overcome the space and time constraints on transforming the globe into a market ruled by concentrated business power. But rather than melt everything in its way, capitalism reshapes and is itself changed by forces that it seeks to control. Chapter 9 extends this argument by introducing the third entry point of structuration.

9

STRUCTURATION: CLASS, GENDER, RACE, SOCIAL MOVEMENTS, HEGEMONY

What is more influential: society or the individual? Are we the product of impersonal structures or are they dependent on us? Do we make history or does history make us? These are enduring questions that have perplexed philosophers and casual observers of social life for centuries. This chapter returns to them because political economy offers important insights and because they offer an opportunity to extend our theory of political economy by building a bridge to social structure and human agency. Moreover, just as spatialization provided a connection between political economy and geography, *structuration* connects political economy with sociology. Political economy starts from an encounter with the economic issues raised by commodification and proceeds to the spatial issues that were once sequestered in the field of geography. But it is not complete without an encounter with the social issues raised by sociologists and specifically with structuration.

Structuration describes a *process by which structures are constituted out of human agency, even as they provide the very "medium" of that constitution.* Social life is comprised of the mutual constitution of structure and agency; put simply, society and the individual create one another. We are the product of structures that our social action or agency produces. To paraphrase Marx, we do make history, but not under conditions of our own making. This chapter elaborates on these ideas by examining them through the lens of political economy, which insists on the importance of power in the relationship between structure and agency. Placing power at the center of the analysis concentrates the study of structuration on social class, race, gender, and social movements that are vital to understanding power relations today. Turning to culture, the chapter concludes by examining how power works to crystallize what is popularly called common sense into hegemony.

Structuration is a concept developed most prominently in the work of the sociologist Anthony Giddens (1984). From the start, Giddens presented the theory of structuration as an effort to bridge what he perceived to be a chasm between theoretical perspectives that foreground structure and those that emphasize action and agency. This encompasses the gap between, for example, the range of structural theories found in the work of Durkheim, Lévi-Strauss, and Althusser, and those action-oriented perspectives that span sociologists, including Max Weber, and such phenomenologically oriented theorists as Schutz and Gadamer.

To accomplish this, Giddens proposes that we consider structure as a duality including constraining rules and enabling resources. No longer the rigid scaffolding that controls and gives form to social life, structure both constitutes action and is reproduced by it. In this respect, structure and action are interconnected in the ongoing patterning of social life. As Giddens himself recognizes, the concept of structuration is not new to social thought. It is certainly a central component to Marx's historical work, featured most prominently in his *Eighteenth Brumaire of Louis Bonaparte* (1963/1869) where he elaborated on the now well-worn phrase that people make history, but not under conditions of their own making. The concept is now widely used in communication research, including attempts to broaden our understanding of media practices (Couldry, 2004), as well as in research on corporate public relations (Durham, 2005), and on collaborative work using new technologies (Evans and Brook, 2005).

One of the important characteristics of structuration theory is the prominence it gives to social change, seen here as a ubiquitous process that describes how structures are produced and reproduced by human agents who act through the medium of these structures. The concept of structuration responds to criticisms directed at functionalist, institutional, and structuralist thought arising out of their tendency to present structures as fully formed, determining entities. These approaches have made important contributions to understanding the operations of structures, but they have not given an adequate accounting of social change. In considering the relationship between structure and agency, we also need to examine the relationship between the maintenance of structures and the inevitability of social change. As the historian Eric Hobsbawn has argued:

> a structural model envisaging only the maintenance of a system is inadequate. It is the simultaneous existence of stabilizing and disruptive elements which such a model must reflect. ... Such a dual (dialectical) model is difficult to set up and use, for in practice the temptation is great to operate it, according to taste or occasion, either as a stable functionalism or as one of revolutionary change; whereas the interesting thing about it is, that it is both. (1973: 280)

This chapter suggests how structuration theory might join with the processes of commodification and spatialization to advance a political economy of communication. Specifically, structuration balances the tendency in political economic analysis to feature structures, typically business and governmental institutions, by addressing and incorporating the ideas of agency, social relations, social process, and social practice. At the same time, joining with Garnham (1990) among others, it rejects as extreme the notion that one can analyze agency in the absence of structures. This is because structure provides the medium out of which agency operates. Structuration theory is an approach to social life that aims to address goal-oriented, reflexive human action, without giving up on understanding the "sutures" of power that mutually constitute social action.

A major problem with Giddens' structuration theory is that it tends to accentuate individual agency, leaving us with a conception of structure limited to a set of *operating rules* and a *store of resources* which individual agents use to meet their needs. Giddens' conception of structuration is not always consistent, but the primary problem with it from a political economy perspective is that it is disconnected from an understanding of power and more generally from a critical approach to society. There are many different kinds of operating rules including, as Thompson notes (1989: 63), "moral rules, traffic rules, bureaucratic rules, rules of grammar, rules of etiquette, rules of football." Admittedly aware of this confusing range of possible referents, Giddens does not provide a satisfactory response, does not offer a clear sense of what are distinctly *social* rules, perhaps because such specificity would make it more difficult for him to establish the *transhistorical* theory essential to his opposition to Marx (Giddens, 1981). One can say the same about resources, which can include everything from the counseling services offered by a social welfare office to the commodity futures traded at the Chicago Mercantile Exchange. Again, arranging resources in a particular form would privilege one type, such as power resources, over others, thereby turning a general theory of social life into a historically specific reading of one among many manifestations. A political economy reading of structuration does just that. Specifically, while it retains Giddens' general notion of the duality of structure and action, it gives greater weight to *power* and to the incorporation of structuration into a *critical* approach to social analysis.

Such a focus deepens the substantive and methodological approach to power in political economy. As earlier chapters have insisted, political economy has made a substantial contribution to social research, including the explanation of communication practices, with a sustained analysis of the commodities, institutions, practices, and consequences that comprise the production, distribution, and use of power. Political economy has accomplished this with concepts and methodologies particularly suited to the large-scale or macroanalysis of power. This has enabled it to examine, for example, how mergers, acquisitions, labor practices, and borrowing have enabled Rupert Murdoch's News Corporation to amass the power to expand the production of media and information commodities and to influence government regulatory policies. The methodology used to carry out such research focuses on data about revenues, organizational structure, employment, as well as submissions to government bodies such as regulatory and policy agencies.

The emphasis on social action or agency that informs the structuration approach also insists on expanding this conception of power by examining how it operates at the constitutive, interactive, or micro-level of power. For example, from among the range of macro-pressures that confront the board of Time Warner, how does it constitute an agenda of priorities that lead it to enter one specific market rather than another, to buy one rather than another company, and to invest in one rather than another new technology? These decisions tend to be normalized as the objective assessments of the "bottom line," which is, in effect, a measure of the balance of macro-pressures. However, these objective assessments gloss over micro-power struggles that can grow out of the narrow interests of specific managers or board members. To expand this assessment involves using different research tools from those that political economists are trained to employ. These include ethnography, ethnomethodology, participant observation, and other means of observing the social practices that constitute the meaning of power for a particular set of actors (Pendakur, 2003).

It is equally important to emphasize the *social* as it is the micro. One of the problems with research on agency, because it addresses the micro-level of analysis, is that it is inclined to focus on the individual. But this departs from the social meaning of structuration. Agency is a fundamentally social conception that refers to individuals as social actors whose behavior is constituted from their matrix of social relations and positionings, including class, race, and gender. These social and individuating tendencies represent an ongoing tension in research on structuration. To recapitulate: structuration is an entry point to examine the mutual constitution of structure and agency in political economy. It is a starting point for expanding the conception of power and, in addition, it provides a lever for understanding the forms that social relations take in political economy.

When political economy has given attention to agency, process, and social practice, it has tended to focus on *social class*. There are good reasons for considering class structuration to be a central entry point for comprehending social life, as studies documenting the persistence of class divisions in the political economy of communication attest. Nevertheless, there are other dimensions to structuration that complement and clash with social class analysis, including gender, race, and social movements that are based on public issues such as access to the Internet. Along with social class, these constitute much of the social relations of communication.

From this use of structuration theory, we can think about society as a field of structuring actions initiated by agents that mutually shape class, gender, race, and social movement relations. According to this view, society exists, if not as a seamless, integrated whole, at least as a field on which various processes mutually constitute identifiable social relationships. The focus on class, gender, race, and social movement relationships is not intended to mean that these are essential ones to which all others can be reduced. Rather, this formulation suggests that these are central gateways to the analysis of structuration and that the social field is not merely a continuum of subjectivities denoted by categories whose value is purely nominal. Social class is real as *both* a social relationship and an instrument of analysis. Furthermore, the process of structuration constructs *hegemony*, defined as the taken-for-granted, common-sense, naturalized ways of thinking about the world. Hegemony includes everything from cosmology (does god or nature govern the universe?), through ethics (what distinguishes right from wrong?), to social practices (what constitutes good behavior?), that are both incorporated and contested in everyday life. It is a lived network of mutually constituting meanings and values.

This chapter contributes to the analysis of class, gender, race, social movements, and hegemony by demonstrating how these terms have been used in political economic research. One goal is to move beyond the notion that these are simply categories on which the media have impacts. It proposes to examine them as means of describing the *social relations of communication practices*, including how they serve to organize the agency of individuals who produce them. Out of the tensions and clashes within various structuration processes, the media of communication come to be organized in their full mainstream, oppositional, and alternative forms.

────────────────**Communication and Social Class**────────────────

Class analysis is one of the more well-trodden fields in social science (Weeden and Grusky, 2005; Wright, 2005). The communication and cultural theorist Raymond Williams (1976) begins his analysis of the concept by recognizing that it is an "obviously difficult" one, both in its range of meanings and in the specific application to a social division. The term appears in the Latin *classis* to describe a division according to property among the people of Rome and made its appearance in sixteenth-century English in a reference, which Veblen would appreciate, to the various forms of vanity. One of the problems with the term is that it evolved in a very general sense to indicate groups of plants and animals, as well as collections of people, without specific social implications. The modern division among types of social class, such as lower, middle, upper, and working, arose with the Industrial Revolution and particularly superseded other notions of division (such as estate) with the increasing awareness that social divisions are created and not just simply inherited.

Debate on the concept revolves around distinctions among categorical, relational, and formational dimensions which are terms usefully applied to all of the major forms of social division, including race and gender as well. Social class is *categorical* in the sense that it defines a category of people who occupy a position in society by virtue of its economic standing measured by wealth and or income. Seen as a *relationship*, social class refers to the connections among people based on their location with respect to the primary processes of social production and reproduction. In this sense, class is not a position that adheres to an individual or group, but a relationship that connects capital and the working class, based on ownership of the means of production. According to the relational view, capital does not exist without the working class and vice versa. Social class is therefore embodied in the shifting relationship that connects and divides them. Finally, class is also, as Williams (1976: 58) notes, "a *formation* in which, for historical reasons, consciousness of this situation and the organization to deal with it have developed." According to this view, class exists to the extent that people are aware and act on their class position. From this perspective, class is not just an external category, nor even just an external relationship. It also is a set of values that form an identity.

Although distinguishable as such, these ways of thinking about social class also overlap considerably. For example, much of the work of the social historian E.P. Thompson (1963) is about social class as relational and formational. His history of the working class in England examines how it arose in relationship to a new class of capitalists, who needed to employ what was once independent craft and agricultural labor in their new factories. In the process, new industrial workers came to identify with new values that formed the core of what it meant to be working class. There is also a long-standing debate about specific dimensions of these definitions. What marks a class category: income, wealth, power, status, some combination of these? What defines the relationship: the means of production? Of reproduction? Of administration? What constitutes class consciousness: individual awareness? Social communication? Organized resistance? Widespread differences about these dimensions and about the compatibility of various positions mark contemporary debates about social class.

The political economy of communication includes a literature on social class, principally from a categorical perspective, exploring the significance of class power. These encompass studies demonstrating how media elites produce and reproduce their control over the communication business, such as analyses of its class composition, as well as forms of integration and division within the media elite. Early studies include Mills' (1956) research on media and entertainment elites in the United States and Clement's (1975) assessment of media elites in Canada.

Several types of study mark contemporary research on social class. The first follows a long tradition by examining the role of media, including both news and entertainment in the construction of social class (Bullock, Wyche, and Williams, 2001; Heider, 2004; Kendall, 2005). This research explores how the media represent class divisions in society and how different social class segments actually behave or should behave in society. Some of these representations reinforce social class stereotypes but in different ways. On the one hand, there is the direct reinforcement that comes from portrayals, for example, of the "authoritarian" working class. On the other hand, there is the popular debasing of the upper class through depictions of their immoral or downright irrational behavior. Such portrayals suggest that those at top are incapable of self-control, let alone the rational and systematic exploitation of an entire society.

Next, contemporary research on social class and the media also pays greater attention to media outside North America and to the growing networks of class rule that link mass media to new communication and information technologies (Chakravartty and Zhao, 2008; Chinn and Fairlie, 2006; Graham, 2002; Mansell, 2002; Pendakur, 2003; van Dijk, 2005). There is especially greater attention on developments in China and India, where the media and information technology have grown spectacularly over the past decade. Research on the digital divide or the unequal distribution of access to new media services is also prominent, including studies of divides within societies and globally. There are also attempts to move beyond the digital divide idea by examining how to develop a package of communication and information services that would satisfy a fundamental human right to communicate.

Third, there are a growing number of studies that follow in the tradition of C. Wright Mills' classic work on the power elite. These examine the dense network that links media entrepreneurs to the rest of the elite class, through the range of connections on corporate boards, business associations, civic organizations, and private clubs (Artz and Kamalipour, 2003; Chomsky, 1999; Edge, 2007; Herman and Chomsky, 2002; McChesney, 2000; Rothkopf, 2008; Sussman, 2005). Specifically, it describes how media moguls like the Asper family in Canada are able to build a media empire and influence governments. It also addresses the processes by which a set of powerful institutional "filters" help to shape the construction of news at elite media like the *New York Times*. Some of this work recognizes that media increasingly spill over into the broader information arena and describe how power is applied to such diverse projects as the construction of a high-tech business district that saps resources from the needier sectors of society and the promotion of the global brands in newly emerging societies.

Fourth, there are studies that concentrate on the process by which class rule takes place in policy-making and regulation (Burkart and McCourt, 2006; Chakravartty and Sarikakis, 2006; Mosco, 2003; Schiller, 2007a). These also range widely to include struggles over the governance of digital music, the Internet, telecommunications systems, and information resources. Specifically, they document the mobilization of class power to construct a profitable regime of digital rights management over music, the expansion of corporate control over Internet governance, and the shift from public interest to market-based pricing in telecommunications and information.

These forms of class analysis are important because they demonstrate that class tells us a great deal about the production, distribution, and consumption of communication in society. Nevertheless, they treat social class largely in *categorical* terms. The primary interest is in determining membership position in a category and in describing related behavioral patterns, including those responsible for the reproduction of class categories. They foreground social class as structure and treat the process of class formation largely as a problem of reproduction. This work has been essential to the critique of liberal pluralist views that deny or ignore the existence of a class structure and which maintain that the production, distribution, and consumption of media is the natural outcome of a democratic marketplace. According to liberal pluralism, the market may need some adjustment but, because the primary unit of analysis is the individual consumer (defined as a person or a business), its proposed adjustments amount to improved market functioning for the individual, rather than the amelioration of fundamental class divisions.

Categorical class analysis provides a powerful critique of the liberal pluralist view, but its critical warrant can be strengthened by greater attention to three points. First, class analysis in communication would benefit by placing greater weight on *relational* and *formational* conceptions of social class. Second, it would be strengthened by addressing the connections between social class and other entry points in the structuration process, particularly *gender, race,* and those *social movements* that organize the energies of resistance to class (and other forms of) power. Finally it needs a tighter link to the construction of *hegemony*, or the social constitution of "common sense."

Whereas a categorical approach defines class by what is contained within a specific category, i.e. wealth or income, a relational method looks for the connections or links between categories. According to this view, social class is not designated by what a class contains or lacks, but by its relationship to other classes. There is no ruling class without a working class and vice versa. What principally counts about class is what defines the relationship between classes, for example, ownership and control over the means of production, reproduction, communication, etc. The relationship can be characterized in numerous ideal types, including *harmony*, where classes are integrated and mutually accept the class relationship, *separation*, where classes are largely excluded from one another, and *conflict* or *struggle*, where class relations are regularly contested.

In actual research practice, categorical and relational approaches overlap because one cannot speak of a category without some reference to the relationships that different categories form. Hence, even research that focuses almost complete attention on the communication elite will likely include material on the impact of this elite on its workforce and on consumers. Similarly, relational approaches necessarily refer to the categories that different relationships connect or divide. Even though the differences amount in practice to matters of degree or emphasis, these can be significant for the overall analysis of social class. One of the important consequences of a categorical emphasis in political economy is a specific view of class that foregrounds the resources that give class power to the top categories and what, as a result, those categories at the bottom lack. Findings based on this view are significant, but incomplete. It makes an important difference in the meaning of resource distribution to determine the nature of the relationships among classes that sustain or disrupt it.

Of equal significance is the problem of defining a class by what it lacks. Again, it is important to acknowledge the significance of a lack of control over the means of production, reproduction, and distribution, and of a lack of the wealth, income, and the opportunities that go along with them. In communication, it is equally significant to document the consequences of a lack of access to the means of communication, mass media, and telecommunications. However, such a categorical view is limited to the conclusion, however important, that the lower classes are defined by the absence of power-generating resources. Some sociologists have addressed this problem by viewing class structure as a continuum of categories (upper-upper, lower-upper, etc.), in which, as one moves down the continuum, classes exhibit diminishing resources. In communication, Fiske (1989) is most notable in his development of the categorical continuum approach to specifically cultural resources. However well this expands the class structure and recognizes some of the fuzziness at the borders of class categories, it does more to obscure real categorical and relational class differences than it does to advance either approach. A social relational approach rejects the calls for eliminating categories because it rejects the conclusion that they are merely artifacts of a real continuum and insists on specifying real relations among categories and on addressing class *formation*.

The concept of class formation is central to a structuration approach because it refers to the process by which social agency creates class through the medium of class structure. From this vantage point, one views class as an active process of social formation that makes use of, and is constrained by, the resources available in the class structure. Social class is therefore less a category relatively full or empty of resources, including communication resources, and more appropriately the set of changing social relationships resulting from the actions of social agents making use of, and limited by, the very structure of those relationships. In the process of social action, people constitute themselves and their class relations. This approach is less mechanical than one concentrating on categories because it permits one to see social class as both a central material force in social life and as the product of social action carried out by people on all sides of class relations.

Given the importance of a categorical view, one does not find many examples of social relational and formational approaches to social class in political economy research. This is understandable considering the ability of class power to deepen a sense of alienation, which Bourdieu once argued rests on "a force of something said with authority" by which subaltern classes are:

> [u]nceasingly asked to accept the point of view of others about themselves, to bear in themselves the viewpoint and judgment of others, they are always exposed to becoming strangers to themselves, to cease being subjects of the judgment they bring to bear on themselves, the centre of the perspective of the view they have of themselves. (Cited in Mattelart and Siegelaub, 1983: 19).

An early starting point for the formational approach is the communication research of Mattelart, who calls this task the search for a "lost paradigm" containing the ways subaltern classes constitute themselves, both in relation to dominant classes as well as from a self-conscious sense of their own needs and interests. Acknowledging the difficulties of moving beyond a categorical view, Mattelart (Mattelart and Siegelaub, 1983) addresses the use of the mass media and popular cultural practices outside the West and the tradition of rank-and-file communication among workers in the West. He does so to demonstrate how these people built their own means of communication, developed their own languages, and their own common sense. In the process, they established their own popular hegemony, which, though constituted along with, alongside and in conflict with a hegemony of the ruling classes, nevertheless provided independent grounds for social action, including class struggle. Political economists have begun to respond more substantially to this call for a formational approach to social class (Artz, Macek and Cloud, 2006; Calabrese and Sparks, 2004; Downing, 2001; Dyer-Witheford, 1999; Fones-Wolf, 2006; Mazepa, 2007; Schiller, 2007b). This research has begun to examine working people as actual producers of communication and culture. It is important to extend this discussion by examining a social class perspective that aims to go beyond the categorical by addressing labor in the communication industries.

Labor and Social Class

The exercise of class power in the workplace has a long history in political economy, with much of the debate in the nineteenth century centering around Marx's brief discussion of the separation of conception from execution at the point of production and reinvigorated in contemporary debates with the work of Braverman (1974). Since there are numerous dimensions to this topic in contemporary research on social class, it is useful to give this more extensive treatment, particularly since there is growing research on the exercise of class power in the communications workplace through the elimination of labor and through the exercise of surveillance-based control over the remaining workforce (Deuze, 2007; Huws, 2003; McKercher and Mosco, 2006, 2007; Mosco and McKercher, 2008). Furthermore, efforts are increasing to build on this research by offering relational and formational perspectives on communication labor and social class.

Because communication and information technology have become so influential, jobs based on these technologies are receiving a great deal of attention with particular emphasis on the class composition of the so-called knowledge occupations. How one addresses this issue has important political as well as theoretical implications. Some have defined knowledge labor narrowly, limiting it to work that directly manipulates symbols to create an original knowledge product, or to add obvious value to an existing one (Florida, 2002). According to this view, knowledge workers are people like writers and artists, web-page designers and software engineers, university professors and film directors. They comprise a so-called creative class that can translate intellectual power into political and economic power, as Daniel Bell predicted they would in his 1973 book *The Coming of Post-industrial Society*.

A broader definition of knowledge work encompasses the labor of those who handle, distribute, and convey information and knowledge. This includes school teachers at both the elementary and secondary levels, most journalists, librarians, media technicians such as telecommunication and cable television workers, as well as those who work in the postal services (see, for example, Day, 2007; Deuze, 2007; Kumar, 2007; Martin, 2007; Tracy and Hayashi, 2007). These are considered knowledge workers because an increasing amount of their work involves making use of information or information technology to efficiently and effectively deliver a product whose value is intended to expand a recipient's knowledge. In essence, they represent a middle class within the knowledge sector.

Finally, there is growing research asserting that anyone in the chain of producing and distributing knowledge products is a knowledge worker. In this view, the low-wage women workers in Silicon Valley and abroad, who manufacture and assemble cables and electronic components, are knowledge workers because they are an integral part of the value chain that produces the essential hardware of knowledge work (Pellow and Park, 2002; Smith, Sonnenfeld, and Pellow 2006). Similarly, call-center workers, who sell products and services over telecommunications networks, would also fall within this broad definition of knowledge work because they are central to selling information and because they make use of the products of communication technology to carry out their work. Furthermore, the management and control of their work would be far more difficult were it not for the advanced surveillance technologies made possible by developments in communication and information technology (Head, 2003).

In essence, a categorical class analysis of media and knowledge labor yields a three-level hierarchy. But that is not sufficient because it is important to look beyond external criteria and examine the subjective experiences of the workers themselves, including the ways they choose to organize or structure their trade unions. This takes us to a relational and a formational view of social class. Trade unions like the Communications Workers of America (CWA) and its Canadian counterpart, the Communications, Energy and Paperworkers Union of Canada (CEP), have brought together a diverse range of workers under the same umbrella – journalists and telephone operators, translators and customer service providers, health care workers and printers, as well as the people who write and broadcast the news and those who work the cameras and sound boards to bring it to viewers and listeners. These two unions have had some success in mobilizing all three social class levels of knowledge workers in effective labor actions. However, the mixed pattern of labor convergence across the communication sector in North America, including the failure of some creative unions to unite, leaves open the question of how trade unions themselves bound the term knowledge worker (McKercher and Mosco, 2007; Mosco and McKercher, 2008).

All of this is directly relevant to addressing the importance of social class because debates about the scope of how to think about knowledge work are also debates about social hierarchies. Since much of the research on knowledge work tends to see inclusion in that category as a positive development for the workers who make the move, the type of definition one accepts is also an implicit decision about who and how many are privileged. Limiting the definition to Florida's creative class, or even to his "super-creative" core, gives greater weight to the privilege of being a knowledge worker than would accepting a broader definition that covers different types of workers, including many, such as call-center employees, about whom it is far more difficult to justify the privileged label. A creative class opens the door to one type of political change, such as a shift in power to knowledge creators. A more heterogeneous vision of the knowledge work category points to another type of politics, one predicated on questions about whether knowledge workers can unite across occupational and national boundaries, whether they can translate solidarity based on a categorical view of their social class position into a formational view. Finally, what should knowledge workers do with their class solidarity?

Another significant division in the concept of knowledge work holds important but different political implications. Think of the continuum we have just described as operating along a vertical hierarchy, with directly creative workers at the top and those who build computer hardware at the bottom. Knowledge workers can also be divided along a horizontal axis, falling into a pure content category at one end of the continuum and a pure technical category at the other, with most knowledge and information workers located somewhere in the middle. Content and technical groups both include creative workers in Florida's meaning of the term, but many other types of workers as well. The content category encompasses artists, entertainers, teachers, journalists, musicians, and others who might also be called cultural workers. The technical category covers software designers, biomedical engineers, audiovisual technicians, and those whose creative contribution is the construction of code, the design and manufacture of technologies, and the production of signals. The work of this category makes possible the labor of cultural and other producers of what is typically viewed as content. Examined this way, the difficulties of calling all these people knowledge workers become readily apparent. What do engineers and writers have in common? Journalists and telecommunications specialists? Musicians and cancer scientists? Regardless of whether the concept of knowledge worker is defined broadly or narrowly along the vertical axis, we are still left with the divide between those who focus on creating culture and those who concentrate on technology. This may make sense in a categorical or relational definition of social class but does it make a difference formationally, i.e. in the class with which these workers identify?

This horizontal divide holds practical significance because cultural and technical workers are increasingly part of the same workplace and participate in the same labor process. This raises the obvious question of whether they can work together in a harmonious way. More importantly, technical and cultural knowledge workers are often included in the same labor organizations. Unions like the CWA and the CEP have brought together very different types of knowledge workers, not just those who are higher or lower in a vertical status hierarchy, but also those who are on one side or the other of the divide between cultural and technical workers. What does this mean for the prospects of building labor solidarity? Can this succeed within a single union, within a single country, across one border, or across one or more oceans? Considering the vertical and horizontal divisions that mark the meaning of knowledge work, it is easy to appreciate the challenge facing those who would unite them. Research in the political economy of communication demonstrates some of the successes and failures (Mosco and McKercher, 2008). But much more needs to be done because the stakes are high. Simply put, answering the question "Will knowledge workers of the world unite?" will go a long way to shaping the global political economy.

Communication and Gender

A political economic perspective makes use of social class as its entry point for examining structuration. The preceding section recognized the value of a categorical conception of social class and described its use in communication research. It also suggested how to build on this conception by incorporating relational and formational conceptions of social class. Such a turn strengthens the political economy of communication by deepening the meaning of social class that underlies so much of its work. Notwithstanding the importance of this project, the analysis of structuration calls for taking up additional conceptual coordinates.

Although social class is a necessary entry point for political economy, it is not a sufficient condition for addressing structuration and its relationship to communication, in part because it leaves the question of gender, in the words of Jansen (1989), "a socially structured silence." As earlier chapters demonstrated, unlike other approaches, political economy has not been entirely silent on the issue of gender, although it typically addresses the subject as a dimension of social class relations. For example, political economic research on information technology and the international division of labor describes the double oppression that women workers face in the microelectronics industry, where they experience the lowest wages and the most brutalizing working conditions (Pellow and Park, 2002). Nevertheless, even though political economy has made important contributions to a gender analysis, it has not aimed to incorporate gender relations as fully as possible within the limits of the political economy perspective (McLaughlin, 2004).

One obvious task is to consider the range of social perspectives on gender and assess their compatibility with a political economic framework. This is important because the goal is not to find a place for gender, or, specifically, for women, in political economic analysis. This sort of "search for women's place" is very much part of the problem. Rather, the goal for political economy is to determine how best to theorize gender within a political economic analysis, i.e. to suggest areas of agreement and, where these are not possible, to identify terms or zones of engagement between the frameworks. It is also important to emphasize that these efforts join those of Micky Lee (2007), McLaughlin and Johnson (2007), Meehan and Riordan (2002), Sarikakis and Shade (2007), and others whose work has taken important steps toward bridging perspectives. Moreover, it also recognizes the significant contribution of explicitly feminist scholarship that starts from the need to address the specific concerns of feminism before beginning to think about connections to alternative perspectives (Chambers, Steiner, and Fleming, 2004; Rakow and Wackwitz, 2004).

Political economic perspectives are most compatible with gender theories that foreground social, rather than biological or psychological categories. Moreover, on a spectrum comprising those social viewpoints from most to least tied to a political economy perspective, we start with gender approaches that begin with *social class as an entry point*, examining, for example, gender and power, next, those that concentrate on *social reproduction*, and finally, on the *duality of gender and class*, or the mutual formation of patriarchy and capitalism.

Perspectives that start with social class foreground the system of production and tend to locate gender within it. This point of view considers, for example, how the international division of labor creates labor hierarchies that locate women predominantly at the bottom, a reserve army of low-skilled, dependent, and flexible workers. A class analysis of communication similarly examines labor hierarchies in the business of producing and distributing media and information by addressing the presence of significant gender divisions within an overall class-divided system (Antcliff, 2005; Huws, 2003; M. Lee, 2007; McLaughlin and Johnson, 2007). Moreover, such an analysis considers the consequences for media access as it situates gender relations within a communication system that stratifies access opportunities by class. For example, class analysis documents diminished access among the poor, but the system of gendered power locates women disproportionately within this category, leaving women more marginal than men in access to media, telecommunication, and information technology, including both the jobs within these industries and the communication resources produced by them.

Theories of social reproduction move political economy closer to gender analysis because these shift the locus of attention from the production of media, or, in the case of access, from the production of audiences, to the reproduction of social relations. Concretely, this means a tendency to shift the center of attention from the workplace to the home, the family, and sexuality. Although operating on the territory that typically occupies gender analysis, political economy takes a major role because the analysis of social reproduction tends to examine the functional connections between the reproduction of capitalism and class structure and the reproduction of social relations in the home and family. From this point of view, the media serve to tie the home, particularly through the activities of women, to the system of production and consumption by replenishing the energies of workers and connecting people to networks of consumption that thicken with each wave of new media and information technology. To complete the cycle, needs, interests, and desires emerging from the process of social reproduction become the source of entertainment and information programming which are used as direct and indirect vehicles for promoting consumption (Dines and Humez, 2002; Lovell, Hartmann, and Karski, 2006; Mosco and McKercher, 2008: Chapter 3).

Explicitly functionalist analyses of social reproduction persist, but most acknowledge the presence of contradictory tendencies and forms of resistance that loosen the link between capitalism and gendered power. For example, as Adam Smith, Marx, and other classical political economists recognized, capitalism tends to move in different directions with respect to gender (as well, *vis-à-vis* race and ethnicity). Even as social class power constitutes hierarchies of production that keep women out or, at best, marginalized, it erodes many of the traditional practices that limited the available human resources. Hence, although capitalism continues to constitute job ghettoes for women, as a result of political struggle it also loosens restrictions on education, occupation, and other forms of women's social activity and social mobility. Similarly, systems of communication that tighten the connections to consumption also provide instruments for breaking with traditional roles, practices, and values. These are further instances of the view that capitalism is both dynamic and contradictory. Moreover, as again is evident in Marx, capitalism creates conflict across the range of social relations, including class and gender. Capitalism uses class power to structure the social relations of production and consumption, but it cannot guarantee that this will work successfully, principally because the people who participate in these structuring practices are self-reflexive and able to act socially on their own needs and interests, however distorted and partially formulated. One consequence is that people recognize the opportunity in the erosion of traditional bonds and take an active role in the process of restructuring them. As a result, the process of reproduction is contested and the sources of social resistance to capitalism are multiplied, but also dispersed.

Both social class and gender become grounds for opposition and resistance, acting sometimes congruently, as when telephone operators, overwhelmingly women, organize feminist caucuses within telephone worker unions to fight for better wages and working conditions. But, as debates within feminist movements indicate, this is not always the case. One source of tension reflecting, perhaps more intensely, fissures within the wider society, is between class and gender solidarity. This tension is manifested in debates over the relative emphasis that one should place on overcoming class divisions by, for example, providing the poor with greater access to and control over the means of communication, or on overcoming gender divisions within classes, for example, by opening more positions within the executive ranks of media companies to women. Social reproduction is contested, but so too are forms of resistance (Bakker and Gill, 2003; Meehan and Riordan, 2002).

Alongside perspectives that begin with class and those that foreground social reproduction, are another set that view gender and class as *independent* categories, each of which provides a grounding for power relations in society. According to this position, society is *both* a patriarchy (gender-divided) and capitalist (class-divided). These co-exist independently within the social field, sometimes interact, and, at times, are mutually constitutive (Steeves, 2001; see also Meehan and Riordan, 2002; Sarikakis and Shade, 2007). An approach based on the duality of patriarchy and capitalism, which has recently emerged in some parts of feminist standpoint theory (see Chapter 6), has the advantage of providing a broad field of analysis because it permits one to concentrate on a specific grounding without ignoring the other, as in studies of capitalist patriarchy or patriarchal capitalism. The approach faces some of the same challenges of any framework based on mutual formation, such as how to characterize the field they occupy – patriarchal or capitalist, and which is adjective and which is noun – and how to describe the nature of their interaction. It faces the additional problem of aiming to address mutual formation without a specific entry point such as class or gender (Dines and Humez, 2002).

These three approaches suggest ways to think about gender within an overall political economy of communication. Their major strength is that, of all categorical approaches, they are relatively simple to apply to specific structural problems in communication studies, such as access to media, to power in media organizations, and to the policy-making process. Their weakness is also that of categorical approaches: they tend to pay less attention to the process of social formation, specifically, to how people actively constitute gender in relation to the mass media, to social class, and to the range of choices within gender (e.g. heterosexuality and homosexuality).

A *formational* approach concentrates on the process of creating a gender identity through the mutual formation of social structures, the means of communication, the product of communication, and the agency of individuals who act as social beings in social relationships. For example, such a perspective examines the formation of gender through the relationships among media institutions, which are situated in a wider political economy, the medium of television, the programs it broadcasts, and the way individuals, who come to the mass-mediated experience with specific, though dynamic, social roles and relationships, understand and act on this programming. Partly because they require that rare transdisciplinary and transnational perspective, spanning political economic and cultural analysis, exemplars remain somewhat sparse (McLaughlin, 2004). Some of the closest approximations lie in social history, where commitments to either of these approaches take a back seat to a social understanding of a particular period (Curran, 2002; DiCenzo, 2004).[1] This work confirms that the term social reproduction is at once too simple and too blunt to describe this process because it implies a "copy" theory of social development and

---

1 DiCenzo's article is particularly important because it provides both a guide to feminist media history and to the many pressure points that it must address, such as balancing the history of women, of media, and of an historical period.

assumes a linear relationship between texts and social experience. Analysts of culture have made progress by reminding us of the polysemic nature of texts, broadly understood to include the full range of media products, but they have tended to fall victim to their own form of simplification, namely a consistent neglect of the relationship between media products and the institutional processes of production and distribution that bring them into being, as well as a tendency to ignore the social embeddedness of individual agency. Furthermore, institutions and social roles are not mere contexts for texts and individual agency, a suggested solution to the institutional and social category blind spot in cultural research. They are full participants in a process of mutual formation. Social histories of mass communication technology have made important contributions to the documentation of this complex process. These include Douglas's work (1987) on the mutual constitution of technology and gender in the relationship of "amateur" radio to the formation of masculinity (see also Douglas, 2004), Beetham's (1996) on the development of women's magazines, Haralovich and Rabinowitz (1999) on women and the history of television entertainment, and Green (2001) on the history of the telephone as seen through the lens of gender and race.

Communication and Race

The powerful and multifaceted effort to theorize gender within areas largely dominated by class analysis holds out the prospect for a renewed political economy of communication that encompasses broader and deeper dimensions of social experience than what is traditionally understood in the discipline. Nevertheless, class and gender, individually or in tandem, do not exhaust the categories that are vital to an understanding of the structuration process in part because, on their own, they do not leave sufficient room for understanding the power of race and related categories such as ethnicity and nationality.

In 1903, the American black nationalist W.E.B. DuBois said that "the problem of the twentieth century is the problem of the color line." For him, the color line was drawn within and across nations as a principal source of divisions within societies and between the rich and powerful nations of the predominantly white West and the poor and dependent rest of the world. Although, as we have seen, communication studies has addressed the question of imperialism extensively, principally by examining the role of the media and information technology in its formation, the discipline has done so to extend a sense of the world as class-divided. It is less frequently viewed as gender-divided (as in the case of studies on women in the international division of labor) and as *race-divided* (Ehrenreich and Hochschild, 2003; Sarikakis and Shade, 2007). That is why it is especially important to identify race as a vital participant in the process of structuration. Racial divisions are a principal constituent of the manifold hierarchies that make up the contemporary global political economy, and race, as both a category and a social relationship, contributes fundamentally to individual and collective access to national and global resources, including communication, media, and information technology (Gandy, 1998).

A categorical understanding of race, like that of class and gender, addresses the differential access to communication that racial divisions bring about. This includes access to ownership and control of communication companies (US GAO, 2008) and to jobs in the media, communication, and information technology industries (Ankney and Procopio, 2003; Benson, 2005; Green, 2001; Thanki and Jefferys, 2007; Wilson, Gutiérrez, and Chao, 2003; Johnston and Flamiano, 2007; Newkirk, 2002). It also encompasses media representations of the range and diversity of minority images (Clawson and Trice, 2000; Downing and Husband, 2005; Gray, 2004; Henry and Tator, 2002; Myers, 2004). Kim (2008) describes how numerous of these stereotypes persist today:

- Black men are threatening
- Black women are "sassy"
- Asian and Asian American women are exotic yet passive
- Asian and Asian American men lack masculinity
- Latinos are presumed not to be citizens
- Middle Easterners are suspected terrorists
- Native Americans are "noble savages"

Tabor documents the historic tolerance of racism in American broadcasting, including numerous cases that demonstrate how the broadcast regulator, the Federal Communications Commission (FCC), tolerated explicit racism in television:

> in the mid-1960s, white supremacists, who managed Jackson, Mississippi television station WLBT, covered the screen with a "Sorry Cable Trouble" sign whenever network programming featured an African-American. Clergy and local citizens banded together to challenge the lack of access given African-Americans on the Jackson station. But the FCC denied the clergy and citizens' standing and conditionally renewed the station's license. (Tabor, 1991: 612)

When a federal court overturned the Commission's decision, the FCC ignored the court and renewed the station's license for a full three-year period. A federal appeals court finally directed the FCC to vacate the license grant to WLBT (United Church of Christ v. FCC F.2d 543, 549–50 (DC Cir. 1969)). Despite 1968 regulations, embraced by the FCC, to eliminate employment discrimination in broadcasting, it was not until 1989 that the Commission upheld a complaint of employment discrimination against a licensee.

From a global perspective, race is a central force in the formation of the international divisions of labor, whose hierarchies include class and gender, but also, vitally, race, in the organization of skills and control situated within a world political economy increasingly defined by the production of microelectronics and information (Smith, Sonnenfeld, and Pellow, 2006).

The racial division of access to media and communication is not without its problems for capitalist development. When ethnic and racial minorities are not incorporated into communication networks, businesses miss opportunities to expand and deepen their markets. As is the case with class and gender, one of the principal fault lines in the construction of markets is the trade-off between incorporating new people and the ground that must be given up with new messages and images that potentially challenge the dominant narratives that occupy most of audiovisual space.

The categorical approach to race and the media documents the significance of race across the various forms of media access. There are fewer studies that address the social relational and formational dimensions of race and the media (Gandy, 1998; Green, 2001; Hunt, 1997; Leung, 2005). These demonstrate that one cannot comprehend the structuration of race in the media without taking into account how it operates through the struggles of minorities to gain access to jobs in the mass media, through the creation of alternative media reflecting the lived experience of minorities, and through pressure to change the presentation of minority information and entertainment in the mass media. As in the case of those studies which foreground gender, some of the most interesting work in this area tends to concentrate in social history. Saxton (1990) demonstrates this in a history of white racism in the United States by identifying those economic levers, from the slave trade to a segmented job market, as well as those cultural instruments, including academic analyses of racial inferiority and popular entertainments like minstrel shows, that reproduced a set of race (and class) relations. These are considerably more than embodiments of white racism. They are also social practices that are constantly put to the test, challenged, revised, and reformulated in the context of racial conflict and wider political economic change. The practices themselves thereby contain evidence of social contestation, as when, for example, black minstrelism became a force of social satire directed at attacking, however gingerly, the very racism it traditionally reinforced. People as diverse as Abraham Lincoln, Mark Twain, and Eugene Debs, who, in Saxton's assessment (1990: 390), were "not so much dissenters as collaborators in the midst of white racial politics, ... nonetheless projected broader visions of human possibility." In addition, at every stage in the construction and reproduction of white racism, oppositional forces like African-American abolitionists, who produced a voluminous anti-racist literature, struck at the heart of racist premises. These embody Sivanandan's conclusion about racism and colonialism:

> I think that it's a mistake to think of colonialism as a one-way street, as something that is done to you, as something that takes you over, something so powerful you can't resist it. There is always a resistance somewhere that comes out of your own culture, your language, your religion. And that resistance first takes the form of an existential rebellion – a rebellion against everything that goes against your grain. (1990: 3; see also Linebaugh and Rediker, 2000)

Communication and Social Movements

The mutual constitution of class, gender, and race is an important dimension of the overall structuration process. A complete analysis of this process would include generational and other processes, although there is the danger that this can all too easily devolve into a pluralistic compilation of equally influential social categories. A political economic approach identifies structuration as a social process which starts from class, as category, relationship, and formation and examines how it is constituted principally with gender and race. Notwithstanding the value of this approach, it contains the added risk of mechanistic thinking about how these terms operate in practice and how they should be brought together in praxis. Arguing from a feminist perspective, Haraway reflects on the difficulty of connecting class, gender, and race, and suggests the need for new geometries of social relations:

> It has seemed very rare for feminist theory to hold race, sex/gender, and class analytically together – all the best intentions, hues of authors, and remarks in prefaces notwithstanding. In addition, there is as much reason for feminists to argue for a race/gender system as for a sex/gender system, and the two are not the same kind of analytical move. And, again, what happened to class? The evidence is building of a need for a theory of "difference" whose geometries, paradigms, and logics break out of binaries, dialectics, and nature/culture models of any kind. Otherwise, threes will always reduce to twos, which quickly become lonely ones in the vanguard. And no one learns to count to four. These things matter politically. (1991: 129)

Haraway's point is important for a political economy of communication, if only because it questions all essentialisms, whether based on class, gender, or race. However, her argument goes beyond these in its pessimism about those approaches, like the one taken here, which eschew essentialism by offering an analysis based on entry points and multiple determinations. Although the thrust of this book is more optimistic about examining the social relations of class, gender, and race, it is useful to consider additional formulations within the general political economy framework. Two possibilities focus on *social movements* and the social relations of *hegemony*.

An analysis organized around social movements holds out the advantage of transcending traditional social categories by concentrating on social agency and social action. Social movements bring together people from a range of social identities who are, more or less, united by a specific interest which includes opposing and seeking to transform established dominant power relations. Social movements can also unite people identified with a particular class position, such as trade unionists, the poor, or business elites. They can also connect people around gender, as does the range of feminist movements, or around race, for example the US civil rights and black power movements. Furthermore, they can mobilize people based on other categorical identities, such as age or nationality. However, the success of social movements typically depends on their ability to transcend particular social categories by uniting a diverse collection of people around a specific interest or cause, such as the movements to support fair trade and oppose corporate-controlled globalization.

In recent years, considerable attention has been directed to movements emphasizing identification with interests and causes that, while not omitting a concern for social categories (the feminist movement is probably the most strongly categorical), are nevertheless chiefly taken up with specific goals. These "new social movements" include pre-eminently those organized around the environment, globalization, health (especially in the fight against AIDS), and sexual preference (gay liberation). They unite people across traditional categories and establish the grounds for greater attention to non-traditional categories.

The line between old and new social movements is not firm, although considerable heat has been expended on defending one or the other as politically superior. Some argue that the global political economy makes class-based movements more important than ever, and others attack this position by claiming that a post-fordist or postmodern information economy diminishes the significance of such categories in favor of movements that unite diverse people behind a general cause, such as environmentalism (Della Porta and Diani, 2006; McDonald, 2006; Meyer, 2006). Old social movement approaches tend to be linked to traditional political economic concerns, while those that call our attention to the new movements tend to place greater emphasis on cultural identification, including the power of various media (social networking sites, reality TV, flash mobs) to forge new cultural links and propel some of these into full-blown movements. Unfortunately, although the literature on new social movements has broken new ground, so much attention has been taken up with the *break* from the old that common ground has been underemphasized and consequently so too the political potential of forging alliances across old and new movements. This has begun to change as new research takes up connections between such enduring categories as social class and newer ones such as environmentalism and sexual preference. There is no doubt that concerns over the environment, gender, and race have provided the basis for major social movements of the late twentieth century. Nevertheless, this does not mean that society is any less class-divided, that labor is no longer a central social activity and a force in social organization, and that trade unionism is politically spent (Mosco and McKercher, 2008). In addition to focusing on the process of political action, a social movement approach is valuable specifically because it rejects categorical imperatives of both old and new varieties.

Social movements are particularly important for a political economy of communication because they have influenced the development of the means and content of communication. In facing up to the inevitable question of how to organize internal and external communication, all of the major social movements have developed communication strategies and policies. Among the most prominent issues are how *democratic* should be the lines of internal communication, the extent to which a movement should adopt mainstream forms of external communication, and the degree of specialized or expert attention a movement should devote to media activity. Early work by the sociologist Todd Gitlin (1980) proved to be especially important because it suggested that a movement's media policy cannot be distinguished from its fundamental goals. Specifically, he showed how the American student anti-war movement lost some of its democratic moorings when it permitted leaders to become media personalities.

The political economy of the mass media itself has contributed to the formation of social movements organized principally around media production and policy. Alternate media movements worldwide have challenged dominant media forms, technologies, images, and messages from perspectives that link political economy to social movement theory (Hackett and Carroll, 2006), to organizational communication theory (Ganesh, Zoller, and Cheney, 2005), and to autonomist social thought (Dyer-Witheford, 1999). These movements range widely to include literacy campaigns, street theater, alternative newspapers, video, and film production, cartooning, public access cable programming, alternative computer networks, video piracy, computer hacking, and other forms of Internet activism. They differ in how they challenge established forms of media. Some, like the massive literacy movements in Cuba and Nicaragua, contested, out of political philosophy and practical necessity, technology-intensive forms of communication and education (Mattelart, 1986). Others, such as video piracy, hacking, and Internet activism take on concentrated control over the means of communication (Hanke, 2005; Kahn and Kellner, 2004). Still others, such as the alternative press and public access radio and cablecasting, offer fundamentally different messages and images from those of the mainstream (Howley, 2003, 2004; Stengrim, 2005; Switzer and Adhikari, 2000; Waltz, 2005).

Social movements have also been prominent in organized challenges to dominant media policies. The movement organized around a New World Information and Communication Order was arguably the most significant international effort to take on dominant forms of media policy-making, particularly the control that Western transnational businesses held over the production and distribution of the major mass media (Sosale, 2003; Traber and Nordenstreng, 1992). The movement continues today in the activities around the World Summit on the Information Society which, among other things, aims to enshrine the Right to Communicate among fundamental human rights accepted by international organizations (Chakravartty and Sarikakis, 2006; Thomas, 2006).

Numerous social movements have taken on national and local policy-making processes, including efforts to democratize decisions about station licensing, spectrum allocation, industry structure, and media content. Historically, these movements have been particularly strong in the United States, which saw intense struggles over the development of the telegraph and telephone, with groups led by trade unions and rural political organizations calling for public ownership or, at least, social control over the development of telecommunications along the model of the public postal service (DuBoff, 1984; Stone, 1991). The development of radio and television broadcasting brought about similar struggles with trade unions and educational interests in the forefront of efforts to promote public broadcasting and strong regulation of commercial channels (Fones-Wolf, 2006; McChesney, 1993; McKercher and Mosco, 2007).

The growth of the civil rights and feminist movements unleashed new energy into the broadcasting reform movement. The former used the courts to gain standing for groups representing the general public interest before the Federal Communications Commission, the federal regulator which had ruled out such standing as a usurpation of its powers. Feminist groups joined their civil rights counterparts to attack established hiring practices and degrading programming (Creedon, 1993). Learning from these left-of-center movements, the right wing organized a strong media movement of its own to attack what it claimed were morally offensive programs (Jamieson and Capella, 2008). Contemporary interest in the development of interactive media, particularly the ferment over media concentration and persistence of inequities in access to new media, has breathed new life into the public interest media reform movement (Communication Workers of America, 2007; McChesney, 2000, 2007).

Hegemony

Hegemony provides another dimension to the process of structuration by describing how our common-sense view of society is constituted, including, for example, the stereotypes discussed in this chapter's section on race and the sense of what it takes to change them. The term achieved prominence in the West principally through the work of social philosopher and activist Antonio Gramsci, who made it a central feature of his intellectual project. Specifically, he sought to understand the specific contours of advanced capitalist societies by concentrating on their capacity to base control on *consent* more than on physical coercion. The concept of hegemony is situated between the concepts of ideology and values. Ideology typically refers to the deliberate distortion or misrepresentation of social reality to advance specific interests and maintain hierarchies of power. On the other hand, values denote those shared social norms connecting the wide range of differently placed people and strata in society. Hegemony differs from these in that it is the ongoing formation of both image and information to produce a map of common sense which is sufficiently persuasive to most people that it provides the social and cultural coordinates to define the "natural" attitude of social life. Hegemony is therefore more valuable than the concept of ideology because it is not simply imposed by class power, but constituted *organically* out of the dynamic geometries of power embedded in social relations and social organizations throughout society. It is more useful than the concept of values because hegemony incorporates both power and common sense whereas values leaves little room for power.

The notion of *tradition* is a powerful instrument in the construction of hegemony. In his attempt to remove the naturalistic gloss that gives the very idea of hegemony its transhistorical quality, Hobsbawn describes "invented traditions" which, like the ceremony surrounding the British monarchy, appear "ancient and linked to an immemorial past." These are, in fact, "a set of practices, normally governed by overtly or tacitly accepted rules and of a ritual or symbolic nature, which seek to inculcate certain values and norms of behaviour by repetition, which automatically implies continuity with the past" (Hobsbawn, 1992: 1). Tradition roots people in a past that achieves a mythic status, setting it beyond the empirical tests of historians and social scientists. The annual celebrations in honour of St Patrick and Christopher Columbus re-enact for Americans a white immigrant narrative of rugged individuals who worked hard to achieve prosperity and acceptance in society.

The invention of tradition is one of the central social processes in the creation of hegemony, one component of which, what Poulantzas (1978) called *individuation*, takes on a life of its own outside tradition. This refers to the tendency of capitalism to transform collective categories and identities into individual ones, thereby diminishing the social power of class, gender, race, and other forms of collective energy. The working class, women, and blacks are thereby reconstituted as individual subjects.

Hegemony is also embodied in a range of substantive ideas such as the widespread acceptance of the marketplace as the cornerstone of a productive economy, of voting as the primary means of carrying out democracy, and of journalistic objectivity as the product of two views on an issue of the day (Goldman and Rajagopal, 1991). Free markets, free elections, a free press, the free flow of information, and other hegemonic ideas are neither politically neutral values, nor ideological instruments of control imposed from above. They constitute the common-sense currency of everyday life, developing out of those social relationships that make up hierarchies of class, gender, race, etc.

Gramsci's analysis of hegemony was inextricably bound to his political project, which would replace revolutionary action and direct military attack, advanced by "enlightened" leaders in the vanguard, with an oppositional and alternative hegemony. This counter-hegemony would constitute a new common sense, a new currency of everyday life that, over the many struggles or "wars of position," would establish a social democratic alternative to capitalist common sense. Gramsci's alternative did not *replace* a political with a cultural strategy. Instead, it broadened the conception of revolutionary politics to encompass the social struggle over cultural and linguistic space.

Given the power of hegemonic ideas, how is it possible to accomplish Gramsci's transformation? The task is all the more daunting, when one recognizes the dynamic power of a dominant hegemony, as it responds to changing political and social relations to take on new forms such as, for example, the expansion of national into continental and global hegemonic blocs, the incorporation of what were once oppositional notions, such as formal gender equality, into the dominant hegemonic constellation, and the reconstruction of ideas about social welfare and private charity. Global neoliberalism, the vision of the world as one large market managed by global business with support from national governments and international organizations constitutes a powerful hegemony. It is little wonder that some intellectuals would go as far as to state that the world has reached the end of history, a time when fundamental social change has ended and all that remains is managing the problems of a global marketplace. Computers and information technology provide the tools to do so and, by enabling instantaneous communication, they also bring us, in the minds of others, to the end of geography and the end of politics as well (Mosco, 2004). But hegemony of this sort was much more powerful in the 1990s when the dotcom bubble was inflating and before two jet planes crashed into New York's World Trade Center.

Notwithstanding the power of a dominant hegemony, there are good arguments to be made for the view that hegemony does not present an impregnable barrier. Yes, hegemony is stronger than ideology because it is based on consent, rather than coercion. But consent is very demanding, calling as it does for the ongoing formation of widespread, willing agreement to accept the dominant view as natural. Unlike formulations based on the logic of capital, of a dominant ideology, or of values embedded in the natural right to rule, hegemonic power is built from social relationships requiring complicity across class, gender, race, and other hierarchies. And this is more difficult to maintain when economic bubbles burst and when terrorist attacks lead to military invasions that remind one painfully that history, geography, and politics inevitably return with a vengeance.

Moreover, once achieved, consent is a powerful form of control; but a process that *requires* consent implies resistance and the potential for alternative forms of common sense. Hence, although hegemony is a central means of accomplishing the structuration of social relationships, it does not guarantee their reproduction. Hegemony is carried out over a contest for consent which, while situated within what Mahon (1980) called an "unequal structure of representation," is sufficiently unstable to admit oppositional and alternative hegemonies (Worth and Kuhling, 2004).

Two major tasks for political economy are to identify the sources of instability in the dominant hegemony and to assess the range of forms taken by oppositional and alternative hegemonies. The former include gaps between what passes for common sense and lived experience. One of the central problems of capitalist hegemony has been to constitute consent for the idea that capitalism produces widespread material abundance in a world full of poverty, including in its own heartland. Numerous defenses offer alternatives to the conclusion that it is the economic system itself which produces poverty. These include references to the *culture of poverty* argument that blames the poor for its own condition. In the extreme, the culture of poverty argument amounts to an academic gloss on racism: blacks, Hispanics, and indigenous people would advance if only they were able to overcome their own social and cultural tendencies, which include the wrong values, work habits, family and sexual practices, and attitudes toward money.

Another favored defense is the "trickle down" view that, over time, economic policies favoring the rich will inevitably trickle down to benefit the entire class structure. This is a variation on the general defense based on the distinction between the short and long run which, in the face of evident short-term consequences (a decision favors one group over another), claims that, in the long run, the consequences will even out. Compaine (2001) offers a trickle-down view to defend the current distribution of communication and information resources. His reading of technological history leads him to conclude that the long run will see access even out across class and other social divisions.

Alternatively, the dominant hegemony often defends itself with an ironic wink, that is, with the stylistic detachment that knows full well that major gaps exist between what passes for common sense and lived experience. As several scholars have documented, political and media institutions have perfected this form of postmodern irony, creating a bond between cynical narrator or plot line and viewers that respond to the gap with knowing recognition that, yes, it exists, but more importantly, "no one is pulling the wool over our eyes" (Glynn, 2000; Miller, 1988). Finally, another major defense relies on no direct defense at all, but rather defends indirectly through the production of entertainment and information that is largely about something else, about attractive distractions that suggest, among other things, that it is better to think about something else, or not to think at all.

Raymond Williams (1980) drew on Gramsci's notion of hegemony to develop the ideas of *oppositional* and *alternative* hegemonies with respect to cultural and media practices. Either form requires the development of a new intellectual leadership which departs from both establishment and revolutionary traditions by rejecting divisions between analysis and political practice, between conceptual and technical knowledge, and between thinking and working. For Gramsci, these leadership qualities constitute "organic intellectuals" who use them to advance the development of oppositional and alternative hegemonies. As a long tradition of informational, dramatic, comedic, and other forms demonstrate, oppositional hegemonies attack the shortcomings in the dominant form by peeling back the glossy covers that mask its contradictions. These cultural practices of opposition and resistance do not necessarily presume an alternative hegemony but, depending on their success, make it easier to create one. Hence, the struggle for media reform leads people to imagine a democratic communication system and the struggle against free trade leads to imagining a fair trade system based on widespread participation in decisions about global governance and a commitment to equal access to all of the resources necessary to lead a full life. Alternative hegemonies, in varying degrees of explicitness and over a range of forms, describe the substance of different ways to make a new common sense of social life, suggesting that it is worthwhile and realistic to think about these differences and to act toward their realization. In this way, the concept of hegemony serves as a broadly based organizing principle or process providing another way of thinking about structuration, one which overlaps, complements, and departs from the processes of constituting class, gender, race, and social movements.

Conclusion

This chapter has examined structuration or the process by which social structures are constituted out of human agency, even as they serve as the very medium of social constitution. Political economy brings an emphasis on power to the structure–agency dualism. Structures constrain individuals by using economic, political, and cultural power. One consequence of this use is the establishment of social class, gender, race, and other social categories that make up the major divisions in the social field. But social class and other divisions are not just a consequence of structural pressure, they also result from the agency of individuals and social groups who use their own power to constitute themselves in the world and in relationship to others. The political economy of communication looks at how these divisions document differences in access to media and information technology as well as to jobs in the media and IT industries. It also looks at how people make use of media and information technology to increase their own power to shape social structures. In addition to examining social class, gender, and race, the chapter considered social movements that use communication to bring about social change, including the movement to create democratic communication systems. Finally, it took up the concept of hegemony or the process of constructing a taken-for-granted world view. Distinguished from ideology and social values, hegemony draws its strength from achieving the consent of those it would control, but it also requires the exercise of power to maintain consent under changing conditions.

Communication plays a central role in hegemony as both old and new media are vital to the successful maintenance of hegemonic control as well as to resistance and the construction of counter-hegemonies.

This brings to a conclusion the analysis of the political economy of communication organized around the three entry processes of commodification, spatialization, and structuration. The discussion broadened the grounds for thinking about communication from a political economic perspective, but it looked outward only within the neighborhood of political economy. The next chapter concludes the book by moving beyond the neighborhood to those disciplines which, though on the boundaries of political economy, nevertheless constitute different intellectual regions. Specifically, it takes up the challenges which cultural studies and public choice theory pose for the political economy of communication. It also suggests new opportunities for political economy beyond these border disciplines.

10

CHALLENGES ON THE BORDERS... AND BEYOND

---------------------------------- **Borderlines** ----------------------------------

The last three chapters provided a theoretical perspective on the political economy of communication from the inside, by assessing the state of the discipline's central questions and ideas. Rethinking and renewing political economy also requires one to look outward, at the relationship between the discipline and those on its borders. Admittedly, one can map the universe of academic disciplines in innumerable ways. Political economy can be situated opposite sociology, political science, geography, and economics, among other approaches. Taking into account the central problems we have identified in a political economy of communication, it is particularly useful to locate the discipline opposite cultural studies, on the one side, and public choice theory on the other.

It would undoubtedly be presumptuous for this chapter to attempt a full-blown critique of these perspectives. The literature in both fields contains excellent maps, analyses, and critiques. Rather, starting from a political economic perspective, the chapter aims to continue a conversation that would benefit each. In addition to this primary goal, the chapter also contributes to identifying strengths and weaknesses within and between cultural studies and public choice that are elements of an ongoing process of rethinking these approaches. As Grossberg (1991: 55) has put it, "The point is not so much to choose between them, although one inevitably must do so, but define new forms of alliance and cooperation amongst them."

Over the years, communication scholars have identified the discipline's principal fault lines in different ways, including the distinction between behavioral and normative, and between administrative and critical approaches. Since the 1990s, the distinction between political economy and cultural studies has attracted considerable attention. This is understandable since cultural studies has grown substantially over the past four decades, has influenced communication studies substantially, and raises fundamental questions about the assumptions, methods, and conclusions offered by alternative approaches, including political economy (Deetz and Hegbloom, 2007; During, 1993; Grossberg, Nelson, and Treichler, 1992; Peck, 2006). Moreover, since communication studies has tended to take root in the arts and humanities divisions of universities, the discipline understandably gravitates to a dialogue with cultural studies. It is therefore essential to take up the challenge of cultural studies in order to establish a sound political economy approach to communication studies.

It is equally important for political economy to critically evaluate its relationship to public choice theory, where, in spite of a substantial increase in the attention of communication scholars, little systematic reflection has taken place. One can define public choice theory in different ways, but this chapter specifically views the field as an amalgam of pluralist thought in political science and neoclassical thought in economics whose goal extends beyond explaining behavior to a normative interest that evaluates and recommends policy courses of action. The pluralist wing has occupied the orthodoxy of political science and public policy research. More recently, neo-classical economists have made use of central assumptions, categories, and theories to shift the center of gravity in policy studies. As a result, approaches variously labeled public choice theory, policy science, and positive political economy now occupy an important place, several of whose practitioners have achieved worldwide notoriety by winning the Nobel prize in economics, including one, Ronald Coase, who worked on major issues in communication policy.

Cultural studies is a broad-based intellectual movement which concentrates on the constitution of meaning in texts, defined broadly to include all forms of social communication. It has grown from many strands, including one based on the drive to oppose academic orthodoxies, particularly the tendency to organize knowledge in disciplinary canons such as English literature. One of the distinguishing characteristics of cultural studies is the tendency to back off from characterizing the field as an academic discipline, in part because it is interested in questioning the foundations of disciplinarity and, in particular, the tendency to create fixed bodies or canons of knowledge. As Johnson (1987: 38) put it, "cultural studies is a process, a kind of alchemy for producing useful knowledge; codify it and you might halt its reactions." Raymond Williams identified the intellectual origins of cultural studies in questions raised about the canon of English Literature:

> So you have in sequence, first, a restriction to printed texts, then a narrowing to what are called "imaginative" works, and then finally a circumspection to a critically established minority of "canonical" texts. But also growing alongside this there is another and often more potent specialization: not just Literature, but English Literature. (1981: 53)

The approach now contains numerous currents and fissures that provide considerable ferment from within as well as without.

From the beginning, especially in the British context, cultural studies has been strongly influenced by Marxian approaches. This includes the tendency to see the cultural as intimately connected to social relations, particularly as organized around social class, gender, and race, especially their asymmetries and antagonisms. Furthermore, Marxian concerns with power, particularly the power to define and realize needs and interests, influenced the development of cultural studies, as is evidenced, for example, in the work of Thompson (1963) and Willis (1977), which brought to the fore the cultural construction of social class relations. Marxian concerns are also exemplified in the work on gender that grew out of, and in response to, the research program carried out at the Centre for Contemporary Cultural Studies in Birmingham (CCCS Women's Studies Group, 1978). Finally, there is the view, prominent in the work of Stuart Hall (1980, 1982) and others, that culture is neither independent nor externally determined. Rather, it is best viewed as the site of social difference, struggle, and contestation. Indeed, commentators have noted that one of the significant differences between British and American approaches to cultural studies is that the former has adopted a more explicitly Marxian and generally political position. Cultural studies in the United States also contains numerous divisions, but one can conclude that there is a greater tendency for it to draw inspiration from a pluralist conception of society and politics which sees power as widely dispersed, from functionalist anthropology and sociology, which concentrate on how cultural practices maintain order and harmony in social life, and from symbolic interactionist social psychology, which uses the language of ritual and drama to examine the production and reproduction of symbolic communities (Carey, 1979). It did not take long for cultural studies in the United States to be singled out for its "affirmative character," essentially offering apolitical, positive assessments of the cultural landscape, and particularly of its audiences. In the view of one influential critique, American cultural studies contained five fundamental flaws:

> First, it overestimates the freedom of audiences in reception. Second, it minimizes the commodification of audiences as analyzed by a political-economic approach. Third, it fails to differentiate between mass advertising and specialized media. Fourth, it confuses active reception with political activity. Finally, it takes the exceptional situation of progressive readings promoted within oppositional subcultures as the norm. (Budd, et al., 1990: 169)

These are important criticisms which hold considerable weight today. Nevertheless, cultural studies can contribute to advancing political economy in several ways. Very importantly, it has taken the lead in constructing a broad-based critique of positivism that foregrounds the subjective and social constitution of knowledge. Starting from the work of Raymond Williams (1961) and Richard Hoggart (1957), cultural studies propelled the shift in literary criticism from the analysis of canonical and elite literature to everyday life.[1] Specifically, they aimed to broaden the sense of what comprises the substance of cultural analysis by starting from the premise that culture is the product of ordinary, everyday life, produced by all social actors, rather than just by a privileged elite. Moreover, although this view is contested and emphasizes shift, cultural studies has maintained that the social is constructed out of gender, race, and nationality divisions and identities as much as by social class (Fiske, 1989; Wilson, Gutiérrez, and Chao, 2003).

---

1 Williams (1981: 65) squarely attributes the shift to Marxism "which instead of privileging a generalized Literature as an independent source of values insists on relating the actual variety of literature to historical processes in which fundamental *conflicts* had necessarily occurred and were still occurring."

Political economy can learn from these departures, but it can also contribute to the development of cultural studies. Even as it takes on a philosophical approach that is open to subjectivity and more broadly inclusive, political economy insists on a realist epistemology that maintains the value of historical research, of thinking in terms of concrete social totalities, of moral commitment, and to overcoming the distinction between social research and social practice. It therefore departs from the tendency in cultural studies to concentrate on subjectivity and the subject, as well as from the inclination to reject thinking in terms of historical practices and social wholes. Political economy also parts company with the tendency in cultural studies to employ a specialized language that belies the original view that cultural analysis should be accessible to those ordinary people who are responsible for its social constitution. Finally, it eschews the propensity in cultural studies to back off from studies of labor and of the labor process in favor of examining the social "production" of consumption and the consequent tendency to reject labor as holding any value in contemporary movements for social change. There are important exceptions to this view (Ross, 2004), but it would be hard to make the case that cultural studies has devoted much attention to labor, the activity that occupies most people's waking hours.

Political economy can also learn from the development of a public choice perspective. The latter encompasses a wide range of thinking with two centers of gravity around which orbit a number of diverse perspectives associated with and reacting against these two leading foci. One center privileges a political analysis that places the *state* in the forefront of analysis. The other gives weight to *economic* arguments that aim to extend the application of neoclassical theory over political, social, and cultural life (Buchanan, 2003; Posner, 1992; Stigler, 1988). Traditionally, political economy has tended to "read" the state and other "superstructural" forces from the specific configuration of capital dominant at the time. It therefore can benefit from an approach that takes seriously the constitutive role of the state. Moreover, political economy shares with public choice theory the interest in extending analysis over the entire social totality, with an eye to social transformation. On the other hand, political economy departs fundamentally from the public choice tendency to adopt a pluralist political analysis that views the state as the independent arbiter of a wide balance of social forces, none of which holds sway. Against this, political economy insists on the power of capital and the process of commodification as the starting points of social analysis. Furthermore, political economy rejects the public choice tendency to build its analysis of the social totality, and of those values that should guide its transformation, on individualism and the presumed rationality of the market. Against this, it insists on starting from social processes, such as social class formation, and on setting community and public life against the market and against a rationality that actually reproduces the power of a dominant social class.

Lessons from the Borders: Cultural Studies

Cultural studies has broadened the range of epistemological approaches beyond positivist and essentialist perspectives to encompass social constructivist approaches to knowledge, which aim to determine how individuals and groups actually participate in the creation of their perceived social reality. It asks how social phenomena are created, institutionalized, and ultimately turned into tradition (Hobsbawn, 1992). Socially constructed reality is an ongoing, dynamic process which people reproduce by acting on their knowledge and interpretations of it.

From a substantive point of view, cultural studies has sided with the view that culture is ordinary, a product of everyday life that is widely produced, distributed, and consumed. Culture is therefore not limited, as defenders of the literary canon would maintain, to those elite practices that have established the cultural orthodoxy for many years. Cultural studies opened the full range of entertainment and information media, including television sitcoms, mass circulation tabloids, Harlequin romances, and Hollywood blockbusters to legitimate critical analysis. More importantly, it distinguished between *mass*-produced and distributed material and *popular* culture or work created and disseminated under relatively democratic conditions (stressing widespread participation and equality) to achieve democratic goals. Ironically, cultural studies often presents itself in an academicized, i.e. relatively inaccessible, idiom that creates an unnecessary gap between the analysis of culture and those cultural workers and consumers who might benefit most from the analysis. There is no gainsaying the need for conceptual sophistication and certainly no need to apologize for acknowledging that research often requires the use of complex theoretical formulations. But, as numerous commentators have noted, some cultural studies work is so inaccessible, so limited to a specialized academic audience, that any democratic inspiration or aspiration seems to be irretrievably lost.

Consider this critique from Harvard University Professor of African-American Studies Henry Louis Gates, Jr., in which he considers the pitfalls of formal cultural analysis, their "alienating strategies," by recounting a painful experience in trying to pass along the canon in the classroom. It is worth a rather lengthy quote:

> One of the first talks I ever gave was to a packed audience at a college honors seminar, and it was one of those mistakes you don't make twice. Fresh out of graduate school, immersed in the arcane technicalities of contemporary literary theory, I was going to deliver a crunchy structuralist analysis of a slave narrative by Frederick Douglas, tracing the intricate play of its "binary oppositions." Everything was neatly schematized, formalized, analyzed; this was my Sunday-best structuralism: crisp white shirt and shiny black shoes. And it wasn't playing. If you've seen an audience glaze over, this was double glazing. Bravely, I finished my talk and, of course, asked for questions. "Yeah, brother," said a young man in the very back of the room, breaking the silence that ensued, "all we want to know is, was Booker T. Washington an Uncle Tom or not?" (Gates, 1989: 44)

Later on, Gates realized that this was a very interesting question, "a lot more interesting than my talk was." It raised questions about the politics of style, about what it means for one person to speak for another, and about how one distinguishes between co-optation and subtle subversion. In essence, it awakened Gates "to the yawning chasm between our critical discourse and the traditions they discourse upon," to the gap between the text and the experience to which it gives rise (Gates, 1989: 44).

Notwithstanding this problem, cultural studies reminds political economy that the substance of its work, the analysis of communication, is rooted in the needs, goals, conflicts, failures, and accomplishments of ordinary people. These try to make sense of their lives, even as they confront an institutional and symbolic world that is not entirely of their own making and which, in fact, appears more often than not as an alien force outside their own control.

Cultural studies has also contributed to the expansion of critical work beyond social class analysis to include research inspired by feminism and those newer social movements committed, for example, to environmentalism. This work has served to remind political economy that, while social class is a central dividing line, or, from the perspective adopted in this book, a starting point, multiple overlapping hierarchies that extend to gender, nationality, race, and ethnicity also constitute the process of structuration. Moreover, although its extreme formulations celebrate the politics of contemporary life as a search for particular identities that fragment oppositional politics, cultural studies has recognized the energizing potential of multifaceted forms of social agency, each of which brings with it dimensions of subjectivity and consciousness that are vital to political praxis and which have received too little treatment in political economic analysis (Kraidy, 2005; Waetjen and Gibson, 2007). Cultural studies is often defined specifically in these terms. According to Johnson (1987: 43), for example, "cultural studies is about the historical forms of consciousness or subjectivity, or the subjective forms we live by... ." Johnson goes on to make the connection between this definition and the Marx–Engels tradition, particularly the early work such as *The German Ideology* (1987/1845). Later on, he notes, in a formulation quite congenial to my conception of political economy, that "the ultimate object of cultural studies is not, in my view, the text, but *the social life of subjective forms* at each moment of their circulation, including their textual embodiments" (Johnson, 1987: 62). Or, as Waetjen and Gibson (2007: 5) put it in their important study of the Harry Potter books, "what is required is a commitment to taking textual meanings seriously, while at the same time situating such textual openings and closures within a diachronic, material analysis of contemporary media production and distribution."

Political economy has been understandably preoccupied with the multifaceted ways in which culture is produced or structured as a result of dynamic imperatives to commodification. Cultural studies reminds political economy to incorporate, in Johnson's (1987: 55) words, "the indirect results of capitalist and other social relations on the existing rules of language and discourse, especially class and gender-based struggles in their effects on different social symbols and signs." Cultural studies approaches implicitly recognize the futility of relying on the outcome of the logic of capital or of organizing resistance solely around class divisions. Instead, it calls for a "political economy from below" to better understand the "micro-productive activities of cultural producers themselves" (Wittel, 2004: 11). Unfortunately, in its haste to turn to new forms of social geometry and resistance, cultural studies has tended, with important exceptions, to simply reject outright those older forms, based on class and, specifically, wage-labor, whose centrality for comprehending and transforming social life political economy quite rightly warrants (McGuigan, 2005; Miller, 2004).

Political economy has concentrated on the macrosocial organization of power and has developed the methodologies to address it. Although cultural studies has, with exceptions, not given the same consideration to power, when it does so, the approach tends to shift attention to the local organization of power, concentrating on how power mutually constitutes intersubjectivity. Moreover, although some streams of cultural studies focus almost exclusively on texts, choosing to "read the social" from its textual embodiments, others have drawn from traditional ethnographic methodologies to understand the social relations of textual, including media, reception and use (Donkor, 2007). By reminding us that power is also local, intersubjective, and accessible through observational techniques, cultural studies enriches the political economic understanding of power.[2] Furthermore, it is evident that some who advance an ethnographic approach to cultural studies recognize its limitations and call for making connections between the global and the local (Ferguson and Gupta, 2002).

Lessons from the Borders: Public Choice Theory

Public choice theory has drawn primarily on pluralist political science and neoclassical economics research to analyze and evaluate alternative courses of action, including communication. Also known as *positive political economy* or the *rational expectations* approach, it is an explicit attempt to apply the tools of orthodox economic research to political science with the aim of creating a policy science (Buchanan, 2003; Murshed, 2002; Posner, 1992; Stigler, 2003). Specifically, public choice aims to create a science whose key concepts are the market, individual choice, and private self-interest. The market provides the structural model for all collective activity, including that of businesses, governments, voluntary associations, interest groups, and families. Collectivities are reducible to the sum total of individual choices which, notwithstanding how they are described, explained, and justified, reflect private self-interest. There is no society or social group *sui generis*, no sum greater than the parts. Studying individuals therefore yields data on the behavior of collectivities because structures are nothing more than convenient fictions for individuals pursuing similar interests. Moreover, the approach privileges private over public interests because it starts from the view that people are, above all else, pursuers of private self-interests. One of the primary tasks of a public choice theorist is to describe the markets in all human activity, including communication. What is your self-interest and how much, in dollars, time, affection, etc., are you willing to pay to achieve it?

For the public choice theorist, social order results from the ongoing process whereby individuals maximize their self-interest by making choices across the range of relatively imperfect markets that constitute social life. From this perspective, a primary moral goal for the scholar or the practitioner is to make markets work better, whether those markets are for information, entertainment, education, communication, creating a

---

2 For a political economic reflection on ethnography, see Pendakur (1993).

family, or making money. For example, from this point of view, policy studies should be taken up with producing strategies for the reduction of those transaction, information, and opportunity costs incurred in the process of choice (Murshed, 2002).[3]

Public choice theory has grown across a range of disciplines and achieved a significant measure of general attention as a few of its founders, notably James Buchanan, Ronald Coase, and George Stigler, have been awarded the Nobel Prize in economics. Its success has emboldened leading proponents, such as Mancur Olson, to call for the development of a unified social science, collapsing all traditional disciplines into public choice theory (Olson, in Alt and Shepsle, 1990: 212–31). Generally aligned with conservative viewpoints, public choice theory has impressed a diverse collection of scholars, including some who advance a Marxian analysis (Cohen, 2000; Tarrit, 2006). From the start, however, leading Marxian theorists have been very critical of the approach because it is fundamentally driven by the application of market principles to social life (Wood, 1989). The approach has been applied to empirical studies of general social behavior, including studies of the family and sexuality (Posner, 1992). Consequently, although public choice theory is only one of several ways of thinking about policy, in the view of some, it is now, or is on its way to becoming, the leading approach in the field.[4] Over the years, the approach has exerted an influence on communication studies through the application to policy questions bearing on such subjects as the value of the radio spectrum and appropriate policies to distribute it, the extent of staff "capture" of regulatory agencies, the costs and consequences of deregulation, and the development of copyright policies for a digital age (Coase, 1991; Crandall, 1991; Derthick and Quirk, 1985; Wilson, 1980; Wu, 2004).

Public choice theory can offer several lessons to a political economic approach to communication. Drawing on the tradition of pluralist political science, most applications of the perspective start from the view that a multiplicity of relatively equal participants are directly involved in the policy process and that one needs to address the specific interests and actions of each to present a full picture of how policy is formed.[5] It tends to resist arguments that maintain, for example, that the logic of capital (or any other singularity) drives public policy. However, public choice does tend to the extreme of a pluralism subject to no overall tendencies, a kind of interest group anarchy which political economy, quite correctly, takes to task.

Just how public choice theory resolves these issues is not central to this chapter. It is more important to recognize that the overall commitment to specific, concrete

---

3 Transaction costs are those incurred in the process of exchange, such as the costs of bringing together a buyer and seller. Information costs are those associated with securing knowledge about products, people, and markets necessary to make the best choice. Opportunity or "sunk" costs are those incurred in previous choices which constrain present ones.

4 There are several journals that feature public choice research. In keeping with the goal of replacing heterodox political economy with a contemporary version of classical economics, a leading outlet is called *The Journal of Political Economy*.

5 For an application to communication studies see Hallin and Mancini (2004).

analyses of clashing interests offers important lessons for a political economy that sometimes reads specific outcomes simply from a thought-experiment on the logical outcome of capitalist processes. Again, there is a tendency for public choice theory to overemphasize government and, particularly, the formal legal-regulatory system for addressing policy issues. This tendency to formalism, which focuses on what happens when a policy issue reaches government, neglects the wide-ranging sources and uses of power outside the legal-regulatory apparatus and the extensive incubation and development process that shapes issues before they reach the formal stage of government consideration. Nevertheless, public choice theory is instructive for political economy because it reminds the latter to resist the tendencies to economism that would read policy decisions from industry structure alone.

There are also lessons to be learned from the economic wing of public choice theory, particularly from its enthusiastic embrace of a broad range of significant questions that have traditionally occupied psychologists, sociologists, political scientists, as well as economists, but which have fallen out of favor as these disciplines have pursued a limited warrant. Not content to remain within the traditional domain of economics, public choice theory has taken the methodological individualism and positivism of traditional economics and applied it to understand decision-making processes in the family, the state, and religious organizations over the widest range of questions encompassing sexuality, bureaucracy, family structure, budgets, etc. Moreover, this approach has not shied away from normative and moral questions that, not too long ago, would have been off limits for mainstream social science. Returning to the values, if not to the precise methodological strategy, that impelled Adam Smith and other classical political economists to take up a wide scope, including the central moral issues of their time, they approach the social with the spirit of pioneers who challenge the timidity of social scientific modernism and the consequent failure to address many of the major social and moral issues of our time. This pioneering spirit is particularly evident in the now classic work of Brennan and Buchanan (1985), who viewed their project of moral reconstitution as nothing short of aiming to create a new "civic religion" in America. Public choice theory is certainly open to criticism for how it approaches these issues, for example, by taking methodological individualism to the extreme and by viewing the state as an independent arbiter of competing interests. Nevertheless, the policy studies approach speaks to a political economy of communication that would reverse research tendencies that reward ever-narrower projects and build walls between social science and moral philosophy.

There are important political consequences that stem from efforts to stress universalism and commonality over fragmentation and division, particularly for those associated with left-of-center political movements that concentrate on the politics of identity and various standpoint theories which accentuate those characteristics that distinguish groups marked by gender, race, ethnicity, age, or sexual preference. Identity politics has admittedly energized a wide range of diverse political and intellectual movements. But it has also helped to reverse traditional Left–Right politics. The Left, which once stood firmly behind universalism, however flawed, now tends to promote a range of fragmented interests. Whereas the Right, which traditionally advanced what amounted to the particularistic standards of elites, now confidently promotes a universalistic conservative populism. It will be interesting to observe whether the return of universalistic ideas in Left discourse, for example, cosmopolitan citizenship, will take root (Brock and Brighouse, 2005; Miller, 2007).

Responses from Political Economy

Political economy offers important lessons that apply individually to public choice theory and to cultural studies, but it is particularly valuable to begin with those it offers both, starting with the centrality of *power* in the analysis of communication. Political economy departs from public choice theory and cultural studies in several ways, particularly by giving considerable weight to power, understood as both a resource to achieve goals and an instrument of control within social hierarchies. Pluralism, the central political tendency within public choice theory, treats power as a widely dispersed resource that is more or less accessible to all interests operating within the political arena (Derthick and Quirk, 1985; Hallin and Mancini, 2004). The distribution of power may be significant for particular cases, favoring, for example, software companies like Microsoft on some issues, telecommunications firms like Verizon on others, and consumer groups in still others, but according to this view, there is no structural tendency for power to be concentrated in one group or interest. From the pluralist viewpoint, it follows that power, generally diffused throughout society, is not at all a central formative influence.

Political economy agrees that it is useful to think of power as a resource, as well as a form of control, but differs significantly on the place of power in its overall analysis. Political economy thinks of power as a resource that is *structured* or rooted in, what Mahon (1980) called, an "unequal structure of representation," a feature built into a system that rewards market position with privileged status within social hierarchies. Moreover, power is more than a resource – it is also a form of *control* that is used to preserve such privileged status against challengers. Although, in practice, public choice and political economy overlap, it is intellectually clarifying to suggest an essential ontological difference in how the two disciplines view power. Public choice views power as diffused and dispersed, one among many forces at work in the social field. Political economy sees it as congealed and structured, a central force in shaping the social field. This is evident in a comparison of any of the numerous political economy analyses of media ownership and concentration with what little appears on this perspective in the public choice literature. Power, in its numerous manifestations, is central to the former, and virtually disappears from the latter.

Cultural studies has certainly not ignored power and presents a variety of ways of seeing it, particularly emphasizing its personal, local, and intersubjective dimensions. Nevertheless, there is a tendency for cultural studies to approach power in ways that put it in closer company with public choice than with political economy. With some notable exceptions (Coombe, 2005; Miller, 2004), culturalist perspectives do not place power at the center of their fundamental way of thinking about social relations. Moreover, their conception of power tends to be rooted in individual sub-jectivities, their identities, and collective action, rather than, as political economy would have it, structured in the institutions of society. Cultural studies tends to step back from conceptions of structure and, in extreme formulations, tends to reject the concepts of society and of social unity, even those presented with caution and con-tingency (Rutherford, 2005).

Political economy responds by reaffirming the value of theorizing the social total-ity, not as the abstract and idealistic conception that systems theory defends, but rather as the concrete manifestation of mutual interests and structures of power. Acknowledging the value of thinking about the subjective dimensions of power, political economy nevertheless maintains that these are mutually constituted with objective conceptions of power that derive from the fundamental rules governing structures in society.

It is interesting to observe that public choice theory and cultural studies, in effect, share a perspective on media content diversity. In their own particular ways, each conflates diversity with multiplicity and tends to discount the view that diversity is difficult to achieve or generally refuses to concede that it requires concerted political action. Among the many tendencies that constitute positions within public choice, one of the central points of view is that content diversity can be equated with the sheer *number* of voices in the market or the community. This point of view opposes media concentration on the grounds that it restricts the flow of information and entertainment, but tends to be satisfied with remedies that expand the multiplicity of marketplace competitors. For example, the typical public choice response to state monopoly control of broadcast channels in Europe is to license private carriers. Its standard response to private monopoly control of North American telecommunica-tions is to support one or a few competitors. Providing access to the Internet adds diversity to a marketplace whose traditional media tends to fall into fewer and fewer hands. From this point of view, the leading measures of concentration should assess the number of producers and distributors in the marketplace to determine whether the market has enough voices to constitute sufficient competition. Or, alternatively, media concentration is a problem only if it has an impact on advertising rates in a marketplace. Put simply, public choice equates diversity with multiplicity and fair-ness with reasonable rates for advertisements.

It is only on the outskirts of public choice theory, where the discipline meets polit-ical economy, especially through critical theories of the state, that one begins to find a sustained effort to unfasten the link between what is viewed, in these heterodox formulations, as the fundamental difference between the sheer number of voices (multiplicity) and the number of *different* voices (diversity), between the number of available media and the ability to use them to produce diverse material and distrib-ute it widely. Public choice argues that diversity tends to flow necessarily from the presence of competing units. From this vantage point, diversity is relatively easy to achieve: simply increase the number of units, of producers and distributors. There is little interest in addressing the thornier problem posed by the conclusion of the political economy literature: however numerous, producers offer and distributors deliver essentially the same messages. Multiplicity does not necessarily lead to diversity. When Rupert Murdoch's Fox network came to the United States, it added more voices into a marketplace led by the oligopoly of ABC, CBS, and NBC. But a political economic view questions whether the news and entertainment which it delivers differs in any fundamental way from standard network fare. It only tends to make already conservative media more conservative. Consequently, political economy contends that there is no net gain, or little, in expanding the number of media voices without any guarantee of increased diversity.

In spite of differences in the general epistemological, theoretical, and substantive positions that cultural studies approaches to communication present in comparison with public choice, they offer similar conclusions about the politics of media diversity (Murdock, 2004; Wood, 1989). Starting from the different vantage point of the audience, cultural studies approaches come to generally the same conclusion: media diversity is not a substantial problem because information and entertainment are *polysemic* or subject to multiple readings and interpretations that, in essence, create their own diversity, whatever the number of formal producers and distributors. The tendency in cultural studies is to see every recipient of a message as a producer, who assigns a different meaning to a message that is based primarily on the receiver's particular "subjectivity position" within the overlapping identities that make up social life. Media concentration does not restrict diversity because the interpretive range is not a function of who formally produces and distributes news, drama, comedy, etc. Rather, the diversity of subjective experiences that audiences bring to communication and information products produce textual diversity. This tendency in cultural studies responds to the twin problems of economism and productivism which, it maintains, confound political economy. In this context, and with notable exceptions, cultural studies sees economism as the tendency to read texts from the logic, structure, and dynamics of the economy and the presumed interests of capitalists. A specific form of economism, *productivism*, reads the text from the circuit of capital that makes up the process of production.[6]

Political economy acknowledges with public choice theory that additional providers can expand the number of messages and political economists have intervened in the policy process to accomplish this. Moreover, it agrees with cultural studies that one cannot read a single audience response from a news or entertainment program.

---

6 Stuart Hall, one of the founding figures in cultural studies, demonstrated genuine ambivalence on this subject, which is reflected throughout cultural studies. In some of his work, Hall assigns powers to capital that defenders of cultural studies would have a hard time distinguishing from work they criticize as economistic. For example, he has suggested that "ownership and control" is sufficiently important that it "gives the whole machinery of representation its fundamental orientation in the value-system of property and profit" (Hall, 1986: 11). Capital, according to Hall, is so powerful that "it prevents new kinds of grouping, new social purposes and new forms of control from entering, in a central way, into the production of culture." In other work (1989: 50), he is sharply critical, charging political economy with "crudity and reductionism" and for having "no conception of the struggle for meaning."

Nevertheless, political economy insists that a thorough understanding of how the process of commodification influences circuits of production, distribution and consumption is vital to comprehending culture. Public choice theory, from its various theoretical standpoints, recognizes this as well. Unfortunately, cultural studies has suffered because its comprehension of economics and of political economy is painfully limited. It has documented very little understanding of the depth, complexity, range of fault lines, and overall diversity of orthodox and heterodox economic and political economic arguments. As a result, rather than address them on their own terms, cultural studies has done little more than reject economic arguments on what amount to categorical grounds. Economic arguments are dismissed because they are economistic. The economic process of producing culture is set aside as productivist. This is particularly unfortunate because such a rejectionist position undermines insights that might otherwise contribute to the creation of useful zones of engagement with those starting from a political economic position. Consider this critique of productivism:

> The text-as-produced is a different object from the text-as-read. The problem with Adorno's analysis and perhaps productivist approaches in general is not only that they infer the text-as-read from the text-as-produced, but that also, in doing this, they ignore the elements of production in other moments, concentrating "creativity" in producer or critic. Perhaps this is the deepest prejudice of all among the writers, the artists, the teachers, the educators, the communicators and the agitators within the intellectual divisions of labour! (Johnson, 1987: 58)

Political economy has no quarrel with the view that the text is different as produced and as read. Nor does it contend with the view that readers produce meaning. Furthermore, political economists have not retreated from examining contemporary traditional and new media as fundamentally *cultural* forces (Baltruschat, 2008; Meehan, 2005; Mosco, 2004; Murdock, 2004). Moreover, political economists have come to recognize the value of ethnographic methods that help to document the social experience of reading, listening, and viewing mass media (Pendakur, 2003; Wasko, Phillips, and Meehan, 2006). However, political economists would disagree with the view prominent in cultural studies that writers and readers are equally the producers of texts, whether these are written, audio-visual, or net-based.

Political economy argues that equating writers with readers neglects the interesting questions, such as, just how powerful are readers and audiences as producers of texts? To what degree can and do producers of texts act on the range of anticipated reader and audience responses? What is the relationship between control over the means of producing texts and the production of meaning? What is the connection between location in social structure and location in the production of meaning?[7] What sorts

---

7 Evans (1990: 150) puts this another way: "Except for the earlier-discussed hypodermic model, no tradition in mass communication research posits a passive audience. Thus, the real difference is not a question of active versus passive but rather the postulation of one kind of activity versus another kind."

of resources are required for opposition and alternatives to arise in the face of what Bakhtin referred to as the "monologic discourse" of the cultural industry? These are areas that, once one stands back from rejectionist positions, offer grounds for useful exchange. However tempting, it is not enough to provide what amounts to "a romantic celebration of the individual's power to evaluate media content critically and consciously" (Evans, 1990: 152).[8] For example, the political economy approach accepts polysemy and the multiple production of texts, recognizes the need to analyze the full circuit of production, distribution, and consumption, and sees these as central moments in the realization of value and in the construction of social life.[9] Nevertheless, it disagrees with the conclusion that diversity is the natural consequence either of the multiplicity of media units or of audiences. Many media units can offer fundamentally the same media substance and form. As Murray (2004) has demonstrated in her research on fan cultures, audience resistance is inscribed within limits established by the media industries.

One result of the focus on audience activity, as the paramount social activity, is to inflate what little social action is encountered beyond reasonable levels of significance (Mosco and Kaye, 2000). Moreover, the very term *audience* is not an analytic category, like class, gender, or race, but a product of the media industry itself, which uses the term to identify markets and to define a commodity. References to audience activity give the term an analytical and experiential reality beyond the evidence and this should therefore warrant greater care in use. At the very least, it is premature to assert that the demographic category "audience" *acts* when we have not established the conceptual value of the term, particularly its relationship to social class, race, ethnicity, and gender, which are more than demographic groupings. They are lived experiences. Organized as social actors in various class, gender, race, and other social dimensions, people carry out activities, including resistance to media presentations, the significance of which is an empirical question testable through a range of procedures. Media power, which gives those with control over markets the ability to fill screens with material embodying their interests, tends to structure the substance and form of polysemy, thereby limiting the diversity of interpretations to certain repeated central tendencies that stand out among the range of possibilities, including those marginalized few that diverge substantially from the norm. Far from

---

8 It is also the case, as Murdock (1989: 437) has noted, that even the first wave of cultural studies, including the work of Hoggart and Williams, "was suffused with nostalgia for worlds that were rapidly disappearing" and "was also tinged by a romantic evaluation of the 'authenticity' of these vanishing ways of life... ."

9 As Evans (1990: 148) has noted, cultural studies differentiates itself from traditional approach by criticizing "hypodermic models" of media effects, which ostensibly warrant the view that media can be injected drug-like into an audience to produce desired impacts. But "those guilty of employing hypodermic models are seldom named; in fact, some scholars suspect that the hypodermic model was never a serious tradition in the discipline and that this direct-effects model has been invoked largely as a polemical strawman against which other positions would easily seem more sophisticated."

rejecting oppositional readings categorically, as those who charge that economism and productivism are the contemporary version of the hypodermic model, political economy situates these readings within the specific power geometry or map of power identified by the coordinates of commodification, spatialization, and structuration.

Accomplishing the task of locating audiences within maps of power is made more difficult by the growth of new media which increases the temptation to abolish the division between cultural producers and their audiences. Aren't blogs and social networking sites eroding the power of media produced by corporate conglomerates? Political economy suggests we temper the inclination to leap to this conclusion. Rather, it proposes that we examine the impact that corporate control over such sites has on what appears (restrictions on content) and on what is done with what appears (violations of privacy for commercial and coercive reasons). Graham Murdock (2004: 19) concludes that by focusing on the "new," the study of communication neglects "historical continuities, structural inequalities, and the scale and scope of economic restructuring" that capitalism is bringing about with new media. Those scholars committed to bringing together a political economic and cultural analysis are optimistic that this can be achieved. In their research on the Harry Potter phenomenon, Waetjen and Gibson (2007: 4) commend political economy for recent work that focuses on texts and see a similar commitment by cultural studies to examine power: " ... within cultural studies, for example, a long preoccupation with the text–audience relation has begun to accommodate a renewed engagement with economic practices and the moment of cultural production" (see also, Deetz and Hegbloom, 2007).

Political economy also offers responses to the specific criticisms that arise individually from public choice theory and cultural studies. In particular, it provides a corrective to instrumentalist, statist, and economistic tendencies. Public choice tends to instrumentalize explanations that address the process of policy formation by describing the actions of groups that pressure government to act according to their interests. It maintains that policy is a function of who succeeds in using the state as an instrument to accomplish specific goals. According to this view, one might explain the trends to liberalize and deregulate telecommunications systems as a result of the ability of large business users to capture the government policy apparatus. As a result, large transnational businesses, such as big banks, make government an instrument to achieve their goals of creating low-cost, customized networks and services to meet their growing business needs. Similarly, an instrumentalist explains the growth in the power and profit of cable television and Internet firms as a consequence of the industry's ability to lobby and out-muscle broadcasters, consumer groups, and others to shape government policy in their interest.

Political economy acknowledges the value of such instrumentalist analyses, but aims to deepen levels of understanding that start from locating the communication industry within the wider totality of capitalist social relations. Specifically, this means situating the various components of the communication industry, the government regulatory and policy apparatus, and civil society groups within the domestic and international political economies that mutually constitute them. In order to understand the specific way in which the liberalization of telecommunication systems has been carried out, in various nations and regions, political economy calls for examining those forces in the domestic and international political economies that pressed large business users to develop both the understanding and organizational capacity to intervene on an unprecedented scale in the policy process. It also examines the forces at work within and around governments that made them more receptive to change, including, for example, the development of activist elements within government agencies that broke from the traditional connections between the government and monopoly telecommunications providers. Finally, political economy calls for studying the forces that opened divisions within civil society groups, with some pressing traditional concerns for public interest regulation and others joining the cause of large users by viewing competition as the best vehicle to bring about industry change.

In essence, political economy argues that understanding *how* requires more than comprehending *who* does *what* to *whom*. Moreover, *how* alone does not in itself explain what is going on. This is accomplished by also determining *why* actions take place, something that requires locating communication policy within the general political economy, including historical and contemporary tendencies. Finally, political economy moves beyond instrumentalism by calling for a critical understanding of the policy process, one that connects a structural and historical understanding to a set of values or to a moral philosophical standpoint that assesses the process for its contribution to democracy, equality, participation, fairness, and justice. This valuational stance also helps to lift policy analysis out of its narrow, descriptive, and positivist tendencies by connecting policy research to the politics of changing policy.

Political economy also affirms the need to balance tendencies in public choice that give excessive emphasis to either the political or the economic dimensions. In the former, or *statist* approaches to policy studies, one proceeds on the assumption, varying with different degrees of emphasis, that ultimate decision-making authority resides with the state. This authority can be formal, denoting government legal control over the process of decision-making, and substantive, referring to the state's power over decision-making content. In the case of either or both, public choice presumes that power resides with government, so that even when it concludes that the state is "captured" by some external (the industry) or internal (its own staff) group that makes the government its own instrument, public choice theory insists that it is the state which holds the power that one must capture in order to accomplish policy goals. The result is a tendency to focus almost entirely on the state, including its regulatory, legislative, executive, and juridical arms, to view it as the center of a decision-making universe that determines the structure of the industry, shapes its capabilities, including prices, services, and revenues, and sets the terms for consumer and public intervention. In essence, the standard statist approach views government as the power that determines the laws of motion of the policy-making process.

More problematic is the tendency of public choice theory to move in the opposite direction, offering an economistic view of the policy process that replaces the institutional language of political structure and power with the economic language of markets, utilities, and preferences. Treating the policy arena as a marketplace that registers the wants of "buyers" looking for favorable decisions and "sellers" who can offer policy outputs, the public choice approach follows neoclassical economic models that aim to ascertain the equilibrium position where the preferences of policy actors presumably meet at the margins. One consequence of this position is a tendency to view government simplistically as the repository of whatever is imperfect, inadequate, or simply wrong with the competitive market system. For Becker and Mulligan (2003), the burdens of administration and procedure leave the state with a tendency to mounting "dead weight costs." Peltzman (1976) argued that the growth of the state can be traced to the rise of special interest groups that feed on, what he perceives to be, the growing entitlement to egalitarianism in Western society. In other words, the state is a parasite on an otherwise healthy economy. Finally, Stigler (1988) claims that even those government agencies, such as regulatory authorities, which ostensibly arise to correct market failures, are really nothing more than inadequate instruments to redistribute income and accumulate power for regulators themselves.[10]

Political economy acknowledges the merit of both statist and economistic tendencies. It credits the former with identifying the independent significance of the state in the policy process against strands of political economy that simply "read" policy decisions from the logic of capital. It also understands the attempt to introduce the language of economics and thereby attenuate statism. Nevertheless, political economy aims to rectify statist and economistic tendencies because they are partial, sacrificing critical elements of either the political or the economic, by starting from the mutual constitution of the political and the economic. Neither is the essential key to the policy process; both are required for a complete understanding. Concretely, this means resisting the temptation to view policy as essentially political because formal authority for the legal-regulatory regime resides with government agencies. Formal authority is only one type of power and is often relevant for little more than providing legitimizing decisions arrived at outside the regulatory process. For example, different forces within business and the academic/intellectual community provided an enormous impetus for the adoption of measures that transformed electronic media, telecommunications, and the Internet through commercialization, privatization, liberalization, and internationalization. This pressure mounted to such an intensity that government adoption of these measures, although contested and significant, was, nevertheless, anticlimactic. Much of the policy research, the assessment of alternatives, the planning, and the mobilization of public opinion took place prior to, or parallel with, but generally *outside* the realm of formal legislative and regulatory consideration. Because of its tendency to concentrate on government-centered activities, much of the public choice literature tends to ignore or, at best, understate these developments. Political economy aims to correct the statist tendency by expanding the conception of the policy process to include those developments that

---

10 In a confidence characteristic of public choice theorists, Stigler (1988: xiii) brushes aside the need to document this view of regulation: "This change in the fundamental role of regulation is so widely accepted, and so copiously documented, that it would be pedantic to cite the vast and growing host of supporting studies."

take place outside the realm of formal government activity including, for example, the activities of policy research and planning centers, and the organizations of corporate, trade union, consumer, and civil society groups. These work to seize the policy agenda and determine how and when policy issues will appear on the government's plate and how policy decisions will be implemented once government has addressed them. In sum, political economy responds to statist approaches by broadening the base of policy analysis, particularly by incorporating those social and economic actors and forces that mutually constitute the political process.

Political economy also aims to correct the particular economistic tendency that public choice approaches bring to bear on policy analysis. Specifically, although it acknowledges the value of introducing the economic, political economy rejects the tendency to incorporate the language and assumptions of neoclassical economics, which understates, or ignores entirely, the exercise of power, the influence of institutional actors, and the formation of social relations that structure individual choice. Moreover, political economy critiques the value of universalizing market models to analyze policy problems and impel solutions. Precisely questioning fundamental public choice assumptions, political economy raises a skeptical eye to the neutrality of markets, their responsiveness to incentives, and their presumed efficiency. Acknowledging the value of identifying the social costs of regulation, political economy reminds public choice theorists that there are social costs to competition that public choice analysts have either ignored or made little more than a half-hearted attempt to determine and evaluate. In essence, drawing on its general critique of neoclassical economics, political economy concludes that since the approach is fundamentally flawed, one can confidently expect to discern flaws in its application to public policy research. In the place of public choice economism, political economy brings a broad-based analysis that centrally includes the processes of commodification, spatialization, and structuration which inform political economy in general. Specifically, it argues in favor of situating the policy process and its actors within the wider context shaped by the current state of commodification, the institutional map that constitutes the spatialization process, and the configuration of the social relations of class, gender, and race, as well as the social movements and processes of hegemony that make up structuration. Although markets, individual preference, and choice play a part in the economic dimension of policy studies, they do so only as dimensions of a wider economic process that political economy provides.

Political economy addresses several responses to the direct and implicit critiques served up by cultural studies. Although there are important political elements in some tendencies within cultural studies, particularly those emanating from Britain and Latin America, the approach has generally lacked a political focus, a sense of political projects and purposes which, over many years, however fiercely contested, have been a central driving force in political economy. There is no denying that political economy, including its application to communication studies, has been a contested terrain, with many different political tendencies aiming to gain the intellectual and political upper hand. But few within, or, for that matter, outside the discipline, dating back to the time of its classical founders, would fail to acknowledge that political economy is a distinctly political discipline, i.e. one that blurs, or eliminates entirely, the distinction between analysis and intervention. That is why praxis is identified among the vital components of a political economy approach.

In its entirety, cultural studies is less than clear about its commitment to political projects and purposes. The discipline is not without those who argue in favor of a political objective that, although different, is no less explicit from what political economy offers. Such thinking tends to shift the focus of political purpose away from social class, to gender, race, and other forms of identity, and to those new social movements that cross class lines to contend over such issues as the environment and feminism. According to this view, by concentrating on those cultural practices and values that constitute social identities and divisions, cultural studies contributes to understanding the central features of the dominant hegemony. This includes, for example, the authoritarian populism that brought so much of the working class into the Thatcher–Reagan fold to support neoliberal globalization and the formation of popular oppositional and alternative movements. But this view is not universally upheld within cultural studies (McGuigan, 2005). Some of its practitioners are considerably more ambiguous about its politics, arguing that cultural studies research contains less certain links to a specific political project or that the primary, if not the only, political activity within cultural studies is the act of research itself. Reflecting on the political uncertainty within cultural studies, Jameson (1989: 43) wondered whether the approach is most comfortable identifying with "an anarchist and populist spirit" that responds enthusiastically to what Featherstone and others perceive to be "a more democratic and culturally literate public everywhere in the world today."[11] Finally, there are those, particularly identifying within post-structuralism, whose view of reality is limited to the construction of texts and discourse. These tend to dismiss any links between the process or substance of research and the political domain. However accurately this description conveys a sense of the range of views, the divisions within cultural studies are not this neatly compartmentalized. Suffice it to say, cultural studies is an enterprise that is entirely more uncertain about its political connections than is political economy.

Cultural studies is also considerably more uncertain about one of the central substantive goals of a political economy approach: understanding social totalities. Tetzlaff (1991: 10) argues that this is rooted in a general tendency in cultural studies, most pronounced in post-structuralism and postmodernism, to equate unification with conceptions of social control and liberation with "the fragmentation of this unity" (Lyotard, 1984). Political economy tends to argue that the social totality exists not so much as a

---

11 It is interesting to observe the support for anarchism from within both cultural studies and the economic wing of policy studies. Both appear to celebrate individual acts of what are interpreted to be resistance to power, particularly to the institutional power of national governments and corporate monopolists. It is also instructive to observe how Jameson distances himself from this position, acknowledging as accurate the criticism directed at his inability to celebrate with sufficient enthusiasm the "new anarchism."

theoretical abstraction that can be necessarily read off the inherent characteristics of systems, but more specifically as the concrete manifestation of empirically observable social relations, specifically those operating within capitalism. Political economy understands capitalism as a particular social whole constituted out of social processes whose starting points are commodification, spatialization, and structuration. These provide one means of comprehending capitalism as a concrete social totality, meaning a specific configuration of interrelated social processes. The nature of the configuration and of the relationships among processes is dynamic and therefore not absolutely specifiable, but it is the goal of political economy to describe, as adequately as its tools permit, both the state of the social totality and the direction to which its primary processes are taking it. Consequently, although political economy is open to a wide range of characterizations of the social whole and of the nature, form, and strength of the relationships that constitute the totality, it maintains that understanding the social totality is unmistakably central to its substantive project.

Cultural studies is considerably less certain about the value of pursuing the social totality because it doubts the empirical reality and theoretical usefulness of the concept. Preferring to concentrate on concepts such as cultural difference, particular subjectivities, and local identities, it approaches with great caution efforts to suggest connections among categories, out of concern that connections can easily mount into systems and forms of objectification that submerge the particular and the local beneath their discursive power. Political economy recognizes that caution is warranted. It acknowledges, for example, that feminist research correctly concluded that efforts to establish a systemic class analysis diminished the recognition of powerful gender divisions within and across class categories. Mindful of the problems that attend to a pursuit of social totalities, political economy nevertheless recognizes the value in doing so (Lee, 2006; McLaughlin, 1999). There is a danger that such a pursuit can result in rarefied systems thinking, what Laclau (1977: 12) called "the Platonic cave of class reductionism." But there is also a danger that emphasis on difference, subjectivity, and the particular can end up with a multiplicity of individualisms whose connections, if there are any, are little more than chance occurrences. It also risks creating a romanticism of difference that recognizes the mere fact of its achievement as an act of political defiance.[12]

Such a view diminishes the significance of concentrated power, including class power, in the face of evidence that global class divisions are massively accelerating within and across nations. It also suggests that political resistance amounts to little

---

12 Frederic Jameson's work offers the unusual defense of the social totality from within a cultural studies framework. His near apologetic tone underscores the exceptional nature of his position:

It has not escaped anyone's attention that my approach to post-modernism is a totalizing one. The interesting question today is then not why I adopt this perspective, but why so many people are scandalized (or have learned to be scandalized) by it. In the old days, abstraction was surely one of the strategic ways in which phenomena, particularly historical phenomena, could be estranged and defamiliarized... . (1989: 33)

more than putting together an appropriate package of symbols that provide a unique spin against orthodoxy. One consequence is a remarkable shift in focus that looks at material divisions, but sees little more than cultural difference.

Consider this analysis of polysemy in a cultural studies text. Noting the limitations of the idea of polysemy, it is nevertheless suggested (During, 1993: 7) that "it did lead to more dynamic and complex theoretical concepts which help us describe how cultural products may be combined with new elements to produce different effects in different situations." "Hybridization" and "negotiation" are cited as examples of different cultural processes which are embodied in the many uses of advertising images, such as that of the Marlboro man whose handsome visage on a package of cigarettes can be "made into a shiny, hard-edged polythene sculpture à la Jeff Koons to achieve a postmodern effect in an expensive Manhattan apartment; ... cut out of the magazine and used to furnish a poor dwelling in Lagos ...; or parodied on a CD/album cover." Notwithstanding the accuracy of this description, it appears out of focus to a political economist because it takes the extremes of class division and seemingly looks right through them to the symbolic uses of cultural detritus that somehow distinguish both the Manhattan apartment dweller and the inhabitant of a Lagos slum, connecting them in symbolic community. Where the political economist would look at the wider social totality linking both people in a power relationship that holds differential consequences for their real lives, the analyst of cultural studies sees the achievement of identity in what amounts to different heterodox uses of cultural symbols, perhaps accurate, but relatively inconsequential in comparison to the canyon-like divide of power that separates their material and cultural lives (see also Kraidy, 2005).

Against this view, political economy maintains the intellectual and political significance of focusing on the social totality. It defends as a central intellectual concern the examination of those forces that link people in symmetrical and asymmetrical social relationships, ranging from power and dependency to equality and interdependence. Political economy also recognizes that the absence of an explicit relationship, demonstrated by some form of reciprocity, does not necessarily mean the lack of significant ties. As social network analysis has demonstrated, linkages are often very complex and some of the strongest ties among individuals and groups are those that connect them *through* others, rather than directly *to* one another (Burt, 1992; Wellman and Hogan, 2004).

Political economy also maintains the political significance of focusing attention on the social totality. Although political economists differ on precisely how to theorize capitalist structures, processes, and consequences, they tend to agree on the need to focus on capitalism as a social formation, a social whole whose parts form dynamic, but discernible, relationships. Admittedly, disagreement continues on how to characterize social relations of domination, hegemony, and resistance, but political economists tend to agree on the need to direct attention to the social or the collective nature of these relationships and on their patterned articulation. One of the primary reasons for upholding these positions is that they embody the nature of political struggles which are integral to the work of political economists, as intellectuals equally committed to explaining capitalism in order to transform it, as they are committed to understanding social relations in order to advance democracy. For political economy, this requires engaging, however critically, with social totalities, such as the capitalist political economy, and with the social relations of class, gender, and race. For political economy, the focal movement is in the direction of unity and the social whole, with difference and particularity contained within these. The critics of political economy within cultural studies have pointed to the shortcomings of this approach, describing the problems of reading too much unity in capitalism and class power and of submerging important differences in social relations and culture. The political economy position and this critique mark one of the more significant boundaries with cultural studies.

To conclude, political economists and other critics have concentrated on three principal points which tend to define the central dimensions of a political economy response to the extremes of cultural studies approaches. First, they raise concerns about the shift from a realist to a nominalist epistemology that rejects the existence of knowable action outside the text, and which also shifts from viewing research as an attempt to produce verifiable statements about action (a process which, in political economy, is connected to social praxis) to merely one intervention in an ongoing conversation. Second, critics argue that this relativist approach to knowledge leads to a wider political relativism which loses a sense of politics as a definitive social project that incorporates the research act and rests almost entirely on politics as a struggle for individual identity. The self-contained nature of the research and the loss of concern for a wider political project foster intellectual insularity, so that the "conversation" takes on an academic quality that is evidenced in a work whose language is inaccessible to all but those few who are intimately part of the conversational flow. Critics, including political economists, call on cultural studies to return to its roots, which maintained that culture is popular and that it reflects the needs and aspirations, including political ones, of widely placed social actors.

Conclusion: A Return to Class Power

It is appropriate to conclude the book with reference to class power because it has historically occupied a central place in political economic analysis and also marks an important boundary between political economy, cultural studies, and public choice theory. This trip through the many rooms of the political economy of communication has been interested in broadening the epistemological, ontological, and substantive scope of the discipline by critically evaluating notions, such as essentialism and class power, which have long been central to debates about social theory. The result is a proposal to build a political economy of communication that:

1. Starts from a realist, inclusive (i.e. non-essentialist), and critical epistemology;
2. Takes an ontological stance that accentuates the ubiquity of social process and social change;
3. Develops a substantive position built on the entry processes of commodification, spatialization, and structuration.

These are the coordinates of social action within a political economic framework. Social class is the starting point for examining the process of structuration. Social class power remains a central element in the political economy of communication, even if it gives up the essentialist view that would make it the position to which all others can be reduced.

Because of its methodological and substantive individualism, and the general tenor of capitalist triumphalism that inflects the work of its supporters, public choice theory has little to say about social class. However, social class and class power are not at all foreign to cultural studies. In fact, early work in the field, including that of Hoggart (1957), Williams (1958), Thompson (1963), Hall and Jefferson (1976), and Willis (1977), maintained a strong commitment to an engaged class analysis, leading one to agree with During's (1993: 1–2) conclusion that "early cultural studies did not flinch from the fact that societies are structured unequally, that individuals are not all born with the same access to education, money, health-care." Over time, particularly as it developed in the United States, cultural studies retreated from class and from the general connection between material inequalities and social power. One of the reasons for this was the understandable interest to expand class analysis to include gender, race, and ethnic divisions, as well as to account for the apparent support for conservative politics within the working class, or at least for the seeming indifference of working people in the face of declining living standards, and for the rise of social movements that cut across class divisions. But in addition to this arguably useful shift in attention, one encountered a growing insularity, what amounts to a withdrawal into the text and a retreat from the world of everyday politics. One of the more significant consequences of such an approach is to eliminate almost entirely any interest in work and the labor process in communication. Although the working class appears from time to time in cultural studies research, it almost never shows up in the factory or the office. There is extensive debate about whether audiences produce texts, but practically nothing on the material or symbolic nature of work itself. The political economist finds this puzzling and troubling. One can comprehend a position that suggests rethinking the meaning and significance of class analysis, but it is difficult to understand the justification for bidding it farewell, in a world where the gap between rich and poor accelerates.

There are a few welcome signs that this view is changing. Led by the work of Andrew Ross (2004), cultural studies has begun to turn its attention to labor, with studies of the workplace (Deetz and Hegbloom, 2007), including strikes and lockouts (Brennen, 2005; Nagy, 2007). Research on the "cultural economy" (Pratt, 2004), on the corporate university (Rutherford, 2005), and on the international division of cultural labor (Miller, 2004) has also demonstrated a renewed interest in power that is beginning to return cultural studies to its roots (see also Denzin and Giardina, 2007).

Whatever the divisions between political economy and disciplines on its borders, the process of research should bring together, not separate, intellectuals and cultural producers. It ought to build a common understanding and common political purpose that can advance the democratization of culture and, through it, the democratization of social life. In making this call, critics, including political economists, remind themselves of their own wider purpose, which includes forging intellectual and political links across disciplinary boundaries. There is value in continuing the conversation, if not, as Williams (1981: 54) wryly observed, so that we can be the "guests, however occasionally untidy or unruly, of a decent pluralism," then certainly in so far as our exchanges are connected to a sense that there is an understandable reality and that intellectual activity is organized to transform it for the wider benefit of all.

Coda: Challenges on the Horizon

This chapter has documented some of the progress in expanding the reach of political economy in exchanges with approaches on its borders. It has also demonstrated that a great deal of work remains to be done. Although its plate remains full, political economy also needs to think about new challenges beyond these borders. The book concludes by suggesting two important ones that will occupy us well into the future: engaging science and technology studies and joining the debate about the relationship between the humanities and the sciences.

Science and technology studies (STS) is a transdisciplinary intellectual movement that addresses the relationships between science and society. Although there is no clear agreement about the scope of the field, STS has established a significant core of ideas led by the work of Donna Haraway (2003), Bruno Latour (1999, 2005), and Steve Woolgar (1988). There are clear affinities between this core and the central themes of political economy. Some have misinterpreted STS to take a relativistic position on knowledge and science, i.e. all truth is relative; there is no reality; science is merely the product of social pressures (Sokal, 2008). Quite to the contrary, STS, like political economy, starts from a realist epistemology. In fact, as Latour describes, it supports a strong realist position because it asserts the reality of both material things and the ideas that describe them. Moreover, like political economy, STS concentrates on the mutual constitution of knowledge and social practice. We learn about the world by acting on it and the world presents itself to us through our ways of understanding it (e.g. experimentation and observation). We and our world become more real and comprehensible by expanding the number of connections we make with it and that it makes with us. Finally, STS shares with political economy an interest in democracy. In fact, Latour's central projects include overturning the "fear of the mob" that Socrates used as his justification to replace popular knowledge with elite science, and overturning the mind/body division that Descartes inscribed in Western thought.

Rejecting Socrates by trusting the mob and replacing Descartes's "mind in a vat" with an interconnected world of people, ideas, animals, technologies, and everything else, is an enormous project. Like political economy, cultural studies, and public choice theory, STS rejects disciplinarity and the border police that accompany efforts to rein in ideas. In fact, what it calls actor network theory aims to understand the social life and relationships not only among people but also, and most importantly, between people, technologies, and what Haraway calls "companion species," or those creatures people have domesticated, hunted, and otherwise called animals and pets. In this respect, STS moves beyond even the most ambitious definition of political economy, which calls for the study of control and survival in social or even organic life. STS does not stop at social life because of the centrality of organic life, but it also wishes to energize technology. The latter is not just an inert mass, the computer on the desk, but a force that grows, retreats, and otherwise interacts with non-technological actors in its network.

There are two major reasons why political economy needs to engage with STS. First, STS thinks beyond human life and, in a world increasingly sensitive to its active environment and increasingly aware of how technologies develop beyond their original design, such thinking is imperative. We have long passed the point where Enlightenment visions of human superiority can be seen as anything more than convenient myths. Although the political economy of communication has addressed technology, the general field of political economy has tiptoed around the world outside human society. Nevertheless, it understands power in ways that STS does not. This alone provides important grounds for mutual exchange. Second, STS suggests the importance of popular knowledge and a democracy of actors, what it calls actants, both human and non-human. Political economy has a strong tradition of thought about democracy, including its necessity and its limitations. Socrates may have been wrong in calling for elite rule and Descartes too may have led us down the wrong path when he called for a hierarchy of mind over body. But without a clear understanding of democracy and its opposition, the drive to trust the mob and the body might lead to authoritarian rule, a painful truth that political economists have demonstrated. This opens another potentially fruitful ground for exchange between the two perspectives.

More than anything else, STS is aiming to reconstitute the relationship between science and the arts or humanities, as they are sometimes called. In 1956 and, more systematically, in 1959, the writer and physicist C.P. Snow (1964) raised the specter of two cultures, comprising the sciences and the humanities, made up of people who have practically nothing to do with each other. Physicists talk to engineers but not to novelists and historians. Film critics and cultural theorists might speak to one another but not to chemists and biologists. Snow bemoaned the loss, if only because a world whose scientists have developed weapons that can destroy the planet needs humanists to control their use. And humanists cannot describe in any convincing way a world shaped by sciences they do not understand or even want to engage. Fifty years later the situation has changed, but not necessarily for the better. The sciences have triumphed and any connection with the humanities is almost always one in which the former dominate the latter. University programs, driven by "practical" concerns, are led by the sciences. The humanities or liberal arts struggle to sustain their role in education and research, and are more likely to succeed when they accept a scientific or technological way of thinking. The humanities may be in decline, but the "digital humanities" are thriving.

There is increasing attention to developing a third way that would neither return to the world in which the sciences and the humanities fill separate spheres, nor to a world in which one dominates over the other. Some have argued that this calls for the formation of a fourth culture, neither science nor art, nor some combination of the two, but rather a new way of thinking and acting in worlds described by the two (Lehrer, 2007). Clearly, this is a project whose enormity is only matched by its necessity. And political economy, especially the political economy of communication, needs to enter the debate. The latter brings together what have traditionally been viewed as a social science (political economy) with an art (communication) and much of its recent attention has been directed to the study of media and other related technology. By definition, its roots are located in multiple cultures and it understands the social relations, and especially the power relations, that constitute them. Whether the reconstitution of the arts and sciences becomes a project of genuine human liberation or merely another way capitalism turns creativity into a profitable industry will depend on who joins the struggle to shape this project. Political economists, especially those who study communication, need to be at its center.

REFERENCES

A Dictionary of Biology (2004) 'Communication', *A Dictionary of Biology*, Oxford: Oxford University Press. Oxford Online, available at: www.oxfordreference.com/views/ENTRY.html?subview= Main&entry=t6.e963, last accessed May 30, 2008.

Abbott, J.P. (2001) 'Democracy@internet.asia? The challenges to the emancipatory potential of the Net: Lessons from China and Malaysia', *Third World Quarterly*, 22(1): 99–114.

Abler, Ron, Adam, John S., and Gould, Peter (1971) *Spatial Organization*. Englewood Cliffs, NJ: Prentice-Hall.

Abler, Ron, Janelle, Donald, Philbrick, Allen, and Sommer, John (1975) *Human Geography in a Shrinking World*. Belmont, CA: Wadsworth.

Aglietta, Michel (1979) *A Theory of Capitalist Regulation: The US Experience*. Trans. D. Fernbach. London: New Left Books.

Agnew, John (2001) 'The new global economy: Time–space compression, geopolitics, and uneven development', *Journal of World Systems Research*, 7(2): 133–154.

Ahmad, Aijiz (1992) *In Theory: Classes, Nations, Literatures*. London: Verso.

Aksoy, Asu and Robins, Kevin (1992) 'Hollywood for the 21st century: Global competition for critical mass in image markets', *Cambridge Journal of Economics*, 16(1): 1–22.

Alt, James E. and Shepsle, Kenneth A. (eds) (1990) *Perspectives on Positive Political Economy*. Cambridge: Cambridge University Press.

Alzouma, G. (2005) 'Myths of digital technology in Africa: Leapfrogging development', *Global Media and Communication*, 1(3): 339–354.

Amin, Samir (1976) *Accumulation on a World Scale: A Critique of the Theory of Underdevelopment*. New York: Monthly Review Press.

Amsden, Alice (1992) 'Otiose economics', *Social Research*, 59(4): 781–797.

Anderson, Gary M. (1988) 'Mr. Smith and the preachers: The economics of religion in the *Wealth of Nations*', *Journal of Political Economy*, 96(5): 1066–1088.

Andrejevic, Mark (2003a) 'Trading space: Monitored mobility in the era of mass customization', *Space and Culture*, 6(2): 132–150.

_____ (2003b) *Reality TV: The Work of Being Watched*. Lanham, MD: Rowman and Littlefield.

Ang, Ien (1991) *Desparately Seeking the Audience*. London: Routledge.

Ankarloo, Daniel and Palermo, Giulio (2004) 'Anti-Williamson: A Marxian critique of new institutional economics', *Cambridge Journal of Economics*, 28: 413–429.

Ankney, Raymond and Procopio, Deborah (2003) 'Corporate culture, minority hiring and newspaper coverage of affirmative action', *Howard Journal of Communication*, 14(3): 159–176.

Antcliff, Valerie (2005) 'Broadcasting in the 1990s: Competition, choice, and inequality?', *New Media & Society*, 27(6): 841–859.

Artz, Lee and Kamalipour, Yahya R. (eds) (2003) *The Globalization of Corporate Media Hegemony*. Albany, NY: State University of New York Press.

Artz, Lee, Macek, Steve, and Cloud, Dana L. (eds) (2006) *Marxism and Communication Studies: The Point is to Change It*. New York: Peter Lang.

Arvidsson, Adam (2005) 'Brands: A critical perspective', *Journal of Consumer Culture*, 5(2): 235–258.

_____ (2004) 'On the pre-history of the panoptic sort: Mobility in market research', *Surveillance and Society*, 1(4): 456–574.

Atkinson, Joshua (2005) 'Conceptualizing global justice audiences of alternative media', *The Communication Review*, 8: 137–157.

Attali, Jacques (1985) *Noise: The Political Economy of Music*. Trans. B. Massumi. Minneapolis, MN: University of Minnesota Press.

Atwood, Rita and McAnany, Emile G. (eds) (1986) *Communication and Latin American Society*. Madison, WI: University of Wisconsin Press.

Aubrey, Rebecca A., Kingstone, Peter R., and Young, Joseph M. (2004) 'Privatization and its discontents: Political mobilization against neoliberal hegemony in Latin America', Paper presented at the annual meeting of the International Studies Association, Le Centre Sheraton Hotel, Montreal, Quebec, Canada. Available at: www.allacademic.com/meta/p73320_index.html, last accessed June 24, 2008.

Babe, Robert (1990) *Telecommunications in Canada*. Toronto: University of Toronto Press.

Bagdikian, Ben H. (1992) *The Media Monopoly* (4th edn). Boston: Beacon Press.

Baker, Drucilla K. (2005) 'Beyond women and economics: Rereading "women's work"', *Signs: Journal of Women in Culture and Society*, 30: 2189–2209.

Bakker, Isabella and Gill, Stephen (eds) (2003) *Power, Production and Social Reproduction*. London: Palgrave.

Baldoz, Rick, Koeber, Charles and Kraft, Philip (eds) (2001) *The Critical Study of Work: Labor, Technology, and Global Production*. Philadelphia, PA: Temple University Press.

Baltruschat, Doris (2008) 'Mapping global production: From cinematic co-productions to TV formats and interactive media'. Doctoral dissertation. Burnaby, BC: Simon Fraser University.

Baran, Paul A. (1957) *The Political Economy of Growth*. New York: Monthly Review Press.

Baran, Paul A. and Sweezy, Paul M. (1966) *Monopoly Capital: An Essay on the American Economic and Social Order*. New York: Monthly Review Press.

_____ (1965) 'Economics of two worlds', in O. Lange (ed.), *On Political Economy and Econometrics*. Oxford: Pergamon. pp. 15–29.

Basu, Kaushick (2000) *Prelude to Political Economy: A Study of the Social and Political Foundations of Economics*. Cambridge: Cambridge University Press.

Baudrillard, Jean (1981) *For a Critique of the Political Economy of the Sign*. St Louis, MO: Telos Press.

_____ (1975) *The Mirror of Production*. St Louis, MO: Telos Press.

Becker, Gary S. and Mulligan, Casey B. (2003) 'Deadweight costs and the size of government', *The Journal of Law and Economics*, 46(2): 293–340.

Beetham, Margaret (1996) *A Magazine of Her Own: Domesticity and Desire in the Woman's Magazine, 1800–1914*. London: Routledge.

Bell, Daniel (1976) *The Cultural Contradictions of Capitalism*. New York: Basic Books.

_____ (1973) *The Coming of Postindustrial Society*. New York: Basic Books.

Bell, Daniel and Kristol, Irving (eds) (1981) *The Crisis in Economic Theory*. New York: Basic Books.

Beltrán, Luis R. (1976) 'Alien premises, objects, and methods in Latin American communication research', *Communication Research*, 3(2): 107–134.

Beltrán, Luis R. and Fox de Cardona, Elizabeth (1980) *Communicación Dominada: Estados Unidos en los Medios de América Latina*. Mexico City: Instituto Latinoamericano de Estudios Transnacionales/Nueva Imagen.

Beniger, James R. (1986) *The Control Revolution*. Cambridge, MA: Harvard University Press.

Benson, Rodney (2005) 'American journalism and the politics of diversity', *Media, Culture & Society*, 27(1): 5–20.

Bentham, Jeremy (1907) *Introduction to the Principles of Morals and Legislation*. Oxford: Clarendon Press (1st edn, 1789).

Benton, Ted (1989) 'Marxism and natural limits: An ecological critique and reconstruction', *New Left Review*, 178: 51–86.

Berberoglu, Berch (ed.) (1993) *The Labor Process and Control of Labor: The Changing Nature of Work Relations in the Late Twentieth Century*. Westport, CT: Praeger.

Bettig, Ronald V. (1996) *Copyrighting Culture: The Political Economy of Intellectual Property*. Boulder, CO: Westview Press.

Bettig, Ronald V. and Hall, Jeanne Lynn (2003) *Big Money, Big Media: Cultural Texts and Political Economics*. Lanham, MD: Rowman and Littlefield.

Bezanson, Kate and Luxton, Meg (2006) *Social Reproduction: Feminist Political Economy Challenges Neo-liberalism*. Montreal: McGill-Queen's University Press.

Bhuiyan, A.J.M. Shafiul Alam (2008) 'Peripheral view: Conceptualizing the information society as a postcolonial subject', *The International Communication Gazette*, 70(2): 99–116.

Bianco, Anthony (2006) *The Bully of Bentonville*. New York: Doubleday.

Boettke, Peter J. and Storr, Virgul Henry (2002) 'Post-classical political economy: Polity, society, and economy in Weber, Mises, and Hayek', *American Journal of Sociology and Economics*, 61(1): 161–191.

Boyer, Robert (2000) 'The political in the era of globalization and finance: Focus on some Regulation School research', *International Journal of Urban and Regional Research*, 24(2): 274–322.

Braman, Sandra (2007) *Change of State*. Cambridge, MA: MIT Press.

Braudel, Fernand (1975) *Capitalism and Material Life: 1400–1800*. Trans. M. Kochan. New York: Harper & Row.

Braverman, Harry (1974) *Labor and Monopoly Capital*. New York: Monthly Review.

Breed, Michael D. (1999) 'How do animals communicate?', *The Quarterly Review of Biology*, 74(2): 204–207.

Brennan, Geoffrey and Buchanan, James M. (1985) *The Reason of Rules: Constitutional Political Economy*. Cambridge and New York: Cambridge University Press.

Brennen, Bonnie (2005) 'Lockouts, protests, and scabs: A critical assessment of the *Los Angeles Herald Examiner* strike', *Critical Studies in Media Communication*, 22(1): 64–81.

Brock, Gillian and Brighouse, Harry (eds) (2005) *The Political Philosophy of Cosmopolitanism*. Cambridge: Cambridge University Press.

Broe, Dennis (2004) 'Fox and its friends: Global commodification and the new cold war', *Cinema Journal*, 4(3): 97–102.

Brophy, Enda (2006) 'System error: Labour precarity and collective organizing at Microsoft', *Canadian Journal of Communication,* 31(3): 619–638.

Bruff, Ian (2005) 'Making sense of the globalisation debate when engaging in political economy analysis', *British Journal of Politics and International Relations*, 7: 261–280.

Brunn, Stanley D. and Leinbach, Thomas R. (eds) (1991) *Collapsing Space and Time: Geographic Aspects of Communication and Information*. London: Harper Collins Academic.

Buchanan, James M. (2003) 'Public choice: Politics without romance', *Policy*, 19(3): 13–18.

_____ (1999) *Public Finance and Public Choice: Two Contrasting Visions of the State*. Cambridge, MA: MIT Press.

Budd, Mike, Entman, Robert M., and Steinman, Clay (1990) 'The affirmative character of US cultural studies', *Critical Studies in Mass Communication*, 7: 169–184.

Bullock, Heather, Wyche, Karen, and Williams, Wendy (2001) 'Media images of the poor', *Journal of Social Issues*, 57(2): 229–246.

Burawoy, Michael (1979) *Manufacturing Consent*. Chicago: University of Chicago Press.

Burkart, Patrick and McCourt, Thomas (2006) *Digital Music Wars*. Lanham, MD: Rowman and Littlefield.

Burke, Edmund (1955) *Reflections on the Revolution in France*. New York: Liberal Arts Press (1st edn, 1790).

Burke, Kenneth (1969a) *A Rhetoric of Motives*. Berkeley, CA: University of California Press (1st edn, 1950).

_____ (1969b) *A Grammar of Motives*. Berkeley, CA: University of California Press (1st edn, 1945).

Burkett, Paul (2006) *Marxism and Ecological Economics: Towards a Red and Green Political Economy*. Leiden: Brill Academic Publishers.

Burt, Ronald S. (1992) *Structural Holes: The Social Structure of Competition*. Cambridge, MA: Harvard University Press.

Butsch, Richard (2000) *The Making of American Audiences, 1750–1990*. New York: Cambridge University Press.

Buxton, William (1994) 'The political economy of communications research: The Rockefeller Foundation, the "Radio Wars" and the Princeton Radio Research Project', in R.E. Babe (ed.), *Information and Communication in Economics*. Boston: Kluwer. pp. 147–175.

Byerly, Carolyn (2004) 'Women and media concentration', in R.R. Rush, C.E. Oukrup, and P.J. Creedon (eds), *Seeking Equity for Women in Journalism and Mass Communication Education*. Hillsdale, NJ: LEA Press. pp. 246–262.

Calabrese, Andrew and Burgelman, Jean-Claude (eds) (1999) *Communication, Citizenship, and Social Policy*. Lanham, MD: Rowman and Littlefield.

Calabrese, Andrew and Sparks, Colin (eds) (2004) *Towards a Political Economy of Culture: Capitalism and Communication in the Twenty-first Century*. Lanham, MD: Rowman and Littlefield.

Calhoun, Craig (1994) *Social Theory and the Politics of Identity*. Oxford: Blackwell.

Camerer, Colin, Issacharoff, Samuel, Loewenstein, George, O'Donoghue, Ted, and Rabin, Matthew (2003) 'Regulation for conservatives: Behavioural economics and the case for "assymmetric paternalism"', *University of Pennsylvania Law Review*, 151(3): 1211–1254.

Campbell, John E. (2005) 'Outing PlanetOut: Surveillance, gay marketing, and Internet affinity portals', *New Media & Society*, 7(5): 663–683.

Campbell, John E. and Carlson, Matt (2002) 'Panopticon.com: Online surveillance and the commodification of privacy', *Journal of Broadcasting and Electronic Media*, 46(4): 586–606.

Cao, Jin and Zhao, Yuezhi (eds) (2007) *The Political Economy of Communication: A Reader*. Shanghai: Fudan University Press.

Cardoso, F.H. and Faletto, E. (1979) *Dependency and Development in Latin America*. Berkeley, CA: University of California Press.

Carey, James W. (1979) 'Mass communication research and cultural studies: An American view', in J. Curran, M. Gurevitch, and J. Woollacott (eds), *Mass Communication and Society*. London: Edward Arnold. pp. 409–425.

Carlson, Matt (2006) 'Tapping in TiVo: Digital recorders and the transition from schedules to surveillance in television', *New Media & Society*, 8(1): 97–115.

Carlyle, Thomas (1984) *A Carlyle Reader*. G.B. Tennyson (ed.). New York: Cambridge University Press.

Castagnera, James Ottavio (2002) 'Groping towards utopia: Capitalism, public policy, and Rawls' theory of justice', *Journal of Transitional Law and Public Policy*, 11(2): 297–308.

Castells, Manuel (2004) *The Politics of Identity*. Oxford: Blackwell (1st edn, 1997).

_____ (2002) 'Local and global: Cities in the network society', *Tijdschrift voor Economische en Socizale Geografie*, 93(5): 548–558.

_____ (2001) *The Internet Galaxy*. New York: Oxford University Press.

_____ (1989) *The Informational City: Information Technology, Economic Restructuring, and the Urban-Regional Process*. Oxford: Blackwell.

Castree, Noel and Gregory, Derek (2006) *David Harvey: A Critical Reader*. Oxford: Blackwell.

CCCS Women's Studies Group (1978) *Women Take Issue*. London: Hutchinson.

Centre for Mass Communication Research (1991) 'Research programme, postgraduate studies, and publications'. University of Leicester, March.

_____ (1984) 'Background to the establishment of the Centre'. University of Leicester, Planning Document Submitted to the University.

Chakravartty, Paula and Sarikakis, Katherine (2006) *Globalization and Media Policy*. Edinburgh: Edinburgh University Press.

Chakravartty, Paula and Zhao, Yuezhi (eds) (2008) *Global Communication: Toward a Transcultural Political Economy*. Lanham, MD: Rowman and Littlefield.

Chambers, Deborah, Steiner, Linda, and Fleming, Carole (2004) *Women and Journalism*. London: Routledge.

Chandler, Alfred D., Jr. (1977) *The Visible Hand: The Managerial Revolution in American Business*. Cambridge, MA: Harvard University Press.

Chang, Ha-Joon (2002) 'Breaking the mould: An institutional political economy alternative to the neoliberal theory of the market and the state', *Cambridge Journal of Economics*, 26: 539–559.

Chapman, Keith and Walker, David (1987) *Industrial Location: Principles and Policies*. Oxford: Basil Blackwell.

Chase-Dunn, Christopher (1989) *Global Formation: Structures of the World-Economy*. Oxford: Blackwell.

Chinn, Menzie and Fairlie, Robert (2006) 'The determinants of the global digital divide: A cross-country analysis of computer and internet penetration', *Oxford Economic Papers*, 59(1): 16–44.

Chomsky, Daniel (1999) 'Mechanisms of management control at the *New York Times*', *Media, Culture & Society*, 21(5): 579–599.

Christopherson, Susan and Storper, Michael (1989) 'The effects of flexible specialisation on industrial politics and the labour market: The motion picture industry', *Industrial and Labour Relations Review*, 42(3): 331–347.

Clark, Barry (1991) *Political Economy: A Comparative Approach*. New York: Praeger.

Clawson, R.A. and Trice, R. (2000) 'Poverty as we know it: Media portrayals of the poor', *Public Opinion Quarterly*, 64(1): 53–64.

Clement, Wallace (2001) 'Canadian political economy's legacy for sociology', *Canadian Journal of Sociology*, 26(3): 405–420.

_____ (1975) *The Canadian Corporate Elite: An Analysis of Economic Power*. Toronto: McClelland and Stewart.

Coase, Ronald H. (1991) *The Nature of the Firm: Origins, Evolution, and Development*. Oxford: Oxford University Press.

Coase, Ronald H. and Barrett, E.W. (1968) *Educational TV: Who Should Pay?* Washington, DC: American Enterprise Institute for Public Policy.

Cohen, Adam (2008) 'The already big thing on the internet: Spying on users', *The New York Times*, www.nytimes.com/2008/04/05/opinion/05sat4.html?_r=1&oref=slogin, last accessed July 4, 2008.

Cohen, G.A. (2000) *Karl Marx's Theory of History: A Defense* (rev. edn). New York: Oxford University Press.

Colander, David, Holt, Richard P.F., and Rosser, Barkley J., Jr. (2004) 'The changing face of main-stream economics', *Review of Political Economy*, 16(4): 485–499.

Communications Workers of America (2007) *Speed Matters: Affordable High-speed Internet for All*. Washington, DC: Communications Workers of America.

Compaine, Benjamin (2001) *The Digital Divide: Facing a Crisis or Creating a Myth*. Cambridge, MA: MIT Press.

Compton, James (2004) *The Integrated News Spectacle: A Political Economy of Cultural Performance*. New York: Peter Lang.

Connell, R.W. (1987) *Gender and Power*. Stanford, CA: Stanford University Press.

Coombe, Rosemary (2005) 'Legal claims to culture in and against the media: Neoliberalism and the global proliferation of meaningful difference', *Law, Culture, and the Humanities*, 1(1): 32–55.

Cooper, Kent (1942) *Barriers Down*. New York: Farrar & Rinehart.

Couldry, Nick (2004) 'Theorizing media as a practice', *Social Semiotics*, 14(2): 115–132.

Crandall, Robert W. (1991) *After the Breakup: US Telecommunications in a More Competitive Era*. Washington, DC: The Brookings Institution.

Crawford, Margaret (1992) 'The world in a shopping mall', in M. Sorkin (ed.), *Variations on a Theme Park: The New American City and the End of Public Space*. New York: Hill and Wang. pp. 3–30.

Creedon, Pamela J. (ed.) (1993) *Women in Mass Communication: Challenging Gender Values* (2nd edn). Thousand Oaks, CA: Sage.

Critical Studies in Mass Communication (1995) 'Colloquy', 12: 60–100.

Crossley, Nick and Roberts, John Michael (eds) (2004) *After Habermas: New Perspectives on the Public Sphere*. Malden, MA: Wiley-Blackwell.

Curran, James (2002) *Media and Power*. New York: Routledge.

_____ (1979) 'Capitalism and control of the press, 1800–1975', in J. Curran, M. Gurevitch, and J. Woolacott (eds), *Mass Communication and Society*. London: Open University. pp. 195–231.

Danielian, N.R. (1939) *AT&T*. New York: Vanguard.

Davis, John (1992) *Exchange*. Minneapolis, MN: University of Minnesota Press.

Davis, John B. (2006) 'The turn in economics: Neoclassical dominance to mainstream pluralism', *Cambridge Journal of Economics*, 2(1): 1–20.

Day, Wan Wen (2007) 'Commodification of creativity: Reskilling computer animation labor in Taiwan', in C. McKercher and V. Mosco (eds), *Knowledge Workers in the Information Society*. Lanham, MD: Lexington Books. pp. 85–99.

de la Haye, Yves (ed.) (1980) *Marx & Engels on the Means of Communication*. New York: International General.

Deery, June (2004a) 'Trading faces: The make-over show as primetime infomercial', *Feminist Media Studies*, 4(2): 211–214.

_____ (2004b) 'Reality TV as advertainment', *Popular Communication*, 2(1): 1–20.

Deetz, Stan and Hegbloom, Maria (2007) 'Situating the political economy and cultural studies conversation in the processes of living and working', *Communication and Critical/Cultural Studies*, 4(3): 323–326.

Della Porta, Donatella, et al. (2006) *Globalisation from Below*. Minneapolis, MN: University of Minnesota Press.

Della Porta, Donatella and Diani, Mario (2006) *Social Movements: An Introduction*. Oxford: Blackwell.

Denning, Michael (2004) *Culture in the Age of Three Worlds*. London: Verso.

_____ (1996) *The Cultural Front: The Laboring of American Culture in the Twentieth Century*. London: Verso.

Denzin, Norman K. and Giardina, Michael D. (eds) (2007) *Contesting Empire, Globalizing Dissent*. Boulder, CO: Paradigm.

Der Derian, James (2001) *Virtuous War: Mapping the Military-Industrial-Media-Entertainment Network*. Boulder, CO: Westview Press.

Derthick, Martha and Quirk, Paul J. (1985) *The Politics of Deregulation*. Washington, DC: The Brookings Institution.

DeSimone, Mark (1992) 'Information is value', *The Globe and Mail*, March 3.

Deuze, Mark (2007) *Media Work*. London: Polity Press.

DiCenzo, Maria (2004) 'Feminist media and history: A response to James Curran', *Media History*, 10(1): 43–49.

Dicken, Peter (1986) *Global Shift*. London: Paul Chapman.

Dines, Gail and Humez, Jean (2002) *Gender, Race and Class in Media*: Thousand Oaks, CA: Sage.

Donkor, David (2007) 'Performance, ethnography and the radical intervention of Dwight Conquergood', *Cultural Studies*, 21(6): 821–825.

Dorfman, Ariel and Mattelart, Armand (1975) *How to Read Donald Duck*. London: International General.

Dorsey, Elizabeth, Steeves, H. Leslie, and Porras, Luz Estella (2004) 'Advertising eco-tourism on the internet: Commodifying environment and culture', *New Media & Society*, 6(6): 753–779.

Dos Santos, T. (1970) 'The structure of dependency', *American Economic Review*, May: 231–236.

Douglas, Susan J. (2004) *Listening In: Radio and American Imagination*. Minneapolis, MN: University of Minnesota Press.

_____ (1987) *Inventing American Broadcasting, 1899–1922*. Baltimore, MD: Johns Hopkins University Press.

Downing, John (2001) *Radical Media*. London: Sage.

Downing, John and Husband, Charles (2005) *Representing Race: Racisms, Ethnicities, and Media*. Thousand Oaks, CA: Sage.

DuBoff, Richard (1989) *Accumulation and Power: An Economic History of the United States*. Armonk, NY: M.E. Sharpe.

_____ (1984) 'The rise of communications regulation: The telegraph industry, 1844–1880', *Journal of Communication*, 34(3): 52–66.

Durham, Frank (2005) 'Public relations as structuration: A prescriptive critique of the StarLink global food contamination case', *Journal of Public Relations Research*, 17(1): 29–47.

During, Simon (ed.) (1993) *The Cultural Studies Reader*. London: Routledge.

Dyer-Witheford, Nick (1999) *Cyber-Marx: Cycles and Circuits of Struggle in High Technology Capitalism*. Urbana and Chicago, IL: University of Illinois Press.

Dyer-Witheford, Nick and Sharman, Nick (2005) 'The political economy of Canada's video and computer game industry', *Canadian Journal of Communication*, 30(2): 187–210.

Eagleton, Terry (2003) *After Theory*. London: Penguin.

Eatwell, John, Milgate, Murray, and Newman, Peter (1987) *The New Palgrave: A Dictionary of Economics*. London: Macmillan.

Edge, Marc (2007) *Asper Nation*. Vancouver: New Star Books.

Edwards, Richard (1979) *Contested Terrain: The Transformation of the Workplace in the Twentieth Century*. New York: Basic Books.

Ehrenreich, Barbara and Hochschild, Arlie (eds) (2003) *Global Woman*. New York: Granta.

Emmanuel, Arghiri (1972) *Unequal Exchange: A Study of the Imperialism of Trade*. Trans. B. Pearce. New York: Monthly Review Press.

Enzensberger, Hans M. (1974) *The Consciousness Industry*. New York: Seabury Press.

Evans, James and Brook, Lawrence (2005) 'Understanding collaboration using new technologies: A structurational perspective', *The Information Society*, 20: 215–220.

Evans, William A. (1990) 'The interpretive turn in media research: Innovation, iteration, or illusion', *Critical Studies in Mass Communication*, 7: 147–168.

Ewen, Elizabeth and Ewen, Stuart (2006) *Typecasting*. New York: Seven Stories Press.

Ewen, Stuart (2001) *Captains of Consciousness*. New York: McGraw Hill (1st edn, 1976).

––––––––––– (1996) *PR!: A Social History of Spin*. New York: Basic Books.

Fanon, Frantz (1965) *A Study in Dying Colonialism*. New York: Monthly Review Press (1st edn, 1959).

Featherstone, Mike (ed.) (1990) *Global Culture: Nationalism, Globalization, and Modernity*. Newbury Park, CA: Sage.

Ferguson, James and Gupta, Akhil (2002) 'Spatializing states: Toward an ethnography of neoliberal governmentality', *American Ethnologist*, 29(4): 981–1002.

Fishman, Charles (2006) *Wal-Mart Effect*. New York: Penguin.

Fishman, Mark (1980) *Manufacturing the News*. Austin, TX: University of Texas Press.

Fiske, John (1989) *Understanding Popular Culture*. London: Unwin Hyman.

Flichy, Patrice (2007) *The Internet Imaginaire*. Trans. Liz Carey-Libbrecht. Cambridge, MA: MIT Press.

Florida, Richard (2002) *The Rise of the Creative Class*. New York: Basic Books.

Foley, Duncan K. (2006) *Adam's Fallacy: A Guide to Economic Theology*. Cambridge, MA: Harvard University Press.

Fones-Wolf, Colin and Fones-Wolf, Elizabeth (2007) 'Labor off the air: The Hearst Corporation, cross ownership and the union struggle for media access in San Francisco', in C. McKercher and V. Mosco (eds), *Knowledge Workers in the Information Society*. Lanham, MD: Lexington Books. pp. 1–18.

Fones-Wolf, Elizabeth (2006) *Waves of Opposition: Labor and the Struggle for Democratic Radio*. Chicago and Urbana, IL: University of Illinois Press.

Foster, John B. (2002) *Ecology against Capitalism*. New York: Monthly Review Press.

Frank, André Gunder (1969) *Capitalism and Underdevelopment in Latin America*. New York: Monthly Review Press.

Free, Marcus and Hughson, John (2006) 'Common culture, commodity fetishism, and the cultural contradictions of sport', *International Journal of Cultural Studies*, 9(1): 83–104.

Freeman, Christopher (2007) 'A political economy of the long wave', in G.M. Hodgson (ed.), *The Evolution of Economic Institutions*. London: Edward Elgar. pp. 75–97.

Freire, Paulo (1974) *Pedagogy of the Oppressed*. New York: Seabury Press.

Friedman, Benjamin M. (1988) *Day of Reckoning: The Consequences of American Economic Policy under Reagan and After*. New York: Random House.

Fuchs, Christian (2007) 'Transnational space and the "networked society"', *21st Century Society*, 2(1): 49–78.

Fürsich, Elfriede and Roushanzamir, Elli P.L. (2004) 'Corporate expansion, textual expansion: Commodification model of communication', *Journal of Communication Inquiry*, 25(4): 375–395.

Furubotn, Eirik G. and Richter, Rudolf (2005) *Institutions and Economic Theory: The Contribution of the New Institutional Economics* (2nd edn). Ann Arbor, MI: University of Michigan Press.

Galbraith, John K. (2004) *The Economics of Innocent Fraud*. Boston: Houghton Mifflin.

––––––––––– (1987) *Economics in Perspective: A Critical History*. Boston: Houghton Mifflin.

––––––––––– (1985) *The New Industrial State* (4th edn). Boston: Houghton Mifflin.

_____ (1958) *The Affluent Society*. Boston: Houghton Mifflin.

Gallagher, Margaret (1992) 'Women and men in the media,' *Communication Research Trends*, 12(1): 1–36.

_____ (1985) *Unequal Opportunities: Update*. Paris: UNESCO.

_____ (1984) *Employment and Positive Action for Women in the Television Organizations of the EEC Member States*. Brussels: Commission for European Communities.

_____ (1980) *Unequal Opportunities: The Case of Women and the Media*. Paris: UNESCO.

Gandy, Oscar, Jr. (2003) 'Privatization and identity: The formation of racial class', in G. Murdock and J. Wasko (eds), *Media in the Age of Marketization*. Creskill, NJ: Hampton Press. pp. 109–130.

_____ (1998) *Communication and Race: A Structural Perspective*. London: Arnold.

Gane, Nicholas (2006) 'Speed up or slow down? Social theory in the information age', *Information, Communication & Society*, 9(1): 20–38.

Ganesh, Shiv, Zoller, Heather, and Cheney, George (2005) 'Transforming resistance, broadening our boundaries: Critical organizational communication meets globalization from below', *Communication Monographs*, 72(2): 169–191.

Gans, Herbert (1979) *Deciding What's News*. New York: Pantheon.

Garnham, Nicholas (2003) 'Class analysis and the information society as mode of production', *The Public*, 11(3): 93–104.

_____ (2000) *Emancipation, the Media, and Modernity: Arguments about the Media and Social Theory*. New York: Oxford University Press.

_____ (1990) *Capitalism and Communication: Global Culture and the Economics of Information*. London: Sage.

_____ (1979) 'Contribution to a political economy of mass communication', *Media, Culture & Society*, 1(2): 122–146.

_____ (1978) *Structures of Television*. London: British Film Institute (1st edn, 1973).

Gates, Henry Louis, Jr. (1989) 'Whose canon is it, anyway?', *The New York Times Book Review*, February 26: 1, 44–45.

Gibson, Timothy (2003) *Securing the Spectacular City*. Lanham, MD: Lexington Books.

Gibson, Timothy and Lowes, Mark (eds) (2006) *Urban Communication: Production, Text, Context*. Lanham, MD: Rowman and Littlefield.

Giddens, Anthony (2000) *Runaway World: How Globalization is Reshaping our Lives*. London: Routledge.

_____ (1991) *Modernity and Self–Identity: Self and Society in the Late Modern Age*. Stanford, CA: Stanford University Press.

_____ (1990) *The Consequences of Modernity*. Stanford, CA: Stanford University Press.

_____ (1984) *The Constitution of Society: Outline of a Theory of Structuration*. Berkeley, CA: University of California Press.

_____ (1981) *A Contemporary Critique of Historical Materialism*. Berkeley, CA: University of California Press.

Gilman, Charlotte Perkins (1966) *Women and Economics: A Study of the Economic Relations between Men and Women as a Factor in Social Evolution*. New York: Harper & Row (1st edn, 1889).

Gilpin, Alan (1977) *Dictionary of Economic Terms*. London: Butterworths.

Gitlin, Todd (1980) *The Whole World is Watching: Mass Media in the Making and the Unmaking of the New Left*. Berkeley, CA: University of California Press.

_____ (1979) 'Media sociology: The dominant paradigm', *Theory and Society*, 6(2): 205–253.

Gittings, Christopher (1998) 'Imaging Canada: The Singing Mountie and other commodifications of nation', *Canadian Journal of Communication*, 23(4): 83–97.

Glenny, Misha (2008) *McMafia: A Journey through the Criminal Underworld*. New York: Knopf.

Glynn, Kevin (2000) *Tabloid Culture*. Durham, NC: Duke University Press.

Godfried, Nathan (1997) *WCFL, Chicago's Voice of Labor, 1926–78*. Chicago and Urbana, IL: University of Illinois Press.

Golding, Peter and Murdock, Graham (1991) 'Culture, communications, and political economy', in J. Curran and M. Gurevitch (eds), *Mass Media and Society*. London: Edward Arnold. pp. 15–32.

Golding, Peter, Murdock, Graham, and Schlesinger, Philip (eds) (1986) *Communicating Politics: Mass Communication and the Political Process*. New York: Holmes and Meier.

Goldman, Robert and Rajagopal, Arvind (1991) *Mapping Hegemony: Television News Coverage of Industrial Conflict*. Norwood, NJ: Ablex.

Gonzalez-Manet, Enrique (1988) *The Hidden War of Information*. Trans. L. Alexandre. Norwood, NJ: Ablex.

Graham, Philip (2000) 'Hypercapitalism: A political economy of informational idealism', *New Media & Society*, 2(2): 131–156.

Graham, Stephen (2002) 'Bridging urban digital divides? Urban polarization and information and communication technologies (ICTs)', *Urban Studies*, 39(1): 33–56.

Gran, Peter (1990) 'Studies of Anglo-American political economy: Democracy, orientalism, and the Left', in H. Sharabi (ed.), *Theory, Politics and the Arab World: Critical Responses*. New York: Routledge. pp. 228–254.

Gray, Herman (2004) *Watching Race: Television and the Struggle for Blackness*. Minneapolis, MN: University of Minnesota Press.

Gray, John (2007) *Black Mass*. London: Farrar, Straus and Giroux.

Green, Mark J. (ed.) (1973) *The Monopoly Makers*. New York: Penguin.

Green, Venus (2001) *Race on the Line: Gender, Labor, and Technology in the Bell System*. Durham, NC: Duke University Press.

Grimes, Sarah M. (2006) 'Online multiplayer games: A virtual space for intellectual property debates?', *New Media & Society*, 8(6): 969–990.

Grossberg, Lawrence (2006) 'Does cultural studies have futures? Should it? (Or what's the matter with New York?)', *Cultural Studies*, 20(1): 1–32.

_____ (1991) 'Strategies of marxist cultural interpretation', in R.K. Avery and D. Eason (eds), *Critical Perspectives on Media and Society*. New York: Guilford Press. pp. 126–159.

Grossberg, Lawrence, Nelson, Cary, and Treichler, Paula (eds) (1992) *Cultural Studies*. New York: Routledge.

Grossman, Elizabeth (2006) *Hi-Tech Trash*. Washington, DC: Island Press/Shearwater Books.

Guback, Thomas (ed.) (1993) *Counterclockwise: Perspectives on Communication – Dallas Smythe*. Boulder, CO: Westview Press.

_____ (1969) *The International Film Industry: Western Europe and America since 1945*. Bloomington, IN: Indiana University Press.

Gunaratne, Shelton A. (2005) 'Public diplomacy, global communication and world order: An analysis based on Theory of Living Systems', *Current Sociology*, 53(5): 749–772.

_____ (2004) 'Thank you Newton, welcome Prigogine: "Unthinking" old paradigms and embracing new directions. Part 2: The pragmatics', *Communications*, 29: 113–132.

_____ (2002a) 'An evolving triadic world: A theoretical framework for global communication research', *Journal of World Systems Research*, 8(3): 330–365.

_____ (2002b) 'Freedom of the press: A world system perspective', *Gazette: The International Journal for Communication Studies*, 64(4): 343–369.

Habermas, Jürgen (1989) *The Structural Transformation of the Public Sphere*. Trans. T. Burger with F. Lawrence. Cambridge, MA: MIT Press (1st edn, 1962).

_____ (1973) *Legitimation Crisis*. Boston: Beacon Press.

Hackett, Robert A. and Carroll, William K. (2006) *Remaking Media: The Struggle to Democratize Public Communication*. New York and London: Routledge.

Hackett, Robert and Zhao, Yuezhi (2005) *Democratizing Global Media: One World, Many Struggles*. Lanham, MD: Rowman and Littlefield.

Hagen, Ingunn and Wasko, Janet (eds) (2000) *Consuming Audiences*. Creskill, NJ: Hampton.

Hagerstrand, Torsten (1968) *Diffusion of Innovation*. Trans. A. Pred. Chicago: University of Chicago Press.

Hall, Stuart (1989) 'Ideology and communication theory', in B. Dervin, L. Grossberg, B. O'Keefe and E. Wartella (eds), *Paradigm Exemplars. Vol. 2, Rethinking Communication*. Thousand Oaks, CA: Sage. pp. 40–52.

_____ (1986) 'Media power and class power', in J. Curran (ed.), *Bending Reality: The State of the Media*. London: Pluto Press. pp. 5–14.

_____ (1982) 'The rediscovery of ideology: Return of the repressed in media studies', in M. Gurevitch, T. Bennett, J. Curran, and J. Woollacott (eds), *Culture, Society, and the Media*. London and New York: Methuen. pp. 56–90.

_____ (1980) 'Cultural studies: Two paradigms', *Media, Culture, & Society*, 2: 57–72.

Hall, Stuart and Jefferson, Tony (eds) (1976) *Resistance through Rituals: Youth Subcultures in Post-war Britain*. London: Hutchinson.

Hallin, Daniel C. and Mancini, Paolo (2004) *Comparing Media Systems*. Cambridge: Cambridge University Press.

Halloran, James (1981) 'The context of mass communication research', in E. McAnany, J. Schnitman, and N. Janus (eds), *Communication and Social Structure*. New York: Praeger. pp. 21–57.

Hamelink, Cees and Linné, Olga (1994) *Mass Communication Research: On Problems and Policies*. Norwood, NJ: Ablex.

Hamelink, Cees and Nordenstreng, Kaarle (2007) 'A short history of IAMCR', in *IAMCR in Retrospect 1957–2007*. Paris: Maison des Sciences de l'Homme, Paris Nord. pp. 5–26.

Hanke, B. (2005) 'The political economy of indymedia practice', *Canadian Journal of Communication*, 30(1). Available at: www.cjc-online.ca/index.php/journal/article/view/1479/1595, last accessed May 23, 2008.

Haralovich, Mary Beth and Rabinovitz, Lauren (1999) *Television, History, and American Culture: Feminist Critical Essays*. Durham, NC: Duke University Press.

Haraway, Donna (2003) *The Haraway Reader*. London: Routledge.

_____ (1991) *Simians, Cyborgs, and Women: The Reinvention of Nature*. New York: Routledge.

Harding, Susan (2003) *The Feminist Standpoint Theory Reader*. London: Routledge.

Hardt, Hanno (1992) *Critical Communication Studies: Communication, History & Theory in America*. London: Routledge.

_____ (1990) 'Newsworkers, technology, and journalism history', *Critical Studies in Mass Communication*, 7: 346–365.

Hardt, Michael and Negri, Antonio (2004) *Multitude: War and Democracy in the Age of Empire*. New York: Penguin.

_____ (2000) *Empire*. Cambridge, MA: Harvard University Press.

Hartsock, Nancy (1999) *The Feminist Standpoint Revisited*. New York: Basic Books.

Harvey, David (2006) *Spaces of Global Capitalism*. London: Verso.

_____ (2001) *Spaces of Capital: Towards a Critical Geography*. London: Routledge.

_____ (1999) *Limits to Capital* (2nd rev. edn). London: Verso.

_____ (1989) *The Condition of Postmodernity*. Oxford: Blackwell.

Head, Simon (2004) 'Inside the Leviathan', *The New York Review of Books*, 51(20). Available at: www.nybooks.com/articles/17647, last accessed December 7, 2004.

_____ (2003) *The New Ruthless Economy: Work and Power in the Digital Age*. Oxford: Oxford University Press.

Heider, Don (ed.) (2004) *Class and News*. Lanham, MD: Rowman and Littlefield.

Heilbroner, Robert L. (1986) *The Worldly Philosophers* (6th rev. edn). New York: Simon & Schuster.

Heller, Walter W. (1967) *New Dimensions in Political Economy*. New York: W.W. Norton.

Henry, Frances and Tator, Carol (2002) *Discourse of Domination: Racial Bias in the Canadian English Language Press*. Toronto: University of Toronto Press.

Herman, Edward S. and Chomsky, Noam (2002) *Manufacturing Consent: The Political Economy of the Mass Media*. New York: Pantheon.

Heyzer, Noeleen (1986) *Working Women in Southeast Asia: Development, Subordination, and Emancipation*. Philadelphia, PA: Open University Press.

Hills, Jill (2007) *Telecommunications and Empire*. Chicago and Urbana, IL: University of Illinois Press.

Hobsbawn, Eric (1992) 'Introduction: Inventing traditions', in E. Hobsbawn and T. Ranger (eds), *The Invention of Tradition*. Cambridge: Cambridge University Press. pp. 1–14.

_____ (1973) 'Karl Marx's contribution to historiography', in R. Blackburn (ed.), *Ideology in Social Sciences*. New York: Vintage. pp. 265–283.

Hodgetts, Darrin, Bolam, Bruce, and Stephens, Christine (2005) 'Mediation and the construction of contemporary understandings of health and lifestyle', *Journal of Health Psychology*, 10(1): 123–136.

Hodgson, Geoffrey (2004) *The Evolution of Institutional Economics: Agency, Structure and Darwinism in American Institutionalism*. London: Routledge.

Hoffman, Bruce (2004) 'What can we learn from the terrorists?', *Global Agenda* (16 January) 32–34.

Hoggart, Richard (1957) *The Uses of Literacy*. Hammondsworth: Penguin.

Holom, Olof (2006) 'Integrated marketing communication: From tactics to strategy', *Corporate Communication: An International Journal*, 11(1): 23–33.

Hoover, Edgar M. (1937) *Location Theory and the Shoe and Leather Industry*. Cambridge, MA: Harvard University Press.

Hope, Wayne (2006) 'Global capitalism and the critique of real time', *Time and Society*, 15(2–3): 275–302.

Hope, Wayne and Johnson, Rosser (2004) 'What is an infomercial?', *Advertising and Society Review*, 5(2). Available at: http://muse.jhu.edu/journals/advertising_and_society_review/v005/5.2hope_johnson.html, last accessed 24 December, 2008.

Horton, Byrne J. (1948) *Dictionary of Modern Economics*. Washington, DC: Public Affairs Press.

Howley, Kevin (2005) *Community Media: People, Places, and Communication Technology*. Cambridge: Cambridge University Press.

_____ (2004) 'Remaking public service broadcasting: Lessons from Allston-Brighton Free Radio', *Social Movement Studies*, 3(2): 221–240.

_____ (2003) 'A poverty of voices: Street papers as communicative democracy', *Journalisim*, 4(3): 273–292.

Hund, Wulf and Kirchoff-Hund, Barbel (1985) 'Problems of political economy', *Media, Culture & Society*, 5: 83–88.

Hunt, Darnell M. (1997) *Screening the Los Angeles 'Riots': Race, Seeing and Resistance*. Cambridge: Cambridge University Press.

Hutton, Will and Giddens, Anthony (eds) (2000) *On the Edge: Living with Global Capitalism*. London: Jonathan Cape.

Huws, Ursula (2003) *The Making of a Cybertariat: Virtual Work in a Real World*. New York: Monthly Review Press.

Ibrahim, S.M. (1981) *The Flow of News into Sudan, the Middle East and Africa*. Khartoum: El Sahafa Press.

Ingram, John Kells (1923) *A History of Political Economy*. Intro. R. Ely. London: A&C Black.

Innis, Harold (1972) *Empire and Communications*. Toronto: University of Toronto Press.

International Chamber of Commerce (2007) *Telecoms Liberalization: An International Business Guide for Policymakers*. Paris: ICC.

'Interview with Harry Cleaver' (1993) *vis-à-vis* 1 (Autumn). Available at: www.geocities.com/CapitolHill/3843/cleaver.html, last accessed June 17, 2007.

Isard, Walter (1956) *Location and Space-economy: A General Theory Relating to Industrial Location, Market Areas, Land Use, Trade, and Urban Structure*. Cambridge: Technology Press of the Massachusetts Institute of Technology.

Jacobs, Katrien (2007) *Netporn: DIY Web Culture and Sexual Politics*. Lanham, MD: Rowman and Littlefield.

James, David E. and Berg, Rick (eds) (1996) *The Hidden Foundation: Cinema and the Question of Class*. Minneapolis, MN: University of Minnesota Press.

Jameson, Frederic (1989) 'Marxism and postmodernism', *New Left Review*, 176 (July–August): 31–45.

Jamieson, Kathleen Hall and Cappella, Joseph N. (2008) *Echo Chamber: Rush Limbaugh and the Conservative Media Establishment*. New York: Oxford University Press.

Jansen, Sue Curry (1989) 'Gender and the information society: A socially structured silence', *Journal of Communication*, 39(3): 196–215.

Jefferson, Therese and King, John E. (2001) '"Never intended to be a theory of everything": Domestic labour in neoclassical and Marxian economics', *Feminist Economics*, 7(3): 71–101.

Jenkins, Henry (2006) *Convergence Culture*. New York: New York University Press.

Jessop, Bob (2002) 'Time and space in the globalization of capital and their implications for state power', *Rethinking Marxism*, 14(1): 91–117.

_____ (2001) 'Bringing the state back in (yet again): Reviews, revisions, rejections, and redirections', *International Journal of Sociology*, 11(2): 149–174.

_____ (2000) 'The crisis of the national spatiotemporal fix and the tendential ecological dominance of globalizing capitalism', *International Journal of Urban and Regional Research*, 24: 323–360.

_____ (1990) *State Theory: Putting Capitalist States in their Place*. University Park, PA: Pennsylvania State University Press.

Jessop, Bob and Sum, Ngai–Ling (2001) 'Pre-disciplinary and post-disciplinary perspectives', *New Political Economy*, 6(1): 89-101.

Jevons, William S. (1965) *The Theory of Political Economy*. New York: A.M. Kelley.

Jhally, Sut (1990) *The Codes of Advertising: Fetishism and the Political Economy of Meaning in the Consumer Society*. New York: Routledge.

Johnson, Paul (1993) 'Colonialism's back – and not a moment too soon', *The New York Times Magazine*, April 18: 22, 43.

Johnson, Richard (1987) 'What is cultural studies anyway?', *Social Text*, 17(Winter): 38–80.

Johnston, Anne and Flamiano, Dolores (2007) 'Diversity in mainstream newspapers from the standpoint of journalists of color', *Howard Journal of Communication*, 18(2): 111–131.

Jussawalla, Meheroo (ed.) (1993) *Global Telecommunications Policies: The Challenge of Change*. Westport, CT: Greenwood Press.

Jussawalla, Meheroo and Taylor, Richard D. (eds) (2003) *Information Technology Parks of the Asia Pacific*. Armonk: M.E. Sharpe.

Kahn, Richard and Kellner, Douglas (2004) 'New media and internet activism: From the "Battle of Seattle" to blogging', *New Media & Society*, 6(1): 87–95.

Kapur, Jyotsna (2007) '"New" economy/old labor: Creativity, flatness, and other neo-liberal myths', in C. McKercher and V. Mosco (eds), *Knowledge Workers in the Information Society*. Lanham, MD: Lexington Books. pp. 163–175.

Keenan, Thomas (1993) 'Windows of vulnerability', in B. Robbins (ed.), *The Phantom Public Sphere*. Minneapolis, MN: University of Minnesota Press. pp. 121–141.

Kellner, Douglas (1990) *Television and the Crisis of Democracy*. Boulder, CO: Westview Press.

_____ (1989) *Jean Baudrillard: From Marxism to Postmodernism and Beyond*. Stanford, CA: Stanford University Press.

Kendall, Diana (2005) *Framing Class: Media Representations of Wealth and Poverty in America*. Lanham, MD: Rowman and Littlefield.

Keynes, John Maynard (1964) *The General Theory of Employment, Interest, and Money*. New York: Harcourt, Brace & World.

Khiabany, Gholam (2006) 'Religion and media in Iran: The imperative of the market and the straightjacket of Islamism', *Westminster Papers in Communication*, 3(2): 3–21.

Kim, L.S. (2008) 'Representations of race', in R. Andersen and J. Gray (eds), *Battleground: The Media*. Westport, CT: Greenwood Press. pp. 452–459.

Kiss, Simon and Mosco, Vincent (2005) 'Negotiating electronic surveillance in the workplace: A study of collective agreements in Canada', *Canadian Journal of Communication*, 30(4): 549–564.

Klein, Naomi (2007) *The Shock Doctrine: The Rise of Disaster Capitalism*. Toronto: Knopf Canada.

_____ (2002) *No Logo*. New York: Picador.

Klein, Peter G. (1999) 'New institutional economics', in B. Bouckaert and G. Geest (eds), *Encyclopedia of Law and Economics*. Vol. 1, *The History and Methodology of Law and Economics*. Cheltenham: Edward Elgar. pp. 456–489.

Klüver, Jürgen and Stoica, Christina (2005) 'On the nature of culture and communication: A complex systems perspective', *Cybernetics and Systems*, 36: 877–902.

Knowles, Richard D. (2006) 'Transport shaping space: Differential collapse in time–space', *Journal of Transport Geography*, 14(6): 407–425.

Kraft, Philip and Dubnoff, Steve (1986) 'Job content, fragmentation and control in computer software work', *Industrial Relations*, 25: 184–196.

Kraidy, M.M. (2005) *Hybridity or the Cultural Logic of Globalization*. Philadelphia, PA: Temple University Press.

Kristol, Irving (1983) *Reflections of a Neoconservative*. New York: Basic Books.

Kuhn, Thomas (1970) *The Structure of Scientific Revolutions* (2nd edn). Chicago: University of Chicago Press.

Kumar, Deepa (2007) *Outside the Box: Corporate Media, Globalization and the UPS Strike*. Chicago and Urbana, IL: University of Illinois Press.

Kumar, Keval J. (2003) 'India and Pakistan: From transitional to network societies', *Development*, 46(1): 41–48.

Kunz, William A. (2006) *Culture Conglomerates:* Lanham, MD: Rowman and Littlefield.

Kyasny, Lynette (2006) 'Cultural reproduction of digital inequality in a US community technology initiative', *Information, Communication, and Society*, 9(2): 160–181.

Laclau, Ernesto (1977) *Politics and Ideology in Marxist Theory*. London: New Left Books.

Lash, Scott and Lury, Celia (2007) *The Global Culture Industry*. London: Polity Press.

Lash, Scott and Urry, John (1987) *The End of Organized Capitalism*. Madison, WI: University of Wisconsin Press.

Latour, Bruno (2005) *Reassembling the Social*. Oxford: Oxford University Press.

_____ (1999) *Pandora's Hope*. Cambridge, MA: Harvard University Press.

Lawrence, Stephen H. (1983) *Centralization and Decentralization: The Communications Connection*. Incidental Paper I–83–2. Cambridge, MA: Harvard University, Program on Information Resources Policy.

Lawson, Tony (2005) 'The nature of institutional economics', *Evolutionary and Institutional Economics Review*, 2(1): 7–20.

Lazear, Edward (2000) 'Economic imperialism', *Quarterly Journal of Economics*, 115(1): 99–146.

Lazzarato, Maurizio (1997) *Lavoro immateriale: Forme di Vita e produzione di soggettività*. Verona: Ombre Corte.

Lebowitz, Michael (1986) 'Too many blindspots on the media', *Studies in Political Economy*, 21(August): 165–173.

Lee, Chin-Chuan (2001) 'Rethinking the political economy: Implications for media and democracy in greater China', *The Public*, 3(5): 1–22.

Lee, Frederic S. (2002) 'The Association for Heterodox Economics: Past, present and future', *Journal for Australian Political Economy*, 50: 29–43.

Lee, Hua L. (2007) 'Peering through a glass darkly', *International Commerce Review*, 7(1): 60–68.

Lee, Micky (2007) 'On the relationship between international telecommunications development and global women's poverty', *The International Communications Gazette*, 69(2): 193–213.

_____ (2006) 'What's missing in feminist research in new information and information technologies?', *Feminist Media Studies*, 6(2): 191–210.

Lefebvre, Henri (1979) 'Space: Social product and use value', in J.W. Freiberg (ed.), *Critical Sociology: European International Perspectives*. New York: Irvington. pp. 285–296.

Lehrer, Jonah (2007) *Proust was a Neuroscientist*. New York: Houghton Mifflin.

Lerner, Daniel (1958) *The Passing of Traditional Society*. New York: The Free Press.

_____ (1949) *Sykewar: Psychological Warfare against Germany, D-Day to V-E Day*. New York: Stewart.

Leung, Linda (2005) *Virtual Ethnicity: Race, Resistance and the World Wide Web*. Aldershot: Ashgate.

Lewis, Justin and Miller, Toby (eds) (2003) *Critical Cultural Policy Studies: A Reader*. Oxford: Blackwell.

Linebaugh, Peter and Rediker, Marcus (2000) *The Many-headed Hydra: Sailors, Slaves, Commoners and the Hidden History of the Revolutionary Atlantic*. Boston: Beacon Press.

Lipietz, Alain (1988) 'Reflections on a tale: The Marxist foundations of the concepts of regulation and accumulation', *Studies in Political Economy*, 26(Summer): 7–36.

Little, David I.M. (2002) *Ethics, Economics, and Politics: Principles of Public Policy*. Oxford: Oxford University Press.

Liu, Chang-de (2006) 'De-skilling effects on journalists: ICTs and the labour process of Taiwanese newspaper reporters', *Canadian Journal of Communication*, 31(3): 695–714.

Livant, William (1979) 'The audience commodity: On the "blindspot" debate', *Canadian Journal of Political and Social Theory*, 3(1): 91–106.

Longstaff, Patricia (2002) *The Communications Toolkit*. Cambridge, MA: MIT Press.

Lovell, Vicki, Hartmann, Heidi, and Koski, Jessica (2006) *Making the Right Call: Jobs and Diversity in the Communications and Media Sector*. Washington, DC: Institute for Women's Policy Research.

Losse, Robert M. (1999) 'Communication defined as complementary informative processes', *Journal of Information, Communication and Library Science*, 5(3): 1–20.

Lukács, Georg (1971) *History and Class Consciousness: Studies in Marxist Dialectics*. Trans. R. Livingstone. Cambridge, MA: MIT Press.

Lux, Kenneth (1990) *Adam Smith's Mistake*. Boston: Shambhala.

Lynch, Mona (2004) 'Punishing images: Jail cam and the changing penal enterprise', *Punishment and Society*, 6(3): 255–270.

Lyon, David (2007) *Surveillance Studies: An Overview*. London: Polity Press.

_____ (ed.) (2006) *Theorizing Surveillance*. Cullompton: Willan.

_____ (2003) *Surveillance after September 11*. London: Polity Press.

Lyotard, Jean-François (1984) *The Postmodern Condition: A Report on Knowledge*. Trans. G. Bennington and B. Massumi. Minneapolis, MN: University of Minnesota Press.

Magder, Ted and Burston, Jonathan (2001) 'Whose Hollywood? Changing forms and relations in the North American information economy', in V. Mosco and D. Schiller (eds), *Continental Order?* Lanham, MD: Rowman and Littlefield. pp. 207–234.

Mahon, Rianne (1980) 'Regulatory agencies: Captive agents or hegemonic apparatuses', in J. Paul Grayson (ed.), *Class, State, Ideology, and Change*. Toronto: Holt, Rinehart & Winston. pp. 154–168.

Malone, Thomas W. and Rockart, John F. (1991) 'Computers, networks and the corporation', *Scientific American*, September: 128–136.

Mandel, Ernest (1995) *Long Waves of Capitalist Development: A Marxist Interpretation* (2nd rev. edn). London: Verso.

Mansell, Robin (2004) 'Political economy, power, and new media', *New Media & Society*, 6(1): 96–105.

_____ (2002) 'From digital divides to digital entitlements in knowledge societies', *Current Sociology*, 5(3): 407–426.

Mansell, Robin and Nordenstreng, Kaarle (2006) 'Great media and communication debates: WSIS and the MacBride Report', *Information Technologies and International Development*, 3(4): 15–36.

Markusen, Ann (2005) 'Communicating political economy', *Review of Radical Political Economics*, 37(3): 269–280.

Marques de Melo, José (ed.) (1991) *Communication and Democracy: Brazilian Perspectives*. Saô Paulo: ECA/USP.

Marshall, Alfred (1961) *Principles of Economics*. London: Macmillan (1st edn, 1890).

Marshall, T.H. (1964) *Class, Citizenship, and Social development: Essays*. Westport, CT: Greenwood Press.

Martin, Christopher (2007) 'Writing off workers: The decline of the US and Canadian labor beats', in C. McKercher and V. Mosco (eds), *Knowledge Workers in the Information Society*. Lanham, MD: Lexington Books. pp. 19–35.

_____ (2004) *Framed! Labor and the Corporate Media*. Ithaca, NY: ILR Press.

Martin, Michèle (1991) *'Hello, Central?': Gender, Technology, and Culture in the Formation of Telephone Systems*. Montreal and Kingston: McGill-Queen's University Press.

Marx, Karl (1976a) *Capital: A Critique of Political Economy*. Vol. 1, Trans. Ben Fowkes. London: Penguin (1st edn, 1867).

_____ (1976b) *Collected Works*. Vol. V. New York: International Publishers.

_____ (1973) *The Grundrisse: Foundations of the Critique of Political Economy*. Trans. Martin Nicolaus. Harmondsworth: Penguin.

_____ (1963) *Eighteenth Brumaire of Louis Bonaparte*. New York: International Publishers. (1st edn 1869.)

Marx, Karl and Engels, Friedrich (1987) *The German Ideology*. London: Lawrence and Wishart. (1st edn 1845.)

Massey, Doreen (2005) *For Space*. London: Sage.

_____ (1992) 'Politics and space/time', *New Left Review*, 19: 65–84.

Mattelart, Armand (2000) *Networking the World, 1794–2000*. Trans. Liz Carey-Libbrecht and James A. Cohen. Minneapolis, MN: University of Minnesota Press.

_____ (ed.) (1986) *Communicating in Popular Nicaragua*. New York: International General.

Mattelart, Armand and Mattelart, Michèle (1992) *Rethinking Media Theory: Signposts and New Directions* (2nd edn). Trans. James A. Cohen and M. Urquidi. Minneapolis, MN: University of Minnesota Press (1st edn, 1986).

Mattelart, Armand and Siegelaub, Seth (eds) (1983) *Communication and Class Struggle. Vol. 2: Liberation, Socialism*. New York: International General.

_____ (eds) (1979) *Communication and Class Struggle. Vol. 1: Capitalism, Imperialism*. New York: International General.

Mattelart, Michèle (1977) 'Création populaire et résistance au système des medias', paper presented at the International Conference on Cultural Imperialism, Algiers, October 11–15.

Maxwell, Richard (2003) *Herbert Schiller*. Lanham, MD: Rowman and Littlefield.

_____ (ed.) (2001) *Culture Works: The Political Economy of Culture*. Minneapolis, MN: University of Minnesota Press.

Mayer, Vicki (2005) 'Soft-core in TV-time: The political economy of a "cultural trend"', *Critical Studies in Media Communication*, 22(4): 302–320.

Mazepa, Patricia (2007) 'Democracy of, in and through communication: struggles around public service in Canada in the first half of the twentieth century', *Info*, 9(2–3): 45–56.

_____ (2003) 'Battles on the cultural front: The (de)labouring of culture in canada, 1914–1944', doctoral dissertation. Ottawa, Carleton University.

McAllister, Mathew P. and Giglo, J. Matt (2004) 'The commodity flow of US children's programming', *Critical Studies in Media Communication*, 22(1): 26–44.

McAnany, Emile G. (1986) 'Seminal ideas in Latin American critical communication research: An agenda for the north', in R. Atwood and E.G. McAnany (eds), *Communication and Latin American Society: Trends in Critical Research*. Madison, WI: Wisconsin University Press. pp. 28–47.

McChesney, Robert W. (2007) *Communication Revolution*. New York: The Free Press.

_____ (2004) *The Problem of the Media: US Communication Policy in Dubious Times*. New York: Monthly Review Press.

_____ (2003) 'The problem of journalism: A political economic contribution to an explanation of the crisis in contemporary US journalism', *Journalism Studies*, 4(3): 299–329.

_____ (2000) *Rich Media, Poor Democracy*. New York: The New Press.

_____ (1993) *Telecommunications, Mass Media and Democracy: The Battle for the Control of US Broadcasting*. New York: Oxford University Press.

_____ (1992) 'Labour and the marketplace of ideas: WCFL and the battle for labor Radio broadcasting, 1927–1934', *Journalism Monographs*, 134 (August).

McChesney, Robert W. and Schiller, Dan (2003) 'The political economy of international communication: Foundations for the emerging global debate about media ownership and regulation', paper no. 11, United Nations Research Institute for Social Development, Technology, Business, and Society Programme. Available at: www.unrisd.org/UNRISD/website/document. nsf/ab82a6805797760f80256b4f005da1ab/c9dcba6c7db78c2ac1256bdf0049a774/$FILE/mcc hesne.pdf, last accessed May 23, 2008.

McCloskey, Deidre N. (2002) *The Secret Sins of Economics*. Chicago: Prickly Paradigm Press.

_____ (1985) *The Rhetoric of Economics*. Madison, WI: University of Wisconsin Press.

McDonald, David A. and Ruiters, Greg (2005) *The Age of Commodity: Water Privatization in Southern Africa*. London: Earthscan.

McDonald, Kevin (2006) *Global Movements*. Oxford: Blackwell.

McGowan, John (1991) *Postmodernism and its Critics*. Ithaca, NY: Cornell University Press.

McGuigan, Jim (2005) 'Neo-liberalism, culture, and policy', *International Journal of Cultural Policy*, 11(3): 229–241.

McKercher, Catherine (2002) *Newsworkers Unite: Labor, Convergence and North American Newspapers*. Lanham, MD: Rowman and Littlefield.

McKercher, Catherine and Mosco, Vincent (eds) (2007) *Knowledge Workers in the Information Society*. Lanham, MD: Lexington Books.

_____(eds) (2006) *Canadian Journal of Communication*, 31(3).

McLaughlin, Lisa (2004) 'Feminism and the political economy of transnational public space', *Sociological Review*, 52(1): 156–175.

_____ (1999) 'Beyond "separate spheres": Feminism, and the cultural studies/political economy debate', *Journal of Communication Inquiry*, 23(4): 327–354.

McLaughlin, Lisa and Johnson, Helen (2007) 'Women and knowledge work in the Asia Pacific: Complicating technological empowerment', in C. McKercher and V. Mosco (eds), *Knowledge Workers in the Information Society*. Lanham, MD: Lexington Books. pp. 249–266.

McMillan, Sally J. (1998) 'Who pays for content? Funding in interactive media', *Journal of Computer Mediated Communication*, 4(1). Available at: http://jcmc.indiana.edu/vol4/issue1/McMillan.html, (last accessed January 5, 2009.

McRobbie, Angela (2005) *The Uses of Cultural Studies*. London: Sage.

Meadowcroft, James (2005) 'Environmental political economy, technological transitions, and the state', *New Political Economy*, 10(4): 479–498.

Meaghar, Gabrielle and Nelson, Julie A. (2004) 'Survey article: Feminism and the dismal science', *Journal of Political Philosophy*, 12(1): 102–126.

Meehan, Eileen R. (2005) *Why TV is Not Our Fault*. Lanham, MD: Rowman and Littlefield.

_____(1999) 'Commodity, culture, common sense: Media research and paradigm dialogue', *Journal of Media Economics*, 12(2): 149–163.

_____ (1984) 'Towards a third vision of an information society', *Media, Culture & Society*, 6: 257–272.

Meehan, Eileen R. and Riordan, Ellen (eds) (2002) *Sex and Money: Feminism and Political Economy in the Media*. Minneapolis, MN: University of Minnesota Press.

Melkote, Srinivas R. and Steeves, H. Leslie (2001) *Communication for Development in the Third World: Theory and Practice for Empowerment* (2nd edn). New Delhi: Sage.

Mellor, Mary (2005) 'Ecofeminist political economy: Integrating feminist economics and ecological economics', *Feminist Economics*, 11(3): 120–126.

Melody, William (2007) 'Cultivating knowledge for knowledge societies at the intersections of economic and cultural analysis', *International Journal of Communication* 1: 70–78.

Mercer, Claire (2004) 'Engineering civil society: ICTs in Tanzania', *Review of African Political Economy*, 31(99): 49–64.

Meyer, David S. (2006) *The Politics of Protest: Social Movements in America*. Oxford: Oxford University Press.

Miège, Bernard (2003) 'Capitalism and communication: A new era of society or an accentuation of long term tendencies', in A. Calabrese and C. Sparks (eds), *Toward a Political Economy of Culture*. Lanham, MD: Rowman and Littlefield. pp. 83–94.

_____ (1989) *The Capitalization of Cultural Production*. New York: International General.

Mill, John Stuart (1848) *Principles of Political Economy*. Boston: C.C. Little and J.B. Brown.

Millard, Bob (2000) *Marxian Political Economy: Theory, History and Contemporary Relevance*. New York: St Martin's Press.

Miller, David (1989) *Market, State, and Community*. New York: Oxford University Press.

Miller, John (1992) 'URPE and radical political economy: Whence we came', *URPE Newsletter*, Fall: 4–5.

Miller, Mark C. (1988) *Boxed In: The Culture of TV*. Evanston, IL: Northwestern University Press.

Miller, Toby (2007) *Cultural Citizenship*. Philadelphia, PA: Temple University Press.

_____ (2004) 'A view from a fossil: The new economy, creativity, and consumption – two or three things I don't believe in', *International Journal of Cultural Studies*, 7(1): 55–65.

Mills, C. Wright (1959) *The Sociological Imagination*. New York: Oxford University Press.

_____ (1956) *The Power Elite*. New York: Oxford University Press.

Milonakis, Dimitris (2003) 'New market socialism: A case for rejuvenation or inspired alchemy', *Cambridge Journal of Economics*, 27(1): 97–121.

Mirchandani, K. (2004) 'Practices of global capital: Gaps, cracks, and ironies in transnational call centres in India', *Global Networks*, 4(4): 355–373.

Mody, Bella (ed.) (2003) *International and Development Communication: A Twenty-first Century Perspective*. Thousand Oaks, CA: Sage.

Monahan, Torin (2004) 'Just another tool? IT pedagogy and the commodification of education', *The Urban Review*, 36(4): 271–292.

Montgomery, Katherine C. (1989) *Target: Prime Time–Advocacy Groups and the Struggle over Entertainment Television*. New York: Oxford University Press.

Morris, Martin (2005) 'Interpretability and social power, or, why postmodern advertising works', *Media, Culture & Society*, 27(5): 697–718.

Morris-Suzuki, Tessa (2005) *The Past Within Us: Media, Memory, History*. London: Verso.

_____ (1988) *Beyond Computopia: Information, Automation, and Democracy in Japan*. London: Routledge.

Morrison, David (1978) 'The beginning of modern mass communication research', *Archives of European Sociology*, 19(2): 347–359.

Mosco, Vincent (2004) *The Digital Sublime*. Cambridge, MA: MIT Press.

_____ (2003) 'The transformation of communication in Canada', in W. Clement and L. Vosko (eds), *Changing Canada: Political Economy as Transformation*. Montreal: McGill-Queen's Press. pp. 287–308.

_____ (1989a) *The Pay-per Society: Computers and Communication in the Information Age*. Toronto: Garamond, and Norwood, NJ: Ablex.

_____ (1989b) 'Labour in the communication industries: A critical sociological perspective', in B. Dervin, L. Grossberg, B. O'Keefe, and E. Wartella (eds), *Paradigm Exemplars. Vol. 2: Rethinking Communication*. Newbury Park, CA: Sage. pp. 213–225.

_____ (1982) *Pushbutton Fantasies*. Norwood, NJ: Ablex.

_____ (1979) *Broadcasting in the United States: Innovative Challenge and Organizational Control*. Norwood, NJ: Ablex.

Mosco, Vincent and Kaye, Lewis (2000) 'Questioning the concept of the audience', in I. Hagen and J. Wasko (eds), *Consuming Audiences*. Creskill, NJ: Hampton Press. pp. 31–46.

Mosco, Vincent and Lavin, David (2007) 'Political economic theory and communication research', *Global Media Journal – Persian Edition*, trans. into Farsi by Hamid Abdollahyan, et al. Available at: www.dcsfs.ut.ac.ir/gmj/, last accessed June 6, 2008.

Mosco, Vincent and McKercher, Catherine (2008) *The Laboring of Communication: Will Knowledge Workers of the World Unite?* Lanham, MD: Lexington Books.

Mosco, Vincent and Schiller, Dan (eds) (2001) *Continental Order? Integrating North America for Cybercapitalism*. Lanham, MD: Rowman and Littlefield.

Mosco, Vincent and Wasko, Janet (eds) (1983) *Labor, the Working Class, and the Media*. Norwood, NJ: Ablex.

Mosco, Vincent and Zureik, Elia (1987) *Computers in the Workplace: Technological Change in the Telephone Industry*. Ottawa: Government of Canada, Department of Labour.

Mowlana, Hamid, Gerbner, George, and Schiller, Herbert I. (eds) (1992) *Triumph of the Image: The Media's War in the Persian Gulf – A Global Perspective*. Boulder, CO: Westview Press.

Murdock, Graham (2004) 'Past the posts: Rethinking change, retrieving critique', *European Journal of Communication*, 19(1): 19–38.

_____ (1989) 'Cultural studies: Missing links', *Critical Studies in Mass Communication*, December: 436–440.

_____ (1978) 'Blindspots about Western Marxism: A reply to Dallas Smythe', *Canadian Journal of Political and Social Theory*, 2(2): 109–119.

Murdock, Graham and Golding, Peter (2005) 'Culture, Communication, and Political Economy', in J. Curran and M. Gurevitch (eds), *Mass Media and Society* (4th edn). London: Hodder Arnold, pp. 60–83.

_____ (2000) 'Culture, communications and political economy', in J. Curran and M. Gurevitch (eds), *Mass Media and Society* (3rd edn). London: Arnold. pp. 70–92.

_____ (1973) 'For a political economy of mass communications', in R. Miliband and J. Saville (eds), *Socialist Register*. London: Merlin Press. pp. 205–234.

_____ (2004) 'Dismantling the digital divide: Rethinking the dynamics of participation and exclusion', in A. Calabrese and C. Sparks (eds), *Towards a Political Economy of Culture: Capitalism and Communication in the Twenty-first Century*. Lanham, MD: Rowman and Littlefield. pp. 244–260.

_____ (1979) 'Capitalism, communication, and class relations', in J. Curran, M. Gurevitch, and J. Woollacott (eds), *Mass Communication and Society*. Beverly Hills, CA: Sage. pp. 12–43.

Murdock, Graham and Wasko, Janet (eds) (2007) *Media in the Age of Marketization*. Creskill, NJ: Hampton Press.

Murray, Simone (2004) 'Celebrating the story the way it is: Cultural studies, corporate media, and the contested utility of fandom', *Continuum: Journal of Media & Cultural Studies*, 18(1): 7–25.

_____ (2003) 'Media convergence's third wave: Content streaming', *Convergence*, 9(8): 8–18.

Murshed, Syed Mansoob (ed.) (2002) *Issues in Positive Political Economy*. London: Routledge.

Myers, Marian (2004) 'African American women and violence: Gender, race and class in the news', *Critical Studies in Media Communication*, 21(2): 95–118.

Nagel, Ernest (1957) *Logic without Metaphysics and Other Essays in the Philosophy of Science*. Glencoe, IL: The Free Press.

Nagy, Ian (2007) 'Labor strife and carnival symbolism', in C. McKercher and V. Mosco (eds), *Knowledge Workers in the Information Society*. Lanham, MD: Lexington Books. pp. 285–298.

Negra, Diane (2001) 'Consuming Ireland: Lucky Charms cereal, Irish Spring soap, and 1-800-SHAMROCK', *Cultural Studies*, 15(1): 76–97.

Negt, Oskar and Kluge, Alexander (1972) *Oeffentlicheit und Erfahrung: zur Organisationanalyse von Buergerlicher und Proletarischer Oeffentlichkeit*. Frankfurt: Suhrkamp.

Newkirk, Pamela (2002) *Within the Veil: Black Journalists and White Media*. New York: New York University Press.

Newman, Saul (2007) 'Anarchism, post-structuralism and the future of radical politics', *SubStance*, 113: 3–18.

Nielsen, Mike (1990) 'Labor's stake in the electronic cinema revolution', *Jump Cut*, 35: 78–84.

Nisbet, Robert (1986) *Conservatism*. Minneapolis, MN: University of Minnesota Press.

Noam, Eli (2008) *Media Ownership and Concentration in America*. New York: Oxford University Press.

Nordenstreng, Kaarle (2004) 'Ferment in the field: Notes on the evolution of communication studies and its disciplinary nature', *The Public*, 11(3): 5–18.

_____ (1993) 'New information order and communication scholarship: Reflections on a delicate relationship', in J. Wasko, V. Mosco, and M. Pendakur (eds), *Illuminating the Blindspots*. Norwood: NJ: Ablex. pp. 251–273.

_____ (1984) *The Mass Media Declaration of UNESCO*. Norwood, NJ: Ablex.

_____ (1968) 'Communication research in the United States: A critical perspective', *Gazette*, 14: 207–216.

Nordenstreng, Kaarle and Padovani, Claudia (2005) 'From NWICO to WSIS: Another world information and communication order?', *Global Media and Communication*, 3: 264–272.

Nordenstreng, Kaarle and Schiller, Herbert (eds) (1993) *Beyond National Sovereignty: International Communication in the 1990s*. Norwood, NJ: Ablex.

_____ (eds) (1979) *National Sovereignty and International Communication*. Norwood, NJ: Ablex.

Nordenstreng, Kaarle and Varis, Tapio (1974) *Television Traffic: A One-Way Street?* Paris: UNESCO.

Nove, Alec (1983) *The Economics of Feasible Socialism*. London: Allen and Unwin.

O'Connor, Alan (1991) 'The emergence of cultural studies in Latin America', *Cultural Studies in Mass Communication*, 8: 60–73.

O'Connor, James (1991) 'Socialism and ecology', *Capitalism Nature Socialism*, 2(3): 1–12.

_____ (1987) *The Meaning of Crisis: A Theoretical Introduction*. Oxford: Blackwell.

Offe, Claus (1984) *Contradictions of the Welfare State*. Cambridge, MA: MIT Press.

O'Hara, Philip A. (2002) 'The contemporary relevance of Thorstein Veblen's institutional-evolutionary political economy', *History of Economics Review*, 35: 78–103.

_____ (2000) *Marx, Veblen, and Contemporary Institutional Political Economy*. Cheltenham: Edward Elgar.

Ortega y Gasset, José (1957) *The Revolt of the Masses*. New York: W.W. Norton.

Owen, Robert (1851) *Labor: Its History and Prospects*. New York: Kelly.

Paavola, Jouni and Adger, W. Neil (2005) 'Institutional ecological economics', *Ecological Economics*, 53: 353–368.

Palgrave, Sir Robert H.I. (1913) *Dictionary of Political Economy*. Vol. III. London: MacMillan and Co.

Palmer, Bryan D. (1990) *Descent into Discourse: The Reification of Language and the Writing of Social History*. Philadelphia, PA: Temple University Press.

Parenti, Christian (2003) *The Soft Cage: Surveillance in America*. New York: Basic Books.

Park, David W. and Pooley, Jefferson (eds) (2008) *The History of Media and Communication Research: Contested Memories*. New York: Peter Lang.

Parker, William (1986) *Economic History and the Modern Economist*. Oxford: Blackwell.

Pasquali, Antonio (1967) *El Aparato Singular: Análisis de un Día de TV en Caracas*. Caracas: Universidad Central de Venezuela.

Peck, Janice (2006) 'Why we shouldn't be bored with the political economy versus cultural studies debate', *Cultural Critique*, 64: 92–126.

Peiss, Kathy (1991) 'Going public: Women in nineteenth-century cultural history', *American Literary History*, 3(Winter): 817–828.

Pellow, David N. and Park, Lisa S. (2002) *The Silicon Valley of Dreams*. New York: New York University Press.

Peltzman, Sam (1976) 'Toward a more general theory of regulation', *Journal of Law and Economics*, 19(2): 211–240.

Pendakur, Manjunath (2003) *Indian Popular Cinema: Industry, Ideology, and Consciousness*. Cresskill, NJ: Hampton Press.

_____ (1993) 'Political economy and ethnography: Transformations in an Indian village', in J. Wasko, V. Mosco, and M. Pendakur (eds), *Illuminating the Blindspots: Essays in Honor of Dallas Smythe*. Norwood, NJ: Ablex. pp. 82–108.

_____ (1990) *Canadian Dreams & American Control: The Political Economy of the Canadian Film Industry*. Detroit, MI: Wayne State University Press.

Perkins, Ellie and Kuiper, Edith (2005) 'Introduction: Explorations in feminist ecological economics', *Feminist Economics*, 11(3): 107–150.

Peterson, Spike V. (2005) 'How (the meaning of) gender matters in political economy', *New Political Economy*, 10(4): 499–521.

Piore, Michael and Sabel, Charles (1984) *The Second Industrial Divide*. New York: Basic Books.

Porritt, Jonathon (1984) *Seeing Green: The Politics of Ecology Explained*. Oxford: Blackwell.

Posner, Richard A. (1992) *Sex and Reason*. Cambridge, MA: Harvard University Press.

Potts, Nick (2005) 'The relevance of Marx to all students of economics no matter what the level', *International Journal of Social Economics*, 32(9): 827–851.

Poulantzas, Nicos (1978) *State, Power, and Socialism*. London: New Left Books.

Pratt, Andy C. (2004) 'The cultural economy: A call for the spatialized "production of culture" perspectives', *International Journal of Cultural Studies*, 7(1): 117–128.

Pred, Alan (1973) *Urban Growth and the Circulation of Information: The United States System of Cities, 1790–1840*. Cambridge, MA: Harvard University Press.

Preston, William, Jr., Herman, Edward S., and Schiller, Herbert I. (1989) *Hope and Folly: The United States and UNESCO 1945–1985*. Minneapolis, MN: University of Minnesota Press.

Prokop, Dieter (1983) 'Problems of production and consumption in the mass media', *Media, Culture & Society*, 5: 101–116.

_____ (1974) *Massenkultur und spontaneität: Zur veranderten warenform der massenkommunikation in spatkapitalismus (aufsätze)*. Frankfurt: Suhrkamp.

_____ (ed.) (1973) *Kritische kommunikationsforschung: Aufsatze aus der 'zeitschrift fur sozialforschung'*. Munich: Hanser.

Rabinach, Anson (1990) *The Human Motor: Energy, Fatigue, and the Origins of Modernity*. New York: Basic Books.

Raboy, Marc (1990) *Missed Opportunities*. Montreal and Kingston: McGill-Queen's Press.

Radziki, Michael J. (2003) 'Mr. Hamilton, Mr. Forrester, and a foundation for evolutionary economics', *Journal of Economic Issues*, 37(1): 133–173.

Rajagopal, Indhu and Bojin, Nis (2004) 'Globalization of prurience: The internet and degradation of women and children', *First Monday*, 9(1). Available at: www.firstmonday.org/issues/issue9_1/rajagopal/index.html, last accessed July 6, 2008.

Rakow, Lana and Wackwitz, Laura A. (2004) *Feminist Communication Theory*. Thousand Oaks, CA: Sage.

Reid, Margaret G. (1934) *Economics of Household Production*. New York: Wiley.

Resnick, Stephen A. and Wolff, Richard D. (2006) *New Directions in Marxian Theory*. New York: Routledge.

_____ (1987) *Knowledge and Class: A Marxian Critique of Political Economy*. Chicago: University of Chicago Press.

Review of African Political Economy (2004) 31(99).

Ricardo, David (1819) *On the Principles of Political Economy and Taxation*. London: G. Bell and Sons.

Riordan, Ellen (2001) 'Commodified agents and empowered girls: Consuming and producing feminism', *Journal of Communication Inquiry*, 25(3): 279–297.

Roach, Colleen (ed.) (1993) *Communication and Culture in War and Peace*. Newbury Park, CA: Sage.

Robinson, Joan (1962) *Economic Philosophy*. Chicago: Aldine.

Rodino-Colocino, Michelle (2007) 'High-tech workers of the world, unionize! A case study of WashTech's "new model of unionism"', in C. McKercher and V. Mosco (eds), *Knowledge Workers in the Information Society*. Lanham, MD: Lexington Books. pp. 209–227.

_____ (2006) 'Laboring under the digital divide', *New Media & Society*, 8(3): 487–511.

Rogers, Everett (1971) *Communication of Innovations*. With F.F. Shoemaker. New York: The Free Press.

Roll, Eric (1942) *A History of Economic Thought*. New York: Prentice-Hall.

Roncagliolo, Rafael (1986) 'Transnational communication and culture', in R. Atwood and E.G. McAnany (eds), *Communication and Latin American Society: Trends in Critical Research*. Madison, WI: Wisconsin University Press. pp. 79–88.

Rorty, Richard (1979) *Philosophy and the Mirror of Nature*. Princeton, NJ: Princeton University Press.

Rosewarne, Stuart (2002) 'Towards an ecological political economy', *Australian Journal of Political Economy*, 50: 179–199.

Ross, Andrew (2004) *No Collar*. Philadelphia, PA: Temple University Press.

_____ (1993) 'The fine art of regulation', in B. Robbins (ed.), *The Phantom Public Sphere*. Minneapolis, MN: University of Minnesota Press. pp. 257–268.

Ross, Karen and Nightingale, Virginia (2003) *Media and Audiences: New Perspectives*. Buckinghamshire: Open University Press, McGraw-Hill.

Rothkopf, David (2008) *Superclass*. New York: Farrar, Strauss and Giroux.

Rothschild, Kurt W. (2002) 'The absence of power in contemporary economic theory', *Journal of Socioeconomics*, 31: 433–442.

Rucinski, Diane (1991) 'The centrality of reciprocity to communication and democracy', *Critical Studies in Mass Communication*, 8: 184–194.

Rusk, James (1991) 'The greatest moral challenge of our time', *The Globe and Mail*, February 19: B8.

Russial, John T. (1989) 'Pagination and the newsroom: Great expectations', Doctoral dissertation. Philadelphia, PA: Temple University.

Rutherford, Jonathan (2005) 'Cultural studies in the corporate university', *Cultural Studies*, 19(3): 297–317.

Rutherford, Malcolm (2001) 'Institutional economics: Then and now', *Journal of Economic Perspectives*, 15(3): 173–194.

Saad-Filho, Alfredo (2002) *The Value of Marx: Political Economy for Contemporary Capitalism*. London: Routledge.

Sahlins, Marshall (1976) *Culture and Practical Reason*. Chicago: University of Chicago Press.

Samarajiva, Rohan (1985) 'Tainted origins of development communication', *Communicator*, April–July: 5–9.

Sanderson, Stephen K. (2005) 'World system analysis after 30 years: Should it rest in peace?', *International Journal of Comparative Sociology*, 46(3): 179–213.

Sarikakis, Katharine and Shade, Leslie Reagan (eds) (2007) *Feminist Interventions in International Communication: Minding the Gap*. Lanham, MD: Rowman and Littlefield.

Sassen, Saskia (2007) *A Sociology of Globalization*. New York: W.W. Norton.

_____ (2001) *The Global City*. Princeton, NJ: Princeton University Press (1st edn, 1991).

Saxenian, AnnaLee (2006) *The New Argonauts*. Cambridge, MA: Harvard University Press.

Saxton, Alexander (1990) *The Rise and Fall of the White Republic: Class Politics and Mass Culture in Nineteenth-Century America*. New York: Verso.

Sayer, Andrew (2001) 'For a critical cultural political economy', *Antipode*, 33(4): 687–708.

Sayers, Sean (2007) 'The concept of labour: Marx and his critics', *Science and Society*, 71(4): 431–454.

Schiller, Dan (2007a) *How to Think about Information*. Urbana, IL and Chicago: University of Illinois Press.

_____ (2007b) 'The hidden history of US public service telecommunications, 1919–1956', *Info*, 9(2–3): 17–28.

_____ (1999a) *Digital Capitalism*. Cambridge, MA: MIT Press.

_____ (1999b) 'The legacy of Robert A. Brady: Antifascist origins of the political economy of communications', *Journal of Media Economics*, 12(2): 89–101.

_____ (1996) *Theorizing Communication*. New York: Oxford.

_____ (1982) *Telematics and Government*. Norwood, NJ: Ablex.

Schiller, Herbert I. (2000) *Living in the Number One Country: Reflections from a Critic of American Empire*. New York: Seven Stories Press.

_____ (1996) *Information Inequality: The Deepening Social Crisis in America*. New York: Routledge.

_____ (1993) 'Not yet the postimperialist era', in C. Roach (ed.), *Communication and Culture in War and Peace*. Boston: Beacon Press. pp. 97–116.

_____ (1992) *Mass Communication and American Empire* (2nd edn). Boston: Beacon Press (1st edn, 1969).

_____ (1989) *Culture, Inc*. New York: Oxford University Press.

_____ (1984) *Information and the Crisis Economy*. Norwood, NJ: Ablex.

_____ (1981) *Who Knows*. Norwood, NJ: Ablex.

_____ (1976) *Communication and Cultural Domination*. White Plains, NY: International Arts and Sciences Press.

_____ (1973) *The Mind Managers*. Boston: Beacon Press.

Schramm, Wilbur (1964) *Mass Media and National Development*. Stanford, CA: Stanford University Press.

Schudson, Michael (1984) *Advertising: The Uneasy Persuasion*. New York: Basic Books.

Schumpeter, Joseph (1942) *Capitalism, Socialism, and Democracy*. New York: Harper and Brothers.

Schwieterman, Joseph P. (2007) *The Return of the Intercity Bus*. Chicago: Chaddick Institute for Metropolitan Development, DePaul University.

Scott, John (1991) *Social Network Analysis: A Handbook*. Newbury Park, CA: Sage.

Scott, John and Marshall, Gordon (2005) 'Communication', in *A Dictionary of Sociology*. Oxford: Oxford University Press. Oxford Online. Available at: www.oxfordreference.com/views/ENTRY.html?subview=Main&entry=t88.e331, last accessed May 30, 2008.

Shannon, Claude E. and Weaver, Warren (1949) *The Mathematical Theory of Communication*. Urbana, IL: University of Illinois Press.

Shiller, Robert (2006) *Irrational Exhuberance* (2nd edn) New York: Random House.

Shimony, Abner and Malin, Shimon (2006) 'Dialogue: Abner Shimony and Shimon Malin', *Quantum Information Processing*, 5(4): 261–276.

Shimpach, Shawn (2005) 'Working watching: The creative and cultural labor of the media audience', *Social Semiotics*, 15(3): 343–360.

Sivanandan, Ambalauaner (1990) *Communities of Resistance: Writings on Black Struggles for Socialism*. London, New York: Verso.

Smith, Adam (1976) *The Theory of Moral Sentiments*. Indianapolis: Liberty Classics (1st edn, 1759).

_____ (1937) *An Inquiry into the Nature and Causes of The Wealth of Nations*. New York: Modern Library (1st edn, 1776).

Smith, Anthony (1991) *The Age of Behemoths*. New York: Priority Press.

Smith, Neil (2005) *The Endgame of Globalization*. London: Routledge.

Smith, Ted, Sonnenfeld, David A., and Pellow, David N. (eds) (2006) *Challenging the Chip*. Philadelphia, PA: Temple University Press.

Smith-Shomade, Beretta E. (2004) 'Narrowcasting in the new world information order: A space for the audience', *Television and New Media*, 5(1): 69–81.

Smythe, Dallas W. (1991) 'Letter to the author', December 4.

_____ (1981) *Dependency Road: Communication, Capitalism, Consciousness and Canada*. Norwood, NJ: Ablex.

_____ (1978) 'Rejoinder to Graham Murdock', *Canadian Journal of Political and Social Theory*, 2(2): 120–127.

_____ (1977) 'Communications: Blindspot of Western Marxism', *Canadian Journal of Political and Social Theory*, 1(3): 1–27.

_____ (1957) *The Structure and Policy of Electronic Communications*. Urbana, IL: University of Illinois Press.

Snider, Laureen (2002) 'Theft of time: Disciplining through science and law', *Osgoode Hall Law Journal*, 40(1): 90–112.

Snow, C.P. (1964) *The Two Cultures* (2nd edn). Cambridge: Cambridge University Press.

Sokal, Alan (2008) *Beyond the Hoax*. New York: Oxford University Press.

Somavia, Juan (1981) 'The democratization of communications: From minority social monopoly to majority social representation', *Development Dialogue*, 2: 13–30.

_____ (1979) *Democratización de las communicaciones: Una perspectiva latino-americana*. Mexico City: ILET.

Sosale, Sujatha (2003) 'Envisioning a new world order through journalism: Lessons from the recent past', *Journalism*, 4(3): 377–392.

Sparks, Colin (2007) *Globalization, Development, and the Mass Media*. London: Sage.

_____ (1985) 'The working-class press', *Media, Culture & Society*, 7(5): 133–146.

Sreberny, Annabelle (2001) 'Mediated culture in the Middle East: Diffusion, democracy and difficulties', *International Communications Gazette*, 63(2/3): 101–119.

Standage, Tom (1998) *The Victorian Internet*. New York: Walker and Company.

Steeves, H. Leslie (2001) 'Liberation, feminism, and developmental communication', *Communication Theory*, 11(4): 397–414.

_____ (1989) 'Gender and mass communication in a global context', in P.J. Creedon (ed.), *Women in Mass Communication: Challenging Gender Values*. Newbury Park, CA: Sage. pp. 83–111.

_____ (1987) 'Feminist theories and media studies', *Critical Studies in Mass Communication*, 4(2): 95–135.

Stengrim, Laura (2005) 'Negotiating postmodern democracy, political activism, and knowledge production: Indymedia's grassroots and e-savvy answer to media oligopoly', *Communication and Critical/Cultural Studies*, 2(4): 281–304.

Steuart, James (1967) *An Inquiry in the Principles of Political Economy*. New York: Augustus M. Kelley (1st edn, 1761).

Stigler, George J. (2003) *Memoirs of an Unregulated Economist*. Chicago: University of Chicago Press.

_____ (ed.) (1988) *Chicago Studies in Political Economy*. Chicago: University of Chicago Press.

_____ (1971) 'The theory of economic regulation', *Bell Journal of Economics & Management Science*, 2(1): 3–21.

Stone, Alan (1991) *Public Service Liberalism: Telecommunications and Transitions in Public Policy*. Princeton, NJ: Princeton University Press.

Stone, Alan and Harpham, Edward J. (eds) (1982) *The Political Economy of Public Policy*. Beverly Hills, CA: Sage.

Stouffer, Samuel Andrew (1949) *The American Soldier*. Princeton, NJ: Princeton University Press.

Streek, Wolfgang and Kenworthy, Lane (2005) 'Theories and practices of neocorporatism', in T. Janoski, R.R. Alford, A.M. Hicks, and M.A. Shwartz (eds), *The Handbook of Political Sociology*. Cambridge: Cambridge University Press. pp. 441–460.

Sussman, Gerald (2005) *Global Electioneering*. Lanham, MD: Rowman and Littlefield.

_____ (1984) 'Global telecommunications in the third world: Theoretical considerations', *Media, Culture & Society*, 6: 289–300.

Sussman, Gerald and Lent, John A. (eds) (1998) *Global Productions: Labor in the Making of the 'Information Society'*. Newbury Park, CA: Sage.

_____ (eds) (1991) *Transnational Communications: Wiring the Third World*. Newbury Park, CA: Sage.

Switzer, Les and Adhikari, Mohamed (2000) *South Africa's Resistance Press: Alternative Voices in the Last Generation*. Athens, OH: Ohio University Press.

Tabor, Mary (1991) 'Encouraging "those who would speak out with fresh voice" through FCC minority ownership policies', *Iowa Law Review*, 76: 609–639.

Tarrit, Fabien (2006) 'A brief history, scope, and peculiarities of analytical Marxism', *Review of Radical Political Economy*, 38(4): 595–618.

Tarrow, Sidney (2006) *The New Transnational Activism*. Cambridge: Cambridge University Press.

Taylor, Phil and Bain, Peter (2004) 'India calling to the far away towns: The call centre labour process and globalization', *Work, Employment, and Society*, 19(2): 261–282.

Terranova, Tiziana (2004) *Network Culture: Politics for the Information Age*. London: Pluto.

_____ (2000) 'Free labor: Producing culture for the digital economy', *Social Text*, 18(63): 33–58.

Tetty, Wisdom J. (2001) 'Information technology and democratic participation in Africa', *African and Asian Studies*, 36(1): 133–153.

Tetzlaff, David (1991) 'Divide and conquer: Popular culture and social control in late capitalism', *Media, Culture & Society*, 13: 9–33.

Thanki, Ashika and Jefferys, Steve (2007) 'Who are the fairest? Ethnic segmentation in London's media production', *Work Organisation, Labour, and Globalisation*, 1(1): 108–118.

Thomas, Pradip N. (2006) 'The communication rights in the information society campaign: Applying social movement theories to an analysis of global media reform', *The International Communication Gazette*, 68(4): 291–312.

Thomas, Pradip, N. and Nain, Zaharom (eds) (2004) *Who Owns the Media: Global Trends and Local Resistance*. Mahwah, NJ: Erlbaum Associates.

Thompson, E.P. (1963) *The Making of the English Working Class*. London: Victor Gollancz.

Thompson, John B. (1989) 'The theory of structuration', in D. Held and J.B. Thompson (eds), *Social Theory of Modern Societies: Anthony Giddens and His Critics*. New York: Cambridge University Press. pp. 56–76.

Thompson, Mark (2004) 'Discourse, "Development" and the "Digital Divide": ICT and the World Bank', *Review of African Political Economy*, 31(99): 103–123.

Thrift, Nigel (2006) 'Re-inventing invention: New tendencies in capitalist commodification', *Economy and Society*, 35(2): 279–306.

Thrift, Nigel and Crang, Mike (2007) *Thinking Space*. London: Taylor & Francis.

Tomlinson, John (1999) *Globalization and Culture*. London: Polity Press.

_____ (1991) *Cultural Imperialism*. Baltimore, MD: Johns Hopkins University Press.

Traber, Michael and Nordenstreng, Kaarle (eds) (1992) *Few Voices, Many Worlds: Towards a Media Reform Movement*. London: World Association for Christian Communication.

Tracy, James F. (2006) '"Labor's monkey wrench": Newsweekly coverage of the 1962–63 New York newspaper strike', *Canadian Journal of Communication*, 31(3): 541–560.

Tracy, James F. and Hayashi, Maris L. (2007) 'A libratariat? Labor, technology, and librarianship in the information age', in C. McKercher and V. Mosco (eds), *Knowledge Workers in the Information Society*. Lanham, MD: Lexington Books. pp. 53–67.

Tran van Dinh (1987) *Independence, Liberation, Revolution: An Approach to the Understanding of the Third World*. Norwood, NJ: Ablex.

Tuchman, Gaye (1978) *Making News*. New York: The Free Press.

Tunstall, Jeremy (1977) *The Media are American*. New York: Columbia University Press.

UNESCO (1979) *International Commission for the Study of Communication Problems: Final Report*. Paris: UNESCO.

Urry, John and Wakeford, John (eds) (1973) *Power in Britain*. London: Heinemann.

US Government Accountability Office (2008) *Media Ownership*. Report to the Chairman, Subcommittee on Telecommunications and the Internet, Committee on Energy and Commerce, House of Representatives. Washington, DC: GAO.

Van Audenhove, Leo, Burgelman, Jean-Claude, Nulens, Gert, and Cammaerts, Bart (1999) 'Information society policy in the developing world: A critical assessment', *Third World Quarterly*, 20(2): 387–404.

van Dijk, Jan (2005) *The Deepening Divide: Inequality in the Information Society*. Newbury Park, CA: Sage.

Van Galen, Jane and Noblit, George W. (2007) *Late to Class: Social Class and Schooling in the New Economy*. Albany, NY: State University of New York Press.

Veblen, Thorstein (2005) *The Higher Learning in America*. New York: Cosimo. (1st edn 1918.)

_____ (1934) *The Theory of the Leisure Class*. New York: Modern Library (1st edn, 1899).

_____ (1932) *The Theory of the Business Enterprise*. New York: Scribner's.

Vernon, Raymond (1992) 'Transnational corporations: Where are they coming from, where are they headed?', *Transnational Corporations*, 1(2): 7–35.

Veron, Eliseo, et al. (1967) *Lenguaje y comunicación social*. Buenos Aires: Editorial Nueva Visión.

Vertova, Giovanna (ed.) (2006) *The Changing Economic Geography of Globalization: Reinventing Space*. London: Routledge.

Vickers, John and Yarrow, George (1991) 'Economic perspectives on privatization', *Journal of Economic Perspectives*, 5(2): 111–132.

Vosko, Leah (2002) 'The pasts (and futures) of feminist political economy in Canada: Reviving the debate', *Studies in Political Economy*, 68: 55–83.

Waetjen, Jarrod and Gibson, Timothy A. (2007) 'Harry Potter and the commodity fetish: Activating corporate reading in the journey from text to commercial inter-text', *Communication and Critical-Cultural Studies*, 4(1): 3–26.

Wall, Derek (2006) 'Green economics: An introduction and research agenda', *International Journal of Green Economics*, 1(1/2): 201–214.

Wallerstein, Immanuel (2004) *The Uncertainties of Knowledge*. Philadelphia, PA: Temple University Press.

_____ (2001) 'Global culture(s): Salvation, menace, or myth?', paper presented at New Cultural Formations in an Era of Transnational Globalization conference, Academia Sinica, Taiwan, October 6–7. Available at: www.binghamton.edu/fbc/iwgloculttw.htm, last accessed May 28, 2008.

_____ (1991) *Geopolitics and Geoculture: Essays on the Changing World-System*. Cambridge: Cambridge University Press.

_____ (1979) *The Capitalist World Economy*. New York: Cambridge University Press.

Walton, Douglas (2000) 'The place of dialogue theory in logic, computer science, and communication studies', *Synthese*, 123(3): 327–346.

Waltz, Mitzi (2005) *Alternative and Activist Media*. Edinburgh: University of Edinburgh Press.

Ward, Adolphus, Trent, William, et al. (1907) *The Cambridge History of English and American Literature*. New York: G.P. Putnam's Sons. Available at: www.bartleby.com/220/1406.html, last accessed May 28, 2008.

Waring, Marilyn (1988) *If Women Counted: A New Feminist Economics*. New York: Harper Collins.

Wasko, Janet (2003) *How Hollywood Works*. London: Sage.

_____ (2001) *Understanding Disney*. London: Polity Press.

_____ (1994) *Hollywood in the Information Age: Beyond the Silver Screen*. London: Polity Press.

_____ (1983) 'Trade unions and broadcasting', in V. Mosco and J. Wasko (eds), *Labor, the Working Class, and the Media*. Norwood, NJ: Ablex. pp. 85–113.

_____ (1982) *Movies and Money*. Norwood, NJ: Ablex.

Wasko, Janet and Erickson, Mary (eds) (2008) *Cross-border Cultural Production: Economic Runaway or Globalization?* Youngstown, NY: Cambria Press.

Wasko, Janet, Mosco, Vincent, and Pendakur, Manjunath (eds) (1993) *Illuminating the Blindspots*. Norwood, NJ: Ablex.

Wasko, Janet, Philips, Mark, and Meehan, Eileen (eds) (2006) *Dazzled by Disney*. Leicester: Leicester University Press.

Waterman, Peter (2001) *Global Social Movements and the New Internationalisms*. London: Mansell.

_____ (1990) 'Communicating labor internationalism: A review of relevant literature and resources', *The European Journal of Communication*, 15(1–2): 85–103.

Wayne, Michael (2003) 'Post-Fordism, monopoly capitalism, and Hollywood's media industrial complex', *Current Sociology*, 6(1): 82–103.

Weber, Max (1946) 'Science as a vocation', in H.H. Gerth and C.W. Mills (eds), *From Max Weber: Essays in Sociology*. New York: Oxford. pp. 126–156.

Weeden, Kim A. and Grusky, David B. (2005) 'The case for a new class map', *American Journal of Sociology*, 111(1): 141–212.

Wellman, Barry and Hogan, Bernie (2004) 'The immanent internet', in J. McKay (ed.), *Netting Citizens*. Edinburgh: St Andrew University Press. pp. 54–80.

Wheeler, D.L. (2003) 'Egypt: Building an information society for international development', *Review of African Political Economy*, 30(98): 627–642.

Williams, Raymond (1981) 'Marxism, structuralism, and literary analysis', *New Left Review*, 129(September–October): 51–66.

_____ (1980) *Problems in Materialism and Culture*. London: Verso.

_____ (1977) *Marxism and Literature*. New York: Oxford University Press.

_____ (1976) *Keywords: A Vocabulary of Culture and Society*. New York: Oxford University Press.

_____ (1975) *Television, Technology and Cultural Form*. London: Fontana.

_____ (1961) *The Long Revolution*. Hammondsworth: Penguin.

_____ (1958) *Culture and Society: 1780–1950*. Hammondsworth: Penguin.

Williamson, Oliver E. (2000) 'The new institutional economics: Taking stock, looking ahead', *Journal of Economic Literature*, 38(3): 595–613.

Willis, Paul (1977) *Learning to Labor: How Working Class Kids Get Working Class Jobs*. New York: Columbia University Press.

Wilson, Clint, Gutiérrez, Felix, and Chao, Lena M. (2003) *Racism, Sexism and the Media: The Rise of Class Communication in Multicultural America* (3rd edn). Thousand Oaks, CA: Sage.

Wilson, James Q. (ed.) (1980) *The Politics of Regulation*. New York: Basic Books.

Winseck, Dwayne (2008) 'Media merger mania', *Canadian Dimension*, 42(1): 30–32.

_____ (1998) *Reconvergence*. Creskill, NJ: Hampton Press.

_____ (1993) 'A study in regulatory change and the deregulatory process in Canadian telecommunication with particular emphasis on telecommunications labor unions', Doctoral dissertation, University of Oregon.

Winseck, Dwayne and Pike, Robert (2007) *Communication and Empire: Media, Markets and Globalization, 1860–1930*. Durnham, NC: Duke University Press.

Winston, Brian (1986) *Misunderstanding Media*. Cambridge, MA: Harvard University Press.

Wittel, Andreas (2004) 'Culture, labour, and subjectivity: For a political economy from below', *Capital and Class*, 84: 11–30.

Wood, Ellen Meiksins (1989) 'Rational choice Marxism: Is the game worth the candle?', *New Left Review*, 177: 41–48.

Woodward, Kath (2004) *Questioning Identity: Gender, Class, and Ethnicity*. London: Routledge.

Woolgar, Steve (1988) *Knowledge and Reflexivity*. London: Sage.

Worth, Owen and Kuhling, Carmen (2004) 'Counter-hegemony, anti-globalisation and culture in international political economy', *Capital and Class*, 84: 31–42.

Woytinsky, W.S. and Woytinsky, E.S. (1955) *World Commerce and Government: Trends and Outlook*. New York: The Twentieth Century Fund.

Wright, Erik Olin (2005) *Approaches to Class Analysis*. Cambridge: Cambridge University Press.

Wu, Tim (2004) 'Copyright's communication policy', *Michigan Law Review*, 103: 278–366.

Yates, JoAnne (2005) *Structuring the Information Age*. Baltimore, MD: Johns Hopkins University Press.

_____ (1989) *Control through Communication: The Rise of System in American Management*. Baltimore, MD: Johns Hopkins University Press.

Ya'u, Y.Z. (2004) 'The new imperialism and Africa in the global electronic village', *Review of African Political Economy*, 31(99): 11–29.

Zhao, Yuezhi (2008) *Communication in China: Political Economy, Power, and Conflict*. Lanham, MD: Rowman and Littlefield.

Zimbalist, Andrew (1979) 'Technology and the labor process in the printing industry', in A. Zimbalist (ed.), *Case Studies in the Labor Process*. New York: Monthly Review. pp. 103–126.

INDEX